PROBLEMS IN FOCUS SERIES

Each volume in the 'Problems in Focus' serie
able to students important new work on key historical problems and
periods that they encounter in their courses. Each volume is devoted to
a central topic or theme, and the most important aspects of this are dealt
with by specially commissioned essays from scholars in the relevant field.
The editorial Introduction reviews the problem or period as a whole,
and each essay provides an assessment of the particular aspect, pointing
out the areas of development and controversy, and indicating where
conclusions can be drawn or where further work is necessary. An annotated bibliography serves as a guide for further reading.

TITLES IN PRINT

List continues overleaf

Problems in Focus
Series Standing Order
ISBN 0–333–71704–X hardcover
ISBN 0–333–69348–5 paperback
(outside North America only)

You can receive future titles in this series as they are published. To place
a standing order please contact your bookseller or, in the case of difficulty, write to us at the address below with your name and address, the
title of the series and the ISBN quoted above.

Customer Services Department, Macmillan Distribution Ltd
Houndmills, Basingstoke, Hampshire RG21 6XS, England

The Origins of the French Revolution

Edited by

PETER R. CAMPBELL

First published 2006 by
PALGRAVE MACMILLAN
Houndmills, Basingstoke, Hampshire RG21 6XS and
175 Fifth Avenue, New York, N. Y. 10010
Companies and representatives throughout the world

PALGRAVE MACMILLAN is the global academic imprint of the Palgrave
Macmillan division of St. Martin's Press, LLC and of Palgrave Macmillan Ltd.
Macmillan® is a registered trademark in the United States, United Kingdom and other
countries. Palgrave is a registered trademark in the European Union and other
countries.

ISBN-13: 978–0–333–94970–2   hardback
ISBN-10: 0–333–94970–6   hardback
ISBN-13: 978–0–333–94971–9   paperback
ISBN-10: 0–333–94971–4   paperback

This book is printed on paper suitable for recycling and
made from fully managed and sustained forest sources.

A catalogue record for this book is available from the British Library.

Library of Congress Cataloging-in-Publication Data
The origins of the French Revolution / edited Peter R. Campbell.
        p. cm.—(Problems in focus)
        Includes bibliographical references and index.
        Contents: The origins of the French Revolution in focus / by Peter
Campbell—The financial origins of the French Revolution / by Joël Félix—Decison-
making / by John Hardman—The Paris Parlement in the 1780s / by Peter Robert
Campbell—From social to cultural history / by William Scott—The intellectual origins
of the French Revolution / by Marisa Linton—The religious origins of the French
Revolution, 1560–1791 / by Dale Van Kley—The contested image: stage, canvas, and
the origins of the French Revolution / by Mark Ledbury—The pamphlet debate over
the organization of the Estates General / by Kenneth Margerison—Peasants and their
grievances / by John Markoff—From the Estates-General to the National Assembly,
May 5–August 4, 1789.
        ISBN 0–333–94970–6 (cloth)—ISBN 0–333–94971–4 (pbk.)
        1. France—History—Revolution, 1789–1799—Causes. I. Campbell, Peter
Robert, 1955– II. Problems in focus series (Palgrave (Firm))
DC138.075 2005
944.04—dc22   2005051385

10   9   8   7   6   5   4   3   2   1
15   14   13   12   11   10   09   08   07   06

Printed in China

Contents

List of Illustrations

List of Figures and Tables

FIGURES

TABLES

Introduction
The Origins of the French Revolution in Focus

PETER ROBERT CAMPBELL

The period of the French Revolution is one of the most important in modern history. The Revolution swept away the old order in France and replaced it with a succession of new regimes, each ultimately unable to win consensus and provide stability. But they were all conscious of being a part of the same great project, to regenerate France, indeed humanity, to make a new world. The Revolution proclaimed equality before the law, the abolition of the vestiges of the feudal regime of peasant dues and services, and gave new social groups the opportunity to exercise power. These were the Notables – a growing combination of liberal nobles and the bourgeoisie of the liberal professions – and, for a brief and intense period of conflict, the artisans and masters of the popular classes. It consolidated the peasantry in their landowning traditions but attacked and alienated the Catholic Church, to which they were also attached. Reactions to the initial constitutional projects, and to the more leveling politics of virtue as the revolution radicalized, created the fundamental division between Right and Left that still characterizes modern politics. Although the twentieth century was profoundly conditioned by two equally great revolutions, the Russian and the Chinese, the nineteenth century lived in the shadow of the French Revolution as its aspirations commanded either allegiance or resistance. New nations adopted the tricolor flag, self-conscious revolutionaries sought to emulate its policies and leaders, while its opponents sought above all to avoid revolution – and of course its true significance began to be evaluated by historians.

The nineteenth-century debates on the Revolution laid out many of the fundamental interpretative positions that once again occupy historians.[1] This fact has often been obscured because for 40 years up to the early 1990s, the debate focused largely on just one nineteenth-century interpretation, the Marxist orthodoxy of a bourgeois capitalist revolution.[2] After

1

the bicentenary in 1989, and the fall of the Berlin Wall, there has been a return to fundamental questions.[3] Early historical debates about the revolution and liberalism, religion, democracy, individualism and the state are once again in the mainstream. These new-but-old views on the nature of the Revolution in general therefore prompt questions about its origins. Moreover, the answers are often very different, for the toppling of the Marxist view of a bourgeois revolution and the rise of cultural history have had a liberating effect upon the study of the eighteenth century. This volume reflects some of the new thinking, and although each chapter is based upon original research, it has been written to be accessible to specialist and non-specialist alike. The first part of this introductory chapter seeks to offer not a general framework of explanation but a cautionary exploration of the problem of the origins or causes of the Revolution. Awareness of these will help us to evaluate various major contributions and situate the offerings in the other chapters in this volume. The second and third parts of this chapter offer an overview that weaves recent work into an argument on the way a revolution grows out of a crisis of the state.

EXPLANATORY FRAMEWORKS

The French Revolution's origins are indeed complex and much debated. Can historians convincingly claim to discern a "causal chain" which links elements together in a way that suggests a progression towards the big event? Some would suggest that such a project could only spring from a very positivist approach to history, and argue that we can do no better than isolate elements in a kind of "genealogy," a sort of upside-down family tree.[4] The latter approach to historical explanation has the virtue of creating an impression of greater fluidity and a wider range of possible outcomes. In either case, the problem of the origins is related to a firm idea of what exactly this revolution was that we are trying to explain. That depends upon our definitions both of the French Revolution and of the concept of "revolution" in general.

First, let us consider what we are seeking to explain. Is our focus the end of the old regime or is it the origins of the Revolution? They are not the same; we must not slip into the assumption that because the regime collapsed into revolution the collapse was caused by "revolutionaries" doing the pushing, nor that the collapse would necessarily lead to revolution. If the former is taken to be the real issue, the questions we ask should focus more upon the long- and short-term failures of a socio-political structure than upon the new ideas that were called upon to rebuild France after the collapse (which can be considered as a separate process in terms of revolution). If, on the other hand, we seek to explain the precise nature of the changes that occurred in the revolutionary period, we will point to a different causal chain or set of origins, and must ask which phase of the revolution we are trying to explain.[5]

There was an explosive revolutionary change from an absolute monarchy to a constitutional monarchy in 1789 based upon a transfer of sovereignty from the king to the nation. This was worked out in a constitutional revolution that lasted until 1791, but such an outcome was not explicitly called for much before mid-1788 or early 1789. But after this, from 1792, came the fall of the monarchy and a republican revolution that for many even in 1789 would have been unthinkable and certainly undesirable. The rise of republicanism had antecedents in classical and eighteenth-century ideology, but circumstances in 1791–2 made an unattractive option in 1789 into a more popular one. Much ink has been spilled of late on whether or not this second revolution was the necessary outcome of the first, or whether circumstances drove the revolutionaries to develop a certain style of politics that made the second revolution not only possible but also probable.[6] These debates are not our main concern here. But it is important to be aware that confusing the origins of 1792 or 1793, the Terror, with the origins of 1789, or the origins of the collapse of the old regime, is to confuse several different explanatory schemas. The end of the old regime was obviously a necessary prerequisite for the more creative revolution. Even then, we need at least to ask whether self-conscious radicals pushed the regime or whether it fell – and what was the relationship between its fall and the development of the revolutionaries' projects.[7]

This has not yet been done systematically, and most studies have considered the revolution to be a unitary whole. It seemed that such a cataclysmic series of events must have had portentous origins that were reflected in its development. For some early analysts, it was the result of the Enlightenment's new ideologies, and particularly "Rousseau's fault." For others, it was a revolt of the masses or a revolt of the bourgeoisie against the aristocracy. By the 1820s it was generally assumed that the revolution was to be taken as a whole bloc, that its origins were long-term, and that its consequences were radical changes in state and society. A class-based interpretation emerged early and soon became very influential: the Revolution was a consequence and reflection of the rise of the bourgeoisie. This was not necessarily a Marxist view that defined the bourgeoisie as a class of budding "capitalists";[8] it seemed, however, to fit the facts, as the not-necessarily-capitalist middle classes did clearly displace the nobility in power, and their position was confirmed by the revolution of 1830.[9] Marx added an economic theory of classes to this paradigm and defined the bourgeoisie more narrowly. Tocqueville, in a book that still inspires historians for its many insights, argued that the Revolution was not so much a radical change as a process that merely accelerated the centralization of France begun by Louis XIV. This kind of argument, which amounts to saying that the revolutionaries deluded themselves about its true nature, has had a future in the hands of historians who want to argue that in the long run it did not fundamentally change society or the state, but merely accelerated developments, as both were evolving in the same direction anyway. Historians living under the Third Republic often saw the Revolution as a patriotic necessity – and this idea had the virtue of making the Terror an integral part of it. However, As Bill Scott shows in his chapter below, the orthodox view established by the middle years of the twentieth century was the Marxist one of a revolution whose politics were generated by class struggle as the economic infrastructure evolved towards capitalism and the dominance of the new bourgeois class.

If the Revolution can indeed be taken as a whole, there is a temptation to argue that it was essentially "about" one particular feature. This error can be termed myth-making and, although more recently associated with the Marxist myth of a bourgeois revolution, it has a long history and continues today.[10] If we take the Revolution as a bloc, as a unitary whole with a single major characteristic, such as the rise of the bourgeoisie or the invention of modern politics, then the search for causes will tend to focus upon the elements leading to this conclusion. Too definite an idea of what the Revolution was "about" inevitably leads to misplaced stress on some causes to the exclusion of others. Much of the chaotic reality that characterized the French Revolution and many of the currents tending in different directions are forgotten or smoothed over in what become teleological narratives. For many critics, the search to explain the essence of the Revolution comes at too high a price in terms of respect for the complexity and humanity of the past. Moreover, the interpretations have been so sweeping that they are impossible to prove, and to discern a clear set of origins would be equally hard.

Even Georges Lefebvre's brilliant, readable and still helpful socialist study argued that in terms of origins not one but four revolutions came together to create the momentous changes in 1789: an attempt at noble reaction, a bourgeois revolution, an urban popular revolution and a peasant revolution.[11] The nobles, ultimately doomed to failure, have their last attempt at wresting power from the too-absolute monarchy in its hour of need; the bourgeoisie seizes the initiative, aided by both an urban class, who would ultimately be unable to prevail, and the peasants, whose aims were more limited and not so very political. The schema helps to explain a single revolution, his bourgeois capitalist revolution. But we could ask how separate these strands really are and whether they best characterize the events of 1787–9. Perhaps the close collaboration of bourgeois and liberal nobles in 1788 and after July 1789 right through to 1791, though not of course in May to July 1789, better suggests the rise of a new elite of notables disillusioned with the absolute monarchy's inability to secure their interests?[12] Surely trying to separate the strands misses the point about the interaction of events in unpredictable ways that is a chief characteristic of a revolutionary situation?

The most recent "myth" was put forward by François Furet, who claimed that the revolution was primarily "about" democracy. He had many precursors of course, but his form of historical explanation is entirely different. For him, it was a largely unsuccessful attempt to create a democratic culture and polity that was doomed to failure in the short term because it suffered from inherent contradictions in its ideology. It was characterized by competition for power and an ideology of popular sovereignty which was derived from Rousseau but which retained the coercive unitary vision of the absolute monarchy, so opening the door to the abuse of individual rights in the name of the state.[13]

One way to avoid this problem of overdetermining the nature of the French Revolution is to define not the French Revolution in particular but the concept of revolution in general. In common parlance we think we know what it means to say "when the revolution comes . . ." but of course there is the danger of making a messy process of the erosion of existing powers and growing competition for social, economic or political power into a thing in itself. We have here a problem of "reification," in which a ready-made idea of revolution is solidified into an entity with certain definite characteristics. Falling into this trap, one then seeks to explain what made its arrival possible: revolution becomes something like the US cavalry charging to the rescue of the beleaguered wagon train, or, to take another metaphor, an actor waiting in the wings for the moment to come on stage. One important effect of this is for events that may be seen as an integral part of the revolutionary process to be labeled as "triggers," "precipitants," or "pre-revolutionary."[14] These merely set the scene for the heroic revolution to arrive on stage. Thus much of what is considered in this book in terms of "politics" would be relegated to this category of "triggers," while the "real" revolution, the one made in men's minds and waiting to happen in 1789, would presumably stem from the intellectual, economic and social developments that led to pent-up dissatisfaction which was unleashed only in 1789. There is a strong tradition in historiography of seeing the events of 1787–8 as a "pre-revo-lution." It is time to rethink this. Several chapters below lend support to the argument that the Revolution began in 1787.

To avoid all this confusion, it would be encouraging if historians could rely upon other disciplines for a helpful definition or model of revolution and its causes which would give us a handy list of things to look for and questions to ask.[15] But sociologists have not been original researchers on the Revolution but simply up to date with the (often misleading) historiography – with the notable exception of John Markoff in the present volume! As research on the French Revolution develops, model-makers have tended to modify their models in the light of the current state of studies on the French Revolution. So it is risky to take from sociological definitions of revolution a checklist of what we histori-ans need to explain in the French case. When social and economic factors dominated thinking on the origins of the French Revolution, most models of revolution in general reflected this. For a long time soci-ologists assumed that all revolutions were rapid processes of societal change necessarily generated by economic and social phenomena.[16]

Since then this idea has been most notably challenged from two perspectives. First came the idea that revolution can be essentially polit-ically motivated: as George V. Taylor famously wrote, the French Revolution was "a political revolution with social consequences and not a social revolution with political consequences."[17] Secondly, criticism emerged from the perspective of post-modernism and the history of ideas.[18] This twin challenge is currently so successful that the economic and social spheres have been sidelined – albeit to the despair of many scholars.[19] The same sort of critique can be made of comparative histo-rians: Alfred Cobban said of R. R. Palmer's explanatory model of the age of democratic revolutions of the later eighteenth century, that it was not generally convincing because it really only fitted one revolution, and that was the French one, because that was the one he had in mind when he thought of the model.[20] No doubt Cobban's critique of Palmer was a backhanded compliment in that at least he (perhaps) thought Palmer was mostly right on France. But what are we to make of models that owe more to Russia or China or seventeenth-century England than to France, but which incorporate the French case? Such books certainly help us to pose better questions about France, but they do not themselves provide satisfactory answers. The specialist on the ancien régime will find just too many misapprehensions about French state and society to accept their model with confidence.

Many historians have offered interesting accounts of the origins of the Revolution, but some have been more ambitious and wider in scope. Let us here focus on just four attempts to provide a general theoretical explanatory framework showing how the transition from old regime to Revolution occurs. Most other interpretations deduce the causes from their view of the Revolution in general, as if causes and consequences had to be the same. Earliest explanations focused upon the idea of a plot, whether by freemasons, Jansenists or *philosophes*. Not until the 1840s with Marx was there a wide-ranging and still-interesting model, of economic and social developments creating a power struggle (a class struggle) as the "feudal" nobility fought to retain its dominance but was successfully challenged by the "capitalist" bourgeoisie. This idea held sway for the best part of a hundred years. Then, in the 1950s and 1960s, R. R. Palmer and J. Godechot's idea that of an "age of democratic revolutions" from the 1770s to the 1790s provoked discussion and found its way into many textbooks.[21] Their contention was that the French Revolution was part of a wave of ideologically motivated revolutions from America to the Low Countries. Next, the 1960s and 1970s saw a successful assault on the Marxist model, but this was more destructive than constructive, for nothing was found to replace it.

The 1980s saw the emergence of new views: these were either materialist and derived from sociology, or idealist and derived from intellectual history. An important debate in sociology has focused on comparative revolutions and has been influenced by two books in particular, one by Theda Skocpol in 1979 and the other by Jack Goldstone in 1991. Skocpol argued that the French, Russian and Chinese revolutions were caused by a failure of "modernization" necessitated by the need for the state to defend its role in the international arena.[22] This idea has been extended to the geopolitical argument that the French Revolution had its "genesis" in demands placed upon the state by its struggle to retain its leading place in an international arena where choices were conditioned by the geographical and international context.[23] In another highly stimulating survey, Goldstone sees demographic change as the key factor. He makes the French Revolution an instance of the multi-sided conflicts produced by various kinds of rigidities (for example, in tax collection) faced by early modern states confronted with rapid population increase. Historians find that his analysis downplays the role of specifically political factors as well as the role of cultural and intellectual changes not related to his major theme.[24] To his stress on the undertaxing of commercial wealth, Joël Félix in the present volume adds the political problems of reform and the nature of the credit system. Nevertheless, his analysis of the long-term effects of population growth upon society should be factored into any long-term explanation.

Within history, François Furet and Keith Baker have opened up an entirely different perspective. Both place stress on language and discourse constructing what we have previously taken to be an objective "reality," an idea Michel Foucault developed in the 1960s. The power of words is combined with the essentially Hegelian idea that the competing discourses contain contradictions whose working-out determined the nature of the Revolution. For Furet the French Revolution is the product of the powerful remodeling effect of new discourses triumphing in 1789. Baker has further suggested (in an argument derived from the German sociologist Habermas, but much modified) that the emergence of a new public sphere helped to generate a new kind of politics, a "politics of contestation." He writes that "three discourses . . . defined the political culture that emerged in France in the later part of the eighteenth century and provided the ideological framework that gave explosive meaning to the events that destroyed the Old Regime."[25] This surprising assertion begs the questions of whether the political culture was indeed fundamentally "new" and whether the ideological framework of meaning was actually created by these discourses (of reason, will and justice) and not by other languages or discourses. Recent research included in this volume suggests a negative answer to both questions.

The danger for these views is that they each focus on one aspect of a revolution that was multifarious and polyvalent. Only Baker's theories sidestep this by adopting a philosophic view that sees everything, all "reality," as constituted by language and discourse. But this philosophic view suffers from the problem of how to bridge the gap between these general discursive forces, be they class conflict, modernization or competing discourses, and the actions of individuals in the storm? How do we get back to the motivations of individuals, who are important and at the very least must be allowed to be bundles of many and often contradictory discourses? This is the problem of "agency." These theories have all been and continue to be very helpful in generating controversy, through which research has advanced, but none is ultimately convincing. The truth is that we have no agreed general theory of why the French Revolution came about and what it was – and no prospect of one. Many historians are tempted to flee the conceptual problems and take refuge in a regularly updated narrative history.

But what story does the narrative tell? Many narrative histories situate the Revolution on the path to modernity. The French Revolution has often been called the "First Modern Revolution." Indeed, one of the major traps into which all these models fall is linked to the idea of a revolution responsible for the "birth of modernity," be it economic and social, or political or ideological. Of particular interest here is the implication that what we have learned about "early modern" revolutions should somehow be irrelevant, because what is "early modern" is "premodern," and therefore not "modern." The Revolution can therefore be explained by stressing all the "modern" aspects of the ancien régime as leading to the Revolution.[26] If we want to argue on the evidence that the origins were actually rather "early modern" in character, then we have to explain how what begins as early modern ends up being the first truly modern revolution: how does this metamorphosis take place? It is therefore very refreshing to have Goldstone, unlike Skocpol, including France in a category of chronologically early modern revolutions. The debate on the "general crisis of the seventeenth century" died down long ago, but the research involved still has much to teach us about the crisis of the European monarchies faced with the mounting costs of war, recalcitrant elites, and unresponsive state administrative systems.[27] The chapters in this book by Félix, Campbell and Hardman provide evidence to support this view.

Having a ready-made idea, a model, of what needs to be explained can be very helpful in widening our explanatory horizons by suggesting questions that need to be asked. Without pretending to provide explanations of the French case, many scholars have come up with helpful insights into the nature of revolution which we might apply to France.[28] Perhaps revolution can be seen as a sudden shift in the paradigm of explaining the world, as T. S. Kuhn put it, or as a "moment of truth" for its participants, or as a carnivalesque moment of liberation, or even as patricide. But let us here retain just one major insight, that of revolution as a process: it is a developing process of the disintegration of existing powers and subsequent competition to fill the vacuum, in which the participants themselves gain awareness and develop strategies they

might previously have thought impracticable. Thus, what are usually
regarded as precipitants or triggers of "revolution" are an integral part
of the process and can have a vital transformative effect. The options
apparent to people change and develop during this process, even leading them to the fundamental choice in times of collapse and constant
uncertainty, of either rebuilding state and society in the old image or
starting afresh to create something in light of old or new utopias. The
participants in the Fronde (1648–53) decided to repair the old structure,
the French Revolutionaries decided to rebuild from the ground up.
Perhaps one could then say that the moment of accepting revolution is
the moment of doing something which feels utterly new and whose
consequences are not known – and such moments may come for different actors at different moments.[29] The National Assembly's defiance of
late June might fit well for one important group. Out in the villages the
revolutionary moment came probably after Mass on some Sunday when
they decided to attack the château rather than the far more traditional
target of a grain convoy. Amongst the elites of the Dauphiné, Brittany
and Provence dates ranging from the summer of 1788 to early 1789
might be appropriate.

One last complicating element is that studies of the Revolution are
an expression of the personal politics of the commentators, as historians
and sociologists have tended to retain a political bias when dealing with
the past. This is especially true of French historians for whom nationalism is an issue, for the very image of France is at stake, but it is also true
of all those who are on the right and left, who tend to be either against
the Revolution, or certain phases of it, or broadly approving of it. This
engagement leads to hazy analysis but good polemics. The left was seeking to explain how momentous change for the better came about and
to secure for future generations the inspiration of the Great Revolution.
They tend to stress the evils of the old regime, and to regard the revolution as necessary. Those on the right, seeking to characterize revolution in general as a chaotic process that destroys all good order and
leads to needless bloodshed, tend to defend the old regime for its
general sense of order, rank and hierarchy, and its moderation, and to
characterize the French Revolution as an unnecessary aberration that
could or should have been avoided in favour of gradual organic change.
This kind of bias has been true of Marxists and Socialists, for whom a
certain idea of the French Revolution served to underpin their whole
philosophy of change for the better, and historians affected by the Cold
War who sought to undermine the legitimacy given to the left by the

Revolution, by undermining their explanation and characterizing it as either a bad thing or redefining it as essentially democratic (in order to undermine the Eastern European idea of centralized democracy). Further to the right is the idea that all revolution is undesirable and can never successfully fulfill the revolutionaries' aspirations. Slow change as advocated by Burke is their ideal (and it suits the defenders of the status quo very well). Interpretations of the Revolution continue to be a battle-ground fought on the terrain of contemporary politics.

THE FRENCH CASE

Stepping aside from the unresolved current debates, let us therefore consider how the factors advanced by historians and sociologists of whatever persuasion fit into a more neutral schema. This is simply one of long-term, medium-term and short-term elements that contributed to the failure of the state in 1789. Like waves destroying a structure on the beach, they will all strike within a short period, but originate further away in some cases than in others. The currents of history one might liken to the big rollers, weakening the structure, the more recent developments destroying specific features, while the constant buffeting from smaller but important waves of immediate crisis finally leads to a dramatic collapse. Such a schema cannot hope to suggest an overall explanation, but at least it helps us to distinguish between various important elements. It may then be possible to suggest some new pathways for us to focus upon.

Long term

The revolutionary crisis of 1787–9 was certainly a crisis of the state (a failure of the state) that had been built up by the absolute monarchy. Although the state organism possessed many features dating from medieval times, such as the structuring principles of hierarchy, order, corporatism, and privilege, its redevelopment under the early Bourbons gave it a basic form that endured until 1789. This "baroque state," as it were, thus survived into the eighteenth century relatively unchanged. Not that there was no development, but the developments that did take place were slow and inadequate. Reforms tended to leave the basic structures and procedures in place in a process of accommodation to social practices and existing power structures.

Some of the state's key features include a decentralized "state of estates," in which, in spite of the theoretical arrogation of powers by the Crown, many tasks continued to be carried out by provincial bodies representing the three orders and by intendants who represented the province as much as the centre;[30] an administration composed of venal officeholders reluctant to undertake new tasks; fiscal privileges favouring the nobility and the Church; and the very fiscal structures, in which reform was almost impossible without attacking the great families who had "captured" the credit system in their own interests;[31] and the fact that decision-making took place in a court society. Although the ancien régime monarchy was involved in war and its financing, it is misleading and reductionist to associate it with the term "fiscal–military state" currently fashionable in British history. The state was not characterized by a modern bureaucracy, it had not become an "administrative monarchy" as some historians claim – indeed had it done so it might have faced its challenges better. Tocqueville's thesis of a successfully centralizing old regime state is misleading, derived from an image of Louis XIV's achievements projected in official documents and artistic fashioning; it simply does not stand up to close examination of practice, as scholars of Louis XIV have long recognized.[32] France after Louis XIV was still characterized by an "absolute monarchy" that operated as a judicial organization, with limited power, in which the king was regarded as an arbiter between competing corporations and jurisdictions. Certainly an ancien régime bureaucracy was forming, but one should stress that the ethics of it were not yet those of a modern bureaucracy. The state possessed an administration that created (and exploited) great friction in society. To function effectively, government also required political management that had recourse both to patronage and clientage directed by the courtly and provincial nobility, and to a cultural hegemony created by the projection of a powerful image of authority reinforced by exemplary but occasional acts of repression. The court at Versailles (often neglected by sociologists who prefer to study bureaucracies) was the central feature of the governing system, for it housed both the central administration and the courtly nobility who retained influence through factions and governing roles. It was thus the centre for negotiated power between sections of the elite, and between king and local and provincial institutions. It is important to grasp that although the king was the head of the body politic, his administration was not above and outside society, but was profoundly conditioned by it – and it reflected as much as it dominated social expectations and practices. Thus its own agents had local and provincial loyalties as well as familial concerns for social advancement and the securing of their patrimony that were often in conflict with their duty to the king. Patronage and clientage networks operated not only in the interests of the state in getting things done, but could work against effective government, and were always as important in the social sphere as in the political. This is not a state to be reified by analysts, but a structure thoroughly intertwined with society and its social values.[33]

These governmental structures and practices, originating in the sixteenth and seventeenth centuries or well before, and modified by Richelieu and Louis XIV in *ad hoc* fashion, had proved barely adequate to meet the huge demands of the seventeenth-century wars. It had required a huge effort of management, concessions and coercion to finance armies and manage the hostility of society to constant fiscal pressure. Like other European monarchies, it seemed as solid as a baroque cathedral but was in fact prone to crisis and near collapse, as in the 1630s and 1640s – and finance was the key area of controversy. Louis XIV's compromise with the nobility enabled the state to survive into the eighteenth century with its room for maneuver constrained by the political and fiscal system dominated by the nobility. It was therefore a colossus with feet of clay.

Instead of asking how such a strong structure suddenly collapsed in 1789, we should be asking how such an apparently strong but actually rather limited set of power structures managed to put off or survive crises for so long. Most of its seventeenth-century weaknesses and strategies were still very much in evidence a century later.[34] The answer to this new question lies partly in the fact that the state's *ad hoc* development, always a response to fiscal necessities, had made it very good at dealing with the traditional tensions inherent in the decentralized structures of parlements, municipalities and provincial estates, but ill-adapted either to the ever-increasing peacetime fiscal needs or to the new ideological challenges. The whole elaborate system of administration tempered and rendered more functional by negotiated power, patronage and clientage, the sense that social interests could be accommodated, was unable to deal with opposition that was based upon ideological commitment. This came in the form of religious dissent and enlightened patriotic opposition, as a *parti patriote* formed from the 1770s. It was hard to buy off a religious zealot or a virtuous patriot. In many ways, then, the structures and practices of the "baroque state" were inadequate to meet the demands of the later eighteenth-century world.

The system of court government made serious reform extremely diffi-cult, as factions inevitably formed and the game of power took prece-dence over the interests of the state. Reforming ministers were almost bound to fail, as support at court ebbed and strings were pulled in the parlement or provincial institutions to generate embarrassing problems for them, while their "credit" was undermined by whispering campaigns at court and pamphlets in Paris. "*Ôtes-toi de là que je m'y mette*" (Get out of there so that I can take your place) was the motto. Machault, L'Averdy, Turgot, Necker, and Calonne were all defeated by this tactic. In partic-ular, the structural problem of court society played into the failure to reform the fiscal system. The fundamental fiscal problem was the contin-ued and long-term failure of the government to increase tax revenues in line with the increase in demands on the state due to the costs of the eighteenth-century wars. The regime escaped fiscal nemesis after the death of Louis XIV only because the John Law experiment created such inflation that royal debts were hugely reduced. Landed wealth continued to be the tax base, so the elite remained relatively undertaxed (though by no means exempt) and moveable wealth in more dynamic areas was not taxed enough. It was not that the finance ministers were unable to diag-nose the problem, but that reforms repeatedly proved impossible to carry through effectively. The scale of the problem meant that adminis-trative reforms and economies usually amounted to tinkering around the edges. But of course the extensive remodeling of the fiscal system would come up against the problems of venality, privilege, and the exploitation of the fiscal system by the courtiers that were all such fundamental aspects of state and society.[35] Thus the problem for the absolute monar-chy was social and political as well as fiscal, as Joël Félix shows in Chapter 1.

One long-term argument that no longer has credibility, however, is that since the sixteenth and seventeenth centuries there had been a decline of the nobility in terms of its political role. Its so-called decline was explained as a consequence either of the rise of the bourgeoisie or of the rise of "the state" to a position of preeminence above all other groups.[36] Louis XIV is supposed to have excluded the higher nobility from important provincial roles and "domesticated" or emasculated the nobles at court. Indeed, important critiques of monarchical authority later developed by the Enlightenment had their origins in theories put forward by such noble opponents of the authoritarian monarchy of Louis XIV as Fénelon and Boulainvilliers. However, the government apparatus of the eighteenth century remained profoundly aristocratic and higher nobles retained influential roles as provincial governors, while almost all parlementaires and all intendants were nobles right up to 1789.[37] Ministers were, if anything, chosen from a higher rank than a century before, and the distinction between robe and sword was certainly much less important, except perhaps in the war ministry and navy. The king in the 1780s still relied upon influential nobles with patronage connections to help govern the provinces and especially to influence the meetings of the still numerous provincial estates. This being the case, historians now treat with caution the argument that the parlements were the spearhead of a noble reaction from 1715 to 1788.[38] There was no need for historians to postulate a reaction or political attempt to regain power lost to the state by nobles; they still were the state.

The survival of the power and prestige of the nobility is demonstrated by the continued attempts of the upper bourgeoisie to live in a similar manner and to acquire venal offices and titles.[39] The *embourgeoisement du sol* so remarked on by seventeenth-century rural historians continued apace in the eighteenth century, as peasant plots were acquired by the urban elites (including the nobility and the clergy). Nevertheless, there is also evidence of a long, slow development of bourgeois values in them-selves, linked to a rise of the professions: an emerging sense of self-esteem, intermarriage with families of similar standing, and an increased irritation with noble social pretensions in the cultural sphere, fuelled by some famous court cases and the use of a rhetoric of virtuous citizen-ship.[40] And there was unquestionably a rise of the bourgeoisie in numer-ical terms. It is no doubt true that a larger and more self-conscious set of groups would find irksome the tripartite division of society into orders, with themselves as the third and least honoured estate.[41] When the government's reforms in the 1780s and the convening of the Estates General starkly posed the issue of privilege, many would take sides against the traditional social divisions and the nobility's perceived attempt to protect its honorific rights.

The government had social and political order at the heart of its philosophy. Royal statements about the monarchy's rights and preroga-tives changed little over two centuries. Preambles to decrees, replies to remonstrances and chastisements in *lits de justice* were based upon the king as absolute sovereign. This did not mean claims to unlimited power, more that sovereignty was undivided and unshared, and that the king was the final judge of the case. Clearly authoritarian in the final assess-ment, though steeped in paternalism, this rhetoric assumed obedience from subjects whose rights to participate were very restricted. The fact that in practice the absolute monarchy needed the elite to function effectively led to a growing contradiction between its rhetoric and its practice. On the one hand it needed to convince people of its power and ability to suppress opposition, as a technique of control in a sometimes relatively weak situation, and on the other hand it actually negotiated and compromised regularly. It attempted to be authoritarian without crossing the boundaries between the legitimate exercise of sovereignty and what was now called "despotism." Over time, the state had succeeded in imposing a sense of its own legitimacy. To the extent that its majestic rhetoric convinced, it also created a divide between subject and ruler. If there was a culture of the state, it was thus mainly one of opposition to the state as oppressor. As social values evolved, and the language of citizenship became current after the 1750s, this needed to be changed to a more positive relationship. Dupont de Nemours, for example, saw this clearly, and indeed quoted the former controller general, L'Averdy, in saying so in his "Memoir on the Municipalities" written for Turgot.[42] But Turgot's projects were still intended to foster a form of civic participation on behalf of the monarchy that was essentially administrative, not to create active, self-reliant citizens who might oppose it. One of the features of the crisis of 1787–9 is the widening appeal of an idea of patriotic citizenship, and this is what made French men and women keen to take an active part in the regeneration of the state.

It is clear then that the relationship of French subjects to this baroque state is an issue of importance. But precisely what was changing? Many long-term cultural currents underpinning the social and political conceptions of the population exhibit remarkable continuity: for example, attitudes held toward the state and taxation, the strong sense of localism and provincialism, patriarchal structures of authority, and conceptions about the nature of, and limits upon, legitimate authority, the continued acceptance of privilege – the sense of local rights and privileges being sacrosanct – with consequent limitations set to the power of the state by these resistances, all remained strong, setting unspoken boundaries to projected reforms. The provincial opposition to "despotism" in the 1760s and 1780s is strongly reminiscent of earlier struggles in its appeal to provincial and social privilege. Clearly the opposition of 1787–9 does not need to be explained entirely in terms of changed attitudes.

On the other hand, in many other areas of life cultural change was manifest. There were developments in terms of individualism, spurred by reading, consumerism, and the growth of the market undermining corporatism. These changes had most effect in the ranks of the social elite. Given the lack of national political involvement by the general population up to early 1789, these cultural shifts were to have their greatest effect when France was faced with the task of rebuilding state and society after the collapse of the old regime. Indeed, the cultural and intellectual changes meant that when the opportunity arose there was insufficient desire to defend the old order. As Bill Scott explains in Chapter 4, the new citizens of 1789 certainly drew upon their new culture in the remaking of France.

One cultural change lower down the social scale, much in evidence in 1789 and with a direct political effect, was a shift in peasant attitudes towards the seigneur. As John Markoff's research conclusively demonstrates, the peasants who opposed state taxation in the seventeenth century now opposed seigneurial dues and the whole "feudal system" in the *cahiers*. This is surely a significant evolution and has yet to be properly accounted for.[43] Perhaps this was a response to the decline of the seigneur as protector and his increasingly evident role as exploiter.[44] Although there is no clear evidence of a seigneurial reaction in the short term in the decades preceding the Revolution, there is evidence of a slower one from the later seventeenth century and evidence of at least constant pressure from lords since then. Moreover, the activities of rural lawyers using newer ideologies such as natural rights and working for the peasant communities stimulated peasant awareness.[45]

One of the characteristic but neglected cultural features of the "baroque state" to which Dale Van Kley has recently drawn attention is the nature of its religious basis. On the one hand, the relationship between the state and religion remained theoretically the same from the early seventeenth century to the eve of the Revolution. On the other hand, the attitudes of many of its subjects were changing. By the end of the reign of Henri IV a working relationship with deep historical roots had been established between Church and State, tested by the Wars of Religion, and reinforced with the new Tridentine Catholicism. In terms of ideological justification and legitimation, this religious underpinning to monarchical power was fundamental, finding expression in rhetoric, ritual and policy. Yet any consensus began to be eroded by disputes over Jansenism from the mid-seventeenth century and was exposed to especially destructive disputes in the mid-eighteenth century. The nature of the religious relationship between the sacral monarchy and its subjects was called into question and theories of the place of the Church in the life of individuals and the state were developed from earlier medieval and sixteenth-century bases.

Not all the important developments conditioning the responses to the crisis can be termed "cultural." The state's preoccupation with order and warfare meant that economic and subsistence issues loomed large in ministers' thinking. There was certainly a relationship between the economy and the failure of the state, for hard times created problems of disorder and reduced tax receipts. The population increase on which Goldstone has set such importance was indeed impressive. After the huge demographic crises of 1694–5 and 1709, the population began its rise from about 20 million to around 28 million in 1789. This created increased competition in many areas of life and a proportionally more youthful population. The bourgeoisie grew disproportionately in the same period, from around 700,000 to perhaps 1,700,000. Land hunger among the peasants led to a rise in rural and urban poor and was indirectly connected to the rise in the urban population in general.[46] Most notably, the Parisian population expanded by a third from around 450,000 to 600,000. The increase was matched neither by arrangements for effective policing nor for food provisioning in critical times.[47] Bread riots, attacks on tolls and grain convoys, vagrancy and severe reductions in expenditure on manufactures became endemic in times of crisis.

A proper understanding of these consequences requires that we recognize not only the economic downturn from the late 1780s, and the manufacturing crisis of 1787–9, but also the century-long shifts and rhythms. Agriculture made only slow advances in yields in most areas during the century, but seaborne trade, especially through the Atlantic ports, was a great success story.[48] The expansion of textile manufacturing and the beginnings of a chemical and metallurgical industry also helped France to have similar overall growth figures to Britain, so to argue straightforwardly that the Revolution grew from long-term economic failure is clearly wrong. A more interesting argument would suggest that the fiscal structures had been unable to develop both sufficiently cheap credit mechanisms and a fiscal structure that could tax the new wealth sufficiently. French finances were overdependent upon internal tariffs (which inhibited trade) and the large but undynamic agricultural sector.

Medium term

In the medium term, French policy-makers had to come to terms with the different global balance of power as it developed in the eighteenth century. The rise of the Atlantic economy and the emergence of Britain as a leading power implied choices for French strategy. France was still the single most powerful and populous state in Europe, but needed to avoid too-costly wars. Yet by mid-century the international situation became unfavorable to a pacific policy such as that of the cardinal de Fleury (1726–43). On the continental side, France had to contend with the rise of a militarist Prussia and Russia's emergence as a power, and needed to maintain a larger army and a policy of Rhineland alliances that would buffer her. At the same time, developing colonial interests needed defending and this implied very costly expenditure on naval armaments. The disaster of the Seven Years' War (1756–63) created a large deficit that constrained choices, as well as dealing a severe blow to French prestige in the international arena. The shifting balance thus set France on the horns of a dilemma, and it was evident to all that fiscal reform was a prerequisite for an effective attempt to recoup the losses suffered in the international arena.[49] But fiscal reform linked to increased peacetime taxation, as in the edicts of 1763, challenged the traditional assumptions of French society as well as raising the issue of provincial and social privileges.

The 1750s and 1760s was precisely the period during which intellectual developments began to have their greatest impact. Although most enlightened writers were both theist and monarchist, the questioning of received wisdom in every area was bound to undermine the older justifications for the state. As Marisa Linton explains in Chapter 5, the Enlightenment produced different attitudes by the elite to the state, to nobility, to citizenship, and to political participation, the latter through developments in ideas of virtue and patriotism.[50] Writers on politics and finance often turned to Britain for comparisons and inspiration, asking how Britain could sustain a role that France was finding impossible. Their answers often drew upon notions of commerce and liberty, both of which they saw as stifled in France. Let us stress, however, that the Enlightenment was not entirely an outsiders' movement critical of the regime. It was linked to the French state and its reforming impulses, it was inside the state in the form of some of its officials and it was, of course, embedded in sections of the nobility as well.[51] So the "absolute monarchy," being a socio-political organization that reflected society, was not only a force for conservatism it was also a force for change, especially from the 1760s. Unfortunately, as we have seen above, the monarchy also contained even stronger forces for the status quo, through its structures of corporatism, its provincial institutions, and, above all, its court-based system of governance. It is not hard to agree with those who stress the role that the contradictions of the regime played in its downfall.

The same monarchy that was espousing fiscal reform was repressing both writers and religious dissidents. It was despotic enough towards these groups to tarnish its own image, delegitimizing itself, but ineffectual enough for them to survive and make telling criticisms.[52] One of the most neglected strands until recently was the Jansenist current. As we have seen, it led to a revival in conciliarist ideas of limitations upon the exercise of sovereignty, and was important in the development of contractual theories and the notion of the Nation.[53] The religious disputes drew in a wider section of the public than did the less accessible writings of the *philosophes*. The churchgoing bourgeoisie of the parishes of Paris acquired an education in activism defending their Jansenist *curés* against the ecclesiastical hierarchy, and the Jansenist parish schools inculcated independence, even democracy, in the artisanal classes.[54] Ideas of natural rights, contracts, and resistance to unjust oppression filtered down to litigious workers and peasants through the activities of lawyers employing the new legal justifications to undermine traditional but oppressive rights.[55]

As an important new set of cultural institutions emerged, the traditional relationship between subjects and the monarchy was undergoing a subtle change. The development of the periodical press, public art exhibitions, salons, academies, reading rooms, clubs, Masonic lodges, and café society all helped to create a "public sphere."[56] This was a forum or critical space for public reflection and debate, embodying the idea of a tribunal of public opinion as the final arbiter. We have seen that Keith Baker has suggested that these developments created a new kind of "politics of contestation." Historians who limit their reading to published pamphlets and works of political theory tend to agree with this view, for in terms of an intellectual construct much evidence exists. But those whose research takes them into the archives of the government tend to stress that decisions were taken with only slight – but increasing – reference to "public opinion." Perhaps it can be accepted that there was indeed contestation in the public sphere, but that a new politics had not before 1788 been created in which the public was a fundamental participant nor one in which rational public debate truly characterized politics.[57] As John Hardman shows, in Chapter 2, it remains very much a closed world of courtly politics until 1787 when the monarchy itself invites wider (but still very limited) commentary.

But let us not be too categorical about this: there are signs of a more general acceptance of public opinion even from ministers, and the subject deserves further investigation. Certainly the calling of an Assembly of Notables was an attempt to create a favorable public opinion that could be used to restrict the parlement's ability to resist the reforms. Even so, that was the brainchild of a finance minister used to the importance of opinion in the markets. One could almost argue that if a new politics of contestation had existed in the minds of the too absolute king and his other ministers, they might not have made the mistakes they did when presenting their reform plans – which of course were so extensive that they needed public approbation to work. As Turgot had seen, France needed a mature public to realize that reforms were necessary. And yet in 1787–8 public opposition throughout France was at first worryingly traditional as people revolted in order to defend or reclaim their provincial and corporate privileges against "despotism." In another area, there was some development, for although ministerial and court politics excluded the "citizens," those who associated in clubs and lodges in forums outside the traditional framework of the monarchy therefore felt a sense of empowerment from their conquest of this freedom to associate. This sense of citizenship was to be a powerful force in the new politics of the Revolution from 1789 onwards – and perhaps in 1788.

Historians have suggested there were processes of "dechristianization" and "desacralization" at work. These terms are a matter for debate, as their precise meaning is unclear, as is the extent of the processes to which they refer. Let us have the temerity to add to them a third: demystification. There was certainly a "demystification" of royal power as the veil was torn away and its workings were exposed to close public scrutiny. This happened not only as a consequence of Jansenism, but also as the public developed an interest in politics during the Enlightenment. The debate over "ministerial despotism" in 1760s, the issues raised as grounds for the expulsion of the Jesuits in 1762, and of course the debate over the Maupeou coup all had an effect.[58] These reasoned critiques appealed to many; others were affected by the scurrilous pamphleteering that tarnished the image of monarchical virtue. A considerable body of recent research has shown how under Louis XV the monarch was portrayed as unvirtuous, and his authority as feminized by the influence of mistresses. Pidansat de Mairobert's apocryphal *Memoirs of Madame du Barry* are an excellent example.[59] This pamphleteering shifted its focus to Marie-Antoinette after 1774, still undermining the masculine authority of the monarchy.[60] There are signs of a decline in the prestige of the absolute monarchy in the medium term as it was undermined in three areas – as a legitimate form of sovereignty, as an effective and respectable form of government, and by foreign policy reverses from 1756 onwards. In 1774 the reversal of policy towards the parlement looked weak to some, and in 1787–8 it was the same story. In a sudden *prise de conscience* in 1788–9, people began to think the unthinkable was possible. The seigneurial regime was under attack, respect for the king seemed in decline and the older forms of Catholic piety were no longer so attractive to French subjects.

Short term

The intervention in the American War of Independence was clearly the most important of the short-term elements of the problem. It stretched the credit mechanisms of the monarchy to the limits, as an expensive naval war was financed at first from loans (and this was notably a choice by Necker who deliberately avoided contentious direct-tax increases). This in turn left a peacetime problem of servicing the debts when continued high taxes (they did have to be increased) seemed less legitimate. Necker's *Compte rendu* of 1781 claiming all was financially sound certainly did not help his successors to deal with the problems. The costs of this war pushed a structural problem beyond compromise short-term solutions. The fact that the war was seen in France as a defense of provincial liberties against despotism fed into the French ideological debate at the most inopportune time. The attempt to levy a stamp tax in 1787 in response to the debts incurred supporting the American insurgents has a nice irony about it.

The *contrôleur général*'s attempts to resolve the fiscal issues from 1783 to 1787 bring to light several issues. As John Hardman suggests, there is the question of the wisdom of the decisions taken and the strategies of political management employed to impose the government's will. Recent research has shown just how disunited that will was, with Louis sidestepping full council meetings and consulting only three ministers, leaving the others less tied into his finance minister's policies. The role and personality of the king must be counted be a factor. Although the reform plans he espoused were Enlightened, deriving in part from Turgot's own earlier projects, Louis himself appears as perhaps the most absolute monarch in his belief in his own God-given powers as king and the least receptive to discussion in council. His political management of the court was very poor – not helped by

Marie-Antoinette's own failings – and the play of faction at court spilled over into the Paris parlement, producing an institutional deadlock by the end of 1786. In 1787 and 1788 when consummate political skills were required, they seemed entirely lacking in Calonne, Loménie de Brienne and Necker, while Louis seemed to have retreated into his shell, overwhelmed by the problems.

Little new work has been done on the question of provincial origins of the Revolution (so there is no chapter devoted to them in this volume) but in a corporate "state of estates" they were important.[61] The 1787 fiscal reform attempts provoked a privileged noble reaction in the provincial estates (which then aroused Third-Estate opposition) and the remodeling of the parlements in 1788 led to the most recalcitrant response from lawyers and magistrates, supported by the populace at times. There was outright violence in several provincial capitals, where the cause of the parlements was often linked to the notion of provincial liberties. This of course posed grave problems for the ministry, whose response thus appeared "despotic," threatening its legitimacy and further undermining credit. The outcome was the setting of an advanced date for the meeting of the Estates General and the recall of the parlements. Three provinces above all deserve closer attention here: Dauphiné, Brittany and Provence. The first two provided a model for the possible evolution of politics in the Estates General, and the third helps us to understand the process of fracturing of opinions under the impact of events.

During the summer of 1788 the capital of Dauphiné, Grenoble, had been a major centre of resistance to the suspension of the parlements. On June 7, 1788 when troops were to ensure the exile of the magistrates, they were bombarded with tiles from the rooftops. On June 14 members of all three orders in Grenoble met to demand the recall of their parlement and the convocation of the Estates General, but they also went on to assert the right of citizens to assemble and deliberate on matters of importance to the nation. In accordance with this last proclamation, the members of all three orders of Grenoble invited other cities and towns of Dauphiné to send representatives to Grenoble to form a new assembly. In defiance of the intendant, the general assembly of all three orders met on July 21, 1788, at the château of Vizille, outside Grenoble. The meeting featured several innovations that caught the attention of much of the rest of France. The Third Estate was numerically predominant, the three orders met in common and issues were resolved through votes by head rather than by order. After adopting resolutions calling for the recall of the parlement and the convocation of the Estates General, the Vizille assembly also called for the reestablishment of the provincial estates of Dauphiné, with double representation for the Third Estate and voting by head. The gathering also offered to renounce the privileges of the province in the interests of the nation, asserting that national unity was necessary for France to move forward.[62]

In Brittany, which also sought the recall of its parlement, events followed an altogether different course. The parlement and the provincial estates were the twin pillars of noble dominance within the province. Clearly dedicated to preserving its traditional privileges, the nobility had difficulty in attracting support from the Third Estate for its cause. Only after a laborious effort was the nobility able to form a deputation of members of all three orders to present a memorandum to the king. The restoration of the parlement of Rennes marked a triumph for aristocratic resistance to "despotism," but the process of mobilization had also led the Third Estate to begin to articulate its own political grievances.[63] This process led in turn to a vigorous effort to reform the Breton constitution by lessening the dominant position of the nobility in the Estates of Brittany, producing sharp conflict between nobles and the Third Estate. Whereas Dauphiné became the symbol of Noble–Third-Estate cooperation and the transcending of privilege in the greater interest of the Nation, Brittany became the model of Noble–Third-Estate confrontation and noble adhesion to privilege over the greater interest of the Nation.[64]

If Brittany and Dauphiné provided models for conduct in 1789, the evolving situation in Provence provides a model for historians of the process by which issues developed and participation widened. As elsewhere, it was less a question of clear social classes than interest groups with a social basis "reacting to opportunities in a fluid situation."[65] It was the issue of the new provincial assembly which first generated discord in Provence. After hearing of Lamoignon's promise to allow variant forms of such assemblies, as in Dauphiné, the fief-holding nobility of Provence determined to seek the reestablishment of the Estates of Provence in abeyance since 1639. The constitution of these Estates gave this section of the nobility complete domination over the distribution of taxes and would preserve their exemptions; in this they were supported by the parlement of Aix-en-Provence. Unable to oppose the revival of the Estates, the leading member of the Assembly of Communities (which since 1639 had administered the unequal tax burden), called for the nobility to give up its fiscal privileges and allow the Third Estate to be represented by more than double the numbers of the privileged orders (because many deputies of the Third would be in the pockets of the nobles). Loménie de Brienne fielded the problem back to the forthcoming Estates of Provence to discuss. In January 1788, a closely united nobility there conceded only equal representation for the Third. Galvanized by 21 deputies of the Third, the municipal bourgeoisie became aware of its opposing interests to those of the enfiefed nobility and demanded its own Assembly of Communities. The May Edicts effected a sort of truce as Provence opposed ministerial despotism, but the quarrel took on new significance when it was known that the Estates General were to meet and it was assumed that the old-style provincial estates would elect the deputies for all orders. In December 1788 a third group entered the debate, the nobility without fiefs, more numerous than their confreres and about to be deprived of representation since they were not in the Estates. In Aix, the capital of Provence, they called for a "general assembly of the Three Orders" to elect deputies to the Provence Estates and reform them. This brought in a fourth group, composed of lawyers, artisans, merchants, and farmers, now affected by the growing interest in public affairs generated by events, who felt the opposition to the enfiefed nobility was led by men who were too timid. Provence emulated Aix and the assemblies that then met were dominated by the councils of the local communities in a clear spirit of revolt. The deputies to the Estates of Provence met at the end of January 1789, with the deputies for the Third Estate elected under many different systems as the whole province followed the lead of Aix. In the Estates, wrote the Intendant, "Authority is neither recognized nor respected." Mirabeau became their spokesman and was cheered; there were "tumultuous gatherings."

Finally, the rural population, politically aroused and hard pressed by the economic situation, began to support reform of the Estates of Provence. Fearing disorder, Necker ruled that the deputies to the Estates General would be elected as elsewhere by assemblies of the seneschalcies. During the elections in late March there were furious popular insurrections directed against not only the seigneurial elite but also the bourgeois municipal governors who levied sales taxes on the poor. "The common people, in their hatred, threaten nothing but death, speak of nothing but tearing out hearts and eating them," wrote the Archbishop of Aix. Another contemporary observation traces a crucial development prefiguring the later revolution:

As the attack by the peasants was directed against everything which seemed to dominate them, the upper Third estate, closer to them, was also the worst treated. This pushed that class, which was greatly opposed to the nobility, toward the nobility, into an alliance against the common enemy.[66]

Provence was a real pioneer in how early its peasants turned to making the seigneurial regime a prime target. Cubells notes how the ideological justifications for the initiatives of the Third Estate developed in arguments and publications in the space of two years. At first, both sides used arguments from distant precedent and history. However, there was soon open affirmation of new ideas, such as the importance of the Third Estate in the social body, with a right to full participation and free representation. There was a process of adoption of Enlightened ideas to the situation in Provence, in terms that also had national significance.[67]

To recapitulate the argument, here is an economy and society in slow transition or at least development, and a state and formal social structure with European and transatlantic commitments that was still rooted in the seventeenth century. Although cultural change was taking place and ideologies were changing, these were less important than the ideology of traditionalism espoused by most of the population and most of the king's ministers. The baroque state – very much a socio-political centre for negotiated power rather than a modern bureaucratic state – was unable to deal with the more pressing demands of the later eighteenth-century world. As a state that had developed through *ad hoc* responses to specific situations, rather than as a clear ideologically motivated construct, it was good at dealing with the specific kinds of political crises that had so conditioned its development, but it remained in a permanent state of tension, far more fragile than it appeared. Its exploitation of imagery and representation was specifically intended to obscure its own weaknesses. Mark Ledbury's essay in this volume explores the significance of changing representations in art and the theatre in undermining this cultural hegemony. Ideological opposition was particularly difficult, be it religious or secular. Its system of political management depended on patronage and clientage and the ability to compromise; real ideological commitment to a position lay beyond the range of negotiated solutions. In this situation the ministries were obliged to propose and manage the most fundamental reforms undertaken by the state since its origins.

And this was exactly the point at which the economic problems began to bite. The hoped for economic gains of the American War never materialized, as the lucrative American tobacco trade was stymied by the vested interests of the Farmers General and traders took up trade with England again.[68] From the later 1770s there was a wider economic downturn. This was greatly exacerbated in Northern France by the effects of the trade treaty with Britain signed in 1786, allowing British manufactures into France at cheaper tariffs. Intended to stimulate competition in France, its more immediate effect was to add to the crisis in the textile industry. Poor harvests also pushed up the price of bread, diminishing the disposable income of the population for manufactures, leading to layoffs of the urban artisans.[69]

Once the crisis of 1787–8 was under way, it acquired its own old-regime style momentum. The ministries were in a corner. Royal prestige, already diminished by scurrilous pamphleteering and the Diamond Necklace Affair, suffered a huge blow with France's debacle of intervention in the Dutch Republic. Threats of war made sound royal finances a priority, and in the event gave the ministries no time for compromise. When the reform agenda ran into stiff traditionalist resistance, there was no alternative to a meeting of the Estates General as the only body able to agree to the financial measures. The previous history of representative institutions shows that they tended to ask for financial controls in return for cooperation, and this of course would imply that some sort of constitutional monarchy would be the outcome.[70] It was the last thing Louis XVI wanted. But from the monarchy there was little recognition of the logic of the situation. Although calling the Estates General was an implicit appeal to public opinion, and even constitutional change, there was almost no attempt to manage these issues in the run-up to the opening session.

Yet a political and financial crisis does not necessarily lead to revolution. Two further processes can help us to understand both the fall of the regime and the attempt to replace it with something better. Between 1787 and the summer of 1789 different groups were drawn into the crisis and, as this happened, the nature of the issues changed. The widening public awareness of the issues began a rapid political education of the French as remonstrances and pamphlets were printed in increasing numbers from the 1787 Assembly onwards, and above all from the summer of 1788. The drawing up of the *cahiers* in 1789 gave rise to debate in villages, chapters, towns, corporate bodies, the clergy and the nobility. Publications, manuscript newsletters and newsmongers made people more aware of national politics than ever before, widening the circle of potential political involvement. (In Paris the centres of this

activity were the duc d'Orléans's *palais royal* and the Tuileries prome-
nade.) This process of broadening the issues and drawing in wider
groups is characteristic of a revolutionary situation, as it politicizes and
creates unmanageable and often contradictory demands. Let us examine this process in more detail.

WHO INTERVENED IN 1787, 1788, AND 1789?
THE REVOLUTION AS A PROCESS

From 1787 to 1789 the very nature of the situation developed as more
groups were drawn in, and perceptions changed. In 1787 the crisis
began at the centre, with reforming initiatives made necessary by long-
term failures in fiscal policy. It was Calonne and the king who involved
the Assembly of Notables, composed of 144 nobles and upper bourgeois
from all over France. The Assembly, convinced that Calonne was trying
to manipulate it, was at first determined to unseat Calonne, whose plans
they thought hastily drawn up and flawed, as well as representing a
significant increase in the despotic potential of the monarchy. As
Leblanc de Castillon said in the Assembly:

> The people should be separated from the upper orders by the reser-
> vation of dignity and power to the latter. The proposed plan has two
> defects: that of having exaggerated the popular element in the parish
> assemblies; and that of giving the intendant too great an authority in
> the provincial assemblies. Republicanism and Despotism.[71]

Loménie de Brienne and the Neckerites were heavily involved in
factional maneuvers.[72] But after they had achieved some success with
Calonne's dismissal, the Assembly was unwisely granted a two-week
Easter break in Paris during which its members turned their attention to
more radical proposals that were less centralizing. These were unacceptable to the new ministry, but, after disbanding, the Notables carried
their ideas to provincial institutions and salons or *sociétés* as Talleyrand
called them. Then Brienne's announcement, in his closing speech, of the
establishment of provincial assemblies sparked off involvement and
protest in some regions by liberals and leading members of the Third
Estate. Although there was to be voting by head and double-sized Third
Estate representation, this would still in practice give power to the most
privileged orders as they had clients in the Third Estate.

At this point pamphleteers were mainly linked to the court and financial factions (rather more than they were embittered freelance inhabitants of Grub Street).[73] Their arguments widened the issues beyond personalities, and the rhetoric of patriotism was employed. Ministerial pamphleteering was one of the sources of anti-aristocratic rhetoric, arguing that the nobility and parlements were privileged and seditious. This argument was linked to the counterweight of a double-sized representation for the Third Estate in the new provincial estates and eventually in the Estates General.[74] The opposition language was also Enlightened, liberal, but it was spoken by members of the elite who were either liberals by belief or liberals by self-interest.[75] Brienne, now a minister, having backed off from this attempt by the Notables to "seize the initiative" took his package of reforms back to the Paris parlement. This institution was both angry at its previous sidelining and influenced by parlementaire radicals. The influential call for the Estates General to be allowed to meet was put forward less as a selfless attempt to involve the nation and more as a rhetorical ploy to embarrass the ministry by radicals and Orleanists, and carried in the parlement by hotheaded youth.

In the summer, to the financial issue was added the challenge to royal authority – and the Crown's response was badly conceived. The exile of the magistrates of the Paris Parlement on August 15 excited support from the *basoche* in Paris – the legal underclass dependent on the various courts – and increased the public disquiet at despotism. "Despotism" was becoming the key word in the summer of 1787, and the Paris Parlement was leading the fight against it. From July 1787 through to the spring of 1788, ministerial despotism continued to be the issue, confirmed by the royal session that turned into a *lit de justice* on November 19, with the subsequent exile of the duc d'Orléans and the arrest of two outspoken magistrates. This evoked enormous interest in the press and in salon talk from a fast-growing public.

Up to May 1788 for the monarchy the crisis was still about finance and authority; for the public it was still about despotism but also, increasingly, about France's constitution. Some saw this as a question of an ancient constitution of provincial rights and self-government, with the parlements retaining their role as a check on despotism. Others like Linguet began to argue that the debt could only be guaranteed by the nation with a constitutional role. Royal fiscal maneuvers led to increased parlementaire criticism, with some very strongly worded remonstrances in the spring of 1788 that not only undermined the financial manipulations but also challenged royal authority on a theoretical level. In May 1788 this led to the Keeper of the Seals' assault on the parlement's ability to block financial solutions, presented as a part of a wider set of reforms. What is interesting in the immediate response by the general public is the lack of it.

The opposition at first stemmed from the courts themselves and the 47 bailiwick courts that traditionally depended upon them, and it was mostly passive – non-cooperation. It is almost as if in most provinces by the 1780s the bourgeois general public, though certainly not the Parisian pamphleteers and legal classes, had become ambivalent about the parlements' claims to defend local and provincial privileges and was thus prepared, given the opportunity, to set its hopes on the remodeled or reinstituted provincial estates.[76] Although several provincial parlements refused to register the royal edicts, the main opposition came in Brittany and Dauphiné.[77] In these provinces sections of the provincial urban elite quickly became involved.[78] Similarly the provincial estates and Assembly of Clergy refused to bail out the "despotic" monarchy with increased grants of taxation. This suggests that the fight against despotism found wide support within the first two orders. However, on the issue of representation in, and taxation by, the provincial estates, a division between the Third Estate and the other two orders was beginning.

A rough measure of public involvement is the quickening rhythm of pamphlet publications. Significantly, until late September 1788, the great majority of Parisian publications were still against ministerial despotism and in defense of the parlements.[79] In some provinces speeches and pamphlets were published reflecting the bourgeois desire to have the privileged pay more equal taxes, to be guaranteed by greater bourgeois representation in the provincial Estates. However, the reappointment of Necker in late August and his recall of the parlements transformed the situation as the literate public really began to believe that the Estates General would be allowed to meet. The ruling by the Paris parlement on September 25, 1788 on the form of the Estates transformed the debate: it created a clear-cut issue about the extent of noble and clerical privilege. This evoked growing resentment from the Third Estate. Necker's second Assembly of Notables in November, which did not recommend doubling the size of the Third Estate in the Estates General, served only to highlight the issue of privilege. In response to this public relations disaster, as Ken Margerison shows, the Society of Thirty campaigned to further its vision of a limited moderate constitution that included a role for the parlements.

By December the royal court and the council of state were split, with

Louis XVI almost inactive. Necker and his allies still dominated the council, but the court factions were mobilized. The *Memorandum of the Princes of the Blood* of December 12 gave later counterrevolutionaries their position, that there was no need for a doubling of the Third Estate because the privileged estates could be relied upon to renounce fiscal privileges themselves. Most were unconvinced. So by the end of the year the main issues had crystallized and sides were being taken. Mallet du Pan, editor of the *Mercure de France*, wrote:

> Public discussion has changed its aspect. It no longer troubles itself except secondarily with the king, with despotism, or with the constitution: it has become a war between the third estate and the two other classes, against whom the court has stirred up the towns. The parlement was an idol six months back; now everyone detests and insults it: d'Eprémesnil, the avenger of the nation, the Brutus of France, is vilified everywhere.[80]

With the elections coming, the ambitious and the young now realized that there was an opportunity to play a role on the national stage. "Regeneration" was the key desire, but the debate was about how best to achieve it, and whether it would be prevented by the combination of the two privileged orders. Early in 1789, observers were well aware of the violence of the Breton situation, and of the compromise in Dauphiné. Meanwhile, the Society of Thirty tried to influence elections and *cahiers* in favour of a union of the three orders. The electoral process, however, deepened and widened splits that had already occurred in the context of the provincial estates. In the nobility, nobles with fiefs or with more than a hundred years of nobility tried, often successfully, to exclude those with newer titles or without fiefs. In the Third Estate, bourgeois often excluded artisans from the assemblies. In response, peasants and more popular urban classes became involved, as they drew conclusions about the link between subsistence and representation. Drawing up *cahiers* only served to crystallize latent tensions. Nevertheless, the *cahiers* do not point unequivocally towards a coming revolution.[81]

When the estates met on May 5, 1789, the deputies were royalist and patriotic, and thought the main issue was how best to achieve national regeneration. Most Third Estate deputies were convinced that the king intended to side with their order against the "privileged" orders.[82] Given the suspicion of the nobility and the upper clergy, who dominated the first two Estates, the Third Estate, equal in numbers to the other two, was determined to secure voting by head rather than by order. If successful, it would always have a majority because there would be support from liberal nobles and the parish clergy. Pamphlet arguments that the Third Estate was effectively the Nation were at first seen as radical. But the Crown failed to intervene effectively in the early days, when such a lead was still acceptable. By June the failure of negotiations and consequential exasperation with the nobility ensured virtual unanimity for the revolutionary step of declaring the Third Estate the "National Assembly" and inviting the others to join it. Such a step was promoted most vigorously by the Breton delegation, influenced by their bitter experience of conflict in Brittany, but other interest groups were also at work. In particular, the assumption of sovereignty by the nation was important for the financial interests who had outstanding loans to the monarchy: a constitutional monarchy was a way of guaranteeing their debt by transferring it from the king, a dubious debtor, to the nation.

Lack of royal initiative, faction, ideology, and therefore the question of voting, were the stumbling blocks. Increasing exasperation at inactivity and apprehension of being disbanded led to a steady rise in support for the seizure of the initiative by the Third Estate on June 17 and 20. But as Michael Fitzsimmons and Ken Margerison show, for many deputies the looked-for moderate compromise of a union of the orders did characterize the outcome in early July (even though it was partly inspired by threats from the crowd). Then, ultraroyalists and conservatives intervened disastrously at court, winning a change of ministry on July 11. By dismissing Necker's ministry, the king showed himself to be apparently in the counterrevolutionary camp.

At this point popular disorder and constitutional crisis came together disastrously for the regime. From 1787 the collapse in the price of wine (a cash crop for peasants) was followed by wet weather which severely reduced yields from farming and on July 13, 1788 a huge storm devastated crops all over northern France. Then the winter of 1788–9 was so severe that rivers and mills froze, preventing the transport and milling of grain. A crisis in manufacturing led to urban unemployment for artisans. From the spring of 1789, fear and necessity drove peasants and urban crowds to riot against seigneurial dues or hoarders trying to profit from famine. Insufficient forces of order were available in this severe subsistence crisis. As the price of bread rose to its highest point (actually on July 14 in Paris), the interaction between subsistence problems and the stimulated popular awareness of politics became explosive. Confronted

by fellow citizens, confused by government policy, the soldiers and officers in the line army failed to perform their task of repression.

From the winter onwards, the economic and subsistence crisis had
been drawing in further groups in the localities, provoking both sympathy and fear from the propertied classes. As John Markoff explains in
Chapter 9, in the countryside antiseigneurialism, as evidenced in the
cahiers, turned words into actions. Complex lines of fracture formed in
local society. The final stages of the collapse in royal authority were therefore a consequence of widespread popular disorder in town and country.
The support of the crowd was essential for frightening the king and nobility into joining with the Third Estate in June and July, and for effecting
the hugely important fall of the Bastille – that very symbol of despotism.[83]
The regime began to collapse like a house of cards. Although a constitutional revolution had become inevitable, the scope and nature of the
revolution was profoundly conditioned by popular involvement.

The widespread disorder redefined some of the issues for the political
classes. The lynchings of July 14 and 22 posed the question of whether
the means justified the ends. Some radicals like Barnave chillingly asked
of the dead, "Was their blood so pure, then?" Most of the propertied
classes were horrified and were determined to reign in popular disorders
in town and country. The very act of doing so, when the government
was unable to act effectively, empowered the bourgeois townsfolk,
provoking municipal revolutions that further undermined the old order.
By raising bourgeois fears, the breakdown of order posed the question of
whether a constitution should include all of the nation – or only the
more respectable part of it. The Night of August 4 has two aspects. As
Michael Fitzsimmons shows in Chapter 10, it was truly revolutionary in
abolishing the old regime. But it was also an attempt to make concessions on the issue of feudal property to calm disorder and rally the propertied classes to the revolution. This ambivalence towards the popular
classes was to characterize the political choices of bourgeois revolutionaries for a decade, until a regime promising order as well as the gains of
the revolution was created by Napoleon.

CONCLUSION

I have tried to show how a crisis of the baroque state developed into a
revolution. The crisis was an essential part of a process of revolution that
grew from a complex interaction of events and ideologies, some old,

some newer. At first, traditional opposition to royal reforms, whether from court faction, parlements, or the nobility, tried to exploit the difficult situation of the seemingly indestructible monarchy to its own particular advantage. Only at a late stage did the likelihood of a fundamentally different polity become clear. At that point the cultural changes of the eighteenth century fed into this crisis, giving it a very different outcome from previous financial breakdowns. To point to cultural changes in some key areas must not be taken to suggest that the crisis of 1787–8 was *caused* by these cultural changes. To do so would be to fall into some of the interpretative traps discussed above. My argument is that cultural and ideological changes help us to understand how this crisis of the baroque state was resolved in a different way from previous ones and turned into a revolution in 1789. The crisis itself, as a process, drew in different groups and gave them the opportunity to express demands that were new, and were increasingly incompatible with the continued existence of the regime. The transformative effect of events is a key element in explaining the Revolution. And even though a sense of citizenship made itself felt in 1789, this alone would not have been enough to ensure that a revolution took place. The surprising extent of the collapse of royal authority was crucial in creating a space for effective action. Uncertainty opened the door to creativity.

1. The Financial Origins of the French Revolution

JOËL FÉLIX

Summary

In his illuminating discussion of the financial system of the regime, Joël Félix somewhat rehabilitates the ancien-régime financial authorities, who were vehemently criticized by contemporaries and historians. His analysis shows that there was not one reason – the fiscal issue for instance – but many reasons why the monarchy faced a financial crisis in 1787. It was not the first such crisis, for financial crises were barely avoidable in a regime engaged in frequent warfare with an inelastic taxation system. For this reason, credit was the most important aspect of finances in the eighteenth century. For whatever we may think about fiscal equality – and political equality – reforming the fiscal system with its many taxes was a long and painful task, and one that could not therefore respond to a short-term crisis. In many respects, French ministers were well aware of these problems. But although some of them simply preferred to perpetuate what was done before them, others believed they would be able to bring a solution to deficits and debts by making the most of a large and potentially wealthier country. So ministers usually overestimated their power, which was always challenged by fellow ministers. Moreover, they were powerless before a growing public opinion, the cultivated elements of which were requesting reforms that were not always politically acceptable or technically possible. In terms of general public opinion, however, most of it had little, indeed barely any, practical experience of administering finance and taxes. What opinions reveal to us was a basic hostility to increased taxation, a sense of inequality and the idea that reforms should bring relief from taxes. Yet, fiscal, financial and economic reforms always challenged the status quo and the crisis tested to its limits the ability of the king and his ministers to bring about a workable solution that would bring greater happiness to his subjects. And kings and ministers, though they would have liked to be able to reduce the burden on the poor, could not contemplate a France without privileges, that is to say, a world in which full equality existed. As a result, when the answer to the financial problems turned out to focus on fiscal equality, political equality remained a major issue. But fiscal equality alone would never be a sufficient reform, for old and bitter issues still remained, such as the control of government expenditures or the liberalization of the economy. Ultimately, the problem was political, in terms both of securing a consensus on potentially divisive decisions and of implementing them.

It appears that the old financial regime will be re-established. One cannot say the old system since it is not quite certain that there was one.   June 5, 1781[1]

Fundamentally, the scope of the debate concerning the financial origins of the French Revolution has changed very little since 1789. When the Estates General began their first session, two very different points of view were already in conflict. According to government ministers, who were seeking to reassure the public after reform proposals made by Calonne and Loménie de Brienne in 1787–8 to balance the budget had been rejected, the *deficit*, though significant, was nothing to worry about for a great nation such as France. Indeed, Necker stated, in his *Rapport sur l'état des finances* (May 5, 1789) to the assembled deputies of the Three Orders, that the kingdom of France was so rich and her people so industrious that with some changes and a handful of reforms it would be extremely easy to make up the deficit quickly *as if by magic*.[2] Thus, far from being a political necessity imposed by the parlous state of the royal finances, the convening of the Estates General was, according to Necker, but an additional proof of the king's affection for his people, and also of the confidence that they were bound to show in his ability and that of the country to face up to the crisis.

These clumsy reassurances were couched in language that was too technical to capture the imagination of an audience enthralled by the event. The deputies easily retorted that the deficit, which had paralyzed the country since 1787, was not quite as fanciful as the minister was claiming, and that, more importantly, they had not been elected to give their support to another programme for rebalancing the finances. The representatives were boosted by their *cahiers de doléances* which asked for the drawing up of a constitution prior to any increase in taxes and presented the political demands of the Third Estate concerning the way votes were counted in the Estates General. They were thus unanimous in their conviction that the crisis in the royal finances required more than the palliative measures advocated by Necker. Coming less than twenty years after controller general Terray's bankruptcy (1770), this new crisis showed clearly how reshaping the structure of the monarchy was needed to avoid an imminent financial collapse of the state and, moreover, to prevent it ever happening again.

In their various ways historians have revisited this initial debate in the same terms ever since, a debate that raises questions about the causes of the crisis, its seriousness and the remedies to be brought to it. A long historical tradition – following on from the criticisms made at the end of the reign of Louis XIV, notably by Vauban and Boisguilbert, about the social and economic fallout of the government's fiscal policy – has stubbornly maintained that the origins of the Revolution were to be found in the archaic structures of an ancien régime that kept the subjects of the king in great poverty. According to this version of events, which was honed by Enlightenment economists, the inequalities and burden of the taxes gathered at great cost by the *financiers* – in addition to the various seigneurial and feudal dues levied by the clergy and nobles – deprived agriculture, the main source of France's wealth, of the investments needed to underpin production and increase the government's income. These ideas, which were taken up by the historian Ernest Labrousse, gave rise to the classic interpretation that the economy of the ancien régime was prone to recurrent agricultural crises of underproduction. By suddenly pushing up the price of bread and wine, bad harvests reduced domestic consumption of manufactured products, raised unemployment and spread poverty. These hardships led to recriminations and acts of violence against the government which wanted for the revenues denied it by a sclerotic economy.

Reacting to this poverty-based version of the origins of the Revolution, other historians, who are usually interested in studying urban rather than rural contexts, have focused on the basic dynamism of the French economy in the eighteenth century, an economy boosted by population growth (going from 20 million to 28 million between 1715 and 1789) and the spectacular development of commerce, especially between France and her colonies. These two phenomena, coupled with other factors such as improvements in hygiene and the development of means of communication, contributed to developing trade, caused a boom in production and consumption, and ultimately led to increasing the wealth of a section of the middle classes. These historians do not deny the existence of some weaknesses in the French economy, particularly the relative slowness of agricultural growth, the lack of a central bank able to control the cost of money, and the fact that France lagged behind Great Britain technologically. However, they have stressed that at the end of a century of growth and on the eve of the Revolution the kingdom of the Bourbons was a leading European economy, if not in qualitative terms then at least in terms of raw figures. With the encouragement of ministers who were anxious to promote growth and progress, France was on the point of catching up with her rival, Great Britain.[3]

Although they are contradictory, these two versions of events are neither completely incompatible nor entirely satisfactory. Besides the fact that they describe two worlds that coexisted in 1789, their contradictions bring to light the limits that ought to be placed on macroeconomic interpretations of the origins of the Revolution. If the society of the ancien régime created poverty such as would lead inevitably to its destruction, it is difficult to understand why this regime collapsed only in 1789 at the end of a period of growth and not much sooner, for example during the reign of Louis XIV in 1694–5, when famine and its attendant ills killed more than two million Frenchmen, or again, as has been suggested, after the Seven Years' War.[4] However, neither is the economic growth theory entirely convincing. Its fundamental optimism leads its proponents to confuse growth with social and political progress and to neglect the short-term impact of the fluctuations in the economic situation that played such an important role in the financial crises of the eighteenth century. It also underestimates the tensions caused by the difficulties of bringing important manufacturing sectors up to date, notably the wool and silk industries. While these were hitherto protected by mercantilist legislation, in the latter half of the eighteenth century they were challenged by international competition, technical innovation, and changes in consumer tastes.

The origins of the Revolution must not only be sought in the performance of the economy in itself, which moreover varied according to sectors of industry, places, and periods, they must also be sought in the Enlightenment's conviction that France was a country with great potential whose government's task was to create an economic policy able to sustain growth, and thus give the State the financial means, by a fiscal reform, of achieving its ambitions. The incongruity between a fast-growing economy and a state regularly facing bankruptcy leads one to arrive at François Crouzet's conclusion that the ancien régime did not perish because of a weak economy but above all because of poor finances. Whether or not one accepts the idea that economic forces at work in the eighteenth century evolved independently of the state's influence – a question which remains unresolved – a proper financial and fiscal approach to the origins of the Revolution raises the problem of the nature of the monarchy under the ancien régime and, in particular, its political and technical ability to gather the revenue it needed to practice its policy of grandeur without harming economic progress and, above all, without being forced into bankruptcy or default.[5]

On these questions historians are no less divided. Some have decided to look for the origins of the deficit in the ineffective and arbitrary fiscal and financial system which favored but a tiny privileged elite who ruined a country worn down by the expenditure of the Court. Others, on the contrary, insist on the presence of essentially competent and honest administrators who aimed at modernizing the structures of the monarchy. However, their attempts were systematically blocked, on this account, by the privileged classes whose members were sufficiently powerful to paralyze or destroy the resolve for reform that existed at the highest level in the state.[6]

As with the arguments over the performance of the economy, adopting one of these points of view would limit severely our understanding of the financial origins of the French Revolution. The development of trade produced new forms of wealth which affected traditional justifications for the social hierarchy without formally changing either the structures of the monarchy or the way in which numerous subjects of the king lived their lives. Similarly, the financial needs of the state forced those in charge to come up with means of finding money – and to make use of language to justify changes – which little by little transformed the relations between the king and his subjects without nonetheless openly calling into question the political foundations of the ancien régime. The structural changes and occasional crises that led to conflict brought about the transformation of the meaning of old concepts and the creation of new ones – such as state, Nation, citizenship, and sovereignty. Then, under the pressure of certain circumstances and the influence of certain men, these changes crystallized to the point of making the Revolution not only possible – because alternative models of financial and political governance had been discussed and even tested prior to 1789 – but also necessary and desirable and, in this respect, perhaps inevitable.

WAR AND PEACE

The importance of war in the Age of Enlightenment, and its impact on society, has generally been underestimated by historians. This is because the eighteenth century was a century of hope and faith in man and in progress; it suffered neither demographic nor climatic disasters nor any major revolts as in the reigns of Louis XIII or Louis XIV, and moreover the economic indicators pointed ordinarily towards growth. It is true that at that time war was normally prosecuted on foreign soil or at sea, and thus was less directly harmful to the kingdom's domestic economy. It is also true that it did not, as in the *grand siècle*, take place in a context of European economic recession. Nevertheless, war remained the central preoccupation of rulers and their subjects in the latter half of the eighteenth century.

After two decades of relative peace following the death of Louis XIV (1715), the European monarchies again went to war over the issue of the succession to the Polish throne (1733). Later, between 1740 and 1783, France was involved in two major international conflicts: the War of Austrian Succession (1740–8) and the Seven Years' War (1756–63). Later still came the American war (1778–83). In total that made 22 years of war and only 21 years of peace, without counting the number of secondary conflicts, such as the invasion of Corsica (1768), and various periods of international tension which, while the ambassadors were in talks, meant that France had to put part of its army on a war footing or begin fitting out battleships. Conflicts thus encroached heavily on the periods of peace. For instance, spending on the American war began shortly after Versailles heard the news of the Boston Tea Party. The government of Louis XVI decided almost immediately to come to the financial help of the Revolutionaries and seized the chance to construct a navy capable of overcoming Great Britain.

If one must seek an overall explanation for the financial crisis of the ancien régime, only war – and the policy of France's grandeur – can provide it. War not only meant great loss of life on the battlefields but also a sudden and significant growth in the government's expenditure, or, in other words, a substantial increase of taxes on the king's subjects. For example, during the War of Austrian Succession, expenditure exceeded normal income by 40 million livres tournois in 1741, 52 million in 1742, 88 million in 1743, 97 million in 1744, 115 million in 1745, 100 million in 1746, 115 million in 1747 and 112 million in 1748: 719 million in total (see Figure 1.1). In other words in eight years the government had to secure a sum of money that without the war it would have taken twelve years to collect.

Given the extent of these expenditures, which would continue to grow throughout the war years, even the smallest financial resource was exploited by the government. Two essential considerations, however, governed their policy. First, the war effort immediately required the gathering of such large sums that rises in taxes, although indispensable, could not alone make up the difference between income and expenditure; suddenly asking the taxpayer to pay half again on his taxes was materially impossible, not to say ill-advised. In addition to the problematic slow process of gathering in the money, overtaxing would have risked stifling an economy that in time of war was bound to suffer from the unavoidable disruption to colonial trade.

In order to pay for the war, therefore, the ministers responsible for finance generally had no other option but to raise existing taxes and have recourse to the so-called extraordinary revenues. These included exceptional taxes levied on certain wealthy groups or goods, borrowing from the public or from corporate bodies (provincial estates, towns, guilds, corporate officers), and securing cash advances from *financiers* who were responsible for ensuring the collection of taxes. The boost from these various means of financing war expenditure amounted to a financial policy which, as will be seen, varied according to period, economic and financial context, and the ideas of the individuals and groups who were in charge of the country.

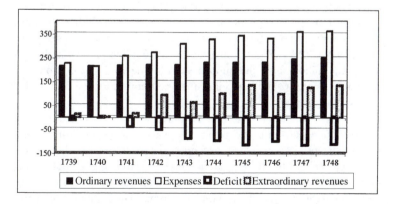

Figure 1.1　*Financing the War of Austrian Succession (millions of livres tournois)*[7]

War faced the government with a second problem: it never knew how long the war would last. Hence the difficulty of preplanning a financial strategy, the success of which would depend upon many variables, notably the outcome of battles or the harvests. Due to these uncertainties, the ministers tried to amass sufficient funds in the Treasury at the outbreak of hostilities to be able to cover the outlay of the first year or two of war, without, as far as was possible, impoverishing the taxpayer or destroying credit. The way to achieve this was either to secure the expected revenue from new taxes as advances from financiers, or to capitalize this new income by borrowing. This method of financing war obviously had its limitations. The interest that the state had to pay to its creditors grew according to the length of the war, the size of the sums borrowed, and the population's ability to pay its taxes, each of which would affect the state's credit rating from one year to the next.[8]

In financial terms, the war brought at least one advantage: it justified in the eyes of the public the raising of new taxes, and sometimes even the need for the government, as controller general Bertin told Louis XV, to take what were essentially financially ruinous steps to avoid military defeat. However, this psychological trump card disappeared when peace was made. The government then had no other choice but to suppress the taxes levied to pay for the war and, as a consequence, to see the king's income suddenly fall spectacularly. In 1762, foreseeing the effects of the peace accord between France and Great Britain, Bertin calculated that the annual income of the monarchy which was set at about 320 million a year, was suddenly going to be reduced by 59 million, or 18 percent. This was due to the suppression of a series of taxes including the third *vingtième* (a direct tax equivalent to 5 percent of the net revenues of property owners) (22.5 million), military taxes (21.5 million), the double *capitation* (12 million) and the supplements to the *dons gratuits* from the provincial estates (3 million), all of them extraordinary revenues levied only for the duration of the war.

The loss of these revenues was a genuine setback for the ministers of finance. In effect, with the return of peace, the expenditure of the monarchy would never return to its prewar levels. Certainly, the government demobilized the troops, but it was already thinking about building up its military strength once more. Above all, it had to meet many new costs which did not exist before the war: in particular, interest on loans, and capital repayments in the case of fixed-term loans.[9] To this public debt in the strict sense of the word – created by virtue of royal order and recorded by the parlements – were added other debts for the payment of which no regular revenue was assigned. In particular these included the *dettes exigibles* (short-term debt), comprising the expenditure of ministerial departments that had not yet been paid, and cash advances by financiers. They also included the *dettes arriérées* (outstanding debt), i.e., usually the payments that in time of war the government ceased to pay or simply froze.[10]

Therefore when peace was made the financial situation promised to be even more difficult than during the war. For example, between 1764 and 1767, controller general L'Averdy paid 209 million livres tournois in cash – 50 million a year – to repay the debts that were considered most urgent. Moreover, he issued 226 million of *reconnaissances au porteur* (bonds bearing an interest) to pay the debts of ministerial departments. The capital of these (437 million) was quite large since it represented nearly half of the extraordinary revenues secured through government levies during the Seven Years' War (1,105 million).[11] As a result, unless the postwar budget reduced certain expenses and increased revenue – notably by supporting economic growth and putting fiscal reform into action – it was destined, for some time at least, to run at a deficit. The problem with deficits was their potentially snowballing effect. Since the government was forced to borrow in peacetime, it ran the risk of deepening its debt day by day and thereby reducing the confidence of creditors in its ability to honour its debts. If the economic situation deteriorated or a particular tax revenue suddenly dried up, the gap between income and expenditure would increase the deficit. The government would then risk losing control of its finances and thus had no option other than to either increase tax in peacetime (thus provoking social and political conflict) or reduce the expenditure in an authoritarian way by declaring bankruptcy or defaulting – a method that could be practiced in the short term but which in the medium term tended to increase the cost of money.

This was more or less the situation that Louis XV, in 1767, and Louis XVI, in 1786, had to face four years after making peace. In August 1786 the controller general, Calonne, told Louis XVI that the third *vingtième*, a tax levied for the duration of the American War of Independence and for a few years after peace was made, was to come to an end. This, he stated, would take the annual difference between expenditure (589 million) and revenue (474 million) to an unsustainable 115 million in 1787 – i.e., to 24 percent of income. To compensate for the loss of the third *vingtième* and to balance the budget, Calonne submitted to Louis XVI a major programme of economic and fiscal reform. Mindful of the dangers of the situation and concerned to avoid foreseeable opposition from the Paris parlement, he secured from the king, who had little affection for the parlements, permission to put forward his projects for the approval of an Assembly of Notables in spring 1787. The subsequent resistance to the reforms by both the Assembly and the Paris parlement set in motion the crisis that led to collapse in 1789.

The nature of the resistance by privileged groups seems to justify the opinion that the fall of the ancien régime was caused by the selfishness and irresponsibility of a privileged aristocracy, and most particularly the *Notables* and the Paris parlement, who did not hesitate to oppose government measures and to some extent encourage the Revolution with the sole aim of maintaining their own privileges. First, they defended their financial privileges which were threatened by Calonne's plan to make the rich pay tax in proportion to their wealth. The other privileges were those of political power and rank which they refused to surrender in the Estates General. The value of this fiscal interpretation of the origins of the Revolution lies in underlining the fact that the monarchy's financial problems were the cause of serious political tensions between the government and the elites. It also shows that the question of levying taxes on the privileged classes was on each occasion one of the principal issues in the conflict.

However, this interpretation has several shortcomings. On the one hand it underestimates the real progress made by the monarchy on the question of fiscal equality during the eighteenth century. On the other hand it confuses finances and taxation, thus forgetting that the question of privileges was exacerbated by the lack of financial transparency, which undermined successive ministers' attempts to establish control of the finances and by the lack of confidence necessary to borrow money at a low rate. Ultimately an analysis based solely on tax policy fails to account for the fact that the existence of privilege was a non-negotiable element of the ancien régime – as was shown by the conflict between the Third Estate and Louis XVI. In such an organic society, social and political distinctions were regarded as providing the foundation not only of public liberties but also of property and public order. In other words, financial crises were fundamentally political.

TAXES AND PRIVILEGES

A long historical tradition attributed the collapse of the ancien régime to the economic and social consequences of the political system of absolutism which set up and maintained the domination of the privileged classes by means of oppressive and unfair taxation, thus sapping the country's sources of wealth. However, since the 1960s this interpretation has been questioned by several authors. In particular, a study by Peter Mathias and Patrick O'Brien focusing on respective taxation rates in France and Great Britain in the eighteenth century shattered conventional wisdom. They showed that the British taxpayer, who, it had been thought, was protected by Parliament from the excesses of the tax office, was in reality more heavily taxed than the French taxpayer who nonetheless denounced ministerial despotism and the excessive rates of taxation. In the opinion of Mathias and O'Brien, the defining element of the Bourbon monarchy was not its ability to oppress the people, but rather the difficulties it encountered during the eighteenth century when it decided to impose new and fairer taxes.[12]

These positions supported the arguments put forward at the beginning of the nineteenth century by Marcel Marion in his biography of the controller general, Machault d'Arnouville, the conclusions of which were in part inspired by Tocqueville's historic analyses of the ancien régime.[13] They have since been taken up by numerous experts of the absolute monarchy. For them, far from serving the interests of the privileged classes, the monarchy since at least the reign of Louis XIV had attempted endlessly to reform its fiscal system to lighten the burden on the most impoverished and make the rich pay a fairer proportion of taxes. Thus, the crisis of the ancien régime should not be sought in the arbitrary character of the absolute monarchy, but on the contrary in its painstaking efforts to abolish privilege, and also in the no less determined resistance that its efforts met among the privileged classes.

Paradoxically, this interpretation, which one could call revisionist insofar as it opposes the Marxist interpretation of the socio-economic origins of the Revolution, has itself been questioned by non-Marxist historians who have focused their attention on the nobility and the elites of the ancien régime. Their refutation of the class warfare theory, notably of the socio-economic opposition between the nobility and the bourgeoisie, highlights the fact that certain members of the privileged classes were far from being fossils, and that they were not the only ones to enjoy privilege. Throughout the centuries the monarchy had made a veritable trade out of privilege, selling numerous positions of authority to the upper classes, granting the holders of such positions – both noble and otherwise – various degrees of immunity. Furthermore, study of the *cahiers de doléances* has ultimately shown that with a few rare exceptions, such as in Normandy or Auvergne, the members of the nobility had by then unanimously expressed the desire to give up their pecuniary privileges and to become full taxpayers. Thus the fiscal revolution was virtually accomplished even before the Estates General met.[14]

The nobility's decision to give up its tax privileges was certainly brought about by its concern to head off the principal demand of the Third Estate concerning the legality of taxes and political equality. However, it must be noted that if the nobles agreed to share the expenses of the nation, it was because little by little they had become taxpayers – certainly privileged taxpayers, as Michael Kwass remarks, but taxpayers all the same. Although the first taxes levied on the nobles were linked to policies concerning the welfare of the state, policies necessitated by periodic crises (in particular wars), these taxes nonetheless contributed to establishing a precedent. The creation of the *capitation* in 1695, a tax on all heads of families, brought into France for the first time the principle of a universal tax. In 1710 the *dixième* (a tenth of revenues), set up by Desmaretz, established for the first time the principle of proportional tax and made it a requirement to submit income declarations to the tax office.[15] Yet these important innovations only bore fruit in 1749 when the controller general, Machault d'Arnouville, decided to convert the *dixième* – a temporary tax imposed or lifted depending on whether the country was at war – into the *vingtième* (a tax of 5 percent on landowners' net incomes). Launched as a mere temporary tax, its revenues were meant to finance a *caisse d'amortissement* (sinking fund) for paying off the capital borrowed by the government during the War of Austrian Succession. However, the *vingtième* was regularly collected until the Revolution, thus making members of the Second Order fuller taxpayers.

Although privilege was far from having entirely disappeared, the monarchy's fiscal policies gradually made all the French subject to taxation. In 1764, L'Averdy gave to his friend the young Isaac de Bacalan the responsibility of passing this message to the parlements in order to obtain their agreement in principle for introducing taxes on interests paid by the state to its creditors who were traditionally exempted by royal edict. To justify these views, Bacalan explained that all income, whatever its origin or the status of the landowner, was subject to tax. This, he said, applied in particular to military pensions which compensated long years of service to the state. Income which allowed for deduction of tax before payment fell even more heavily under such rulings, and this explains why the peacetime suppression of war tax, such as the *dixième*, was never applied to interest payments or salaries funded by the state. In 1745 a pension of 1000 livres tournois netted in reality only 860 livres, while 16 percent went to the tax office. From the 10 million paid by the state to magistrates and judges – 8 million for *gages* (revenues) and 2.4 million for the *franc-salé* (salt franchise) – the government only paid out 5 million livres, an amount equal to a tax at source of approximately 50 percent.

Of course, it is very difficult to ascertain the proportion of tax paid by the nobles and other privileged groups on the eve of the Revolution, and to compare them with other social groups, notably the merchant bourgeoisie. However, it is no exaggeration to suppose that on average the nobility paid a direct tax equal to between 10 and 12 percent of their net income. From 1756 onward, nobles in peacetime were obliged to pay direct taxes of *deux sols pour livres du dixième* (1.66 percent), two *vingtièmes* (10 percent) and the *capitation* (1 to 1.5 percent). To these taxes would be added a third *vingtième* and a double *capitation* during wartime. It is true that since the fiscal administration was prevented from system-atically checking tax declarations but had the right to grant exemptions to individuals, the two *vingtièmes* were never effectively levied. According to Calonne, tax fraud in this area cost about 25 million a year. Moreover, nobles could get back part of the tax by securing lucrative positions either at Court, in the army, in finance, or in the administra-tion.

But these taxes were not the only ones the nobility paid. In the *pays de taille réelle*, located in the south of France, nobles who owned non-noble land paid the *taille*, the commoner's tax. Moreover they benefited from the *taille* exemption only for a limited portion of the land which they farmed directly. According to the admission of many nobles, the tax levied by the state on the commoners was also reflected in the value of the leases on their land. Lastly, nobles paid many indirect taxes. As Calonne reminded the *Notables*, "every last subject of the King, whether prince, noble or churchmen, must, like the humblest of the People, pay capitation, the *aides*, the salt tax, and tax on all drinks." Although they were socially regressive, indirect taxes hit large-scale consumers, while the rich, both bourgeois and noble, were particularly hit through the *contrôle des actes*, a tax on private contracts, which was introduced during the reign of Louis XIV.

This labyrinth of taxes, franchises and laws surely amounted to the most powerful block on the monarchy's desire to tax the French more equitably. In effect, in a tax system dominated by inequality, adding on a fair tax would only magnify its discrepancies. This problem explains the mid-eighteenth-century enthusiasm for the physiocrats' proposal to replace all taxes with a single direct tax on landowners' income. Such a tax would, they argued, be the best form of tax, for it would operate directly on what they regarded as the true and only source of wealth. It would also reduce the cost of tax collection by freeing up the *commis* of the General Farm used in the fight against fraudsters who could then work on the land and be productive. The influence of liberal economic thought on government policy must not, however, make us forget that, unlike the intellectuals who redesigned the world on the basis of their political arithmetic, controllers general had to balance the budget. As L'Averdy told the parlements, taxes were not a *décor de théâtre* which could be brought in and removed at a whim. In 1763 Bertin explained the government position on taxes and privileges, which did not change until the Revolution: "Everyone must contribute because everyone is obliged to come to the help of the State. But what establishes the level of contribution can vary according to an individual's status and the range of taxable products. For there are privileges that your Majesty must maintain and there are goods on which a heavy tax would impede production and circulation."[16] In line with these views, Calonne's plan was to make up the deficit by an increase in direct tax on properties and by proposing in return to exempt the nobles and clergy from the *capitation*. Henceforth, like the *taille*, the *capitation* would be reserved for members of the Third Estate. Of course, this initiative was worth the trouble. According to Calonne's estimates, if land revenues were taxed fairly they were bound to bring in twice as much. As these examples show, the abolition of tax privileges was not so much the aim of government fiscal policies as one of the many means by which ministers tried to collect more revenue.

INCOME AND EXPENDITURE

The question of the financial origins of the Revolution is to some degree distorted by the size of the deficit, which came as a real shock. The annual deficit Calonne revealed to the *Notables* in 1787 was truly gigantic: 115 million – later recalculated at 140 million – which amounted to more than half the budget of the Habsburg monarchy and equivalent to the annual revenues of Spain. Clearly it was impossible to eliminate the deficit without taking far-reaching measures and raising taxes considerably. To meet this enormous deficit, Calonne suggested to the king and the *Notables* that direct taxes paid by landowners, nobles and bourgeois be raised from the yearly level of 55 million (76 million if calculating from the levies on landowners during the war) to 105 million. This was 66 percent higher than wartime tax levels and 90 percent higher than those in peacetime. Although the social, economic and political situation of modern democracies bears no resemblance to that of the ancien régime, one can easily understand the reaction of the rich to Calonne's proposals if one compares it to present-day criticisms of tax increases and their effect on economic growth.

In 1787 the size of the deficit was a reality all the more difficult to swallow because the monarchy's income had risen continually since the War of Austrian Succession, particularly during the Seven Years' War (1756–63), when on average the per capita tax paid by French subjects was at its highest since the War of Spanish Succession in the last decade of Louis XIV's reign.[17] As Figure 1.2 shows, ordinary income doubled in 40 years, going from an average of 200 million a year (212 million in constant money) between 1736 and 1739 (when the country was at peace) to 405 million between the years 1777 and 1783 (when the country was at war), amounting to a rise of about 1.6 percent per year. It is true that the rise in prices and the economic growth – fixed by the most recent estimates at 0.6 percent per year for agricultural production and

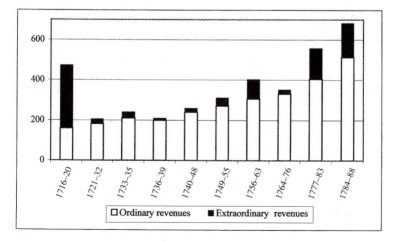

Figure 1.2 *Annual average of ordinary and extraordinary revenues in periods of peace and war, 1716–88 (millions of livres tournois)*[18]

1.5 percent per year for commerce and manufacturing – certainly contributed to minimizing the real growth of the tax burden on the French taxpayer. However, besides the fact that these estimates are not very reliable, such macroeconomic considerations do not take into account the taxpayers' perception of the change in their tax burden nor the impact of short-term crises on production and prices.

From 1740 to 1763, the rise in tax receipts was especially rapid, being in the order of 2.5 percent per year. Since the price of grain at that time was very low, these tax hikes hit landowners badly. From 1756 onwards they paid two *vingtièmes* in peacetime and three *vingtièmes* in wartime, and thus some of them sought the suppression of legislation forbidding the exportation of grain, laws which contributed to a fall in prices when grain yields were high. Despite getting rid of war tax, the government was forced to pay its debts by raising tax revenues from 303 million to 348 million between 1767 and 1772, a rise of 15 percent. The dizzying rise in the price of foodstuffs certainly did not make up for tax losses, since the wheat and wine yield was on the whole very poor. Moreover, the bankruptcy of abbé Terray levied, as it were, a covert tax by default-ing on part of the state's debt.

Since the government in peacetime and in wartime continued to borrow to finance its extraordinary expenses and deficit, the French understandably had the impression that the source of these problems lay essentially in excessive expenditure and not at all in insufficient income. After all, between 1775 and 1787 the monarchy's income rose from 370 to 475 million. For the taxpayer, the history of tax amounted to major rises during war which, in spite of government assurances, were always followed in peacetime by the extension of some of the taxes levied orig-inally just for the duration of the conflict, and by tax rises intended to cover the budget deficit. For instance, the original 4 sous in the livre, additional taxes levied since 1715 to top up indirect taxes, rose step by step from 5 sous in 1760 to 6 sous in 1764, 8 sous in 1771 and 10 sous in 1781, an overall rise of 25 percent on certain goods (alcoholic bever-ages, tobacco, salt) and all services (taxes on legal registrations).

Certainly Louis XV's and Louis XVI's subjects were not entirely misled by their impressions of excessive expenditure or their reluctance to pay taxes. They knew that war was very expensive and that paying off the debts accumulated during the conflict meant that maintaining a certain level of tax revenue in peacetime was necessary. However, given that the monarchy's accounts, unlike Great Britain's, were not public, and also given that the system of absolute monarchy rejected all formal control on its finances, it was never possible to ascertain the level of taxes necessary, a permanent complaint of the parlements. Nor was it possible to discuss the best methods to make up the deficit. Ministers both bene-fited and suffered in this situation. Hiding the reality of what was required enabled them to maintain confidence (which governed the cost of borrowing money) and to maneuver on credit in a way that favoured the government. After his resignation, Calonne thus admitted that the financial situation was so desperate when he arrived at the ministry in 1783 that "nothing was less likely to re-establish confidence than reveal-ing the enormous deficit before the debts were paid (since they) could not be paid except by borrowing heavily."[19] In other words, the secret status of state finance allowed the government to use the reputation of France's wealth to manipulate opinion and thus the money markets.

Though useful in times of crisis, these advantages did not make up for medium- and long-term disadvantages. Insofar as the government was not legally obliged to provide details of its expenditure each year, the controllers general only had inexact or partial information on finance, especially in wartime when numerous breaches of accounting rules were authorized. In terms similar to those used by L'Averdy in 1768, Calonne explained to the *Notables* the technical problems encountered by the controllers general in carrying out their duties:

> In my first and second year of office, I knew no more than my prede-cessors about the true situation of the finances; I needed all that time to go through the enormous number of details . . . My first calcula-tions could only be based on previous records . . . I had to believe them to be true; and they were in effect true as far as they went . . . But they hardly portrayed the day-to-day situation, because of the then inevitable and necessary, albeit somewhat confused, pooling of temporary resources and fixed revenues, the costs of the war and annual expenditure, the outstanding debts, a few suspended payments; inactive revenues and anticipated or late incoming monies.[20]

It is true that the role of the controllers general consisted in sorting through this confusion which came with the war, and in drawing up the accounting rules that would prevent a return to such a situation. But at the end of the war it was already too late and the problems recurred endlessly. The measures taken successively by L'Averdy (1765), Necker (1781) and Brienne (1788) to centralize income and expenditure showed up clearly the limits of the controller general's authority. During the American war, clashes between Sartine, secretary of state for the navy, and Necker on the subject of navy expenses highlighted the fact that rules made by the finance minister to stop his colleagues spending without authorization – expenditure for which no reserves were set aside – were not respected. The minister responsible for authorizing payment was not even informed. L'Averdy had already discovered this unpleasant reality in 1767. Three years after peace was made, when he thought that he had dealt with all debts, he suddenly discovered an unknown 250 million floating and outstanding debt, a year's worth of net revenue. What was true of expenditure was also true of income. In the absence of an efficient and centralized treasury, ministers were often forced to borrow from financiers sums of money that they already had in their own coffers. Under these conditions, as John Bosher shrewdly remarked, balancing the budget was like trying to fill a barrel with no bottom, i.e., funding the budget of such a great power "with the help of palliative measures and temporary resources that were unequal to the seriousness of its problems."[21]

CREDIT AND BANKRUPTCY

Such financial mismanagement was not the chief cause of the crisis of 1787. With the return of peace, they only made the ministers' task more difficult, or even impossible. This crisis was essentially caused by a series of three major wars, each more costly than the last. In spite of a rise in taxes in real terms (see Figure 1.3), these wars were financed more and more by loans so costly that economic growth and fiscal reforms could not absorb the public deficit quickly enough or without generating a serious political crisis. The funding of the first war, the War of Austrian Succession, was not really problematic. Essentially, it was financed by tax rises, since extraordinary revenues had only provided 35 percent of the increase in revenue, or on average 21 million a year. From the second half of the eighteenth century, the balance between taxes and borrowing was reversed and the gap grew wider. Extraordinary revenues represented 71 percent of additional income during the Seven Years' War (126 million a year) and 67 percent during the American war (228 million a year). In other words, the last two wars of the ancien régime were mainly financed by credit and not by an increase in ordinary or extraordinary taxes.

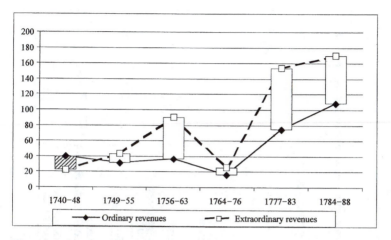

Figure 1.3   *Origin of revenue increases in periods of war and peace, 1740–48 (annual average in millions of livres tournois)*

These changes to the way wars were financed came at a time of important modifications to the state's extraordinary revenues (see Figure 1.4). The War of Austrian Succession was principally financed by a mixture of loans (fixed-term loans and loans secured on the credit of *pays d'états* and towns or one-off revenues coming from the alienation of extraordinary taxes and the clergy's *don gratuit*) – altogether 111 million livres tournois – to which were added life annuities to the amount of 69 million. During the Seven Years' War the ministry continued to borrow in life annuities (147 million) and to raise money through loans/extraordinary taxes, but above all it had recourse to loans in *rentes perpétuelles* (252 million) to which were added a total of 196 million siphoned from corporate bodies of *officiers* (the sale of new *offices* and a forced increase in the capital value of existing offices) or financiers (cash advances). By contrast, during the American War, the government drew the main part of its extraordinary revenues in the first instance from life annuities (584 million) and, as during the War of Austrian Succession, had recourse to large sums in the form of perpetual or fixed-term loans and extraordinary taxes (348 million). Very little income, however, derived from the financiers' advances or the sale of offices.

The deficit of 1787 consisted of three elements: the cost of the American war which was the most expensive of the three wars, the

Joël Félix

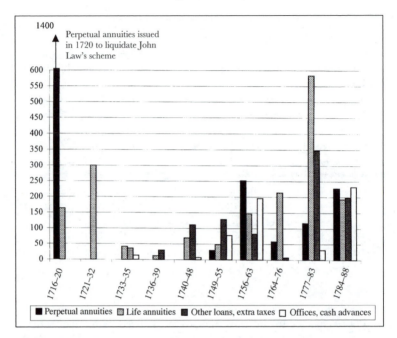

Figure 1.4 *Extraordinary revenues, 1716–88 (millions of livres tournois)*

undertaxing of the French compared to the extent of war expenditure, and lastly the borrowing in costly life annuities which were subject to high interest (see Table 1.1). On these grounds it is understandable that Necker who, more than any other finance minister, had recourse to life annuities to finance the monarchy's expenditure, was considered – as he sometimes still is – the gravedigger of the ancien régime, the man who ruined the monarchy through relying on overly expensive loans. However, the ministers of Louis XVI did not always have a choice as to the means available.

Except for Turgot and some administrators who were unsympathetic to the American War, ministers and public opinion pushed the government to support the American Revolutionaries in order to avenge the defeat suffered by the French in the Seven Years' War. Since Versailles continually told British ambassadors that France did not want war, and even delayed its declaration to make good the preparations, it was impossible to raise taxes to meet the costs incurred by the build-up to war. Raising taxes in peacetime would have been immediately interpreted in

Table 1.1 *French loans, 1740–83 (millions of livres tournois)*

	Perpetual annuities	Life annuities	Others	Total
1740–63	282 (24%)	264 (23%)	603 (53%)	1149
1763–83	175 (13%)	798 (59%)	387 (28%)	1360
1740–83	457 (18%)	1062 (42%)	990 (40%)	2509

Great Britain as a declaration of war, or at the very least as a clear indication of France's desire to enter the conflict. Necker's policy was meant to increase net income by reorganizing some of the monarchy's administrative services (such as the numerous officers in charge of payments in the king's household) or by reducing the cost of revenue collection and of benefits for financiers who were responsible for gathering in taxes. It is understandable then that Necker secured the support of his colleagues, as well as a section of the French who, since the end of the seventeenth century, had continually singled out the king's financiers – and their wealth – as the cause of the crisis.

As soon as war was declared, the government's options with regard to loans were dictated by the money markets. Weir estimated that the cost of servicing debt in France was much higher than in Britain (7.5 percent against 3.8 percent) even though the debt itself was much smaller in France (56 percent of GDP against 182 percent for Britain).[22] According to Velde and Weir, money was particularly dear in France because, unlike the British political system which provided sufficient guarantees to issue low-cost loans in nonredeemable stocks, the monarchy was forced to use the considerably more expensive life annuities integrating a premium risk against the possibility of bankruptcy.[23] Certainly, interest on the monarchy's loans was never set by chance, as some authors have suggested, but responded to the market. It followed the rise and fall in the cost of money, which in turn depended on whether interest payments to creditors could be reliably guaranteed, though these fluctuated according to creditors' confidence in the government's financial well-being. But in the eighteenth century it was not so much the fear of bankruptcy, but rather the financial mechanisms engendered by bankruptcies that determined the kind of loans the government made and set the cost of borrowing.

To understand this, one must go back to 1720 and the collapse in the value of the *billets de banque* (banknotes) and stock of the *Compagnie des Indes* (India Company). These had been floated by the Scotsman John

Law who had used them to replace France's debts upon the death of Louis XIV. Law's bankruptcy was immediately followed by the so-called *visa*, an operation which led to the conversion of Law's *billets* and *actions* into the sizeable sum of 1700 million *rentes perpétuelles* on the Hôtel de Ville in Paris at denier 40 (2.5 percent). Naturally this conversion was followed by a fall in the value of these stocks as some holders had chosen or had been forced to sell them at a loss, leading to the discrediting of the operation. This resulted in an increase in the real interest of money since the purchasers bought the fixed revenue of the capital on the cheap.

For the government, the best solution would have been to continue borrowing in long-term annuities, even if that meant, in the first instance, paying a relatively high rate of interest, while assuring, as in Great Britain, the redemption of a part of the capital and making the trade in these bonds easier to allow a progressive reduction in the interest rates.[24] However, in the 1720s, a decade of economic difficulties, ministers could not foresee that the country was about to enter a period of sustained growth that would reduce the cost of the perpetual debt. Above all they were obsessed by the pressing question of the debts left by Louis XIV to his grandson. In an attempt to make up the deficit by avoiding as far as possible mortgaging the future, they chose to borrow in life annuities because the fall in the value of non-redeemable stocks on the Hôtel de Ville meant that this type of loan was not much dearer. Most especially it offered the benefit of redemption of the debt with the death of the creditor, and allowed corporate bodies and individuals to continue to borrow or invest their money at the legal rate of 5 percent.

The main reasons for the crisis of the ancien régime are to be sought in Louis XV's ministers' inability to follow the British model developed by Walpole and Pelham and to set up a viable system of debt conversion before the wars of the second half of the eighteenth century took their toll on the monarchy's finances. The clergy's success in securing from Louis XV an exemption from the *vingtième*, which other landowners had to pay, was not the only reason for the failure of Machault d'Arnouville's *caisse d'amortissement* (sinking fund) established in 1749. By dint of using a part of the *vingtième*'s revenue earmarked for debt management to pay off the deficit and increase expenditure, the government lost the confidence of the upper classes and gave credence to the idea that the deficit did not result from a lack of taxation but from the court's excessive and unrestricted expenditure. The second *caisse d'amortissement* established by

L'Averdy in 1764 ensured, as it had done for Machault, that when peace was made the parlements again accepted the establishment of new taxes. Income from the new taxes made it possible to convert the short-term unfounded war debts into long-term capital and also to reduce the cost of money to sustain economic growth. Yet the bulk of the debts which this *caisse* was to meet exceeded its revenue to such a degree that it did little for the cost of money. Faced with a massive deficit in its budget and a serious economic crisis, the government preferred to suspend repayments, to default on part of its debts and to seize the revenues earmarked for the *caisse d'amortissement* to balance its budget (1770).[25]

As in 1720, Terray's bankruptcy inevitably and significantly raised the cost of borrowing money because the price of long-term stock was no longer sustained by the process of repayments. The volume of these stocks moreover had risen considerably following the conversion of a portion of the debts of the Seven Years' War into nonredeemable annuities. According to Necker, these stocks, set at 4 percent, changed hands only at a 40 percent loss before preparations for the American War began. Thus, "capitalists could speculate on their funds at an interest rate of 6 and 2/3% by reacquiring the capital of 1000 francs at a cost of 600." Necker drew the conclusion from this loss in value:

> Even if one easily feels that during peacetime one could use money in that way, it was not possible in wartime to build up a lot of capital by limiting oneself only to borrowing through nonredeemable or long-term stocks. Otherwise one would have had to accept conditions, the excesses of which would soon have destroyed all credit.[26]

To find large sums of money, therefore, the government had no other choice but to seek public loans on the international market, the cost of which depended amongst other things on the real interest of the nonredeemable stock. Unless it could secure money from captive markets but of limited means, such as provincial estates, towns and corporate bodies of officers who would agree to guarantee loans at the lower rate of 5 percent, the government had no other choice when it wanted to borrow substantial capital, as was the case during the American war, but to offer a return above real interest on nonredeemable stocks, i.e. above 6 percent. Even with a healthy economy, the cost of money was too high not to create a major financial and fiscal crisis in peacetime.

FINANCE AND POLITICS

Turgot's famous letter was hardly prophetic when, in 1774, it warned Louis XVI at the beginning of his reign of the dramatic consequences that would follow the opening volley of war. Six years previously L'Averdy had already drawn this conclusion and told Louis XV:

> If, Sire, there is a means of being able to prosecute war without later bankrupting oneself, it is only through reducing expenditure in peacetime, by redeeming part of the debt and a reduction in interest equal to the cost of loans which the war will bring and the debts it will create. And these loans made during the war will only be successful insofar as credit is re-established in peacetime. Otherwise it will be useless to offer loans. They will be of interest to nobody unless they comprise benefits that are usurious and ruinous for the State.

But thirst for grandeur was scarcely connected to finance. France was thought of as a rich country, and thus for the government the question of financing the war amounted to finding the right man for the job. Through the confidence he would inspire in the public, such a man would be able to levy the taxes needed to pay the troops while causing as little upset as possible. Then, with the return of peace, he would find the means to pay off the debts. Necker was very successful during the war because he was able to secure the interest on new loans through savings on Court expenditure and reductions in the cost of tax collection – two solutions that met the expectations of the public. As Robert Harris has shown, Necker's loans (530 million) were not as ruinous as has often been said since on average the interest rate payable was 6 percent.[27]

However, during the war years, confidence in the government's ability to pay its debts inexorably diminished, and Necker was obliged to offer increasingly advantageous conditions to the capitalists. His final annuity loans were subject to an interest rate of between 6.5 and 9 percent depending on the age of the lender. To fight against this loss in credit which drove up the cost of loans, the government broke with its traditional secrecy over finances and allowed Necker in his famous *Compte rendu au roi* (1781) to make public the monarchy's budget of income and expenditure which at the time ran at a surplus of 10 million, as he claimed. His successor, Joly de Fleury, was able to make use of a name that was famous among the parlements. Thus, through the Paris parlement he was able to register a rise in income tax consisting of a surtax of *deux sous pour livre* on indirect taxes (25 million) and a third *vingtième* (21 million), thus pushing the monarchy's income up to 500 million. The interest on money nevertheless remained very high, and the signing of peace did not change the situation much for the Treasury, which had to continue borrowing to repay war debts. Between 1783 and 1786, Calonne offered an average interest of 7.34 percent for the 488 million he had borrowed to convert the war debts into capital stock, to cover the deficit to the budget and pay for rising expenditure. This amounted in total to an annual surcharge of 36 million.

Since credit was so expensive, the crisis was inevitable. However, it was bound to be all the more serious since the government, under the influence of physiocratic ideas, deceived itself about the French economy's ability to absorb the budgetary deficits through economic growth. If France was a country where opportunities were great, it was also a vast country where growth occurred either through considerable investment in infrastructure (for which the state had no financial means) or by fiscal reform (which was always a delicate undertaking). Growth could also be stimulated by relaxing commercial legislation, but this clashed with the Colbertist vision of an unchangeable economic order in which the interests of producers and consumers were protected by state control.[28] As L'Averdy observed, unhappily contemplating the failure of his policy for economic growth and for reducing the cost of money, "without the government having well-disciplined finances, all [these] efforts to balance income and expenditure are fruitless, and cause more problems. Their effects in any case are so slow that one can utterly discount them."

Calonne understood that it was no longer possible to solve the deficit by half-measures without pushing the country further into another crisis; to restore France's finances to health, the time had come for the monarchy to pursue the reforms begun in the middle of the eighteenth century. Louis XVI's error was not to have realized that it would be extremely difficult to put the program of financial reform into the hands of a minister who, whatever one might think of his financial management, had to acknowledge the existence of a gigantic deficit four years after the end of the war. Ultimately, the ministers of the king bore a collective responsibility for not having seen that although Calonne's central project was based on a praiseworthy desire for fiscal justice, it was but the dream of a man so obsessed by the desire to solve the deficit that he had lost all contact with reality. As the Notables remarked straightaway, the plan of replacing the two *vingtièmes* by a territorial subsidy (a tax to be collected in kind) was not only impractical but also contradicted the views of the king expressed in the speech of the Garde des Sceaux (Keeper of the Seals) "to make tax collection simpler and less onerous." Also, Calonne explained to the Notables that the financial records shown each year by the minister to the king did not enable him to get an exact idea of the level of the deficits and announced that, contrary to what Necker claimed in his *Compte rendu au roi*, there had never been a budget surplus but only deficits. He thereby unhappily confirmed the suspicions of the public who ever since the failure of Machault's *vingtième* had continually blamed the deficits on poor royal administration and on the expenditure of the Court, rather than on the cost of war and the burden of privilege.

A number of factors raised the question of the king's ability to exercise an effective oversight of the finances, a royal prerogative which was at the heart of the political system put in place by Louis XIV when he took power in 1661: the impossibility of deciding between the accounts of Necker and Calonne who, with figures to hand, accused each other of being the cause of the deficit; the reiterated assurances on the part of the minister that the king was completely informed of the financial situation and supported his projects; and finally the difficulties encountered by the Notables when they decided to ascertain the exact size of the deficit. In all, Calonne's failure confirmed the prescience of one government member who, when asked about the minister's plans, had wondered whether there was not cause

> to fear that the carrying out of this plan would provoke the strongest protests, and that an insurrection of the clergy, the major landowners and all those whose interests were served by opposing it, would create such great difficulties that the King would be faced either with abandoning plans already solemnly announced, and thereby compromise his sovereign dignity in the eyes of all Europe, or with having to put down constant resistance, which could disturb the peace of his reign.

Altogether the Assembly of Notables realized what the government most feared: bringing out into the light of day the seriousness of the financial situation without being able to provide a concrete solution. As in 1760, the lack of information about the monarchy's finances and administration meant that the government quickly found itself overwhelmed by an outbreak of political and financial commentaries which spread amongst the public the vocabulary of the Enlightenment and the ill-digested ideas of the physiocrats.[29] Unlike 1763 the Paris parlement was of no help to the government. During the Seven Years' War the parlements came forward to lead the opposition and champion reform. To justify his reforms Calonne had reminded Louis XVI that his plans were so much in line with the views that the high courts had made known in their various protests that it seems in some respects that the plan was shaped by following their opinions and memoranda:

> Let us refer to those of the Parlement of Paris in 1754 and 1760, the Parlement of Rouen in 1756, the Parlement of Bordeaux in 1764 and lastly the Cour des Aides in 1770: we will find that the procedures of the new financial administration correspond perfectly to the principles established in all their remonstrances.

In 1787 the Paris parlement was of no help in reestablishing public order. As the magistrates would say to the king in their protests against the introduction of the *timbre* (stamp tax), the parlement was now accused by a section of the public of having failed to prevent the deficit without offering the least resistance: it had permitted all increases in taxes and especially in borrowing during the war, and even afterwards. A few magistrates naturally tried to take advantage of a most delicate situation for the government in order to recover some of their authority lost since 1774. This they did by asking for statements on income and expenditure, which were of course refused, and by helping to restore parlement and the king's prestige by proposing to organize Calonne's trial. But the king, still remembering the Diamond Necklace Affair, had no intention of handing himself over to the goodwill of the parlement. As for the magistrates, even if in the interests of calming public unrest some of them wished to lay the foundations of a compromise with the government, the majority of them having recently entered parlement had given up any wish of playing a political role which was refused to them. The parlement responded to usual ministers' accusations of having betrayed their duty by declaring itself not competent to register the new taxes, and by reiterating to the king its request to convoke the Estates General.

In fact neither Calonne nor Necker, nor the king nor the parlements, emerged victorious from this crisis. As George Weulersse remarked with reference to the evolution in economic thinking, and as Michael Sonenscher reflected concerning the development of political thinking on public debt, the collapse of Calonne's projects in the Assembly of Notables on territorial taxes and the means of covering the deficit led to a kind of "disintegration, if not general confusion of economic doctrines" and "stretched the categories and capacities of eighteenth century political thought to the limit."[30] The unveiling of the deficit had shown that it was impossible to continue to borrow without increasing taxes, and at the same time maintain a tax system that was condemned by everyone, the government and its opposition. At the end of the Notables' gathering, the very brother of the king, Monsieur, had drawn the simple conclusion that if the salt tax was bad it would have to be suppressed. Time was obviously ripe for a financial revolution, a revolution which was not only necessary but universally hoped for. But still unrecognized was the desirability of the political changes which would be required to establish an efficient new financial system in which the king's subjects would become citizens and the ministers would be accountable to a nation of equal taxpayers.

2. Decision-making

JOHN HARDMAN

Summary

Misled for generations by the argument that the absolute monarchy had become a "modern administrative state," historians have only recently begun in earnest to research and reflect upon the nature of the courtly system of governance of the baroque state. It is now the continuities of the system of patronage, in the influence of the court factions, in the strategies of political management of the various institutions of the (not centralized but) decentralized system of power, that seem most relevant to the problem of the collapse of the state. Piecing together the structures and procedures of the royal council, John Hardman gives us an analysis of how two vital decisions were taken. The entry into the American war, ultimately so significant in financial terms for the regime, was discussed logically and with due analysis of the circumstances. Even if the judgement could be considered unwise, it was free from factional influence, and in some ways reveals Louis XVI at his best. The second decision, to support Calonne and present a wide program of reforms for approval by an Assembly of Notables, is a different matter. Departing from the traditional conciliar processes, Louis avoided consulting all but three of his ministers on this matter, implicitly leaving them free to oppose what they had not approved. Given that the ministry was split into warring factions and that Calonne's reforms were in need of all the support they could get, this was a bad mistake. The factional strife and mistakes in political management suggest that the dissolution of the regime began at the centre.

This chapter will examine two decisions taken by Louis XVI which are often considered to have had a direct bearing on the outbreak of the Revolution or at least (a slightly different thing) on the fall of the ancien régime: the decision taken in February 1778 to assist England's American colonies in their War of Independence and that taken in

December 1786 to convoke the Assembly of Notables. The two decisions were linked because the war created a deficit that the parlement would not finance through increased taxation, causing the king to bypass it by convoking the Notables. An analysis of how these key decisions were reached throws light on the nature of the late-ancien-régime monarchy, its procedures and how the various balances of power operated through them.

THE STRUCTURE OF DECISION-MAKING

In theory, the decision-making process was straightforward. In the early evening, generally about 7:P.M., the king assembled his higher council, the *conseil d'en haut* (simply called the *conseil d'état* under Louis XVI) on Sundays and Wednesdays to determine foreign policy, and the *conseil des dépêches* on Tuesdays and Saturdays to determine home policy. The councils consisted of departmental ministers, plus the odd minister-with-out-portfolio in the *conseil d'état*, plus junior technicians, councillors of state and masters of requests as appropriate. All the men sitting round the magnificently inlaid and ormoulu-mounted table in the council chamber were, in an ideal world, freely chosen by the king and would give him dispassionate advice for the "good of his service" which was equated with the good of the country. This advice would be given in reverse order of precedence, which was determined by date of entry to the council unless the minister held a title which superseded this, such as cardinal, chancellor or head of the royal council of finance.

Each man was required to give his opinion even if he had nothing in particular to say or was indeed entirely ignorant of the matter in question. When everyone had spoken, the king, who was not supposed to reveal his own stance, counted the votes and opted for the majority opinion whatever his own private view, which was not necessarily disclosed even at this stage. When Louis XVI maneuvered the *conseil des dépêches* in December 1788 to grant double representation to the Third Estates in the forthcoming Estates-General, he was considered by one junior minister to have acted despotically.

This process may come as a surprise to readers, many of whom whilst accepting the conventional view of Louis XVI as a *roi fainéant* hidebound by tradition do not realize just how stylized was his theoretical role. This was an administrative and juridical ideal, that of the absolute administrative monarchy, the absolutism of the monarchy being unaffected by the personal role of the transient king. Politics, as we understand it, simply did not exist: *la politique* is translated as "foreign policy," the politics of the powers. How far this ideal obtained even in 1661 when Louis XIV set up this system at the start of his personal rule is debatable; certainly it was not the case under Louis XVI. The composition of the council was now determined by the influence of court factions, financiers and even public opinion quite as much as by the free choice of the king or the prime minister when there was one.

What might be termed this politicization of the council led to the rapid development of the committee system to enable the king and/or prime minister to get his way over policy-making but it was an imperfect solution since the basis of the decision was narrowed and the opposition to the measure was merely deferred: this was what happened with the decision to convoke the Notables. The committee system was invented by the comte de Maurepas, the young Louis XVI's mentor and *de facto* prime minister from 1774 until his death in 1781. He wanted to restore the old parlement which Louis XV had abolished in 1771 but could not use the council because it was still dominated by Louis XV's old ministers, Maupeou, d'Aiguillon and Terray. A further problem was that Louis XVI supported them. So Maurepas sent a disingenuous letter to the other ministers informing them that he could not execute his task of teaching the king his métier in the large formal body and that he intended to do this in committees consisting only of the relevant ministers. The new system was aimed quite as much at reeducating the king on the parlementaire question as excluding Maurepas's opponents. The scheme worked but only at the price of instilling in the king a vague sense of betrayal and an abiding distrust of ministers. The committee system however survived once its original purpose had been accomplished by the removal of Maupeou and Terray and the recall of the old parlements. And it survived largely because the king himself, who had been its principal victim, realized that he could turn it to his own advantage to secure his ends by bypassing those who opposed his policies.

FACTION AND THE COMPOSITION OF THE MINISTRY

By the time of Louis XVI's accession in 1774 the king no longer possessed untrammeled freedom to choose his ministers, though his ability to dismiss them was less impaired for, as Maurepas quipped, "the indispensable minister has yet to be born." In practice the various interest groups or factions influenced the king's choice in the kingdom, probably to as great an extent as that of the King of England. But in England the process crystallized into the need to command a majority in Parliament and so can be analyzed more easily and indeed quantified by the number of votes each interest could deliver. But in France there was no formal mechanism for the representation of influence; the composition of the ministry very often did not reflect the interests accurately; and this itself could be a source of instability. In any case there were only six departmental ministers, far fewer than there were factions. The influence of faction can be shown by an analysis of the composition of the ministry in 1786, the last year in which the ancien régime operated normally and a year important for the present purpose because it was that in which the decision was taken to convoke an Assembly of Notables.

The chancellor, Maupeou, was in exile. His attack on the parlements had been reversed in 1774. But convention had it that a chancellor could not be dismissed without being put on trial. The new king's policy of balance would have been upset by such an extreme action so, since Maupeou could not be induced to resign, Miromesnil was appointed to perform his functions with the title of Keeper of the Seals. (Does anything better illustrate the constraints on Bourbon absolutism?) Miromesnil was the architect of the 1774 settlement with the old parlement but was felt by many, because of his antecedents, to favour the restored parlement's pretensions at the expense of the king's authority – a false distinction he would have said but one which the king ultimately came to regard as valid.

The foreign secretary, Charles Gravier, comte de Vergennes, was an elderly career diplomat with an exalted and somewhat old-fashioned view of the king's authority, a distrust of the Enlightenment, Protestants and the parlements. He stood for defense of the church and strict censorship. In professional terms he was cool about the new (1756) alliance with France's traditional enemy, Austria, and was at daggers drawn with Marie-Antoinette. These were the tenets of the *parti dévôt*, the tradition in which Louis XVI was reared, though the king was more liberal than his minister. Vergennes was the leader of the king's party in the council and had no significant support save that of the king.

The controller-general, Charles-Alexandre de Calonne, was also a "king's man" in the sense that he believed passionately in the absolute administrative monarchy. He had been one of the 30 intendants who administered the provinces. Until about 1760, secretaries of state were normally recruited from the ranks of the intendants and had a common ethos, but thereafter members of the court aristocracy, with a military rather than a legal background, were increasingly entering the royal councils. Such men tended to favour a form of aristocratic, decentralized, constitutional government such as they believed had existed before the accession of the Bourbons to the throne; this sapped the morale of the Bourbon monarchy from within. Then, suddenly, the convocation of the Assembly of Notables enabled such ministers to link up with the Notables to try to enforce their ideas on a weakened king. Calonne deplored the rise of the new-style minister long before he witnessed its consequences at first hand during the first phase of the Notables and, from exile, during the even more dangerous second phase when, having defeated the king's reform programme and driven his minister into exile, the Assembly sought to limit his monarchy with commissions staffed by non-government personnel. Calonne also deplored the politicization of the court and the courtierization of politics, which the new breed of minister tended to produce, as well as their lack of professionalism.[1]

Yet for all that, and despite his undoubted loyalty to the traditional monarchy, Calonne did not owe his appointment to the king, who initially distrusted his public morality, but rather to the dominant faction at court (the Polignac coterie) and to *"la finance."* This was a group of often-venal officeholders who managed the king's credit, tiding him over with loans until taxes came in or, in the case of the Farmers General, actually buying the revenue stream from the indirect taxes.[2] The Polignac group sometimes called the *"société intime de la reine"* consisted of some dozen men and women centered on the queen's favorite and governess of her children, the duchesse de Polignac. Nevertheless, for a variety of reasons, whilst the group formed the queen's social circle it was allied politically to the king and served to neutralize the political influence of Marie-Antoinette.

However, the queen's influence on major political appointments – Maurepas had always allowed her a say in military and ecclesiastical ones – could not be postponed indefinitely, particularly after the birth of a dauphin in 1781. But her unpopularity grew with her political influence until in 1786, after the disastrous conclusion of the Diamond Necklace Affair, it had reached dangerous proportions. In that year no fewer than three ministers regarded her as their *patronne*. The first was the naval minister from 1780 to 1787, Charles-Gabriel de la Croix, marquis de Castries. He had been one of the few successful generals in the Seven Years' War, and a diary, which he dictated to his mistress, still survives. This reveals his disillusionment with the absolute monarchy in general and with Louis XVI in particular. Typical entries for 1787 include: "It would be too distasteful to serve such a master if one were serving him alone and not the state as well" and "The nation makes great strides towards liberty . . . this safeguards the people from giving the sweat of its labours to an implacable and oppressive master."[3] Personal loyalty to the king had hitherto been an article of faith among the old nobility but if Castries is typical, and there are indications that he was, the troubles that lay ahead for the monarchy in the *révolte nobiliaire* of 1787–8 need not surprise us.

It suited both Castries and the queen to assume a client–patron relationship but the main agent in Castries's appointment had been Jacques Necker, finance minister from 1776 to 1781. Despite or perhaps because of his plebeian origins, Necker favoured court aristocrats in the ministry, for which Calonne took him to task. Necker resigned in 1781 but he planned a return to office, having made the task of his successors difficult by publishing a misleading *Compte rendu au roi* in 1781 which claimed that the king's revenues were in surplus. Castries was the spokesman in the ministry for Necker's powerful faction at court and in Paris.

Philippe-Henri, marquis de Ségur, the minister for war and the queen's second minister, was a paler version of Castries, whose lead he tended to follow. He is perhaps unfairly best remembered for the 1781 *ordonnance* which bears his name and restricted commissioned entry into the army to those whose great-grandfathers were noble.

The queen's third minister was Charles-Louis Le Tonnelier, baron de Breteuil. He was a member of the administrative nobility, the *noblesse d'état*, but of a rather grand kind, like Maurepas, with family alliances among the court nobility. He had been ambassador to Vienna until 1783 when the queen had had him appointed minister for the Maison du Roi. This position, apart from regulating the court and supervising the policing of Paris, had many of the functions of a modern minister of the interior. Breteuil told the Austrian ambassador that Marie-Antoinette should only sanction the appointment of ministers who "felt that they could only perform their duties to the extent that they allowed the queen to reign."[4] But his incompetence led Marie-Antoinette into dangers and unpopularity, notably in the Diamond Necklace Affair; the French, as Marie-Antoinette was well aware, did not like queens who reigned.

It can be seen from this analysis of the composition of the ministry in 1786 that the king had only limited control of his cabinet. One can express this merely in terms of intrigue, of faction, the king's, the queen's, Necker's, the Polignacs', remembering also that not all interests could be adequately represented by six men. But by the end of the ancien régime, faction often masked ideological differences. Only Breteuil and Marie-Antoinette were motivated simply by questions of personality. In this respect they deserved and indeed remained faithful to each other through thick and thin. In ideological terms only two ministers shared Louis XVI's conception of the monarchy, Vergennes and Calonne. Calonne put this explicitly when he wrote that Vergennes's death and his own dismissal had deprived the king "of all the ministers truly loyal to him."[5]

Miromesnil favoured or rather facilitated an increase in the power of the parlement at the king's expense though, again, he would not have accepted the distinction and in any case he did not want a return to the chaos of the 1760s. Castries may have thought that he was advocating a pre-Richelieu monarchy, but in practical terms his alliance with Necker would have led to an assimilation of the French monarchy to the "Venetian" constitution of England, the aristocratic oligarchy denounced by Disraeli in *Coningsby*. On leaving office, Castries told the queen that he was relieved that the insupportable tension between his duty as a minister and that as a citizen was coming to an end. He concluded by telling her: "as a Frenchman I want the Estates-General to meet but as a minister of the crown I feel bound to tell you that they would destroy your authority."[6]

What were the chances of such a motley crew of ministers deciding anything of importance or anything controversial in 1786, let alone what Castries called "the most important event of . . . [the king's] reign," the convocation of the Assembly of Notables which was decided at the end of the year? In order to implement his policies, Louis XVI was driven to take liberties with the procedures instituted by Louis XIV to regulate and regularize personal monarchy. However, before considering the decision to convoke an Assembly of Notables it is instructive to examine an area where the old Louis-Quatorzième procedures retained greater vigor, that is the field of foreign policy (preeminently the *métier du roi*), and to ask why this should have been?

FOREIGN POLICY AND THE DECISION TO ENTER THE AMERICAN WAR OF INDEPENDENCE

The clue is found in Sorel's masterpiece, *Europe and the French Revolution*, which contrasts "the extreme complication of the internal situation and the comparative simplicity of external affairs."[7] In the absence of a genius such as Richlelieu, who could reduce external and internal policy to a seamless whole, Louis XVI, at the start of his reign, turned to Turgot and Vergennes. Turgot failed not just because he attacked vested interests but because many considered his grain policies misguided: the country was split down the middle between supporters of free trade in grain and supporters of state regulation. Vergennes's objectives, on the other hand, were shared by just about everyone: first, to turn the Austrian alliance to France's advantage rather than Austria's and, secondly, to take revenge on England for the humiliating peace of 1763. Louis, as Soulavie and Sorel observed, possessed intellect but no willpower. But since the nation was united, it did not require any willpower on Louis's part to support Vergennes, since "all that was needed was an honest intention and knowledge of the permanent interests of France in Europe, both of which Louis XVI had." Consequently, "he could accept good counsels and give good advice."[8] On this reading, faction is not divorced from ideology and it thrives when the king, either from personal weakness or because the divisions are too deep, cannot impose a unified policy.

In the field of foreign policy there were really only two factions in play: the queen on her own, and the king and a united cabinet against her. In 1778, when France entered the American war, there were two wars on offer: one against Frederick II of Prussia to secure the territories of the late Elector of Bavaria for Marie-Antoinette's brother, the Emperor Joseph II; the other against England to exploit her difficulties with her North American colonies. The Seven Years' War had exposed the folly of fighting a war on two fronts, and in any case, if it had come to it, the king and his ministers would have preferred to fight on the side of Prussia rather than of Austria, France's ally in name, enemy in fact, as Vergennes put it.

The first steps to aid the American colonists were clandestine: on May 2, 1776 Louis XVI signed an authorization to give the Americans one million livres through intermediaries. This followed Vergennes's request for position papers from the ministers on the American issue in his Considerations in March. The most pacific of the papers came from the controller-general, Turgot. However even his position was not clear-cut: his position paper of April 6, 1776 makes it clear that Turgot would have countenanced war provided that it was short and above all financed by increased taxation. What he could not stomach was re-armament without war because though the parlement might accept increased taxation for war they would not for rearmament.[9] Yet massive naval rearmament without war was precisely the course of action upon which Louis was embarking. However Turgot and Maurepas, among others, were wrong in arguing that rearmament was almost as expensive as war. It was not. Naval expenditure in 1776 was some 47,000,000 livres, and in 1777, the last year of peace, 59,000,000. In 1778, however, it reached 150,000,000 and 155,000,000 the following year.

On October 18, 1776 Louis XVI sent Vergennes a detailed analysis of the political and military situation following the recapture of New York by English troops. It went as follows: England's preoccupation with her revolted colonies gave France the opportunity to build up her fleet which England might otherwise have tried to prevent; furthermore, beyond a certain point rearmament passed from being a provocation to being a deterrent. France's international prestige also, again without war, increased proportionately. Meanwhile England was sinking deeper and deeper into a war from which she could not profit: either the colonists would gain their independence without the expenditure of French lives and treasure or England would win at the cost of ruining her own colonies. Any English victory, such as the reconquest of New York, would have the dual benefit of committing England more deeply to a struggle she could not win and of shoring up the ministry of Lord North which was well-disposed toward France – allowing her to rearm and even to supply America clandestinely, provided only that England's face was saved.[10]

The baffling question is why, having made this lucid and sustained analysis, did Louis, some sixteen months later, decide to enter the war? The stock explanation is that what had changed was the capitulation of the English general Burgoyne's 5000 troops at Saratoga Springs, news of which reached Versailles on December 4, 1777. This seemed to initiate the endgame and France might as well cash in on it. On December 5 the naval minister, Sartine, wrote to Vergennes: "[Saratoga] will determine victory but our course of action merits serious consideration."[11] The way Vergennes presented the case, however, was very different. Saratoga might indeed initiate the endgame, but when the war was concluded, England would use the troops already in the American hemisphere to attack French and Spanish colonies and obtain *dédommagement* (compensation) for her losses. In this attack France would be without an ally, so she must acquire the American one before it was too late.

These fears on Vergennes's part were completely groundless – there is no evidence that England was planning an attack on French and

Spanish possessions. So the question arises of whether he actually held them. The American historian C. H. Van Tyne, writing in 1925, argued that Vergennes did.[12] In favour of this line of argument one can adduce the fact that if Vergennes did not believe that England would attack, he never, in public or private correspondence, dropped his guard. Perhaps he was influenced by a guilty conscience towards England for France's clandestine aid to the Americans and by the essentially French concept of *dédommagement*. In other words that is how *he* would have proceeded if the boot had been on the other foot. Jonathan Dull, however, writing 50 years later, questions not only Van Tyne's argument but also the relevance of Saratoga. Vergennes, Maurepas and Sartine were determined from an early date to take advantage of England's difficulties with her colonies to avenge the defeats of the Seven Years' War. Louis XVI, however, scrupled to embark on a war which France could ill afford in support of the rebel subjects of a king with whom France had no immediate quarrel. To overcome these royal scruples they fabricated the line of an English attack on French and Spanish possessions. The timing of France's alliance with the Americans (February 6, 1778) had nothing to do with Saratoga but was dictated solely by the completion of France's naval re-armament.[13] Louis, incidentally, was as keen on naval rearmament as were Sartine and Vergennes but did not see a logical connexion between rearmament and war, rather the reverse. In this he may have been indulging in wishful thinking.

For whatever reason, *post hoc* or *propter hoc*, news of Saratoga was followed immediately by French discussions on an alliance with the Americans. What seems to have happened is that the "hawks" in the cabinet used Saratoga in an attempt to bounce the king into entering the war but at the same time tried to make him take responsibility for the risky strategy of going to war with England without having first secured the agreement of Spain, whose ships were needed to give France naval parity with England. The two principal hawks were Vergennes and Sartine; Maurepas inclined towards war and Montbarey, the minister for war, was against. Necker, the finance minister, was scarcely consulted. Sartine suggested using D'Aranda, the Spanish ambassador who was far more hawkish than his government, to soften up Louis. Then Louis was prevailed upon to decide in a process recalled to him by Vergennes himself two years later, when the war was going badly:

This question [of treating with the American delegation] was examined in depth in the various memoranda which were submitted to

Your Majesty at the time. Your Majesty examined them himself; then he had them discussed by those of his ministers he saw fit to summon to this important deliberation and he is humbly beseeched to remember that when the moment came to decide on whether to treat with the Americans, M. le comte de Maurepas, provoked by Your Majesty to let him know his advice, demurred on the grounds that the matter having been weighed and debated in the memoranda and discussions, it was up to the king in his wisdom to pronounce and all his ministers could do was respectfully to await his orders.

It was in executing Your Majesty's orders that I began the negotiations with the American deputies and concluded two treaties with them in February 1778.[14]

One could say that Maurepas was passing the buck but what he is objecting to is not giving his opinion – which he must have already done unofficially or in private – but speaking *ex cathedra* as *de facto* prime minister. It was for the king to take the sense of the meeting, if need be with a vote. But if his ministers thought they had brought the king to the point of making a decision they were mistaken. He did indeed authorize Vergennes to open discussions with the Americans but insisted that they be kept secret to enable his uncle, Charles III of Spain, to choose the moment to "go public." Charles soon made it clear that he had no interest in fighting England on the side of the Americans because, among other things, he did not want to set the example of revolt in his own American colonies, North as well as South: his own colonies in North America were more extensive than those of George III.

In what is only an apparent paradox, it was on the very day, January 6, 1778, that Charles's negative and tetchy reaction was known at Versailles and only then that Louis XVI started to take the negotiations with the Americans seriously. The news from Spain was devastating and it meant that in order finally to drag Spain into the war in 1779, France would have to make promises, notably no peace without Gibraltar, which would make it dangerously difficult to conclude peace. But on January 6, news also arrived that the Elector of Bavaria had died. It was known that Louis's brother-in-law, Joseph II, the Holy Roman Emperor, would ask for French assistance to make annexations in Bavaria. This Louis, and his entire council, was determined to resist. It was a breach of international law, it would upset the balance in Germany, cause war with Frederick II of Prussia, and open up the south of France to a future Austrian invasion. The problem was Joseph's sister,

Marie-Antoinette, who put enormous pressure on her husband to help Joseph. Louis knew that if he already had a war in hand, overseas, he could on those grounds refuse to be involved in Europe; after the experience of the Seven Years' War, there could be no question of a war on two fronts. I am not suggesting that Louis XVI would embark on a risky war simply to spite his wife and brother-in-law, and it is true that the arms race with England, which Louis inaugurated, made war difficult to avoid, because arms races, especially naval ones, tend to lead to war. What the news from Germany did was to enable the king to see the logic of this and to yield gracefully to the pressure from his ministers.[15]

As we have seen, faction played little part in decisions relating to foreign policy. If there was disagreement about whether to enter the American war, the divisions occurred along departmental lines: Turgot did not want to have to finance the war, Sartine was engaged in departmental empire-building, Vergennes wanted to win prestige for himself as well as for his king. Only the minister for war, Montbarey, offered the disinterested advice that France should stay out of the war. The absence of factional motivation is best seen in the decisions relating to the Austro-Dutch crisis of 1784–5. The Emperor Joseph II wanted to increase the utility of the Austrian Netherlands by opening up the Scheldt to international traffic in defiance of the Treaty of Westphalia. The Dutch had inserted this clause into the treaty to prevent Antwerp from becoming a rival to Amsterdam. When Joseph sent a symbolic ship down the river to buy French wine, the Dutch stopped it by firing across its bows. Joseph threatened war and asked what assistance his French ally proposed to give. Louis was under considerable pressure from his Austrian queen to support her brother, the emperor, so to stiffen his resistance he asked all the *ministres d'état* to read out position papers in the *conseil d'état*. At the end of the meeting he collected the papers in, so, provided one arranges them in reverse order of precedence, we have a rare chance to reconstruct a meeting of the council.

Prima facie, Louis was taking a risk in formally consulting his council because no fewer than three members, Breteuil, Castries and Ségur, were the queen's protégés. But most Frenchmen, of whatever faction, were united in their distrust of Austria, the traditional enemy. Breteuil, for example, though a rival for Vergennes's ministry had, like him, been a member of Louis XV's secret diplomatic service designed to counter the influence of Austria. In the council, the condemnation by the queen's protégés of Joseph's action was louder than was Vergennes's. And for Breteuil, the queen's protégé par excellence, was reserved the harshest criticism of all: the emperor "seems to think that the man who annexes the most territory will go down as the greatest prince in history."[16] French policy towards her Austrian ally can best be described as malevolent neutrality. The upshot of the conciliar discussions was that France provided the Dutch with 6,000,000 gold florins to give the emperor in satisfaction for the insult to his flag – a derisory sum which nevertheless gave rise to the widespread myth that Marie-Antoinette was systematically sending her brother French money.

When, foiled in his attempt to open the Scheldt, Joseph II resurrected his pet project of swapping the Austrian Netherlands for Bavaria, Louis repeated his ploy of convening the *conseil d'état*. This time Louis cynically announced to the emperor that, not to mention his own interests, he must consider the impact of the exchange on Germany and in particular on the King of Prussia. Since Frederick the Great had mobilized in 1777 to prevent an earlier version of the exchange, this was tantamount to blocking the project. Marie-Antoinette had difficulty concealing her chagrin, telling Castries, "I feel that when one votes against the emperor I should at least be informed and I should have been annoyed if you had not said anything." Castries himself realized, though he was prepared to play his role in the charade, that consulting the council had been a "useless formality."[17] Whether the king and Vergennes consulted it on major matters was entirely political: during the five years of the American war, Vergennes had brought little of importance before this body, which continued nevertheless to meet twice a week, because he seems to have suspected that Necker, who was not a *ministre* but was informed by his ally Castries, was in the pay of England.

WHY CALONNE DECIDED TO PROPOSE AN ASSEMBLY OF NOTABLES

In 1786 Louis XVI faced a multifaceted crisis. His ambitious foreign policy was beginning to unravel as the "patriot" party in the Dutch Republic, with whom he had signed the Treaty of Fontainebleau in 1785, came under increasing pressure from England and Prussia, who backed the Prince of Orange. Louis's failure in 1787, through financial pressure, to resist the Anglo-Prussian invasion of Holland, with the attendant loss of diplomatic prestige, can be seen as a contributory factor in the fall of his regime.

At the same time, the desperate relations between his finance minister, Calonne, and the parlement made it impossible for him to raise another loan, let alone impose new taxation. The link between the breakdown in relations between Calonne and the parlement and the decision to convoke the Notables is demonstrated by a memorandum which Calonne sent to the king in November 1786 informing the king that he has been pondering his reform package for "several years" but that he has been "particularly occupied with it for the last ten months."[18] This curiously precise number of ten months strongly suggests that Calonne's mind had been concentrated by the furore surrounding the registration of his loan in the parlement of December 21, 1785. This had been accompanied by an *arrêté* stating that the loan had been registered "du très exprès commandement du roi," the formula used in a *lit de justice*. And Calonne rightly concluded that this would stale the appetite of subscribers. On December 23 the king summoned the parlement to Versailles, angrily removed the offending *arrêté* with his own hand, and told the parlement that he was fed up with it "criticizing his administration at all times and in all places."[19] In the memoranda with which he plied the king between August and December 1786, Calonne reiterated that the parlement would not sanction another loan. Since 1778, royal finances had been kept afloat by loans and, though by 1786 Calonne had funded the debt, its actual size continued to increase, since taxation was inadequate to pay even the interest on it, let alone repay the capital. Calonne had personal quarrels with the parlement but he admitted to the king that that body would be right to refuse further loans unless steps were taken to remedy the underlying situation. In any case royal credit was so bad that the king had to pay 2 percent a year more than his English counterpart, which would prove the difference between salvation and disaster. On top of it all, the third *vingtième*, which brought in about 20,000,000 livres a year, was due to expire at the end of the year.

There was a crisis, then, but it was a concealed one: people basked in France's renewed diplomatic prestige, her daring alliances and far-reaching commercial treaties and enjoyed the somewhat factitious prosperity engendered by the coming of peace and Calonne's construction boom. There was a crisis and something would have to be done but there was no pressure on the king to attempt the radical financial, administrative, and indeed constitutional reforms Calonne proposed, still less to send them before a body, the Assembly of Notables, of which no one had heard. Since the Maupeou coup of 1771 had created a sense of institutional instability, there had been some agitation for a convocation of the Estates General, whose inadequacies had been forgotten but none for an Assembly of Notables, whose last meeting in 1626 had left no imprint on the popular psyche.

Calonne's programme was comprehensive, including as it did the establishment of a national bank, the abolition of internal customs barriers and the phasing out of the *gabelle*. But the twin kernel of the matter was the replacement of the *vingtièmes* with a land tax assessed as a proportion of the crop yield and so keeping pace with inflation of which the price of corn was the main element. Calonne's collaborator, P-S. Dupont, believed that without this link France would cease to be an absolute monarchy since the king would have to keep asking the parlements for money.[20] The new tax was to be payable by all equally and without exception, irrespective of local or social status and was to be assessed by an elected three-tier system of assemblies, parish, district and provincial, whose composition was determined exclusively by the possession of landed wealth. It was not an egalitarian system, since the rich would have more seats than the poor in the assemblies, but it was radical in completely ignoring the traditional division of political society into orders. The *taille* and the *gabelle*, the main taxes on the peasantry, would be mitigated but retained but Lavoisier expressed the hopes of many and the fears of some when he told the agricultural think tank which Calonne had instituted:

> The speech that M. de Calonne addressed to the Assembly of Notables represented only isolated portions of a very vast plan; that the portion so far revealed seemed to have two main objectives: the first was to extend the *vingtièmes* to the clergy and all the privileged groups; the second was to establish a land tax which would one day make it possible to know the net and gross value of the kingdom's product and which could serve as the basis for a tax which could replace the taille; that it was already a great achievement to have established a first tax from which no one would be exempt; that perhaps it would not have been prudent or wise for the king and his minister to attempt too much at the same time by aiming to subject the clergy at one fell swoop to a tax representing the *vingtièmes* and the *taille* combined; that the difficulties that the *controleur-général* was experiencing over the single measure to which he confined himself proved beyond doubt that he had made an accurate calculation of the strength of the opposition but that it would have been risky to attempt any more.[21]

Calonne's proposals would be presented to a specially convoked Assembly of 144 Notables. The king would nominate the members but they would be taken from the same categories as in 1626, leading ecclesiastics, parlementaires, *conseillers d'état*, etc. The assembly would need to have prestige because the idea was that its endorsement of Calonne's programme would enable the king to have it registered immediately, easily and simultaneously in all the parlements by *lit de justice* without creating an impression of "despotism."

It was a high-risk strategy because of the certain opposition from vested interests, to which Lavoisier alludes only a day after the opening of the assembly: opponents who feared that Calonne's proposals were only the tip of the iceberg and that he planned to destroy the whole social order. There was also the risk of the king's likely irresolution in the face of such opposition. These factors had doomed much more limited attempts at reform under both Louis XV and Louis XVI. Calonne did not disguise these twin risks in the copious memoranda with which he plied the king but he affected a confidence he did not entirely feel, whilst the king was piqued by the suggestion that he might not stand firm into discounting that impediment. So what options remained to the king other than the disastrous one he adopted?

The early historian of the reign, J-F-X. Droz, considered that when Calonne announced the size of the deficit to the king, Louis should have promptly dismissed him and recalled Necker. Necker's popularity was such that he could have implemented the reform package without recourse to the Notables.[22] However this view does not take account of the king's personal antipathy to Necker and his belief that Calonne's accounts rather than the Genevan's were accurate. Moreover Necker's reforming style was very different from Calonne's. He implicitly favoured an evolution toward an English form of government, which his method of raising credit and reliance on public opinion tended to promote. The effect of Calonne's measures, however, would have been to strengthen Bourbon absolutism by securing for the king an inflation-proof income stream which would have relieved him of the necessity of going cap in hand to the parlements.

Bosher has argued that Calonne's reforms were an irrelevance, since the underlying problem was not fiscal (expenditure exceeding revenue) but administrative (the private management of public monies, which Necker had all but eradicated and his successors, including Calonne, had all but restored). For Necker, his recent biographer, Harris, and Bosher, then, the problem lay in the cost of collecting taxes rather than in tax assessment and evasion.[23] Nevertheless, it was Calonne's viewpoint rather than Necker's that the king came to share.

Since the gridlock with the parlement resulted mainly from the personal antipathy of that body to Calonne, one option open to the king was to buy time by dismissing his controller-general. In such cases, that had been the normal outcome over the previous 50 years. A finance minister would be appointed who was acceptable to the parlement, perhaps taken from its ranks. Such an arrangement had obtained during Louis's adolescence in the 1760s, and he was not inclined to revisit the humiliations his grandfather had suffered. Besides, Louis scrupled to sacrifice Calonne because if he was unpopular with the parlement it was precisely because he was the exemplary servant of the absolute monarchy. The opposite option would have been to register all Calonne's edicts simultaneously in all 13 parlements by *lit de justice* and dare the parlements to break the terms of the 1774 settlement by going on strike or arresting the collectors of the new tax. With the prestige of a victorious peace under his belt, Louis might just have pulled this off.

HOW THE DECISION TO CONVOKE AN ASSEMBLY OF NOTABLES WAS TAKEN

The decision-making process which led up to the convocation of the Notables was as follows. From August until November Calonne plied the king with memoranda covering every aspect of the matter, practical and theoretical, seeking to answer every imaginable objection.[24] The king read these on his own, annotated them, and discussed them in his weekly *travail* with the minister. At the same time, and with the king's permission, Calonne showed the thornier aspects of his projects first to Vergennes and then to Miromesnil. Then the three of them had "several *conférences* [ministerial committees without the king]." Miromesnil and Vergennes, according to Calonne, "were happy to be quoted as saying that they were persuaded both as to the necessity and the utility of the programme." Indeed, their approval went as far as "enthusiasm." So Calonne, in the memorandum known as the *Objections et réponses* of c. November 23–30 , asked the king to preside over a *comité* of the three ministers "by the end of the week," that is, by December 1.[25] Calonne assumed that only one such *comité* would be necessary. In fact there were several meetings of the *comité*, long meetings according to Castries, and the *conseil des dépêches* did not meet to ratify the plan until December 29.[26]

Though Castries bitterly resented his own exclusion, he saw that there was some functional logic to the membership of the *comité*: Calonne obviously, Vergennes in his capacity as *chef du conseil royal des finances*, or *chef des finances* as Castries put it, and Miromesnil who had to oversee the drafting of the necessary legislation. He also recognized that the three ministers had been acting as a "triumvirate" or *comité de gouvernement* for some time. But he felt that in "major matters" all the ministers should be heard even when their specific departmental competence was not required, as they had in the Austro-Dutch crisis of 1784–5. So on December 28 Castries wrote to the king complaining that he had "decided perhaps the most important event of his reign without deigning to test his loyalty." There were many matters, he explained, which were strictly departmental, but those matters "which touch on the very constitution of the state" cannot be dealt with "exclusively" by the specialists. Louis gave him the disingenuous reply that the measures in question, "merely concern the arrangements to be made for apportioning the burden of taxation and have absolutely nothing to do with any department save that of finance."[27]

Castries accused the king of manipulating the decision-making process to suit his needs: a wide discussion in the council when his views were likely to prevail and a narrow one when that was not guaranteed: "the king prefers the unanimity which enables him to sleep o'nights to a frank discussion which leads to a better decision."[28] However, Castries was wrong in saying that the king *had* secured unanimity in the small *comité*. Or rather, even if he did, it was simulated, for in a long letter dated December 28, the day before the meeting of the *conseil des dépêches*, Miromesnil tells the king that there were a number of objections he had wanted to raise in the *comité* of December 27 but had decided instead to put in a letter.[29] He had adopted this approach, he claimed, because he might have lost his temper in the *comité* which would have shown disrespect for the king and not have conduced to a rational discussion. In fact, Miromesnil's real motive in choosing the well-trodden epistolary approach to the king was that Calonne, Vergennes and the king would have simply outvoted him in the *comité*. The letter, he hoped, would keep the ball in play.

Had he not decided, out of respect for the king, to hold his peace in the *comité*, Miromesnil said, he "had been planning to ask Your Majesty what character he proposed giving to the Assembly?" In particular, would it be a mere rubber stamp, or would it be allowed to make "*de très humbles représentations*" concerning the matters presented to it (a phrase which would have sounded to the king suspiciously like the "très humbles remontrances" of the parlement). If the former, "the utility of the assembly will not be great"; if the latter, the king had better be fore-armed with answers to possible objections. This was doubly astute: for, as Calonne's memoranda to the king abundantly testify, the minister wanted to eat his cake and have it. The Notables would have the respect of the public but would be essentially yes-men – a role which they, with Miromesnil's encouragement, were emphatically to reject. The incompatibility of the two approaches was a serious and possibly fatal flaw in the enterprise and Miromesnil put his finger on it. The need to answer possible objections also gave Miromesnil the excuse to attack Calonne's measures themselves. Calonne had ignored the question of:

> How to raise the land tax throughout your estates [sic]. The difficulties it may encounter when applied to Brittany and the Languedoc, bearing in mind that you have just allowed these two provinces to settle for a lump sum [*abonnement*]. The measures to be taken in respect of Burgundy and Navarre and the estates of the little provinces adjoining Navarre such as . . . Bigorre. Provence which has its own individual regime, Flanders, Artois and the Cambrésis, in short all those of your provinces which have estates or the equivalent. . . . All these highly important matters have only been treated very superficially in our *conférences* and very slightly in the *comités* where Your Majesty has been good enough to hear us.

But this was not negligence on Calonne's part: the imposition of uniformity was a matter of deliberate principle. A man as astute as Miromesnil must have known this. But he wanted to press upon the king the idea that what Calonne was proposing was unjust, and appeal to Louis XVI's sense of fair play. There is a defense of the historic rights of the provinces – those which Calonne had dismissed as "superannuated," a concept which meant nothing to Miromesnil. But, more telling, Louis is reminded that he personally has "recently" signed contracts, registered in the parlements, with the estates of Brittany and the Languedoc, giving them *abonnements* (lump-sum payments in lieu of taxes).

As regards the content of the proposals, Miromesnil's letters fore-shadow precisely the casuistical line that would be adopted by the Notables. Namely that although all orders and regions must pay their fair share, respect must be paid to the contracts entered into when the various provinces became part of France and to the rights of corps to pay in the traditional way and notably the clergy by its notoriously inadequate "free gift." In short, as Calonne's chief clerical opponent, Loménie de Brienne put it, "equality" was acceptable but not "uniformity."[30] So although Miromesnil was rightly accused of colluding with the Notables to defeat Calonne, he cannot be accused, as the king was to accuse him, of changing his stance.

Miromesnil tried to escape from his invidious position in the small committee by asking the king to include the other secretaries of state and some state councillors, at least to help in the drafting of the edicts, claiming that the task was too much for three men. Of course he had an ulterior motive in that he was pretty sure that the excluded ministers would support him and even vote down the measures: Breteuil for personal reasons, Castries and Ségur on ideological grounds. But it could be argued that his motives were honorable: if the king could not carry the council with him, how could he carry the Notables and the country? Would it not be wiser to give up before the regime itself was compromised?

However, Miromesnil was wasting his time. Indeed, his letter may at last have convinced the king that further discussion was pointless. For the very next day, December 29, Louis simply announced as a fait accompli to a stunned *conseil des dépêches* that an Assembly of Notables would meet the following month to implement a radical reform package. The council did not take minutes but the king's words were probably based on the draft found in his papers entitled "*Projet d'annonce de l'Assemblée des Notables à faire au Conseil du roi*":

> I am occupied with extremely important measures designed to ease the lot of my peoples, to eliminate several abuses and to restore order to my finances. Before ordering their implementation, I have decided to consult an Assembly of Notables. I have chosen its members. Each secretary of state must without delay send out letters of convocation, based on the one which the keeper of the seals will supply, to the people covered by his department. The proposals I will successively lay before the Assembly will be examined in advance by my council.[31]

To add insult to injury, the king tossed this bombshell casually at his ministers at the end of the council.[32] Did Louis XIV ever act in so high-handed a manner?

I have examined Louis XVI's decision to convoke the Assembly of Notables at some length because of its gravity, because it is the first link in an unbroken chain of events which led to the outbreak of revolution in 1789; because we have fairly detailed information on how it was arrived at; and because weakness in the structure of decision-making contributed in part and in a predictable way to the failure of this, the most ambitious reform package ever attempted by the Bourbon monarchy. The procedure adopted by Louis XVI – a protracted examination by a small group – achieved the worst of both worlds. Calonne had stressed to the king that the financial aspects of his measures – the new land tax, stamp duty and the inaugural loan to the state of the National Bank – must be in place before the third *vingtième* expired at the end of December. This was not achieved, so that even if things had gone well in the Assembly, it would have been impossible to have the new taxes in place in 1787. At the same time, the narrow basis of the decision – a minority even of the royal council – augured badly for an attempt to persuade the holders of entrenched fiscal privilege to make sacrifices without at least the prospect of increased political power. For what factions were represented by the men who took the decision? What one might call the "king's party" represented by the king and Vergennes, who merely reflected the king's light; and Calonne who additionally represented both *la finance* and the Polignac group or *société intime de la reine*. The queen herself, informed by Calonne at the last minute, was hostile, refused to attend the opening ceremony of the Notables and was to tip the balance in bringing about Calonne's fall. The failure to bring Miromesnil, the head of the judiciary, on board guaranteed the hostility of the parlements. Throughout the session of the Notables, the excluded Castries acted as the ministerial spokesman for the Notables' opposition in general and for Necker's powerful faction in particular, angering the king with his intemperate and disrespectful criticism. Breteuil, meanwhile, the minister for the household, and another of the queen's protégés, attempted to topple Calonne even before the Notables had opened by attempting to have him denounced in the parlement for borrowing more than had been stipulated in the edicts creating his previous loans.[33] Perhaps never before had a King of France gone into battle (literal or metaphorical) with less chance of success.

Once the Notables had met, the transformative nature of the situation itself came into play, illustrating the point that everything about a revolution cannot be derived from its wider origins. Whilst Calonne had remained in office, the Notables had concentrated on defeating his measures. But after they had forced the king to dismiss him, they moved to the offensive and made radical, even "revolutionary," demands to limit his monarchy. They held it as axiomatic that Necker's *Compte rendu* was accurate. It therefore followed that Calonne had squandered four billion livres in less than four years and that the king was responsible: (a) for appointing him; (b) for not supervising his administration; and (c) for personal extravagance. They therefore demanded, first, that institutional steps be taken to prevent a recurrence of such waste: a finance council on which would sit not only ministers but laymen representing the different orders of society with no links to the administration; and the annual publication of accounts, including pensions and favours from the royal domain. Secondly, they demanded that taxation should be for a given purpose over a finite period and that expenditure should be tailored to revenue not vice versa. Dupont de Nemours thought that this in itself spelled the end of the absolute monarchy because, given infla-tion, the king, now no more than a "a magistrate decorated with the title and honours of royalty" (compare the constitution of 1791, first draft) would have to appeal regularly to the representatives of the nation cap in hand. He also thought it would lead to a corrupt system *à l'anglaise*. The third demand was that redress of grievances should precede supply; in other words, the safeguards the Notables demanded should be imple-mented whilst the Notables were in session. Finally, the society of orders should have an institutional political base through the financial council and the provincial assemblies.

At this point the king dismissed the Notables, with only one of the seven bureaux endorsing any increase of taxation. A few Notables (for example, La Fayette) asked for the convocation of the Estates General; a more common position was that the king could only implement changes of the magnitude of those presented through the estates.

At the same time the Notables feared that Calonne's published programme was only the tip of the iceberg. These fears are confirmed by Dupont, who was not only Calonne's close collaborator but the *éminence grise* behind his successor's brief ministry, that of Bouvard de Fourqueux. Dupont stated what he believed to be the king's ultimate intention: "the *taille* will be abolished, its total being added to that of the *subvention terri-toriale* which should be borne in the same proportion by the lands of the citizens of all the orders, princes, nobles and ecclesiastics."[34]

CONCLUSION

Do procedures matter in decision-making? People at the time thought that if a decision purported to have been taken by the council then that actually should be the case; the alternative was ministerial or royal despotism, which everyone united in condemning. The principle was that the king should act on advice duly delivered, which distinguished the French monarchy from the Ottoman despotism. Were these just pious platitudes or does it relate to the modern notion of proper consultation? Castries said that rather than a proper debate, the king preferred unanimity which enabled him to sleep at night, but this was to lead to a rude awakening.

The question of when to consult vested interests is a tricky one, or rather one that I have answered by the use of the pejorative term "vested." Clearly, if a regime is stable and at peace with itself, a wide consultation, even taking unofficial soundings as Louis XVI and Necker both did, is desirable. But by definition this is unlikely to lead to change. If a country is undergoing immense stresses, as France under Louis XVI was, particularly if it was deeply divided about the necessity of change, as Sorel argued, then consultation may not be the most effective way of managing change. In such a situation the king could not win (except in his foreign policy). In convoking the Notables he ignored vested interests, which quickly conspired to defeat his reforms. So should he have done nothing? The trick in terms of political management is to understand where power lies, at court and in the country; to make sure that the number and influence of your supporters exceeds that of your likely opponents and (this is the lesson of the *révolte nobiliaire*) can be mobilized effectively; and to recognize that whereas action is often dangerous, inactivity can be more so.

Put in another way, there were some decisions which had to be taken and others which did not. Three of the decisions of Louis XVI's reign – those to recall the parlement in 1774, to sign an alliance with the Americans in 1778 and to convoke the Notables in 1786 – did not have to be taken. There was an expectation of a decision in 1774 and 1778, but it did not have to be satisfied; that taken in 1786 was a complete surprise. So we are confronted with the paradox of Louis XVI, the man who hated making decisions, making three supererogatory ones. Moreover, these three decisions in a sense all brought about the very consequences they were designed to avert. For example, Vergennes argued that France must enter the American war to ensure she had an alliance with the colonies in place before England attacked French colonies. That is why the only condition France put in the generous terms of her treaty of alliance was that the signatories would not sign a separate peace with England. Yet this solitary condition was broken in

spirit if not in letter by the Americans signing separate peace preliminaries, which meant that if Spain had persisted (as she was entitled by
the convention of Aranjuez) in refusing peace unless Gibraltar was
returned to her, the French navy and finances could have been
destroyed in 1783 and with them, perhaps, the regime itself. The convocation of the Notables was destined to cure a financial crisis, but the cure
was worse than the disease. As Calonne had prophesied – but still he
went ahead – to reveal the size of the deficit, without at the same time
implementing measures to deal with it, risked financial meltdown.

It can be said that the decision to enter the American war was taken
after full observance of the regular consultative procedures – they may
indeed be considered to have been unduly protracted. Protracted also
were Louis's deliberations about whether to summon the Notables, but
he failed to secure the unanimous endorsement even of the small
committee he consulted so that, after Vergennes's death, it was the king
and Calonne against the entire political establishment. The words "fool-
hardy" or "despotic" might be applied and the lethargic king of historical myth might be more properly dubbed *Louis le téméraire*. On the other
hand, due observance of procedures does not in itself guarantee a wise
decision: many of the decisions taken regularly by his ancestor, Louis
XIV, may be said to have been ill-advised if also fully advised, and Louis
XVI should have stuck to his original analysis of Anglo-American
conflict, ignored Vergennes, and waited for the ripe plum to drop into
his lap.

Consider the decision to intervene in the proceedings of the Estates
General in the *séance royale* of June 23, 1789. This decision was taken after
the widest consultation, even including royal princes – a throwback to an
earlier period of the monarchy. And it was a disaster. The lesson takes
the form of a truism: if you consult the establishment you will preserve
the status quo if the establishment is in good shape; if it is not you will be
swept aside with it. And the question remains: could Louis XVI ever
have implemented his reform programme in 1787? And, if so, how?

3. The Paris Parlement in the 1780s

PETER ROBERT CAMPBELL

Summary

It was long thought that there was a clear rise of parlementary and aristocratic opposition to the absolute monarchy from 1715 to 1771, crushed by Maupeou only to resume in 1785, and motivated by an ideology of aristocratic reaction. This chapter argues against these older historical explanations for being misleadingly simple. Close examination of the sociology, procedures, and arguments, and their context, suggests there were important constant elements. The structure of the various crises was similar and so indeed were the magistrates's motivations. The defense of their jurisdiction is the real constant in Crown–parlement relations, but this desire could be manipulated by court factions or interest groups like the Jansenists; this and poor political management from the centre largely explains the numerous crises. The key new element was the *parti janséniste* which played the leading role up to 1771, and this included elaborating a "new" history of the parlement that appealed to a so-called "ancient constitution" in which the judges were the depositories of the laws. Thus ideology is recognized as important, but its use is interpreted more as rhetoric than ideological motivation. The parlement's role is here seen more in terms of institutional strategies and court politics than in terms of more general ideological or social contests. Therefore, and perhaps controversially, doubts are cast upon the current notion of "parlementary constitutionalism" as being the principal motivation of the judges. Since jurisdiction, the defense of corporate honour, was at the root of the confrontations, parlementary constitutionalism would therefore be left as an influential rhetoric adopted by the judges in various crises to legitimize more conservative aims. Nevertheless, as Margerison shows in this volume, for the wider public and pamphleteers, this parlementaire rhetoric took on a life of its own and was the basis of division between opposing sides in the pamphlet debate over the future constitution of France.

INTRODUCTION

The quarrel between the Crown and the parlements dominates the politics of the pre-revolution. The Paris parlement in particular was a crucial and hallowed element in the political system of the monarchy. It was the most important of 13 parlements and sovereign courts, with a jurisdiction extending from Paris down to Lyon and Poitiers amounting to more than two-fifths of France. In the 1780s the Paris parlement was composed of about 144 magistrates who convened in the *palais de justice* in the heart of Paris in courts staffed by about 400 clerks and bailiffs, attended by perhaps 100 lawyers. It had 164 lesser courts under its jurisdiction. All the parlements were the supreme courts of appeal in their regional jurisdiction, and were very necessary to the functioning of the legal system. Their political and jurisdictional quarrels are only the most visible elements of their role. As the monarchy of France was essentially a legal system in which laws were cast as judgments, and this included royal pronouncements, much of what we call "administration" was supervised by the parlements (who often clashed with intendants). They dealt with municipal government, public order, grain supply in bad times, and were thus essentially part of local and regional government, ruling though legal pronouncements called *arrêts*. They were therefore as much a part of government as they were of opposition

Their oppositional potential stemmed largely from the fact that the courts were regarded as a depository of the laws, with the right and duty to verify that new legislation conformed to existing laws and principles (and in the provinces with all their different legal codes, this could be important). This verification and registration of legal and fiscal legislation was both practically useful and was also intended to reassure the public that the monarchy was limited. They therefore had the right to point out problems in letters and remonstrances to the king. According to them, the king should neither innovate nor transgress; but of course the king, facing new problems and acting in a tradition of making policy decisions in an *ad hoc* fashion, felt obliged to alter past policies and introduce new ones, with the result that the courts would sometimes protest and block new legislation. But everyone accepted that the final word remained with the "absolute" monarch, whose sovereignty was not to be shared or divided.[1] Nevertheless, if the courts felt strongly, they could make life very difficult for the king and his ministers. By registering laws and loans with caveats and restrictions that undermined them and by repeatedly remonstrating, when pushed they might suspend their functions of providing justice and administration, partially paralyzing the state.

Moreover, given the hazy nature of the constitution of the monarchy, it is not surprising that such bodies should claim as many rights as they could get away with, so that they were involved in a perpetual war of jurisdictions with other courts and even with the king's council. In trying to confirm and even extend their jurisdiction (for example, in tussles with the financial or ecclesiastical courts), they often encroached on what the Crown, in the council of state, regarded as its own powers as supreme legislator. This caused considerable but tolerable frictions that were part of a *modus vivendi* between the king and his courts. Some of the most difficult episodes concerned loans and taxation, and a breakdown in relations could be serious. The Paris parlement had to register fiscal legislation and it could therefore pose a serious threat to policy as it believed new taxes should be limited to a wartime necessity and that loans should be properly secured and not turn into a new tax. In an age of expensive maritime warfare and developments in military commitments in the competitive arena of the Atlantic world, the monarchy needed more money and had trouble getting it. The courts represented the innate conservatism of a backwards-looking society that understood very little of finance and still thought the king should live off his own estate income. Clashes were inevitable, driven by issues of jurisdiction and the fact that the old fiscal system of the baroque state did not provide enough revenue even with the addition of another peacetime tax such as the *vingtième* after 1749. Whatever view we hold of the motives of the magistrates, it is certain that their actions could prove troublesome for the royal ministers when it concerned provincial privileges, corporate privileges, religion and the church's jurisdiction, and, of course, fiscal objectives.

Historians and contemporaries have all accepted that the actions of the Paris parlement, and those of the provincial parlements as well, played a crucial role in the events leading to the end of the old regime. From 1783 to 1788 a progressive breakdown in relations between the Crown and the parlement occurred. Without its opposition there might not have been a revolution, for France was not overtaxed. Its role certainly undermined credit and focused attention on the issue of despotism, which dominated the ideological debate in 1787–8. But behind these bare facts the issues are more complicated. Questions need to be asked about the motives of the magistrates and their oppositional tactics, and the answers lead us away from broad generalizations towards a far more complex picture.

Did the judges really have a will to opposition? Were they a coherent group with unified views? Did the courts even have an overall political agenda? Was their activity the result of a century-long desire to acquire power at the expense of the monarchy, with the magistrates forming a sort of vanguard of "aristocratic reaction"?[2] Were the magistrates perhaps defenders of liberal values against a despotic monarchy that was insistent on its undivided (hence "absolute") sovereignty? Or were the judges in fact nothing more than a selfish oligarchy of nobles defending their privileges against reform from a progressive monarchy? There are so many good questions to re-examine, and there is some evidence for all these views. Perhaps the single most telling piece of evidence is the decree by the parlement on September 25, 1788 that the Estates General should meet according to their form of 1614, meaning in three equal-sized orders each with one vote. It seemed to imply taking sides with the two privileged orders against reforms wanted by the Third Estate, and was so out of touch with the public mind that the Paris parlement's influence promptly disappeared forever. Coming as it did at the end of a bitter struggle, it seems to throw a clear light on their motives. But even in this case questions have been raised about the judges' intention.[3] Clearly, we need to know more about why and how this breakdown in relations occurred, and whether it had a long history. Even if it did, were new elements to be found in the 1780s?

THE NATURE OF EARLIER CRISES

Historians have highlighted the previous crises because they add drama to a narrative and because they produce manageable bodies of evidence to consult. So one could easily come away from the specialized studies with the impression that the relations between Crown and parlement were on a wartime footing for most of the time. That is not the case, and yet the period was punctuated by serious disputes in the following years: 1648–52; 1675; 1718, 1730–2, 1753–4, 1756, 1763, 1770–1, and the final crisis of 1786–8. Of these disputes, two are worth a short discussion both for their illustrative value and their intrinsic significance. The crisis of 1730–2, for example, is interesting not only for the parallels with those of the 1780s but also for revealing the importance of political management, which is necessary in all regimes and which was so conspicuously absent in 1786–8. In terms of this basic ingredient for all successful politics, the skills of Louis XV's first minister Cardinal Fleury, his Keeper of the Seals Chauvelin, and Chancellor Daguesseau in the 1730s were head and shoulders above those of *premier ministre* Loménie de Brienne and, particularly, Lamoignon, the head of the judiciary, in the later 1780s.

From 1729, the parlement had become heavily involved in the controversy over the Bull *Unigenitus* and the defence of persecuted Jansenists. From 1730 to 1732 the magistrates protested the use of evocations of cases to the king's council as undermining its hallowed right to protect French subjects from abuses of "papal" ecclesiastical justice through the courts's right to judge appeals from decisions by church courts (a procedure known as *appel comme d'abus*). After remonstrances, deputations, strikes, and exiles, the courts suffered a defeat, though with face saved, at the hands of a skilful, united, and determined ministry under Cardinal Fleury. This crisis set a pattern that was to be repeated up to 1771. In these affairs, we have recently discovered that the small but cleverly organized *parti janséniste*, composed of perhaps thirty lawyers and about fourteen committed magistrates, with wider links to priests and theologians, was extremely influential (and this has important implications for the historical evalution of the parlement).[4] They cleverly manipulated their less-committed colleagues for their own ends by appealing to their sense of jurisdiction and corporate honour. Their main end was, however, to use the parlement to defend their co-religionists outside the courts, because these persecuted individuals' only recourse against the authority of the bishops was by way of a legal appeal against abuses of ecclesiastical jurisdiction to the parlement as the highest regular appeal court in the land. The issues are detailed and complicated, but in brief the Jansenists denounced threats to the parlement's jurisdiction time and again, and this tactic led to an escalation of rhetoric on both sides (that is, between the council of state and the courts), until patience was exhausted and the king retaliated by exiling or arresting magistrates as troublemakers. At that point, chosen royal servants would negotiate with the leading magistrates to effect a compromise that enabled the courts to return to work chastened but honour intact, and the king to win on the essential points. At least he was supposed to win, but some felt that royal policy under Choiseul (1758–70) came dangerously close to capitulation.

How could a small group of zealots influence the larger body of judges? The truth is that most judges were apathetic unless galvanized – only a zealous minority dealt with any significant number of cases – and jurisdiction was the issue that all found important, as it related to the prestige of their venal offices. Some have argued that the magistrates' motivation was primarily ideological, prompted by "Gallicanism" or "parlementary constitutionalism," but if that was the case surely the magistrates would have been expected to take up almost all cases relating to these issues.[5] The only ones they did take up were on occasions when they were prompted by concerned counsellors around issues of jurisdiction, and these concerned judges were invariably linked to the *parti janséniste* in those years. It is thus safe to conclude that more issues were involved than just the legal and constitutional ones, and that defense of their jurisdiction is the main key to understanding the judges. This interpretative model has been shown to be equally true of the 1750s and 1760s.[6] The Jansenist period of influence (1718–71) had lasting consequences, as it brought the parlement back into politics, and led to popular esteem and to the refinement of oppositional tactics such as strategies for manipulation and the publication of remonstrances. In the 1780s other factional interests replaced the Jansenists as movers in the courts, but they used the same tactics.[7]

Our second example, the conflict that led to the Maupeou coup in 1771, reveals many of the same elements, but with a crucial difference. In 1770–1 this uncomfortable ritual was to end in tears. The Maupeou coup was related to both the religious factions and court politics, and to the poor relationship between the ministry and the courts over the previous 15 years.[8] The Jansenist-inspired resistance to the refusal of sacraments to dying Jansenists in the 1750s, the successful assault on the Jesuit order in 1762 in the Paris parlement, the determined resistance of several provincial courts to the forcible registration of controller general Bertin's fiscal edicts of 1763 (imposing new taxes and prolonging wartime taxes in preacetime), the theory that the various parlements all formed a part of a single body (the theory of classes) – all these served to create two views of the parlements amongst ministers. Some like Bernis and Choiseul were for careful management; others like Maupeou and d'Aiguillon, the governor of Brittany whose brother-in-law was a secretary of state, were for crushing the magistrates's pretentions. The Maupeou coup grew directly out of the Brittany affair. From 1763 the Rennes parlement was at loggerheads with the harsh and provocative governor d'Aiguillon over taxation. In 1765 the magistrates played their last card, which was mass resignation; the Crown riposted by having the distinguished Jansenist *procureur général* (attorney general) of the Breton parlement arrested along with four other magistrates and gave the court one more chance to return to work, which almost all the judges rejected. The king then trumped them by setting up a new court. The Paris parlement became involved by protesting at the treatment of its colleagues, arguing that all the parlements were in fact one body. Louis replied to the Parisian remonstrances with the famous *séance de la flagellation* of 1766 in which he rejected the parlements' constitutional claims and strongly reasserted the principles of absolute sovereignty.[9] The *parti janséniste* saw it all as a *dévôt* (or Jesuit) plot, and after their reinstatement in 1769 (for the recently appointed chancellor Maupeou was then acting as the soul of moderation), the Breton parlementaires wanted to impeach their governor on what amounted to charges of despotism.

The Paris parlement became embroiled again when d'Aiguillon opted for trial in the parlement sitting as the court of peers. In the summer of 1770 the case was being turned by the magistrates into an attack on the royal style of government, so Louis XV intervened to revoke the case to his council and declare d'Aiguillon innocent. Faction was involved: Choiseul's whole policy of moderation with the parlements was called into question, as was his very position at court. Because d'Aiguillon was linked to the *dévôt* anti-Choiseul faction at court, Chancellor Maupeou felt it wise to abandon Choiseul and side with the beleaguered duke. To protect himself, the chancellor in November provoked the parlement to the point of uncompromising opposition, by reiterating the king's position very brusquely. The angry and offended judges played into his hands with remonstrances, iterative remonstrances and finally a strike, and refused to obey orders to return to work. This provided Maupeou with the excuse he was looking for to remodel or "reform" the judicial system in what became known as the Maupeou coup. The magistrates were exiled and a new system of courts established. New parlements or "superior councils" replaced the old courts almost throughout France, with venality of office and the system of "gifts" for judges abolished – and of course the political role of the new courts was considerably reduced. The way was open to authoritarian reform – but this never took place. However hard Maupeou tried to portray himself as a real reformer, few historians today would give him credit for that, and most feel that the origins of the coup lie in his factional choices.[10]

The consequence of the coup was a torrent of pamphlets in opposition to Maupeou and in defence of the exiled magistrates. The anti-Maupeou camp mustered hundreds of publications, while the royal propagandists were drowned out. The "patriots" raised the dangerous constitutional questions already agitated by Jansenists through the parlements and in pamphlets over the preceding 40 years.[11] The monarchy was behaving "despotically" and questions were raised in the political nation about the rights of the Crown and those of its subjects. As political debate took hold of France for a year, political awareness seeped further down the social scale. Ideological divisions about the monarchy and despotism were now fully in the public sphere: perhaps the ideas were rooted in the sixteenth century, but now they were expressed in a new language of rights and patriotism. Much of the authority of the French monarchy rested on the illusion that it was a moderate arbiter between conflicting jurisdictions. The Maupeou coup shattered this illusion; it tore away the veil traditionally cast over the "mysteries of state." People were beginning to reason that without the parlements, there was no one to speak for the nation; if the will of the king's ministers had no opposition, France must be a "ministerial despotism." Still royalist to the core, the patriots argued that the king himself was not a despot, but that he had been "surprised" by his ministers.[12] Needless to say, this crisis had a profound impact on the political culture of the next two decades. Many of the arguments re-surfaced in 1788.

HISTORICAL APPROACHES

Earlier historians of the parlements fall into three main schools, each of which paid close attention to the official statements of the Crown and the courts and to propagandist eighteenth-century histories. The first might be called that of the nineteenth-century liberals, epitomized by Jules Flammermont, which regards parlementaire opposition to the Crown as paving the way for parliamentary democracy. It takes the parlement's own statements (which were often propaganda) too uncritically. The second, including Marcel Marion, Alfred Cobban, and recently Michel Antoine, regards the parlements as selfish and obscurantist oligarchs impeding the efforts of an enlightened monarchy to modernize France, and in particular to introduce uniformity to institutions and equality to the tax system.[13] These historians regard the parlementaire statements as special pleading, and consider they are illegitimately encroaching upon royal prerogatives: they therefore take the royal critique of courts too literally (but they were also propaganda). The third and most recent school is more nuanced, seeing them as neither heroes nor villains but as jobbing judges treading through a minefield of conflicting jurisdictions and claims on their loyalties.[14] A weakness with the first two approaches in particular is their tendency to neglect the overall context in which events unfold. All three leave the king and his ministers – the dominant part of the partnership of Crown and parlement – out of the equation.

Indeed, once it is fully recognized that we are dealing with a *relationship* between the two principal parties of Crown and parlement, fresh questions emerge. A fourth view therefore – that of this essay – responds to this by investigating the role of the king and his ministers as well as that of the courts. Benefiting from a new current of historiography that has taken court politics seriously and explored the institutional functioning of the courtly governance of France, it stresses the part played by the Crown in generating and resolving conflicts. The approach does of course draw upon earlier analyses, but above all it has sought to write microhistories of events. Several recent studies focus in great detail on the causes of the various crises, but three also ask questions about the periods of good relations with the government.[15] Emphasizing the role of the Crown brings out new factors such as the surer grasp of the political issues by the ministers, the issue of jurisdiction, the importance of political management, the role of patronage and clientage, the risks of giving offence to honor and ambition, the role of faction, and the significance of rhetoric. With these views in mind let us consider the question of the motivation of the courts in opposing royal policies.

As we have suggested above, historians looking at the general characteristics of the magistrates have tried to address questions like whether or not the magistrates as a group had a will to opposition, or any unified views at all, or whether the courts had any overall political ambitions. A social analysis shows that the counsellors were fairly recent nobles who for the most part owned landed estates with seigneurial titles, and Parisian property. The oldest families of magistrates had been part of a wave of recruitment to the nobility in the sixteenth century when the concept of virtue expanded to include renaissance learning alongside military prowess as a claim to nobility. By the early seventeenth century tenure of office in the parlement carried with it a noble title after twenty years' service, but the office was, like almost all offices, purchased by the holder or his forebear, and could be passed on to his heir as a property, provided a tax were paid annually. Financial or legal families bought their way into the magistrature for status, and by the eighteenth century the parlement was almost exclusively composed of robe nobles with a strong tendency to intermarriage. Judges would be related to each other and to sword and robe families of similar standing.[16]

Within the courts several dynasties existed who were themselves related to numerous other judicial families: the Daguesseau, Lamoignon, Joly de Fleury, Voisin, and d'Ormesson families, for example. In the eighteenth century, at the top of the hierarchy in the courts, the grander families of judges were increasingly related to courtier dynasties and the great robe families of the secretaries of state. They all tended to share the values of the nobility of the robe, which meant having a sense of duty to the laws and to their corporate body whose rules governed their lives. They were certainly bound by the corporate ethic of outward unanimity (even if the courts were riven with factions internally). They were very conservative, legally minded members of a privileged corporation who saw it as their duty to defend the laws and, just as importantly, to defend their jurisdiction against all encroachments, be they by the king's council or other bodies. For the 1770s and 1780s, Bailey Stone has refined this approach, and concluded that they were attached to the divisions of society into three orders and strongly believed in the justness of privilege. In politics they displayed an ambivalent royalism, which resulted in their being devoted to the monarchy but denying it the wherewithal to function. He stresses that they "championed a perplexing variety of special interests" and many came to identify the regeneration of France with their own partnership with a periodic Estates General. A few radical judges, influenced by the Enlightenment, saw the future in the subordination of the courts to the commonweal.[17]

If some general sense of motivation can be inferred from a sociological analysis, more precise information can be gained from studying what the courts actually said (as Bailey Stone has indeed also done). When they opposed royal policy, they made statements of their position in *arrêtés*, deputations and remonstrances. In their *arrêtés* and remonstrances (collected together and published by Flammermont) the parlements tend to appeal to four newer notions, each with antecedents but developed more cogently from the 1750s.[18] First, they begin to argue that the laws were above the king, thus separating the king and laws; soon they were to separate the king and the Nation. Then they claim that the parlement is a depository of the law. Free verification of the law is a necessary right, for the king did not have time to discuss everything with his ministers, so he can be "surprised." From the 1730s the parlements make increasingly frequent references to the idea of a contract between king and Nation, in which the courts represented the Nation. In this way a different idea of the "fundamental laws" of the state emerges, with the idea that the courts are intermediary powers necessary to balance the tendency for the monarchy to become despotic. In the 1750s the "theory of classes" is stressed, linked to a history of the parlements that legitimizes, in their own eyes at least, their claims.[19] A fascinating amalgam of Jansenist and Enlightened theories emerges by the end of the 1750s.[20] Although the idea of classes faded away, all the other ideas were to be appealed to in the 1780s.

Nevertheless, as we have suggested, to deduce their intentions from the official statements alone is a mistake. So many statements juxtaposed one after another in Flammermont give the impression that the debate was essentially about theories and jurisprudence. That is to forget the nature of ancien-régime politics, which was mostly about the defence of jurisdiction and privilege, the concern for which was often concealed behind more general principles. Courts were perpetually skirmishing with one another, and problems that we today see as administrative or institutional they interpreted in terms of the rights and powers of corporate bodies. They were all involved in an ancien-régime game of bluff, negotiation, and compromise. Statements were used rhetorically – these judges all had training in rhetoric – and tactically. They tended to extrapolate the worst-case scenario from royal legislation or actions, and conceal the lesser issues by reading some fundamental theoretical point of jurisprudence or sovereignty into the case. Indeed, it was perfectly possible for small groups to manipulate their colleagues by appealing to the universal desire to defend their jurisdiction, by finding some such issue to unite everyone around, when their real aim was quite different. Not everyone had to be won over, for even a majority of one bound the institution as much as unanimity.

Detailed studies of events, such as those of our examples in 1730–2 and 1770–1, and others on the 1750s, have shown that behind the apparently unanimous corporate statements the magistrates were not in fact united in their legal and political views.[21] Their internal debates reveal shades of opinion and quite often narrow majorities for more radical steps during disputes. It was not always hard to persuade just enough colleagues to swing the debate. Many judges were idle and many were inexperienced; most felt condemned to remain in their place with no prospect of advancement until they became an honorary judge in retirement; some saw opposition as the only way upwards and out; few were competent in matters of state finances and the lawyers were much more expert in legal matters than most judges.[22] A further important point is that, as these and other case studies show, the structure of crises repeats itself throughout the century.[23] There is a tendency to escalation in these confrontations, broken by bluff, negotiation, and compromise. To defend its claim to supreme authority, the Crown could not be seen to negotiate with its courts, so official dialogue was almost impossible and affairs had to be resolved behind the scenes and a "compromise" reached that saved face on both sides. But it could all too easily go wrong.

Therefore, to understand the diverse factors involved in the generation of opposition statements and stances we have to take into account both how the courts functioned in terms of procedure and each highly specific political situation.[24] In the corrupt system of old-regime justice for the elite, it was often a question of which party could influence the most judges, and it was the same for political matters in the courts. The Crown had an advantage because it could use its official representatives as well as give pensions to senior magistrates to encourage loyalty. Inside the parlement, hierarchy was extremely important. During its general assemblies, opinions were given in strict order of seniority after the suggestions of the king's lawyers had been heard. So it was usually possible for the "ministerial party," as it was known, to control the outcome. It included several royal appointees, namely the First President, and the *rapporteur* who put the king's case, with the solicitor general and his lawyer colleagues, collectively known as the *gens du roi*. It was usually more productive to influence senior judges because debate was not structured democratically but hierarchically. The most senior gave their opinion first, and after the first few views had been expressed the other judges could effectively only agree or disagree with them, as any new view was unlikely to get a majority (because all previous votes could not adhere to their view). So some of the members of the highest court, the *grand' chambre*, received government loans and pensions.

The system usually worked quite well, as long as the ministry was united. But there were some structural limitations. In practice the "royal" appointees could only be chosen from two or three possible candidates, such was the role of propriety and precedence, so the control through appointments could become more theoretical than real. The fact that some of the leading robe dynasties had increasingly close relations with the court nobility in the eighteenth century takes on a new significance. Some developed ministerial ambitions, and lent succor to courtly factions and ministerial rivalries. Furthermore, each minister had some clients in the courts (relations, legal advisers or judges hoping for advancement to intendant, say), and if the ministers were at war with one another the system could break down as strings were pulled in different directions. Talleyrand wrote of the parlement in the 1780s that "intrigue penetrated it from every angle. M. Necker, M. de Calonne, M. de Breteuil each had their creatures there who defended or attacked the measures of the minister they wanted to help or do down."[25] The external face of corporate unanimity that we see in the written pronouncements often obscures factional splits (that were often linked to factions outside the parlement, at Versailles for instance). Other factors were just as important: internecine rivalry, hotheaded youth, ambition and disaffection. As we have seen, ambitious souls had little hope for advancement unless they made a nuisance of themselves.[26]

Excessive royal demands were an important cause of friction too, especially with regard to fiscality. Wars were so costly that taxes and loans were necessary in a state in which the medieval belief that the king should only raise extra taxes in wartime still held sway. In 1648 and 1787 the problem was that too great a burden was placed on the parlement for it to retain its credibility with the people without protests. So even if there was usually the potential to handle the parlement carefully, some fiscal crises were too severe for the system to cope with. Trapped in a socio-fiscal system that came into existence under Louis XIV, the monarchy never could fundamentally reform its finances to a level at which it could escape recurrent fiscal crises in wartime. Quarrels about religion were troublesome, but in the eighteenth century were not likely to bring the state to its knees, whereas the resistance to fiscal proposals was very serious.

All in all, the government's control was somewhat precarious.[27] It was better to avoid confrontations if at all possible because of their tendency to escalate, as cardinal Bernis, who dealt as minister with the courts in 1757–8, recognized:

> All affairs that can agitate the parlement, especially those that concern religion, ought to be smothered at birth and destroyed in their germ whenever men of wisdom in these assemblies, however few in number, are able to quench at its origin the progress of the fire. But when matters have once started, judicial forms and methods carry them rapidly along, and a decision once given, the wisest minds find themselves linked to the hottest heads; they cannot then, without violent shocks, abolish or reform the decrees of parlement.[28]

This process could only be broken by good political management. The *parti ministériel* (ministerial group) was expected to employ all the tricks of the trade: "Pains must be taken to govern the parlements and to prevent the storms that arise there. By a few deserved distinctions, by confidence, by concert of feeling, it would be easy to maintain the calmness and subordination of those great bodies."[29]

Management inside the parlement was far easier if only the government ministers were far-sighted enough to plan things properly: "The whole secret of legitimate and recognized authority consists in never compromising itself, and consequently, in estimating correctly the resistance that projects may encounter in execution."[30]

This was necessary because, in effect, the ministry's hands were tied:

> It is impossible to exile and supercede the parlement of Paris without all the other parlements in the kingdom espousing its cause. . . . You cannot destroy in a day bodies which have sent such deep roots into the very foundations of the monarchy. . . . It is rash to attempt suddenly, by the employment of force and authority, to chain up the most vigorous and most powerful bodies in the State.[31]

It was far better to use the carrot than the stick when managing the courts – but as a quarrel turned into a crisis, intimidation could sometimes be effective. The most impressive action the Crown could take was for the king to embody royal justice in person at a session of the parlement known as a *lit de justice*. After a highly formal consultation of the magistrates, the king as judge insisted upon his will being registered forthwith. If the parlement persisted in its refusal to register an edict, the Crown would certainly withhold patronage, and even make an example of rebellious magistrates by exiling them. (Needless to say, such tactics, used injudiciously, could be equally counterproductive, stiffening resistance.) In the ministers' bottom drawer were plans for disciplinary regulations or the remodeling of the court; another threat was to deprive the courts of jurisdiction by giving the *grand conseil* powers of registration.[32] In the Fronde, in 1732 and 1737, on several occasions during the 1750s, and in 1770, such tactics were used. After the reinstatement of the parlement in 1774, its feud with the *grand conseil* continued. Foolishly, the Keeper of the Seals Miromesnil allowed the courts to win in 1777. That deprived the ministry of one arrow in its quiver.

And yet, Miromesnil did this because he was confident he could control the courts. His view was shared by distinguished advisors and ministers in this period. The marquis d'Argenson, Jacob-Nicolas Moreau, cardinal Bernis, all held similar views. Looking back on the parlements's pre-revolutionary opposition, Sénac de Meilhan, an Enlightened intendant, did not regard them as an insurmountable obstacle for the government. He emphasized the limitations in their outlook and the possibilities for ministerial control.

> The parlements, attached to their old forms, sometimes gave rise to opposition, but they were easy to defeat, by negotiation and by favours secretly offered to those who had the most *crédit*. This grand corps was characterised by ignorance of affairs of state, their wisdom was always far behind their century, and it was easy for an adroit minister to present affairs to them in a favourable light; their remonstrances were often agreed in advance with the Court and the reply ready prepared, and the most eloquent of them were quite commonplace.[33]

Perhaps this "commonplace" character to the remonstrances is significant: it shows their awareness of the importance of public opinion, which did not understand finance either. From the 1730s onwards, the parlement's opposition gained strength from the support of the public. Having successfully used public opinion against the parlement in 1758, Bernis reflected that: "The parlement has force only through that of the voice of the people; the fermentations in its assemblies are nothing if not supported by a public fermentation . . . the parlements must yield as soon as they are abandoned by the public."[34]

The publication of the traditionally secret remonstrances, a new development from the 1730s, gave people an education in political language and the theories of monarchy and opposition: the evident newsworthiness of internal debates during crises is certainly evidence of growing political consciousness. The Parisians certainly took an interest in the "politics" of "their" courts and ministry. They read the banned Jansenist newspaper the *Nouvelles ecclésiastiques* (*Ecclesiastical News*) detailing the developments in the refusal of sacraments controversy, in which the parlement sided with the persecuted Jansenists, and discussed developments in the cafés, where police spies eavesdropped on them.[35]

After 1774 it would be more difficult to dominate the parlement. Historians have differed on whether the recall in November 1774 was a simple mistake, or whether it was justified because the Maupeou courts had not bedded in properly and appeared no better than the old ones.

Probably it was a mistake then, and certainly seems so with hindsight. The magistrates returned not chastened but defiant and vindicated, with their powers to oppose ministers almost intact. The repeated disciplinary threats, retractions, exiles, and recalls in the 1750s, the abolition of 1771, and the recall itself, all encouraged the idea that relations with the Crown were a "game" and that the government would always compromise. In the 1780s it therefore seemed as if risks could be taken. Magistrates and most ministers thought the monarchy was as solid as a rock, and continued with these games of bluff, when in fact this time the fiscal problems were overwhelmingly dangerous. There was, moreover, a self-centred arrogance in their approach, as they seemed to think they could judge the consequences of their actions to a nicety. We shall see that it does also matter who the individuals were and what political games they were playing. To fulfil the promise of this new approach, let us now examine the period 1774–89 more closely.

1774–1789

In 1776 the parlement certainly made its presence felt in opposition to Turgot's reforms, for its remonstrances against the abolition of the guilds are a ringing defense of the corporate order. Nevertheless, under Necker controversial rises in direct taxation were avoided, but, after his resignation in 1781, relations between the controllers general and the parlement were increasingly strained. The loans of 1782 and taxes, the *vingtièmes*, were registered easily only because it was still wartime. Indeed, it could be argued that relations were apparently good because it was difficult for the parlement to refuse loans in wartime when it was traditionally accepted that the king had far wider prerogatives.

By 1783 there were internal rivalries in the courts, making it more difficult for the ministry to manage them. President Lamoignon was opposed to First President d'Aligre because he wanted to become Keeper of the Seals, while *rapporteur* d'Amécourt wanted to replace Calonne. In the parlement there were serious differences on the issue of judicial reform, championed by the president, Lamoignon, who was using the issue to appear worthy of a ministry. From 1783 to 1787 faction at court created further divisions which were reflected in Crown–parlement relations. The Queen's faction suffered in 1783 from the realignment of the Polignacs towards the controller general Calonne, who could certainly do more to meet their financial demands.

Vergennes had backed Calonne's appointment and benefited from this new alliance, and the Keeper of the Seals Miromesnil was of necessity with these ministers. This situation drove the ambitious minister for the king's household, Breteuil, an adviser to the Queen, to intrigue against Calonne, seeking to have one of his clients, Foulon, replace Calonne, while he himself hoped to take Vergennes's place as foreign secretary. The war minister, Ségur, and Castries, secretary of state for the marine, were in the Queen's faction. The split between a king's party and the queen's was a sign of poor political management by Louis XVI. Its consequences were to be played out over the Diamond Necklace Affair and the registration of loans.[36]

In the Diamond Necklace Affair of 1785–6, the cardinal de Rohan was arrested and charged with complicity with the fraudsters. He chose to be tried by the parlement as a court of peers rather than the lesser châtelet court, and the queen was badly advised to accept this by Breteuil. Despite the implications for the queen if Rohan were cleared of guilt, the affair became factional. Vergennes wanted to repay a debt to the Rohan clan by finding witnesses to clear him, and Calonne used the trial against the queen's party to damage them by using his influence with "his" judges to make the prosecution fail. Calonne hoped the failure would lead to the dismissal of Breteuil, so that he himself could change ministries to avoid the financial calamities he could see coming. There was thus the unsavoury spectacle of the *parti* in the parlement being opposed by Calonne's and Vergennes's allies who were for acquittal. Rohan was indeed acquitted, and this outcome did more than tarnish the queen's reputation, it dealt the monarchy itself a blow.[37] More trouble was in store over the vital issue of loans. The *parti* was absolutely determined to block Calonne's loans, to discredit him, and so Calonne tried to have the First President dismissed, but Miromesnil was playing a double game and defended d'Aligre to the king. Augeard, a well-connected financier and memorialist, says that after the attempt to get rid of d'Aligre failed, "It was impossible for M. de Calonne to think of negotiating with the parlement: the king's lawyers, the grand bench, except M. de Lamoignon and M. de Saron who were neutral, and all the presidents were against him; he had no more than eight counsellors on his side."[38]

This impossible situation was what led Calonne to try to avoid the parlement, by calling an Assembly of Notables. Hardman has argued that at this point the classical political system had been stalemated. He is thinking of the inability to get taxes approved by the parlement, but although this was the case it is also true that the sheer scale of the problem made it difficult for the courts to agree to such large taxes in peacetime and retain credibility with the people. And in this sense their call for the Estates General could be interpreted as reasonable, because the burden of assent to such wide plans was too heavy for their shoulders.[39]

The period of the Assembly of Notables saw the parlement pushed to the background. In June 1787, after the Assembly of Notables had been dismissed, the parlement returned center stage. It was then asked to register the new taxes and new provincial arrangements for collecting them. But the magistrates felt slighted by the attempt to get around their jurisdiction and were not in a receptive mood. Moreover, various interests were now attempting to exploit the parlement to further their own aims. In the background was the Orléans faction, sidelined during the Notables, but which always had royal ambitions that surfaced in times of crisis. With Calonne and Miromesnil gone and Brienne appointed first *chef du conseil royal des finances*, then principal minister when Laurent de *Villedeuil* became controller general, and with Lamoignon as Keeper of the Seals, the ministerial factions looked a little different. Loménie de Brienne was relying on an ambitious and overconfident Lamoignon to manage the parlement for him, but that was going to be difficult. The parlement had an undistinguished *grand'chambre*, second-rate presidents of its chambers and its upper echelons were riven with rivalries, while Lamoignon himself was particularly disliked. "The *grand'chambre*," wrote Pasquier, "and the magistrates forming part of it, did not obtain from the rest of the house the recognition which should have been theirs. Youth had shaken off the yoke of its elders."[40] The way was open for radicals to exploit the situation.

Although the parlement accepted Loménie de Brienne's provincial reform proposals, its resistance to the fiscal proposals in the package remained strong. On July 16, 1787 the courts sitting as the full court with peers of the realm present, even echoed the marquis de Lafayette's call in the Notables for the Estates General to be allowed to meet.[41] This was a very public challenge to royal authority. It is unclear where this specifically originated. On the one hand it had become a rhetorical appeal to embarrass the government; it was used by the parlement of Rouen in 1759 and 1771, and taken up by other courts.[42] It certainly served a factional purpose as well. According to a leading magistrate: "In fact, everything that they put forward against the edicts [stamped paper and land tax] was only a pretext on which to base the demand for the Estates General. It had been organised in several committees and the call for it was made by that wretched *abbé* Sabathier."[43] Ferrand also says that the

First President chose not to oppose it because he saw it as a maneuver against Lamoignon, whom he hated.

At this point, a small group of radical counsellors in the chambers of inquests led by Duport, Fréteau, Robert de Saint Vincent, Duval d'Eprémesnil, and Huguet de Sémonville was very influential. They were thoroughly imbued with virtuous and patriotic concepts and saw themselves as fighting against "ministerial despotism." D'Eprémesnil was vehemently opposed to the queen and declared that her separate household was a scandal. Their patriotic ideology took precedence over political acumen, for they really seemed to believe that the king was being misled by evil ministers and that all would be well if the king could only be enlightened by the Nation. As they were fine orators, masters of the new rhetoric, and prestigious members of the Company, their younger colleagues were putty in their hands.

As Sallier observed:

> The young men of the chambers of inquests came to the assemblies as if they had been marching into battle and everything assured them of victory in a fight that was too unequal. Apart form superior numbers, they had more unity than those they were attacking. They even had some allies in the *grand'chambre*. Their orators pleaded a cause susceptible to those eloquent moments that always produce a great effect upon large assemblies. They appeared to be defending the rights and interests of the nation. Nothing was done to counter them ... the *parti* of the *grand'chambre* was silent ... The parlement above all lacked a first president who ... might have known how to make himself heard both by the [royal] court and his company at the same time. Either from pride, or through lack of concern, the ministry had always neglected much too much the means that could preserve harmony between the court and the parlement; and having no means of corruption, it appeared to have not the slightest idea of the skill needed to mold and maintain the spirit of such an assembly.

He also points out that Lamoignon was not a good choice as chancellor, because he was already distanced from many judges.[44]

The call for the Estates General in the session of July 16 that was embodied in the remonstrances presented on July 26, 1787, although proposed by radicals (and by the Orleanist *abbé* Sabatier de Cabre),[45] seems to have been carried by the majority as a tactical way of forcing the ministry to withdraw the declaration on stamp duty by raising the stakes.[46] Sallier explains that the rhetorical escalation was not unreasonable given that the ministry had already ignored the parlement's jurisdiction by calling the Assembly of Notables, had set no time limit for the new taxes and had begun to implement the new provincial assemblies before full registration, and that the parlement did not have the power to ensure that budgetary cuts were accepted at court: "Every session added to the strength of feeling and the gravity of the language."[47] To this was added the glory to be had from an impressive classical republican gesture of self-abnegation. The reiteration of this demand for the Estates in response to the *subvention territoriale* on July 30, 1787 was passed by an increased majority as patriotic rhetoric now conjoined with the scent of victory, and youth was encouraged by the *basoche*.

Ferrand, the loyalist who wrote the remonstrances, wanted the ministry to reply with delaying tactics to calm things down, but Brienne insisted on a *lit de justice*. This was held at Versailles on August 6 – followed up by the judges the next day by a fairly narrow majority of 64 to 51 for an *arrêt* declaring the registration to be null and illegal. On August 10 they began proceedings against Calonne and then condemned the royal procedures. With foreign war a possibility, the ministry could not afford the luxury of a drawn-out dispute, and, because a big procession that included the magistrates was due on the Feast of the Assumption, disturbances were feared. At 2:A.M. in the morning on August 15, *lettres de cachet* were delivered to the homes of the magistrates, exiling them immediately to Troyes. This only served to strengthen the belief amongst the public that the monarchy was behaving despotically. The result was riots from the *basoche* and generalized resistance from the lower courts all over the parlement's area of jurisdiction.[48] Loménie de Brienne then made the mistake of negotiating with the parlement too soon, when the radicals still felt they were winning; he had to accept the unfavourable compromise of withdrawing the new edicts and prolonging existing taxes. Momentously, the ministry gave in to the call for the Estates General, promising it would meet in five years' time.[49] This compromise had been worked out in September behind the scenes, and was broadly acceptable – but of course it also compromised royal authority and increased political tensions by occasioning a dangerous pamphlet debate.

The deal was supposed to be acted out in a royal session of the full parlement with the peers, but the way the "royal session" was concluded angered many judges. When Louis declared the edicts registered, after listening to "advice" but crucially before votes had been counted, he was challenged by the duc d'Orléans with the ringing phrase, "Sire it is illegal." Louis replied, "It is legal because I will it." This was actually not an attempt at despotism but a statement of the theory that in the king's presence only non-binding advice could be given, after which the king decided. But the counsellors felt it had been turned into another dishonoring and unnecessary *lit de justice*. What did look despotic to the public and the magistrates was the subsequent arrest of two of their number and the exiling of the duc d'Orléans by *lettres de cachet*: "Never had a government played so well into the hands of its opponents."[50]

In spite of all this, what most disrupted the whole enterprise were the "despotic" plans by the ministry to collect more in taxation than originally decreed, and the harsh tone of royal replies to requests for the return of the arrested magistrates (couched undiplomatically, by the courts, as an attack on *lettres de cachet* in general). Pasquier's analysis is particularly valuable, because he later became chancellor and knew all about political management:

> The king's answers, as inspired by his ministers, were not only always couched in the sense of a refusal, but even in very dry form. As a result, instead of an isolated matter being debated, general questions were taken up. Remonstrances were drawn up in the matter of compulsory registrations, *lettres de cachet*, and the danger resulting from a power which should be kept within bounds by its will alone. These remonstrances, ever respectfully couched, nevertheless set forth strong arguments in their support. Hence they acted powerfully on the mind of the nation, and then it was that the Parlement enjoyed the highest degree of public esteem and popular favour.[51]

The magistrates realised that work was afoot to curtail their political power by a judicial reorganization. (These plans had been mooted abroad in the hope of intimidating the parlement, as early as the previous September, as in the several threats during the century to employ the *Grand conseil* to register legislation.)[52] This provoked something of a battle fought through remonstrances and royal replies. In January the parlement attacked a symbol of despotism, *lettres de cachet*, invoking the liberty of the Nation amongst its arguments; as the king had the decree struck from the registers, remonstrances on March 13 denounced this form of response. On April 13 the royal session in November was the subject of remonstrances which raised the rhetorical stakes: the free deliberation and right to vote in the king's presence were a national right required by the public interest and by the Constitution. The will of the King alone is not sufficient for a law; the simple expression of this will is not a national form [of law]; the will, to be obligatory, must be legally published; for it to be published legally, it must be verified: such, Sire, is the constitution of France and it was born with the monarchy.[53]

At the end of the month reiterative remonstrances were decreed in reply to the king's accusation that they wanted an aristocracy of magistrates. There followed the final famous and preemptive action by the parlement of May 3. The courts denied the accusation and listed the "Fundamental Laws" which ministerial despotism had infringed and, necessity being the mother of invention, added a new one on the inviolability of magistrates. It would all seem so new if it were not so old.

The blow planned by the Keeper of the Seals, Lamoignon, fell almost immediately. On May 5–6, at the end of a very theatrical display of royal power and judicial defiance in a plenary session, two magistrates distinguished for their troublesome opposition had been arrested in the chamber. On May 8, 1788 Lamoignon promulgated a long-overdue wholesale reform of the judicial system that was coupled with the setting up of a plenary court designed to replace the parlements in the registration of royal edicts. It was carried out unwisely. Pasquier points out that Lamoignon's speech gave this royal act the character of a private vengeance against the court. The arrest of the two judges had been a pointless error: "It is hard to understand how, at the point of dissolving the parlement, the ministry had not felt it should abstain from a vengeance henceforth without object."[54] The magistrates went quietly, though forbidding the courts under their jurisdiction to cooperate. Nevertheless, in Paris there were no popular disturbances in their favour, even from the dependent clerks of the *basoche*; in the provinces it was different. Governors took similar legislation to the other parlements; in Navarre, Brittany and Dauphiné in particular there was strong popular support and even violence on their behalf.[55] There were renewed calls for the Estates General. The stubborn defence of the provincial parlements in the summer of 1788 by their supporters was a significant step in the compromising of royal authority. By brutally remodeling the courts in the manner of Maupeou in 1771, the monarchy only looked even more despotic, and this drew other sections of the community into the fray. A despotic monarchy subject to no restraints could repudiate its debts, it was feared, and so the creditworthiness of the monarchy fell to a new low. Mallet du Pan observed, "Louis XIV, at the height of his glory, with complete peace in his realm, with vigorous and respected ministers, would hardly have conceived of the idea of such a revolution."[56]

Nevertheless, if the Lamoignon coup at first elicited little response from the public in Paris, by mid-June it had transformed the nature of the crisis in public's eyes, as the cause of the parlement gradually became accepted as a battle against despotism, in which the virtuous magistrates appeared to be taking the lead. In this struggle the urban protests in support of the provincial parlements of Rennes, Toulouse, Bordeaux Pau, and Grenoble had played an important part.[57] The fears aroused led of course to a failure of credit, greatly exacerbated by the Assembly of Clergy's vote of no-confidence in June. The Assembly of Clergy was clearly influenced by the air of despotism and refused to bail out the ministry with a large loan in addition to its customary "free gift."[58] So Loménie de Brienne had on August 8, 1788 to announce that the Estates General would meet in May 1789 and postpone his plenary court. Too late: even this was not enough to sustain credit, and the king had to give in to calls for the return to office of Necker, the reputed financial wizard. Louis was hardly in control: Loménie de Brienne resigned, Necker whom he disliked was recalled, and Lamoignon was dismissed two weeks later. The financier's very presence promptly restored confidence, but he confirmed that the Estates General would meet in January 1789 and reinstated the old parlements on September 23. The parlement was hugely popular; the magistrates were seen as heroic senators defending the hallowed order of things, prepared to endure exile in the fight against despotism.

Then they threw it all away. On September 25, 1788 when registering the royal legislation of September 23, they attempted to defend their future role and jurisdiction in France by ruling that the Estates General should meet according to the apparently regular form of 1614. They opted for the 1614 structure because it was the last one that had met in due and verifiable form: in this they were acting as conservative judges. However, public opinion in the Third Estate saw it in a very different light, as a defection from the struggle to defeat despotism and regenerate France, towards a defence of their privileged status as nobles. The magistrates had failed to read the signs of the times, the political game was changing rapidly, and they were soon sidelined. There is truth in Bailey Stone's point that the fateful September decree played a part in crystallizing the social issues that were raised by the issues of reform.[59] Suddenly it seemed as if the privileged orders would stick together to defeat social and political change. Duval d'Eprémesnil tried desperately to regain the public's confidence by having the courts pass a new resolution in December 1788. But it was too late and in the cacophony of opinions as the elections approached, hardly anybody was listening. "Its importance was wiped out, no one gave it a thought, nobody was any longer under its spell," wrote Pasquier. In a bitter twist of fate, a pamphlet of early 1789 was entitled "The Despotism of the Parlements, or Letter from an Englishman to a Frenchman."[60]

CONCLUSION

The debacle of their endgame should not blind us to the importance of the judges' actions in creating a revolutionary situation. In short, the parlement had affected royal credit at a time of fiscal crisis, had blocked royal policy, and had helped shift public debate on to the familiar terrain of a struggle against ministerial despotism. The political debate in France from the 1750s had for 40 years been predicated in terms that were set by the remonstrances of the courts and the historical justifications for their existence that pamphleteers and contemporary historians had produced. But with the waning of the parlements in the autumn of 1788, and the imminence of the Estates, the politics moved on.

In many respects the crisis of 1787–8 had much in common with earlier crises in Crown–parlement relations. It was not the product of growing militancy or aristocratic reaction, nor was it produced by a particularly liberal legalistic attitude, as other historical explanations of the parlement's conduct have suggested. All the ingredients stressed in recent historiography for the earlier period are in still evidence: ministerial splits, factions pulling strings, internal rivalries in the courts making management ineffectual, youthful hotheadedness, injudicious royal statements, escalation in the absence of dialogue, and the importance of bluff and negotiation, with the magistrates apparently unaware of how serious the situation actually was. Where the crisis differed was in the failure of the ministry to win a kind of royal victory or at least a satisfactory compromise without conceding the essential point (which was to get its plans through without having to call the Estates General that, everyone knew, were bound to compromise royal authority for ever). Perhaps the ministries had no choice because the issue was the failure of royal finances, and they had no time for maneuver before the debacle of a forced rescheduling of debt overtook them.[61] But it certainly seems as if a massive failure of political management was a very important feature, due both to the incompetence of individuals and to the nature of the court system as it had been allowed to evolve by Louis XVI.

4. From Social to Cultural History

WILLIAM SCOTT

Summary

Bill Scott here charts the attack on a restricted kind of social history, the Marxist interpretation of the French Revolution. Just as a new revisionist political history of the revolution was coming into being on the one hand, wider intellectual movements in the 1960s led to a rise of "cultural history" that was much broader than the political approach. Undoubtedly stimulating, opening up new perspectives, this new history is nevertheless akin to interpretations put forward as early as the revolution itself, and in the nineteenth century. Too-rigid lines of demarcation can create new blindnesses. Cultural history does not supersede previous approaches, but ideally should complement them. In some areas it has yet to fulfill its promise, notably by taking up the challenge of reintegrating the missing commercial bourgeoisie into revolutionary history.

INTRODUCTION

The French Revolution was immediately seen by participants and observers as a movement that would change the world. Immediately, too, its origins became a matter of impassioned debate. They were certainly seen as complex. And some of the Revolution's origins were traced well back into history. Two closely-linked forces were often seen as crucial: the growth of commerce since the "discovery" of America and the equally impressive expansion and spread of *"lumières"* or Enlightenment. In these intimately conjoined areas, liberty was a demand before it became a rallying cry of 1789. So no real distinction was made between what we might term the "social" and the "cultural" origins of the Revolution. The exchange of both goods and ideas, and the increasing consumption of both, was widely regarded as accompanying, indeed contributing to, the growing importance of a class of "middling" men, "*les classes moyennes,*" destined to play the leading role in the Revolution. These men came to power in 1789 and largely molded the Revolution to advance their purposes and interests.

Ever since 1789, successive generations of historians have interpreted the origins and history of the Revolution from different perspectives. One difference, of course, was between those who favored the Revolution and those who saw it, and the principles behind it, as harmful, even disastrous. Nineteenth-century historians of both persuasions often saw the Revolution as the triumph of the middle classes or bourgeoisie, to be celebrated or deplored. But this early "social interpretation" in no way excluded analysis of political developments: parliamentary government was likewise welcomed or regretted as essentially bourgeois. Nor were the religious and antireligious aspects neglected: the Church's role was trimmed to suit bourgeois interests and for the victors God protected the new order of property and profit. Perhaps "culture" was not seen as an independent factor or as embracing all aspects of individual and collective life, as it often is by today's historians. But if the Revolution replaced, socially and politically, a noble hegemony with the supremacy of the bourgeoisie, this was also a profound *cultural* change. For bourgeois manners, lifestyle and attitudes differed markedly from those of the old Court and aristocracy – and also from those of the "inferior" classes.

More radical historians, such as Jules Michelet (1798–1874), did indeed emphasize the role of the people in the Revolution. These were not the destructive "mobs" of conservative historians but the proud bearers of their own uplifting values, notably those of equality and fraternity. These values, certainly, grew from social roots, in the often grim experience of workers and peasants. But they also inspired "political" demands: for democracy, a *social* democracy based on a less unequal distribution of wealth and finding expression in universal manhood suffrage. Such values were sustained by popular forms of cultural activity, in various forms of fraternal unions and associations. Solidarity was a key value of a distinctively popular culture. The struggles stemming from the Revolution dominated the subsequent century. What remained unfinished business for those favouring revolutionary principles was a constant threat to their opponents, seeking to turn back the tide threatening to engulf *all* they held dear. Historians of both camps, therefore, who often engaged in these struggles as politicians and ideologues, were not inclined to divide history into distinct subdisciplines, each considering only part of the picture.

Following these general considerations, the present chapter surveys some of the major currents of interpretation of the Revolution, after a century in which history's subdivisions (intellectual, political, social, economic, cultural, gendered, etc.) proliferated, sometimes in rather unfriendly relationships to each other. The chapter's title suggests a recent movement away from social history, in which social structure, and especially class, was seen as dominant, to a present-day predominance of "cultural history." This, its practitioners maintain, has broadened the concerns of historians to cover all aspects of life, from the high culture of the arts and sciences to the "popular culture," or modes of life, of ordinary men and women. Culture is now analyzed in its own right, and in its amazing variety, *not* as primarily (and banally) expressing allegedly more basic social or economic interests. Hence, as will be illustrated later, cultural historians accord themselves a freedom and scope transcending what they tend to see as the more restricted, more closely determined and more narrowly defined sphere of social history.

To emphasize different dimensions of history is probably unavoidable. Moreover, a shift of emphasis may illuminate new or neglected areas. However, it is here suggested that any too-rigid demarcation is to be regretted if it, in turn, produces a new blindness. As already implied, this would seem particularly inappropriate in considering the French Revolution. Certainly, to establish a newness of approach, historians tend to exaggerate the limited nature of their predecessors' work. A very pronounced instance of this occurred, as we shall see, in the 1960s, when the "social interpretation" of the Revolution was given a particularly restricted character by revisionist historians claiming to revive "political" history.

Insofar as cultural history does indeed broaden the range of historical concerns, its undoubted impact appears most positive. However, as I shall seek to indicate, the most stimulating social and political historians – if we must use these terms – were very much alive to the cultural dimension. Cultural history, it will be argued here, does not miraculously supersede earlier histories. Ideally, it should complement or supplement them. Traditions of interpretation should not of course be revered. But neither should they be ignored. Moreover, a point which will only be alluded to but which informs the general approach of this chapter: the French Revolution was an extremely reflexive movement, its participants deeply concerned with values and principles. Few issues, including origins, were not debated intensely by the Revolutionaries themselves. They were (mostly) men of culture and ideas, engaged not only in changing the world but also in interpreting it.

MAINLY "MARXISM"

A century ago, Jean Jaurès wrote an impressive "socialist history" of the Revolution.[1] This, while openly positioned in the "progressive" tradition, was neither narrowly partisan in its politics, nor restricted in its more general approach. Jaurès, an outstanding statesman and intellectual, offered to the French people an all-embracing and generous account of a revolution which was certainly mainly bourgeois in inspiration and undertaking, but which had also expressed the hopes, aspirations, fears and worries of ordinary men and women struggling for a better life. They had sought decency, dignity and recognition, not just material necessities or advantages. Jaurès saw the working people of France, his desired readers, as potential heirs to all that was best in the revolutionary project, itself heir to the Enlightenment. They were to enjoy all the progressive benefits of French culture, including achievements which, like the "rights of man," had often been seen as specifically bourgeois but which could be extended to all men and, ultimately, to all women (and internationally too).

Arguably, Jaurès's generosity of spirit was not replicated in the much less optimistic atmosphere following World War I, a period of intense social and political upheaval. One strand of revolutionary history achieved preeminence. This, the social interpretation, suited a period of dearth and deprivation, in which masses (or classes) of men and women were forced to obey the diktat of remorseless historical laws of a fundamentally economic nature – hardship and unemployment imposed by a ruthless postwar capitalism but also by the rigours of the Russian Revolution of 1917. Albert Mathiez was the leading revolutionary historian of the 1920s, dealing, in a prose lacking the warmth and richness of that of Jaurès, with political struggles of a somewhat arid sort, strictly tied to basic social conflicts and class war.[2] Mathiez's grim masterpiece, *La Vie chère et le mouvement social sous la Terreur*, was on food shortages: the struggle for existence was similar in 1793 and 1917. Making parallels between Jacobins and Bolsheviks, between Robespierre and Lenin, Mathiez drew on a Marxist schema which saw economic forces as fundamental in history. They determined all aspects of life, giving rise to social classes, the main agents in history. In the French Revolution, the nobility were overthrown by the bourgeoisie. Now, in the USSR, observed Mathiez, the bourgeoisie had been overthrown by the working class or proletariat. With the change-over of classes, *all* aspects of life would change, including, ultimately and inevitably, culture (religion would now wither away, together with all the cultural forms it supported). It was believed that revolutions, the locomotives or motors of History, drove it progressively forwards. Their combattants, classes, strong and determined, fulfilled an historic task. In the French Revolution, aristocratic landed wealth, extorting revenue from a subservient peasantry, ceded to trade and industry exploiting a downtrodden working class. Yet this capitalism was vastly to expand production. It was therefore progressive. However all profits went to the capitalists. The next, proletarian, revolution would change this, again expanding production, but now for the real producers.[3]

This schema underlay the approach of Mathiez. Subsequent historians of this school, Georges Lefebvre and Albert Soboul, painted a much more varied, animated and in some ways contradictory picture of the Revolution. Lefebvre had an unrivalled knowledge of, and sympathy for, the peasants – to use a single word to embrace the complexities and contradictions he revealed in rural society. Soboul produced a magisterial study of the Paris *sans-culottes*, the politically radical "people" of Paris, most active during the Terror, in 1793 and 1794.[4] The two historians highlighted areas of the Revolution (and sometimes resistance to the Revolution) hardly fitting neatly into a "Marxism" insistently stressing only the struggle between bourgeoisie and aristocracy, capitalism and feudalism, and allowing only one possible victor to take all the spoils.

However, certain key historical points may be made here. The nobility *was* abolished in 1790. The revolutionary bourgeoisie did indeed free economic enterprise by deregulation, the creation of a national market, the abolition of guild restrictions on industry, the abolition of monopolistic trading companies, and the admission of men of talent – themselves – into all political, administrative, judicial and church posts. These reforms had often been demanded by writers of an Enlightenment often itself seen by Marxists as basically reflecting bourgeois interests. Even in the Revolution, its ideals – such as the rights of man – were seen as disguising bourgeois interests. "Liberty" included the economic right freely to hire and fire. "Equality" certainly did not include social equality, or equality of property. And the new bourgeois rulers showed little "fraternity" to their inferiors. Hence, we would add, the broad currents of Marxist interpretation had considerable support from within the

Revolution itself, and from subsequent "bourgeois" historians celebrating the triumph of their class. Marx acknowledged that his idea of history as essentially a class struggle came from such bourgeois historians of the Revolution.

MARXISTS UNDER ATTACK

In 1964 Alfred Cobban published his *The Social Interpretation of the French Revolution*. This severely criticized the Marxist interpretation. Cobban's "revisionism" denied the relevance of class analysis to eighteenth-century France. He rejected any idea of the French Revolution as a bourgeois revolution. Taking English empiricism to extreme lengths, Cobban broke down any possible generalization, or indeed any general term, into a potentially infinite number of isolated instances, each of which spoke for itself alone. History as a study of linkages and relationships – certainly too one-sidedly imposed by the economy in the most rigid Marxist works – was entirely repudiated. Only fragments of a picture remained. Yet Cobban claimed to have a positive purpose, to rescue *political* history from enslavement to the economic and social imperatives of the Marxists. He identified the social interpretation exclusively with Marxists, though a much broader and more varied social history, exemplified in France since the 1920s by the journal *Annales* and in Britain, much more recently, by *Past and Present*, had attained wide currency. Moreover Cobban contributed little to any revitalization of political history.

Describing the Revolution as a "myth" was, for him, to downgrade the importance of what Marx had described as an unprecedented outburst of political energy.[5] Many would argue that a truly mythic event galvanizes enormous energy, breaks down the flimsy barriers historians erect between different types of history and inspires bold action in all spheres. And appealing as much to the emotions as to reason, arousing fears and doubtless exaggerated aspirations, the "mythic" Revolution did indeed inspire a wide variety of cultural forms – songs (the *Marseillaise*), slogans (*Liberté, Egalité, Fraternité*), and innumerable symbols, rituals, and festivals, as well as plays and paintings. This creative, Promethean aspect reverberated throughout Europe, notably in Romanticism, inspiring the great "romantic" historian Jules Michelet. (Even Marx was not unaffected.) For many, the Revolution was a struggle between good and evil. Its enemies saw the demon of "democracy" released, a leveling fury that recognized no bounds. Middle-class ideologues had opened Pandora's Box.

Less dramatically, historians such as François Furet[6] and Keith Baker[7] do see the French Revolution as the "inventor" of modern democratic political culture. Furet's *Penser la Révolution française* (1978) owed much to the sudden collapse of Marxist hegemony in French intellectual life. Though severely critical of the revolutionaries, Furet's crediting them with the invention of democracy, the political force destined to triumph across the world, enabled him further to discredit antidemocratic regimes and parties, notably of course the USSR and the French Communist Party (to which he had once belonged). Gravely compromising their achievement, however, was the fact that, in Furet's view, the politics of the actual years of the Revolution was "excessive," prefiguring Bolshevism. Politics rapidly lost touch with a social reality fundamentally resistant to rapid change. For like Marx, ironically, Furet believed that the revolutionaries succumbed to the "political illusion," whereby all problems, including the social, were solvable by political means (for example, to *decree* the abolition of "poverty"). Especially in the Terror, the revolutionaries' political will and energy far outran a more normal history, slower-moving but inexorable. This was, it seems, social history. Like Cobban, Furet argued that the Revolution changed society much less than the revolutionaries, or most Marxists, asserted. But in claiming that the France of Louis-Philippe (1830–48) was hardly different from that of the 1780s, Furet seemed to downplay the *political* revolution too. After all, Louis-Philippe was often termed a "bourgeois monarch," a title hardly suitable for Louis XVI. In a subsequent work, Furet gave "the French Revolution" a timespan of well-nigh a hundred years, seeing the definitive triumph of its political principles as won only in the 1880s. He also reinstalled the "revolutionary bourgeoisie" as a crucial actor in history.[8]

But by the late 1880s, it seemed to Furet, politics and society were reconciled. The violent revolutionary current had exhausted itself in futile reenactments of 1789 (in 1830, 1848 and 1871). A more moderate, yet modern and fairly democratic politics converged in the 1880s with a slow-moving social history. Universal manhood suffrage, first introduced disastrously in 1792, ushering in the Terror, was now established on the secure, and recently educated, base of bourgeoisie, petite bourgeoisie and prosperous peasantry. Thus, for democratic political culture to take root, it needs to permeate not only the political sphere but also to enter the social and cultural *mores* of the bulk of the male population. This took time. And women were "given" the vote only in 1944.

Thus, for Furet, the "gap" between political and social history needs to be filled. Recurrent elections not only provided a political mechanism for the expression of political demands but also served as a civic pedagogy. Also vital were a free press, free assembly, and freedom of religious belief and non-belief. The "excess" of the Revolution was the illusion that these could be successfully introduced between 1789 and 1793, before "society" was ready. They *were*, however, successfully reintroduced by the Third Republic before 1914. Perhaps only with the total separation of Church and State in 1905 did this regime go significantly beyond the horizon of a century earlier – and even this was attempted in 1795. Furet seemingly returned to something of a social interpretation, by demanding that politics await the more basic movement of society. He also came to realize, with most modern historians of nineteenth-century France, that one cannot do without the bourgeoisie.

ON ORIGINS AND SOCIAL CLASS

Crucially, for Furet, the course of the Revolution cannot be deduced from its origins. It was no mere working-out of preexisting causes originating at some deep level of the socioeconomic structure – as if one could have foreseen the Revolution in, say, 1780. What Furet found most striking was the Revolution's radical newness. Especially new was the language and ideology of extremism, by which rival groups outbid each other in a rush towards the most extreme, tolerating no hesitancy, far less opposition. Initially, in 1789, the revolutionaries' imagery of a "new creation," of emergence from darkness into light, expressed high hopes of unity and reconciliation. The French came together to create a *nation* from a rather chaotic collection of provinces, laws, customs, languages, and social groupings often antagonistic to each other. Even educated Frenchmen lacked political experience, there having been virtually no assemblies outside church. France had indeed had an impressive body of political thought, with Montesquieu, Rousseau, Mably, and others, and institutions such as the parlements which raised constitutional issues. But from 1788, with the calling of the Estates General providing the indispensable focus (and forum), political debate exploded. Unfortunately, via ruthless "outbidding," a narrow Jacobin orthodoxy emerged, armed with a fanatical language as, in Furet's account, an ideological and linguistic determinism drove the Revolution headlong into the Terror.

Perhaps, however, Furet might have broadened *his* treatment of the Revolution's political culture. Jacobinism was not as narrow and monolithic as he (and his disciples) allege. This might have enabled Furet more fully to establish more convincing connections with France's intellectual and cultural life of the pre-revolutionary decades. For 1789 cannot be totally split from what went before. Here, Furet's intellectual hero, Alexis de Tocqueville, is relevant.[9]

Writing in the 1850s, Tocqueville argued that the revolutionaries had greatly exaggerated the newness, and success, of their enterprise. And Furet, not wholly consistently, maintained that the revolutionaries disastrously replicated the old regime's view that supreme power, or sovereignty, must be undivided to be strong and effective. It therefore became despotic. For the Jacobins had the means to create a state machinery of unprecedented power, crushing all opposition, resistance or dissent. The fantastic range of opinions expressed in the upsurge of liberty in 1789 was suppressed. The imposition of total uniformity and obedience on a divided nation and a complex society inevitably brought Terror. Furet clearly saw Soviet parallels.

If, previously, French kings had ruled in the name of God, the fact that the new despots ruled in the name of "Nation" or "people" did not justify tyranny. The real people (or society) were denied even a voice. For Furet, as for Tocqueville, the free "liberal" phase of 1789–91 had been almost an interlude, as inexplicable as unexpected. However, Tocqueville helps to explain why the window of liberty was open so briefly. He argued that the "absolute" monarchy had trained the French in servility, unfitting them for liberty and independence of thought and action. They expected the government to do everything. Unlike in Britain, there was no culture of political liberty. French political writers such as Rousseau purveyed dreams and illusions.

Certainly, by the 1780s, many considered that any "real" politics was secretive, an artificial art of deceit and self-seeking.[10] This moralistic view had given rise to a desire for a more open politics, not centred on intrigue but more accountable to men of talent and enlightenment who were imbued with patriotic zeal. A new, informed public opinion was being formed in private institutions of sociability – masonic lodges, reading societies, clubs – while even staid, official academies were encouraging ordinary people to write about matters of public concern.

Tocqueville regarded this as more a social than a political opinion, concerned with equality, not liberty. Like his contemporary Marx, Tocqueville saw the Revolution as bourgeois. It had long been prepared by the steady advance of bureaucracy, whose value of uniformity tended towards an administered rather than a politically free society. The Revolution's destruction of the nobility removed the last vestiges of independence. The bourgeoisie could not be relied on to uphold liberty. Here, surprisingly, Marx is more generous: in 1789 the bourgeoisie championed interests wider than their own, certainly much wider than the backward interests of the nobility. Their patriotic idealism, expressed in the Declaration of the Rights of Man, largely the fruit of Enlightenment, did cover class interests. But the liberal freedoms it proposed were not mere camouflage, or to be enjoyed only by the bourgeoisie. And (economic) enterprise was praiseworthy. Reforms of the Revolution, formulated in theory in the Enlightenment, were now enacted, making enterprise, if for the common good, a virtue.

For Tocqueville the bourgeoisie were narrow-minded and mediocre, essentially uncultured. He pictured the "patriots" as composed of a stratum of petty intellectuals, enamoured of impractically abstract ideas, men without responsible positions in society. Leading the bourgeoisie ideologically in 1789, they made the people impossible promises, leading inevitably to disillusionment and social conflict. However, recent historians have drawn our attention to a broad, "middling" class of men, holding respectable if subordinate public posts nationally or, more often, locally. These included bureaucrats in the Church, the armed forces and the civil service, doctors, lawyers, engineers, and merchants, these last often holding various official posts in commercial cities. Such men often produced well-argued and circumstantial reform proposals. They felt frustrated when these were ignored. Robert Darnton and Daniel Roche show the importance of such practically orientated men to the great *Encyclopédie* and the academic movement.[11] Towns were centers of this activity. If the Marxist bourgeoisie of trade and industry was hardly prominent, the expanding networks of cultural sociability and intellectual endeavour prospered from the wealth commerce generated. The number of books published and newspapers circulated rose. But Tocqueville and Furet underestimated this opinion's commitment to liberty. The incisiveness of the extremely liberal constitution-makers of 1789 derived from the backing of the alliance, broadly interpreted, of commerce and Enlightenment, carried forward by history. Many of the reforms introduced in 1789–91 endured.

The fact that Lefebvre and Soboul studied social groups, the peasantry and *sans-culottes*, hardly renowned as champions of the capitalist enterprise allegedly boosted by the Revolution, undoubtedly weakened a social interpretation abusively identified exclusively with Marxist historians. While Tocqueville, as a conservative rural nobleman, may be excused researching urban society, neither Cobban nor Furet allowed their lack of research to inhibit pronouncements on the "absent bourgeoisie." However, even in countries where most legislation seems tailored to capitalist interests, entrepreneurs hardly thrust themselves to the front of the political stage. Yet many merchants, and some manufacturers, published pamphlets in 1789. Certainly, principles usually bent before interests. But an impressive "discourse of wealth" circulated in old-regime France. The widespread view that commercial wealth was being absorbed and wasted by the government and its parasitic Court financiers was backed by the "scientific" analysis of political economy. Economic ideas criss-crossed the English Channel. The general European advance toward "commercial society," led by Britain and France, was the "grand narrative" of the cultivated classes who, rather complacently perhaps, saw commerce and Enlightenment combining virtuously.

Very little hard economic material has reached the revisionist discussion of the origins and course of the Revolution, with even the major French works on the port cities largely ignored by "Anglo-Saxon" historians.[12] Perhaps, at least, the revived interest in "world history" will place France and the French Revolution in the world's march towards capitalism. Emma Rothschild's work on Adam Smith and Condorcet expands horizons, not least by its attention to economic *sentiments*, exploring commerce's crucial role within a discouse of political and social morality. Clearly commerce was becoming a vital *cultural* force.[13] Metaphors of exchange permeated society. Groethuysen's brilliant work of cultural history, *The Bourgeois: Catholicism versus Capitalism in Eighteenth-Century France* (1927), has unfortunately not encouraged similar explorations of contiguous fields.

Commerce might have received greater attention from those historians who, some years ago, argued that, before the Revolution, an Enlightened elite was being formed, composed of wealthy, reform-minded noblemen, well-endowed ecclesiastics and distinguished, talented and moneyed commoners.[14] Some evidence supports this – as wishful thinking. It was too little, too late. Any such alliance would have been resented by those excluded, and few historians seemed inclined to include rich and Enlightened merchants within the charmed circle. Even those who in the 1780s vaguely favoured such a rapprochement failed to see the need for wide-ranging reform and profound changes of attitude.

What perhaps needs emphasizing once more here is the depth of resentment and frustration at the effects of the regime's *structural* rigidities. Much criticism was couched in moral terms. Commercial wealth rewarded foresight, knowledge, thrift, moderation. A bourgeois ethos grew stronger, expressed in plays, paintings, novels. It championed domestic values, which might attain civic or even patriotic status.

However peaceable these values seemed, they amounted to an indictment, even a scapegoating, of those violating them – flashy financiers, profligate prelates, unpatriotic courtiers. The 1780s, culminating in 1789, saw the demonization of such villains. Cultural historians are particularly sensitive to the symbolic expression of such antagonism in verbal and visual imagery. The splendidly vivid work of Antoine de Baecque on metaphors of the body politic and studies of caricature, exaggerating the perverse and the disreputable, and the cornucopia of images in Michel Vovelle's collection, display a menagerie of degenerate monsters.[15] Long-repressed hatred exploded in 1789. Peaceable bourgeois, in their private letters, rejoiced at the humiliation of "*les grands*."

A CHANGING CLIMATE

Explanations for the increased prominence of cultural history are many and varied. By the 1970s the social sciences, among which some historians had wished to place history, were undergoing a crisis of confidence. Their "hard" methods, often relying on quantitative data, seemed to be yielding meagre results. For hard-core social scientists, the accumulation of facts would enable laws of human behavior and organization to be formulated. Clearly individuals could not but conform, in an almost preprogrammed way. Not surprisingly, liberation was sought. Rigid research programmes and narrow parameters were to be discarded. In seeking meanings, so often subjective, rather than an often deterministic explanation, more imagination might be deployed. This suited the climate surrounding the Paris upheavals of May 1968, which shook up certain institutions of cultural control, including academia. Moreover, the greater affluence of some social categories, accompanied by an expansion of higher education, boosted cultural consumption: travel, exhibitions, films, recorded music, arts festivals, sports, and leisure opportunities multiplied. With experience so diversified, questions of identity and self-expression challenged old solidarities, often imposed or inherited. (In France, allegiance to the Communist Party declined drastically.) Questions of gender and sexuality attained a new openness. New links and loyalties were forged, from choice and affinity.

For historians, this encouraged new curiosities regarding a past which now appeared more diversified, with more opportunities for identification and empathy with men and women whose experiences were seemingly similar to one's own – and were certainly not to be reduced to inert data. The sheer pleasure of a wider choice of research topics cannot be overestimated. With more fascinating stories to be told, history might come alive, history-writing become more lively.

Historians of France could not but be aware of the new intellectual currents from Paris. Michel Foucault opened up for unprecedented scrutiny both new areas of enquiry and old institutions and activities. Prisons, hospitals and clinics, and asylums, though often secretive and murky, had produced ever-expanding discourses of power and knowledge. Claims to expertise were used to justify the extension of their powers of control over matters of health and sexuality and therefore over each person's body. The historian's task was to use a "genealogical" method to trace back such discourses to their often ignoble origins, to use "archeological" means to uncover structures, in order to subvert them. What was taken as true, normal, or natural had often triumphed by underhand means. Pierre Bourdieu's concepts of cultural capital, distinction, and habitus provided tools to analyze struggles for influence and prestige. Roland Barthes and the American Hayden White exposed the rhetorical tricks whereby historians gave their stories (or "fictions") the authority of "the real," of truth. All these intellectuals derided any "scientific" pretensions history might have. Truth was relative to positions occupied in the contest for power.

History borrowed from rival disciplines: Foucault was (arguably) a philosopher, Bourdieu a sociologist, Barthes a literary critic. Anthropology likewise broadened horizons. Claude Lévi-Strauss held that culture functioned like language: one could *read* relationships like a text. Clifford Geertz's work on Bali convinced him that "the culture of a people is an ensemble of texts," from which the sensitive reader could tease out meaning and unravel secrets. Myths, festivals, symbols, rituals offered entry into the beliefs which gave coherence to a culture. Bakhtin's notion of carnival inspired much writing on festivals and encouraged the treatment of riot, revolt and revolution as festive occasions. Persons of authority were (un)ceremoniously humiliated as coarse derision and lewd humour erupted, as in 1789, in "a world turned upside down."

Geertz, like other anthropologists and anthropology in general, has been criticized for portraying a culture as too cohesive. Conversely, perhaps, Bakhtin's work may be used to glorify often cruel upheaval. At best, moreover, disorder was only a momentary escape from drudgery. With the safety valve closed again, structures of power reasserted themselves. While urging resistance, Foucault tended to stress their oppressive power, but many "culturalists" and cultural historians celebrate the liberating forces. This is doubtless a tension never to be resolved.

CULTURAL HISTORY

Cultural history is text-orientated. The move away from explanation by social structure to interpretation has made textual analysis crucial. The nature of written texts, their exposed or hidden resources of language or idiom, of rhetoric and metaphor, their genre and tropes, their narrative strategies, all have to be revealed and decoded. The reader's relationship with the text demands careful scrutiny. But texts are *all* artefacts which confer meaning or on which meaning can plausibly be conferred. They may include material objects like clothing, buildings, bodies – even noises and smells. Events, too, are read as texts. Written texts are often grouped as discourses, organized around problems (economic, judicial, or penal reform, for example) and related to relevant nonwritten material (ships and commodities; judges and prisons). Indeed *relationships* are specially privileged by cultural historians, as for instance gender relations. Most discourse on women has, until recently, been male. Many types of signs and symbols illuminate relationships. But the vast expansion, and variety of *written* texts in 1789 means that questions of authorship, readership and reception, as studied by Roger Chartier, are not eclipsed but are supplemented by attention to the visual. In all cases, the impact of "text" on the receiver is crucial but maddeningly difficult to gauge.

Cultural historians often exploit quite humble, even crude, texts: newspapers, brochures, chapbooks. They also seek traces of oral culture, teased out of very disparate sources, often from indirect sources like court records. Cultural practices like religious observance, but also all "leisure activities" and all aspects of intimacy, have been tracked in a variety of ingenious ways. Much more is extracted than the explicit meaning. Yet a single text can sometimes disclose key elements of a group's culture, their systems of meaning or patterns of belief, their deepest values. And emotions are as important as more "rational" activities, especially in periods of excitement like the Revolution. Participants were preoccupied with the comparative roles of reason and the passions. Notions of "the self" were challenged in those testing times; some saw the Revolution as drama.[16] Virtually all the concerns of the cultural historian were of even deeper concern to the revolutionaries themselves. Often it was a matter of life and death.

Those in happily less fraught circumstances, using notions of culture, encounter problems of limits or boundaries between the general and the particular, the inclusive and the exclusionary. However, "culture" risks becoming too broad and vague a concept, without discriminatory power, when used in what was, until fairly recently, the basic anthropological sense, to emphasize shared meanings. "Culture" may then seem to soften antagonism, even to obscure the differences which cultural historians profess to disclose. It may also occlude processes of historical change and neglect problems of agency, of those who attempted to bring change about. But cultural historians do often examine the cultures of distinct groups or milieus: popular culture, peasant culture, or the culture of women, city, street or workplace. These are sometimes seen to overlap with the cultures of different professions such as merchants, lawyers, or clergy. With such a proliferation of "cultures," however, fragmentation threatens and no general picture emerges. Moreover, the possibility of shared meanings was restricted, in pre-revolutionary France, by different languages or idioms, literally (with *patois*) as well as metaphorically. Town and country could not always converse easily with each other, for example. But we can trace interactions between, say, elite and popular cultures using notions of cultural intermediaries and spokesmen (more rarely women). And we can study how specific institutions sustained, preserved, modified, and handed down cultural practices, becoming traditions. Sometimes, as with the Court or with the higher law courts, this served to exclude those unable to attain the required standards of manners, knowledge, nobility, dress, or language (Bourdieu's "distinction").

Voluntary, private associations, multiplying before 1789, aided cultural exchange and transmission, but the privileged corporations were felt to be restrictive, perhaps increasingly so, dividing the public sphere. If the advance of commerce and Enlightenment was cosmopolitan, access to "cultural capital" was restricted, within and between countries. Chartier shows how print culture was socially stratified, how modes of reading differed between social groups. Educational provision, and ambition, varied too with gender and geography, as did access to good French. "Prejudices,"or unexamined attitudes, seemed prevalent among the "ignorant" lower orders, acting from instinct rather than reflection. But to assume this too readily was itself a *"préjugé"* of the "cultured" classes.

Was there, then, a "French culture" before the Revolution? The upsurge of patriotism in 1789 suggests a deep, underlying feeling, urgently demanding open expression. Some adduced a general "love of the king," a king now responding to the people's wishes, as uniting all but the most selfishly narrow-minded. Perhaps, also, Tocqueville's argument that the vast majority of the French desired "equality" bound most together in a common endeavour. But such feelings, expressed in the *cahiers* and countless pamphlets, may have sharpened frustration at the persistence of disputes between rival corporate groups and localities, each seeking petty advantage, decorating privilege with principles, with fine talk of liberty. Certainly, some had already aspired to crosscultural boundaries, as when guild masters in craft industries (or their lawyers) had tried to appropriate, from "higher," "distinguished" culture, concepts of natural law.[17] However, the awkwardness of such strategies suggests the real incommensurability of opposing cultural worlds. Now 1789 also exposed concepts such as "natural law," and such abstractions as "nation," "liberty," and "equality" to the deconstructive, destructive power of unrestricted controversy and struggle. Words were treacherous. Language buckled under the strain. Women's failure to "master" the "male language of virtue," and citizenship, likewise exposed the limitations and exclusionary power of what professed to unite.[18] Such difficulties underlined the deeply divided nature of French society – of France. This helps to explain the failure of both old regime and Revolution to unite the nation.

With no parliament, parties or national elections before 1789, patriotic reform proposals lacked both a forum and a focus. Certain reforms were belatedly introduced (Protestant toleration in 1787) but often only partially. Others were sabotaged by vested interests. A confused jumble of disputes may well have formed the expectational horizon of many disenchanted subjects – who aspired to become citizens. Versailles seemed distant, politics was the preserve of cliques of rich aristocrats. Corporations like the Church or, much more humbly, the guilds, where fair representation of members was an ideal, were divided, having their own "aristocracies," self-perpetuating and corrupt. Ideas of representation, of accountability heralded a new culture of openness, of transparency.

Aspects of this outlook – an accountability involving calculation – might seem narrowly *bourgeois*, yet interest did not exclude "virtue." Virtue, as has been shown recently, had many dimensions.[19] But most Enlightenment writers saw virtue in social terms: a virtuous man helped his fellows and, by natural extension, their common *patrie*. Public and private morality should harmonize. Extremes – of self-sacrifice and privation on the one hand, and of the ruthless, extortionate pushing of selfish interests on the other – were to be shunned, especially if the latter was at the expense of the weak. Virtue lay in moderation. This demanded a degree of self-control in every station and aspect of life. Politically, virtue was often seen as a form of civic and patriotic conscience, or consciousness, forming the ethos of an idealized citizenship. This might have "republican" dimensions, but was also philanthropic and utilitarian. Classical citizenship, as championed by Mably for instance, might be too demanding (and too "antique") a model. Social usefulness was a stronger, more modern ideal. A *social* conscience informed those many, almost obligatory, private but published projects to help the deserving poor. Socially, or economically, virtuous actions and writings sought to ensure a moderate prosperity for all honest French men and women. Virtue, as morality, could exist neither in the excessively rich nor in the extremely poor.

Excess tended to be related to various forms of violence. Much recent cultural–historical literature has explored questions of sexuality, perhaps giving insufficient attention to sexual violence. Excessive wealth and privilege facilitated abuse. Denunciations of the predatory sexuality of the lay and secular aristocracy fuelled the moral indignation of the middle classes. A striking number of pamphlets portrayed the wives and daughters of bourgeois, artisans and even peasants, seized, bought or seduced by financiers, nobles and, especially, bishops and priests. This was seen as symptomatic of wider relationships of exploitation (and impunity). This, probably more than the pornography so emphasized by Lynn Hunt and Robert Darnton, influenced and unified moral opinion.[20] Since political females had allegedly been behind the most corrupt politics of the old regime, a self-righteous culture of virtue and decency might serve as a pretext to confine women still more securely within the domestic domain and, literally advocated by some ultramoralistic writers, within the house. For sexual profligacy seemed contagious, threatening even the bourgeois domestic sphere, fostering a panic over prostitution. Fears of contamination by dirt and disease circulated widely, provoking oppressive, "excessive" schemes of discipline, surveillance, and control, well-meaning but all too dismally fitting Foucault's grim scenario. The metaphors as well as the matters of health and hygiene darkened middle-class discourse. So whereas historians too numerous to mention have stressed that "no one wanted a revolution in 1789," cultural history would suggest the intensity with which many wanted, even longed for, what was perhaps even more dangerous: a moral regeneration.

CULTURAL VERSUS SOCIAL HISTORY?

Violence might have occurred in 1789 without the bad harvest of 1788, and without the deep-rooted economic and social problems in an economy which, despite talk of commerce and *lumières*, was still based on subsistence agriculture. But the economic and social problems analyzed by Marxist and other historians, have not been dissolved by the subsequent emphasis on cultural history. They have been put in a deeper and richer interpretative context by treatment of their symptoms or consequences. Cultural-historical attention to signs and symbols, to spectacle and representation, to the production and reception of images, enriches the significance of events. Perhaps such events as the taking of the Bastille and the great revolutionary festivals hardly need this.[21] But others, less outstanding, get added significance if placed in networks of symbolic associations involving hopes and fears, some of which, as grim forebodings or ideally imagined projects, perhaps contributed to their coming. Even the most humble riot can be illuminated by "anthropological" approaches – but also by notions of an age-old "moral economy" as well as millennial hopes and fears. Thresholds of violence – indeed liminal, tension-ridden situations in general – are likewise marked by various rites which need decoding. More recent Marxist historians such as Vovelle and Maurice Agulhon have always been interested in, and contributed enormously to, this kind of "cultural history."[22] But Lefebvre's *Great Fear* (1932) is an excellent example of a history which might now be termed cultural – to which his unequalled knowledge of rural society is absolutely essential. The immediate fear of peasants in the summer of 1789, that their crops would be destroyed by brigands paid by "aristocrats," reactivated memories of how the Saracens (in the "Dark Ages") and then the English (in the Hundred Years' War) ravaged large areas of France, ruining the peasantry. Complex notions of time and memory are often at the centre of cultural historians' preoccupations but often still need to be thus socially situated.[23]

As time speeded up, and became more precise and purposeful, in the Revolution, historians exaggerate the "immobility" of the bulk of ancien-régime society. It is all too easy to repeat contemporary stereotypes regarding the unchanging nature of rural life and its parochial horizons, the backward-looking attitudes of a peasantry sunk deep in unthinking routine and harboring age-old resentments. Yet the persistence of such a picture may suggest that it was not totally divorced from "reality." It may at least suggest that certain interests wished to confine the rural population in a state of inertia and ignorance. The "awakening" of the peasantry to modern politics, to the timetables of club and electoral meetings, wrenched out of routine (and the old religion) by the imposition of the new calendar divided into ten-day sections in its twelve new months, with its pattern of civic festivals, aroused misgivings among many Revolutionaries as well as resistance from their opponents. Time, so highly symbolic, was also so down-to-earth. A working "week" of nine days and only a tenth day of rest hardly made the Revolution more attractive to the "laboring classes."

Thus social "reality," with its often material preoccupations, might set limits to symbolic representation and transformation. Certainly, cultural history provides many opportunities to try to relate representation and reality. The exploration of body imagery in relation to the body politic offers inexhaustible possibilities of confrontation with the Revolution's treatment of "real" bodies. If, in cultural history, "the real" seems sometimes to vanish behind the symbolic, to dissolve as all representation melts away, Bakhtin's influence is so strong that a purely immaterial body seems inconceivable.[24] Moreover, regarding Revolutionary festivals, if the spiritual and aesthetic dimension justifiably appeals to cultural historians, they cannot ignore the brutal questions posed by contemporaries as to their real significance and impact. Revolutionary festivals were very similar to blueprints published, or at least penned, by would-be reformers in the last decades of the old regime, designed to encourage patriotic unity, enthusiasm, and idealism. But, in the event, sceptics asked if Revolutionary festivals were not designed (as always) to distract the people from "real" problems, problems of social and economic distress: Mathiez's "vie chère." Did not festivals, like elections (so essential to modern political culture), "waste the people's working time," elevating them to "sovereign" status while leaving real relationships unchanged? Problems contributing to the "origins" of the Revolution continued into and beyond the Revolution.

If cultural historians such as Chartier sometimes see history exclusively formed by the potentially infinite play of representations and interpretations, it is all the more necessary to note that notions of representation and interpretation, spectacle and appearance, were already seen in prerevolutionary France as an important but problematic part of reality. Rousseau condemned most representation as fraudulent and deceitful – but regrettably powerful. The nobility's preeminence depended, some thought entirely, on *appearances* of bravery, loyalty, generosity, disinterestedness. This was condemned as "a world of illusions" well before 1789. More prosaically, merchants were sometimes suspected of keeping up a facade of probity, propriety and solvency (the "virtue" of their calling). Representation often collapsed suddenly in 1788–9. Politically, the parlements' self-image as guardians of the nation's "fundamental laws," as "protectors of the people," was irredeemably shattered. They were exposed as allegedly always having been concerned with defending their own, often pecuniary, interests. Thus, to repeat, spectacle and appearance were key aspects of a certainly complex, often bewildering, reality. They were not, however, the whole of that reality. Nor were they taken as such.

Clearly, cultural historians must – as most do – explore sensitively interpretations given in the past. They would not, of course, fall into the trap warned against by such analysts as Marx and Furet – of taking at face value the words and explanations of the historical actors. For cultural historians' tendency to treat all events as texts often discloses multiple meanings, some of which escaped the actors themselves. Even if we regard both Enlightenment and Revolution as exceptionally self-reflexive and even self-critical, they hardly raised and far less answered all interesting questions about themselves or, in the case of the Revolution, about its possible "origins" in the Enlightenment. Controversially, Lynn Hunt's *The Family Romance*, gendering and sexualizing revolutionary relationships, is a fascinating example of the renewal of questions by a cultural historian finding (or imposing?) a new layer or level of interpretation, here psychoanalytical.[25] More generally, the idea that the long-repressed reemerges in revolutions, or other troubles, when the "crust of civilization" breaks, already underlay fears of disorder, even premonitions of revolution, in the decades before 1789. Confirmed all too rapidly in 1789, it was a commonplace among counterrevolutionaries, to be lovingly elaborated by later antirevolutionary writers such as Taine (the people as monkeys gambolling on the corpses of their victims).[26]

Less repulsively, the millennial image of "the world upside down" appears in 1789 as the peasant riding the nobleman (with a female version too). The "festive," carnavalesque aspects of riot drew on ancient (primeval?) feelings. More respectably, a traditional upper-class view saw the peasants as similar to their beasts: stubborn, rather stupid, usually docile but liable to turn very nasty if goaded beyond endurance. This image, reinforced by collective memories of "jacqueries" (rural revolts or "peasant furies"), contrasted with an equally venerable view of rustic life as natural, innocent, and healthy. This, in turn, was countered by a moralistic, but realistic, emphasis on the peasants' all too frequent moral degradation (drunkenness and wife-beating) due to wretched poverty. Such views, held for example by many country priests, now coexisted with a "scientific" analysis of the unequal relationships of rural society (landholding, tenancy, seigneurialism, problems of communication and dispersed habitat, etc.). All these "discourses on the peasant," together with hard information retrieved as relevant by historians (tax burden, service in the militia, army recruitment, literacy rates, wages and prices) need to be evaluated collectively, with any testimony from peasants themselves being especially prized, since so rare. While not needing, thankfully, to spend months studying tax records, a cultural historian, in assessing attitudes and images, cannot ignore such evidence when published. Such attitudes and images were part of the Revolution's origins. At the very least they highlighted problems of rural deprivation, moral and cultural as well as material. They sharpened the reformist thrust. They perhaps awakened the people's hopes, while reinforcing the fears of many property-owners. Hopes aroused but not satisfied, as Tocqueville noted more generally of the Revolution's genesis, contributed powerfully to the outbreak of the rural revolution. But these hopes and fears, however intensified by the (exaggerated?) disorders of the summer of 1789, clearly crossed from prerevolution to Revolution.

Revolutionaries, often themselves landowners faced by peasant opposition and insurrection, legislated, almost at pitchfork-point, on peasant problems. If some were, from experience and/or study, extremely well-informed on rural conditions, others may have voted out of prejudice or following unreflectively one or other of the "images" long available in common discourse. Only when considering all these aspects can the historian, cultural or uncultural, evaluate changes effected, or claimed to have been effected, by the Revolution. For it is impossible fully to understand the Revolution's origins without some knowledge of its course and, even, consequences.

ASPECTS OF POLITICAL CULTURE

Chartier notes the inevitability of hindsight, unless a virtue is made of ignorance. Certainly, a teleological view of origins, suggesting that everything in eighteenth-century France led on straight lines to the Revolution, is to be avoided. Notions of revolution before 1789 tended to refer to the circular motion of a wheel, returning to its point of departure. The idea of revolution as an effort of substantial change stemmed largely, but by no means exclusively, from the Revolution itself. However, as already suggested, many of the ideas, attitudes, and emotions of the Revolution had roots in the old regime (itself of course designated retrospectively). The dimension of violence, already alluded to and so obviously crucial to the Revolution, may be further underlined. Verbal violence, endemic in the daily life of the people in the old regime, has been brilliantly explored by Arlette Farge. Cynthia Truant, in a broad chronology, charts some of the rougher aspects of workingmen's lives. The violence of "the crowd" has been examined by Colin Lucas, developing the work of the "Marxist" George Rudé. Olwen Hufton has delineated a specifically female violence.[27] Thus the violence of 1789, though shocking, was hardly a bolt from the blue. It fulfilled many people's worst fears.

Unfortunately, some influential cultural-historical works on origins, notably Chartier's, underplay the passionate, and at least potentially violent, nature of much writing and reading before 1789. Chartier's brilliantly sophisticated and theoretically informed account of print culture is extremely formalistic. He signally fails, unlike Farge, to convey the strength of feeling with which many texts were, as it were, inflamed. The designation and demonization of enemies had preceded 1789. Vindictiveness, a desire for vengeance, hardly needs to be read retrospectively into many texts. Also anticipated was a feeling that any serious reform plans, designed, not always wisely, to improve the people's conditions, were bound to be sabotaged, as was already the case with those attempted by Turgot in 1776. So the many-headed hydra of aristocratic conspiracy featured in many crude woodcuts of 1789. The riots in town and country from March 1789 onwards owed much to bad material conditions. But popular violence also responded to an age-old violence of the authorities and "aristocracy." The brutal legal and penal systems, the "spectacular" punishment of wretched smugglers or poachers, caused middle-class reformist opinion to weep with pity but also to choke with indignation. Here, print culture was impressively argued and incandescent. August 4 was prefigured if not quite preordained.

In this light, Timothy Tackett's study of the deputies of the Constituent Assembly (1789–91) is all the more vivid and instructive.[28] Tackett recaptures their excitement, elation, and sometimes despair. An examination of how, within the middling reaches of old-regime society, these men came by their ideas – what they read and wrote, and what experience their careers had furnished their minds with, complements attention to their performance and feelings in the Assembly. Dismay at the bitter squabbles between different egos and interests mingled with very physical feelings of inadequacy or discontent, aggravated in the noisy and overheated assembly room. In such a feverish and fetid atmosphere, belief in "plots" was almost inevitable. The "contagion" of a large assembly, virtually unknown in the old regime, the heady nature of political oratory (perhaps learned in or from the pulpit but now inflamed with new zeal) seemed to confirm the fears of those who before 1789 had wished to keep politics and debate strictly restricted. Yet, it was persuasively argued too, these very restrictions (censorship, corporatist divisions of the public sphere, chronic distrust of any assembly outside church) had made the "eruption" of public opinion, in all its discordant voices, all the more uncontrollable once it occurred. To delay and finally to frustrate reform had, many alleged, led to a revolution of "volcanic" force.

Divisions, partly inherited from the old regime and which had contributed to its downfall, influenced what many saw as the deplorable emergence of factions in the Assembly, notably the sort of aristocratic opposition which had already been apprehensively anticipated by prerevolutionary reformers. The degree to which the issues of a political culture involving an unprecedentedly intense and comprehensive attempt to translate principles into policies were viewed through old-regime ideals, prejudices and categories (and language) is debatable. The extent to which revolutionary experiences themselves changed ideas and attitudes (and language), deserves, as it did then, an examination of the relationship between two complex phenomena, Enlightenment and Revolution. Tackett again, drawing on his earlier work on religious problems – which also combined social and cultural history, with the Revolution confronting the acrimonious legacy of the old regime – illuminates this disputed cultural domain where, again, battle lines had been drawn in the old regime.[29]

Both Revolutionaries and Counterrevolutionaries sought, often rather unscrupulously, inspiration and legitimacy from prominent Enlightenment and Counter-Enlightenment polemicists. The Revolutionaries especially, having no organized Church and dogma to draw on, were keen to praise "precursors," men so farsighted, so far above prejudice, as to have, like Voltaire, Rousseau Mably, Raynal, indicated the need for serious change, if not to have predicted (still less desired) the Revolution. But Rousseau, especially – and we must include his life – supplied such an inexhaustible and arguably contradictory fund of ideas and feelings that they excited the passions of the most antagonistic groups. Rousseau, optimistic about human nature, pessimistic about society, seemed to legitimize readings by both Revolutionaries and Counterrevolutionaries. But certainly, with Rousseau, ideas torn out of context, ignoring his most explicit warnings, provisos, and qualifications, were explosive. If all this today underlines the limitations of an exclusively *intellectual* reading, the current of cultural criticism suggesting that an author, when writing, is not the master/mistress of his or her text, and according readers considerable liberty to interpret – even almost to create – the text to their own liking and in their own interest could perhaps exonerate Revolutionaries and Counterrevolutionaries alike from the accusations of distortion which historians might make against both – and which were traded freely between enemies. However, for historians less blinded by partisan passion than combatants, and perhaps seeking truth beyond the polemics, this is the slippiest of slopes.

To deny that a text has one *true* meaning may provoke fascinating interpretations, though it risks legitimizing interpretations that reflect more the preoccupations of the interpreter today than those of the author of the text. How far these may stray from a literal interpretation (perhaps a meaningless concept) is debatable. Lynn Hunt's *Family Romance* at least disproves that the issues raised by the Revolution are "finished." Its gendered interpretation heightens its interest for non-specialists, non-historians and nonacademics. If the revolutionaries, by "killing the father" (and not just the king) instituted a republic of brothers, and condemned sisters to what one can hardly term impotence, this change in the idiom of interpretation obviously affects the "true" significance as well as the "true" meaning of the Revolution, making it very different from what the revolutionaries thought they were doing – a point levied against Marxist historians, imposing *their* truth on the past.

Any identification of true meaning is, we are told, always deferred and therefore ultimately impossible. But "Truth takes many forms." Or truth can be partial – there may be "some truth" in an original interpretation (as in a literary or filmic interpretation: Buchner's *Danton's Death*, Wajda's *Danton*).[30] There might also be a "poetic" truth, seized in revelatory moments: Wordsworth's "bliss" at being present at 1789's "dawn." Tocqueville, perhaps regretfully, confessed that the upsurge of liberty in 1789 was, finally, inexplicable, despite his impressively thorough study of original documents. But the brilliant newness of 1789 – opening out untold possibilities – cleared the road not just for light but for darkness. However, this also had been anticipated by those who thought that, in the religious sphere, *any* change, any movement towards toleration of Protestants and Jews, would open the floodgates to impiety and atheism. From 1789, counterrevolutionaries, pitting "original sin" against man's "natural goodness," seeing the Revolution as a frenzy exacerbating the Enlightenment's sinful pride (for which God punished the French by the Terror) may come closer to some modern interpretations than liberals might like (or these interpreters acknowledge): to Adorno and Horkheimer's emphasis on the oppressive effects of a reason vested with mythic, potentially destructive power;[31] to a Foucauldian Enlightenment advancing the tentacular grip of discipline and surveillance;[32] to scholars who emphasize the relevance to our times, as well as to the Revolution, of de Sade's "perversion" of Enlightenment values, by basing a regime of utter control, exploitation and cruelty on the ideals of "nature" and "philosophy." In such an enlarged but treacherous context of debate – which would bring in not just literary texts but, today, film – the idea that 1789 can be redeemed, as attempted by liberal opinion during the bicentenary, as a creative moment, uncoupled from the Terror and promising universal benevolence and rights all round, seems superficial. While liable to exaggeration, and raising most acutely problems of anachronism and hindsight (inevitable, but not to be pushed beyond certain limits, difficult to define) those political philosophers such as Hannah Arendt and Claude Lefort who reinterpret the French Revolution in the light of twentieth-century "totalitarianism" contribute to a deeper understanding just as Mathiez did, despite my earlier criticism, when interpreting 1789 through 1917.[33]

Nevertheless, if writing or reading history involves conversations between successive generations, we must not undervalue, in the present context, the acuteness of analysis from within the Revolution itself, notably its own discussions of its origins. But, also, these debates cannot be abstacted from the nondiscursive elements, often of a "social" nature, often not readily translatable as, or reduced to, text. If, in the depths of December 1793 amid food shortages and guillotinings, a Paris journalist discoursed on "Voltaire and Rousseau as revolutionary writers" (his title), the fact that Voltaire was rich, loved society and his creature comforts, and preached to kings was adduced to explain his emphasis on liberty and free thought, and thus his works' influence in 1789. Jean-Jacques, poor, declaiming against the rich, preaching equality, simplicity, and natural virtues to the people, became an icon of the *sans-culottes* in the harsh days of 1793. Such discriminating recognition that the Enlightenment was diverse helped to distinguish the different stages, or even parties, in the Revolution, with the social element being important for bourgeois in 1789 and for artisans in 1793. This (though hardly the crude summary offered here) suggests interesting avenues of interpretation for *us*.

For this journalist, Voltaire epitomized the "*commerce/lumières*" equation, which I too have emphasized. But the counterrevolutionaries stressed Voltaire's impiety. His disastrously effective preaching of irreligion was, to them, *the* crucial "origin" of a Revolution all of whose ills stemmed from accomplishing the *philosophes'* design to dethrone God. Diverse interpretations are possible. Perhaps these two very different interpretations can be related, if not reconciled. Certainly to explore their relationship would shed light on origins. Excessively stark oppositions, uncritically inherited from the past, may, if replicated by the historian, mislead. They run counter to cultural-historical approaches emphasizing the undecidable, the indeterminate, the ambivalent, the hybrid, and the in-between. For much in the Revolution and its origins was equivocal, unclear. Its participants, tragically, tried starkly to separate "for" and "against." Today, multiple perspectives, and differing views, viewers, and viewpoints offer hope of deeper understanding. This need not smother real differences of principle and value in a deadening consensus.

HISTORY OR HISTORIES?

To conclude: concerning the origins of a revolution which, for good or ill, reevaluated all values, it is especially harmful to exaggerate the divisions between different types of history. Emphasis on multiple perspectives should reduce this danger. Perhaps the more intensely and imaginatively one writes other types of history, the more likely they are to be(come) cultural, which ideally does encourage a variety of approaches. That the Revolution itself inspired a diversity of historical schools and approaches, each of which had and still has, if in attenuated form, a political dimension, suggests that no single one will attain the truth. While all should be evaluated critically, it is unlikely that any will, or should, be completely discarded. History-writing, like history, is not a process of rigidly demarcated stages. Moreover, productive tensions have always existed between types of history, with boundary-zones often being particularly fruitful, perhaps because disputed. So weak consensus is unlikely to last long either. The issues raised by Enlightenment and Revolution will continue to divide and inspire. Jules Michelet, whom many historians, of whatever school, see as the greatest historian of the Revolution, is unclassifiable – partly because of his passionate engagement with the issues, shunning the alibi of cold objectivity. Michelet's interest in popular beliefs, customs, folklore, myths, forms of sociability; his sensitivity to feeling; his attention to the cultural role of women; the evocative poetry of his descriptions; the power of his imagination; even his own contorted psychology – all make him especially attractive to cultural historians. But his times and ours are very different. The perhaps rather uncritical prominence of cultural history today may reflect a world in which the old social formations have declined or disintegrated; the loyalties they inspired have fractured or disappeared, without new movements as yet appearing. Absent too are vigorous ideologies and "big" ideas – with the lowest common denominator of "democracy" the norm; it is a world where images and representations are as substantial – or, rather, insubstantial – as what they purport to represent, and where no powerful languages or forms of discourse compete, offering the prospect of a brighter future worth struggling for, with commitment and enthusiasm.

If such commonplaces of today's academic discourse do accurately depict the current "post-historical" condition, this may itself be of limited, temporary consequence. Furet pronounced the French Revolution "over," its positive ideals comfortably absorbed into today's culture (and society), with anything too dangerous for today's dull politics discarded and the subject itself cold rather than cool. The vigour and variety of new works – including the heatedly polemical and aggressively combative – suggest otherwise. Whether "revolution" is a thing of the past or not, the end of the history of revolutions and their origins has evidently not yet arrived.[34]

5. The Intellectual Origins of the French Revolution

MARISA LINTON

Summary

The intellectual changes taking place in eighteenth-century France have long been cited as a cause of the Revolution. In this chapter Linton stresses the complexity of the relationship of the Enlightenment to the outbreak of revolution. She shows how traditional interpretations have been affected by new perspectives in political culture and the social history of ideas. She considers some of the leading eighteenth-century participants in radical political polemics, and looks at key concepts in the development of those polemics. Recognizing that discourse theory has been a fruitful approach, she nevertheless points to problematic features of the approach of Baker and of Furet. With regard to Baker, she critiques three features: firstly, the schematic claim to boil down the ideological origins into three particular discourses, those of will, reason, and justice; secondly, the ideas-driven approach that gives insufficient place to the impact of context and events; thirdly, the neglect of the motivations, intentions, and rhetorical strategies on the part of authors of discourses. To illustrate these points she shows how the discourse of virtue also played a significant role in the ideological origins of the Revolution, a role that must be interpreted in terms of the rhetorical and strategic development of this concept within specific historical contexts. Nor was this idea new in 1789, molding its users in a determinist fashion, as Furet suggested. By 1789 a language had been fashioned (consisting of such key words as virtue, patrie, nation, despotism, privilege) armed with which participants could enter into the new realm of politics and struggle to control the political debates for the future of France. But the shape of that future was still very much under contestation, and would be further transformed in the context of revolutionary and counterrevolutionary politics.

INTRODUCTION

The question of how eighteenth-century ideas were related to the outbreak of the French Revolution has been discussed and analyzed many times since the Revolution first broke out. No definitive answer has ever presented itself, nor is it likely that the debate will ever reach a conclusion that satisfies all the possible permutations. Part of the problem is that we as historians are looking back on the years before the Revolution from the inevitable perspective of hindsight. We know what was going to happen – that the seemingly fixed regime, which had endured with relatively few changes for several hundred years, would be swept away, almost overnight, by a Revolution founded on the principles of liberty and equality. We know, too, that the attempt to set up a new and stable form of government based on a constitutional monarchy would founder and that within four years a reign of Terror would be instituted which would call into question the very principles on which the Revolution had been founded. Given this hindsight, the link between the radicalism of the French Revolution and the radical ideas that circulated in Paris in the years before it broke out seems – at least at first sight – to be obvious. Paris, of course, was a focal point of the European Enlightenment, and one might be tempted to assume that Enlightenment ideas must have dealt an ideological deathblow to the authority of absolute monarchy that contributed to the disintegration of the ancien régime, paving the way for the outbreak of Revolution. But the danger is that if we do not separate the two phenomena – Revolution and ideas before the Revolution – we will fall into the trap of attributing the former to the latter – and no such easy connection exists. There was no equivalent of Marx amongst the writers of the eighteenth century, planning and predicting a revolution before it happened. There was no preexisting intellectual blueprint for the revolutionaries to adopt as a model on which to base their plans for the future. On the contrary, few events have been so unanticipated as was the French Revolution.

One of the oldest explanations of how the Revolution came about was that the Enlightenment was – literally – to blame, and that the Revolution was the work of a conspiracy of intellectuals. Conservative writers in the years immediately following the Revolution freely attributed it to the devious and subversive activities of *philosophes* and freemasons. For de Maistre, the arch conservative and ardently pro-Catholic writer, there was little question but that the traumas of the Revolution should be laid at the door of meddling intellectuals and freethinkers;

though these men died years before the Revolution actually broke out, they could not escape responsibility for the impact of their words.

> What does it matter to me that the weak, timid and reticent Rousseau never had the wish or the power to stir up revolt? What does it matter to me that Voltaire defended Calas to get his name in the papers? What does it matter to me that, during the appalling tyranny that has fallen on France, the philosophers, frightened for their heads, have withdrawn into prudent seclusion? Once they put forward maxims capable of spawning every crime, these crimes are their work, since the criminals are their disciples ... The tiger that rips men open is following his nature; the real criminal is the man who unmuzzles him and launches him on society.[1]

This belief was acted out in pointed fashion after the restoration of the monarchy in 1815, when the remains of Voltaire and Rousseau were summarily ejected from the Panthéon where the revolutionaries had installed them as "great men," and cast onto a rubbish heap as an explicit repudiation of their subversive ideas.

Thinking on the relationship between ideas and Revolution has come a long way since that simplistic and retributive treatment. In more recent years, rather than seeking a direct causal link between ideas and Revolution, questions are much more likely to be framed in terms of the kinds of ideas that were conducive towards revolutionary thought. Rather than asking whether the Revolution had intellectual "causes," it has proved much more fruitful to think in terms of "intellectual origins," a wider climate of ideas that encouraged some people to be more receptive to the Revolution. As Roger Chartier put this, the Revolution became possible, in part at least, because it became conceivable.[2] Building on this perspective, historians have been asking questions about the relationship between ideas and Revolution, questions that involve a mingling of social and cultural historical methods, as well as the more traditional text-based approach associated with the history of ideas. The first major area of questioning focuses on the kinds of people who had access to new and radical ideas in the eighteenth century. What sort of people wrote the works that were to influence the Revolution? What sort of people read those works, and provided interested audiences for their ideas? Secondly, what were the key words and concepts that linked eighteenth-century thought to the Revolution? Thirdly, a question that can be seen independently, but which relates very closely to the first two:

how did these words and concepts work, how were they used, applied, and understood? For this third question we must also consider the problems of agency and intentionality, as well as the effect of the application of words in specific contexts. This chapter will explore some of these questions, and look at recent approaches that historians have adopted to explain them. The first part of the chapter will consider how historians have been reassessing the kinds of people who contributed to the ferment of new ideas in the eighteenth century and their possible motivation. The second part will ask what were some of the key words and concepts that had the greatest impact on radical thought in the later eighteenth century together with a significant influence on Revolutionary thought. It will then examine how these ideas were shaped and applied in specific contexts, looking at how words were used and manipulated, and consider the impact that this may have on our understanding of the relationship between ideas and Revolution.

WHO CONTRIBUTED TO THE NEW POLITICAL CULTURE?

The radical Enlightenment thinkers make up the group that has been been most consistently linked with the ideas of the Revolution. Here too, however, the nature of the link is hard to clarify. In part, the problem rests with the question of *how* one defines "Enlightenment" in the first place, as well as *whom* one includes under the heading of "Enlightenment thinkers" – both questions that have provoked some contention. One might define the Enlightenment as both a body of ideas and the adoption of new approaches to an understanding of the nature of science and, by extension, of the moral, social, and religious organization of human society. Many of the thinkers associated with this movement were far from radical in their politics. Though there was a strand of more radical thought associated with the Enlightenment, the question of how far this extended and how great an influence it asserted over a "prerevolutionary" readership is one that remains contentious. Within the ranks of the French *philosophes* there was little concurrence about how best to rethink the political and social structure of France – and little appetite for actively challenging the social order. They embraced a variety of political positions from the "enlightened despotism" associated with Voltaire, to the proparlement and pronoble politics of Montesquieu. Neither of these men was what we would term a political radical, let alone a democrat, though both of them – particularly Montesquieu – were to prove sources of inspiration to the Revolutionaries. As late as 1791, the future Montagnard, Saint-Just, in his *L'Esprit de la Révolution et de la constitution de la France* (*The Spirit of the Revolution and the Constitution of France*) was using Montesquieu's political structures as a basis for his own revolutionary projections.

Of all the *philosophes*, the one who has been most frequently associated with the Revolution is Rousseau, a connection that was made as early as L. S. Mercier's *De J.J. Rousseau, considéré comme l'un des premiers auteurs de la révolution* (*Jean-Jacques Rousseau Considered as One of the First Authors of the Revolution*) (1791). More than one observer has pointed out ominous resonances between his idea of the "general will," and the radical revolutionary ideology of coercion by the nation that was the intellectual basis of the Terror under the Jacobin republic – though the question of how far Rousseau's philosophy can be said to bear some responsibility for the Terror is one that has been highly contested. To return to the question of the Revolution's *origins*, however, it was Daniel Mornet who first noted that *The Social Contract* appears to have been little read before the Revolution. Mornet examined the lists of books in 500 private book collections before the Revolution and found *The Social Contract* featured only once. On the other hand, Rousseau's more emotionally engaged books were well represented: Mornet found nine copies of *Emile*, and no fewer than 126 copies of Rousseau's great paean to virtuous sensibility, his novel, *La Nouvelle Héloïse*. It was not *The Social Contract* but *La Nouvelle Héloïse* that went through no fewer than 50 editions before the Revolution. It could be argued that Rousseau's influence on the Revolutionary generation was strongest in the sphere of the emotions rather than in political theory.[3] Mme Roland, for example, stated that it was Plutarch rather than Rousseau who had inspired her interest in republicanism, whereas "Rousseau showed me the possibility of domestic happiness and the delights that were available to me if I sought them."[4] Once the Revolution broke out, some kind of link between Rousseau and Revolutionary politics was evident from early on. From October 1790, for example, his bust, along with a copy of *The Social Contract*, resided in the meeting place of the Constituent Assembly. Even so, the evidence for his having had an explicitly *political* significance in the earlier phase of the Revolution remains somewhat ambivalent. Joan McDonald argued that his political works were little used in the early years of the Revolution and, more recently, Timothy Tackett, in his detailed study of the intellectual background of the men who made the Revolution, claimed that the deputies of the Constituent Assembly took little inspiration from

Rousseau's politics, and that the deputies "in their diary entries and letters home, alluded more frequently to history and the classics, than to reason and the general will or to Rousseau and Voltaire."[5] Up until at least 1791, opponents of revolution were just as likely to use Rousseau to buttress their arguments as were advocates of it.[6] The evidence is contradictory, though, as Bernard Manin has stated, there is a strong case for arguing that the Revolutionaries took Rousseau's ideas and shaped them into an argument to suit their own position: "In a sense, therefore, the Revolution imposed its own meaning on Rousseau's complex thought."[7] We need to distinguish between the ideas and intentions of an author and the way in which those ideas are subsequently appropriated and used by the author's readers. In other words, it was the Revolutionaries who created Jean-Jacques Rousseau as the founder of the Revolution.

The search for intellectual origins impels us to move away from a narrow definition of the Enlightenment as a canon of "great thinkers" who can be studied in isolation from their social and cultural context. It was Daniel Mornet who pioneered this move as he broadened his focus to include the development of a wider mentality that took hold amongst a significant swathe of educated society in eighteenth-century France. His book, *Les Origines intellectuelles de la Révolution française, 1715–1787* (*The Intellectual Origins of the French Revolution, 1715–1787*) was first published in 1933 and has been profoundly influential, though it has never been translated into English. It set the terms of reference for subsequent generations of historians. Mornet's contention was that the intellectual origins of the French Revolution could be traced through the ideas of a "a very large minority, more or less enlightened" who comprehended the faults of the political regime, had in mind the kinds of fundamental reforms that they wanted to see instituted, and, little by little, influenced the shaping of public opinion.[8] For this task, he said, it was necessary not just to examine the ideas of the acknowledged "great authors," but to widen one's net considerably and explore a whole range of writers who were widely read in their day. He argued that one must look also at writers in the second, third, and even tenth rank, because writers whom we may rank as "tenth rate" often turn out to have been of major importance for their contemporaries and to have exerted a substantial influence over the development of ideas. Mornet highlighted two critical moments in the transformation of ideas. The first was around 1748 to 1750, a period which saw the publication of several key works, including Montesquieu's *De l'esprit des lois* (*Spirit of the Laws*), and Toussaint's *Les Moeurs* (*Morals*) (both in 1748); and the *Prospectus* and *Preliminary Discourse* of the *Encyclopédie* (the first volume of which appeared in 1751). These works, said Mornet, marked the point at which earlier ideas were crystallized into a conscious project of Enlightenment reform. The second key period began around 1770. At this point the battle of the *philosophes* to win acceptance for their ideas amongst the educated elite was largely won. Thereafter, Mornet traced the diffusion and spread of their ideas in the period up to 1787 when the threatened collapse of the old regime began to materialise.[9] It was Mornet who was the first to explore a number of ideological influences current in their day – including the key concepts of patriotism and of virtue (in the sense of active social morality), and the impact of the American Revolution. He argued convincingly that such ideas were diffused or disseminated through French society through a variety of institutions that he also explored, including freemasonry, journalism, education, and café society. As such he can fairly be said to have been the founder of the social history of the intellectual origins of the Revolution. On the other hand, he did not really demonstrate the means by which such ideas were diffused, or examine the ways in which people appropriated new ideological concepts and how they understood them. It is these problems of the cultural appropriation and adaptation of ideas that subsequent historians have gone on to investigate.[10] Thus, it is not enough, says Chartier, to show that certain ideas were current in educated society and consider only the diffusion and reception of these ideas; one must go a step further and show *how* such ideas were understood and used:

> Reception always involves appropriation, which transforms, reformulates, and exceeds what it receives. Opinion is in no way a receptacle, nor is it a soft wax to be written upon. The circulation of thoughts or cultural models is always a dynamic and creative process. Texts . . . do not bear within them a stable and univocal meaning, and their migrations within a given society produce interpretations that are mobile, plural, and even contradictory.[11]

If Mornet initiated the idea that obscure and heretofore unconsidered writers merited study for their contribution to the intellectual origins of the Revolution, it is to Robert Darnton that we owe the inspirational development of this approach. In a series of writings, beginning with the publication of "The High Enlightenment and the Low Life of Literature in Pre-Revolutionary France" in *Past and Present* in 1971, and culminating in his latest major work, *The Forbidden Best-Sellers of Pre-Revolutionary*

France in 1996, Darnton has shown that the intellectual origins of the Revolution were not confined to acknowledged thinkers such as Voltaire, Rousseau, and Montesquieu and their political and philosophical theory. Ideas that contributed to undermining the ancien régime could equally be found amidst the less edifying underworld of Parisian society. They could be seen in the political *libelles* of "Grub Street" hacks, some of them future revolutionaries such as Brissot, Carra, Gorsas, and Fabre d'Eglantine. The doors of the best salons, and hence the socially exclusive world of Enlightenment society, were closed to them. Darnton argued that the frustration and embitterment engendered by this rebuttal fuelled their readiness to embrace radical revolutionary ideas – though not all historians agree with this ready link between resentment at social exclusion and revolutionary ideology.[12] From the hired pens of such impoverished but ambitious men stemmed a series of scathing *libelles* on the ruling elite: anonymous attacks on the alleged moral, financial, and sexual corruption of leading courtiers, members of the clergy, and even the monarchy itself. These writings were often spiced up by lurid accounts of the alleged sexual debaucheries of key players. No one was more vulnerable to this kind of clandestine attack than Marie-Antoinette herself. Attacks on her supposed sexual corruption and political interference began relatively early in her married life, but took hold particularly after the debacle of the Diamond Necklace Affair of 1786 when the image of a profligate, debauched, and unscrupulous queen was circulated in a series of clandestine and highly damaging writings, despite the efforts of the police to track them down. Darnton contends that the impact of these damaging writings contributed to an ominous "delegitimization" or "desacralization" of the French monarchy.[13]

In his book, *The Forbidden Best-Sellers of Pre-Revolutionary France*, Darnton took up the challenge of the questions originally posed by Mornet and asked what books people actually read. As the culmination of his work over many years on book publishing and readership, Darnton sets out to examine the aspects omitted by Mornet, and to "map the forbidden sector" of literature. As he makes clear, "that sector was enormous. In fact, it contained almost the entire Enlightenment and everything that Mornet was later to identify with the intellectual origins of the French Revolution."[14] As Darnton concedes, this includes a vast number of texts, for almost all the books that we think of as original or thought-provoking in eighteenth-century literature were ones that came under the category of "forbidden books" because they failed to pass the criteria for accessibility of the censors. Despite the fluency of Darnton's writing and his engaging depictions of the world of books in eighteenth-century society, he has generated his share of controversy – indeed, a whole book has been devoted to the examination of Darnton's work by his fellow historians, in which enthusiasm and criticism share in about equal measure.[15] Some of the most deep-seated problems relate to his apparent reluctance to engage on a more complex level with the ideas and words of the books and writers he has studied. As one of his critics puts it, "In Darnton's work, too much focus on books as objects, too much emphasis on their commercial production and circulation as things, has taken him away from the less concrete but all-important subject of words, their meaning and their power. It is striking that nowhere in his work has he paid attention to the formation of a revolutionary vocabulary prior to 1789."[16] This question of the generation of a Revolutionary vocabulary and how historians have dealt with it, is one to which we shall return. But firstly, let us turn to the question of how we can move beyond the study of books as artefacts and uncover the cultural world that produced them.

Much recent historical work has explored the political culture of the ancien régime, by which is meant the shared assumptions, practices and interactions around the practise of politics. The possibilities and limitations of these new approaches have been examined in Roger Chartier's study, *The Cultural Origins of the French Revolution* (1991). Chartier argues that, hitherto, historians of ideas sought to impose a retrospective specific meaning and hierarchy of importance to eighteenth-century ideas in order to fit them into the mold of protorevolutionary ideology. To say that the Enlightenment was about ideas that can be designated as "modern," and that these ideas somehow inspired the Revolution, is to take what is essentially a teleological approach. Rather, Chartier suggests, the perception could be reversed: "Should we not consider instead that it was the Revolution that invented the Enlightenment by attempting to root its legitimacy in a corpus of texts and founding authors?"[17] Chartier contends that it was the Revolutionaries who created the modern image of "the Enlightenment" as a body that appeared cohesive and unitary, emphasizing those eighteenth-century texts that appeared to give legitimacy to the Revolutionary enterprise. The Revolutionaries were searching for retrospective justification and for paternity in philosophy. Cultural historians, therefore, do not to try to find an endorsement of revolution in the texts of particular writers. Chartier illuminates this shift from the traditional history of ideas toward cultural sociology; that is, away from a narrow group of thinkers toward an appreciation of the wider social mentalities that made the ideas of leading thinkers possible.

No concept is more central to the cultural origins of the Revolution than that of public opinion. The recent focus on the importance of this concept owes much to the influential work of the German philosopher, Habermas. He argues that the eighteenth century saw the rise of a new category of the "public sphere" that would lead to the formation of the modern world of journalism and other critical media.[18] According to Habermas, the "public sphere" was a form of intellectual space between the state and civil society, where private individuals who heretofore would have had no opportunity to develop their ideas about politics and government could come together and voice their views on public and political events of the day. For Habermas this was primarily a "bour-geois" public sphere, indicative of the rise to prominence of a new intel-lectually – but not yet politically – emancipated social class: the bourgeoisie. They met in the growing number of institutions that catered for new ideas: in the salons, Masonic societies, provincial academies and societies, clubs, cafés, and journals (though censorship narrowed the permitted scope of authorized journals and gazettes). Their voices grew ever more confident and articulate in giving their opinions on matters of politics and government, whether on the conduct of wars, prominent court cases, or disputes between the king and the parlements. Their voices took shape and hardened into a new phenomenon, that of public opinion. Right up until the collapse of political authority in 1787 (the so-called pre-Revolution) the laws of censorship of publications, including newspapers, meant that access to political issues was limited (though the clandestine press, as we have seen, continued to put forward alternative views, albeit to a limited audience). Nevertheless, censorship did not impede the progress of public opinion, and it gradually undermined the authority of government. Even Louis XVI, it seemed, was not impervi-ous to public opinion. When he took the decision to restore the Paris parlement on his accession to the throne in 1774, he stated, "It may be considered politically unwise, but it seems to me to be the general wish and I want to be loved." In his youth, whilst he was still the dauphin, Louis had written, "I must always follow public opinion, it is never wrong."[19] Despite his efforts, Louis's biographer, John Hardman, notes that Louis was singularly inept at winning the popularity he so deeply desired.[20]

Yet public opinion was the very institution set up to judge the merits of kingship. Public opinion was frequently said to be a "tribunal" whereby the educated elite could engage in public debate, freely express their views and judgements on events of the day, and even speak out on those political matters from which they had heretofore been barred. According to Keith Baker, the first use of public opinion as a tribunal dated back to controversies within the parlements over the rights of the Jansenists to access to the sacraments and thus to freedom of religious beliefs. At around the same time, the *philosophes* likewise adopted the notion of public opinion as part of an intellectual campaign, a kind of "tribunal" for the "men of letters" to express their judgements on current issues. Writers and thinkers of the day used the rhetoric of public opinion, not to empower the lower orders but to act as an authorized voice on behalf of men of letters, lawyers, and other intellectuals who were without a means of legitimate expression. Public opinion was thus an invaluable linguistic weapon for the reading classes in a society characterized by censorship and lack of political representation: it provided "a voice for the voiceless." However, public opinion, it must be noted, was not the same thing as "popular opinion." Indeed, the writers who used this term were careful to distinguish "opinion," which they perceived as educated, sophisticated, and cultured, from what they considered to be the vagaries, ignorance, and brutality of the common people.[21]

There is much evidence to indicate that it was not primarily the disaffected, or "Grub Street" radicals, who spearheaded the challenges to monarchical authority; the poor and dispossessed were of still less significance in the intellectual origins. On the contrary, it was within the ranks of the elite that much of the most wounding ideological criticism appeared and was nourished. The prominent role played by nobles in the Enlightenment, both as writers and readers, has been well attested. Even some members of the higher clergy were enthusiasts for aspects of the Enlightenment, though somewhat qualified by their religious perspectives.[22] Even more remarkable is the extent to which members of the inner elite of the ancien régime, from the ranks of the judiciary, administrators, and office holders were prepared to voice criticisms of the conduct of government. The ancien régime was undermined as much by powerful critics within its ranks as by the discontents of those outside the elite. As these were the very men who wielded most power during this period, the extent of their influence is hardly surprising. Whilst Darnton lays stress on the underdogs and social marginals of "Grub Street" who actually wrote most of the pamphlets, and claims that they were motivated by social resentment, one should note that very often these pamphleteers were in the pay of members of the elite and wrote partly at their bidding and instigation. Thus many of the most critical *libelles* owed their origins to people who moved in exclusive circles. Such pamphlets were secretly sponsored by disaffected courtiers who acted from personal, factional, and familial motives in portraying political rivals, including members of the royal family and government ministers, in the most scathing terms.

THE REPERTOIRE OF POLITICAL WORDS AND CONCEPTS

Rather than see the ideological critique of monarchy as particularly "aristocratic" in inspiration, it is more helpful to characterize these new ideas as part of a "common culture" that developed in the last decades of the ancien régime, and in which all members of the educated classes might participate.[23] The existence of a common culture does not imply that the elite shared a common ideology or set of political beliefs, far from it. But a common repertoire of concepts of political ideas existed with which participants in this culture were familiar and on which they might draw in order to develop specific political arguments in particular contexts. Of course, the very idea of a common culture in some ways militated against the old idea that the nobility were superior in either birth, prowess, or intellect. But the antiaristocratic tendencies of some of these ideas only became really apparent in the context of the Revolution. Most of the culture of opposition to monarchical authority before the Revolution was about reform of the system, not its destruction. There was a revolutionary potential about some of the language but, without the collapse of the political regime, potential is all that it would have remained. One may ask at this point, what were the elements of this "common culture"? What kind of ideas and concepts constituted part of the available repertoire of critique of absolute monarchy? And how can we best study the relationship between such words and access to political power? One such concept, as we have discussed, was that of "public opinion." But there were a number of others.

One of the most sophisticated and coherent concepts was that of natural law theory, developed by such thinkers as Pufendorf, Grotius, Locke, and (especially influential in France) Burlamaqui. It was a legally based alternative theory of morality and political authority. It set out a contractual theory of government that implicitly – and sometimes explicitly – challenged the premises on which the legitimacy of absolute monarchy was founded. Diderot demonstrated the radical potential of this theory in his article "*Autorité politique*" which appeared in 1751 in the first volume of the *Encyclopédie*. The article developed a polemic based on the justification of natural law that began with the stirring lines: "No man has received from nature the right to command other men. Freedom is a present from heaven, and every individual of the same species has the right to enjoy it as soon as he enjoys reason."[24] The explosive nature of this political theory was acknowledged by critics who were still launching attacks on the offending article 20 years later, and it was a factor in the first suspension of publication of the *Encyclopédie*. Natural law theory, with its legalist foundation, also paralleled some of the proparlementaire rhetoric in resistance to absolutist politics; though many of the more conservative magistrates would not go so far as to countenance it, some did adopt it, as did many proparlementaire supporters in their own polemics. Diderot's article was explicitly implicated in the bitter conflict between the monarchy and the parlement in 1753 and 1754 over the administration of the sacraments to Jansenists.[25]

Another concept that exerted a major influence was that of republicanism. There were different versions and derivations of republican ideas – but there were a number of themes common to all republican thought. Amongst these themes was the centrality of civic virtue to politics, a phrase that was understood to mean that citizens of a republic should be devoted to the public good. Although a republic did not necessarily have to be without a king, the king (or any executive power) would also be subordinate to the public good. Of all the different versions of republicanism, classical republicanism was at once the most ancient, of course, and the original inspiration for its more recent manifestations. Throughout much of the eighteenth century, the republic seemed an outmoded form of government, confined to a few minor city states.[26] This changed with the advent of the American Republic. Much work has been done on the impact of the American Republic on French radical thought in the final years of the ancien régime. This influence was of much significance in the years between 1776 and 1789, not least because America showed that republics were not confined to some golden age of antiquity, but could be given a politically viable form in the modern world. This influence endured to some extent up until the overthrow of the monarchy in 1792 when the gaps between the two conceptions of politics became much more evident, particularly the French adoption of direct democracy – embodied in the right to insurrection.[27] Another strand of this tradition was that of English republicanism. Again, the influence of English republicanism in France on the eve of the Revolution has been well attested. Most French thinkers – like Mirabeau – who admired the English model did so because they were drawn to the idea of a constitutional monarchy, a form of limited, somewhat pragmatic government, where the separation of executive and legislative powers formed a constitutional barrier against "absolutist" rule. But there was also some interest in the more radical, republican strand of thought that stemmed from the period 1649 to 1660 when Britain had been without a monarch. As an inspiration to French radicals, however, this English example had its limitations, partly because of its radical religious elements, but also because Cromwell was widely seen to have reinstated a form of despotism, based on military force. In 1789 such an idea seemed anathema to French radicals.[28]

HOW THE LANGUAGE WAS APPLIED

The question remains, how do we understand such ideological concepts and their significance in an eighteenth-century context? Words alone did not make the Revolution. We have to ask how people used words, and how such words took on a specific relationship to power. The development of discourse theory, particularly in the hands of Keith Baker, has to be our starting point here. Baker's understanding of "discourse" owes much to Foucault's argument that a discourse is a form of language and association of words that gives access to power.[29] Baker's approach to discourses of power has had a great impact on studies of the political culture of the ancien régime and most writers on the ideological origins acknowledge their immense debt to him. Along with François Furet, Baker has played a pioneering role in the revisionist history of the ideological origins of the Revolution. Beginning in the late 1970s, he published a number of pathbreaking articles, collectively published under the title *Inventing the French Revolution* (1990). In these articles he followed a consistent approach, which he set out most systematically in "On the Problem of the Ideological Origins of the French Revolution."[30] Here he criticized older approaches to the history of ideas and the assumption that ideas carried a consistent meaning that existed outside the specific historical context and events. He argued that there were three discourses that took on new meaning in the later eighteenth century and went on to play a significant role in the ideology of the Revolution. The first of these was the discourse of justice. This was based on the idea that the king should not abuse his power and that the people should have their limited rights within the monarchical constitution. He associated this discourse above all with the parlementaires and their supporters, and writers in that tradition, most notably Montesquieu. The second discourse was that of will. According to this view, popular sovereignty (the will of the people) was superior to the will of the monarch and could rightfully oppose it. Baker associated this discourse with Rousseau and, to some extent, Mably. The third discourse was that of reason. This was grounded in the idea of enlightened reform imposed by state officials, and involved transposing problems of social order into the language of social science. Turgot and the physiocrats attempted to put some of this reform into practice, but its theory had originated with the "enlightened absolutism" espoused by Voltaire. During the Revolution it was the Rousseauist discourse of will that triumphed over the other two and thus paved the way for the radicalization of politics. Taken together, Baker argued, "these three discourses . . . defined the political culture that emerged in France in the later part of the eighteenth century and provided the ideological framework that gave explosive meaning to the events that destroyed the Old Regime."[31] Like Furet, Baker has stressed the causational role of eighteenth-century language as a force that not only described, but also shaped events. Although Baker has done much to reinstate the centrality of the relationship between words, politics, and power, he has not been without his critics.

Firstly, the division of political culture into three competing discourses has seemed to some observers to be an overly schematic and artificial contrivance. Why should the three discourses of will, reason, and justice be so much more significant than any other oppositional discourses of the eighteenth century? One might point to other concepts that could be said with equal validity to have lent themselves to an oppositional role, such as *patrie*, despotism, privilege, citizen, Nation, and virtue, amongst others. All these ideas played a prominent part in polemical critiques of absolute monarchy, and their development is important for any exploration of the intellectual origins of the Revolution, as recent scholars are beginning to demonstrate.[32] Baker's archaeology of knowledge has followed what is, in some ways, a somewhat schematic framework, in that the discourses of justice, will, and reason are said to correspond to the traditional conceptions of, respectively, Montesquieu, Rousseau, and Voltaire. There are other discourses, as well as other ways of categorizing discourses. One might

further categorize or redivide conceptual categories amongst different
lines than the three divisions picked by Baker: for example, into classical
republicanism, religious (particularly Jansenist) critiques of absolutist
policies, and public opinion.[33] All these concepts play a part in the
discourses as analyzed by Baker, and he has written illuminatingly on the
use of classical republicanism.[34] Indeed, more recently Baker has
emphasized the importance of classical republicanism as a "diagnostic
language" rather than a political model to be adopted uncritically.[35] But
the question here is how one conceives of overall analytical categories for
an understanding of the intellectual origins of the Revolution; in effect,
how one decides what a discourse is "essentially about." Does it have to
be essentially about anything? Does it not depend more on how a
concept is deployed or used within a specific context; that is, how it is
appropriated?

A second criticism made of Baker's approach is that he has tended to
neglect the context, particularly the social context, within which ideas
were developed and within which they derived a specific meaning.[36]
Chisick, for example, has argued that "neo-revisionists" (under which
banner he includes Baker and also Furet) have an ideas-driven view of
political culture that leads to a reification of ideas, and takes insufficient
account of both social factors and the ways in which ideas are developed
and manipulated within particular contexts.[37] This reification can lead
to misreadings of both the derivation of ideas and their causation. For
example, Baker's argument that the Revolutionaries learned the idea of
popular sovereignty largely from Rousseau has been countered by
Tackett who argues that the radicalization of ideas in the Constituent
Assembly in the second half of 1789 and the adoption of the ideology of
popular sovereignty came about largely in response to tangible fears of a
real counterrevolutionary force.[38] This has implications, not only for our
understanding of the ideological origins of the Revolution, but also for
the origins of the Terror. For Baker explicitly states that when the
National Assembly adopted what he terms the Rousseauist "language of
political will" in September, 1789, already the Assembly "was opting for
the Terror."[39] Tackett's very different reading of the political context
leads to a much less determinist interpretation, where the causes of the
Terror lie more in the continuing political conflict in the early years of
the Revolution than in any inherent propulsion towards terror in the
discourse of a dead *philosophe*.

A third problem, which relates to the reification of ideas, is whether
Baker's approach to discourse as power gives sufficient space to questions

of motivation and intentionality. The elevation of discourse to a primary shaper of historical events tends to flatten out the registers in which language is used, the purposes for which it is enlisted, and the motives and aims of the person who employs that language. One has the impression at times of the tail (the discourse) wagging the dog (the person who speaks the discourse).

One way through this problem may be to think again about the ways in which we describe how words function in relationship to political power. Thus, we can distinguish between three ways of conceptualizing political language. These are, respectively, language as a discourse, as an ideology, and as a rhetorical strategy. A political discourse is a group of linked words by means of which a speaker gains authority and power. Yet these linked words may be accessed by different groups, put together in different ways, and thus have different consequences. For example, the discourse of the "Nation" meant something very different in the hands of the monarchical government, attempting to mobilize public opinion in support of the Seven Years' War, from what it meant to revolutionaries in 1792 in the build-up to war with Austria.[40] By contrast, an ideology indicates a set of consciously held beliefs which are drawn together in support of a particular political stance. Many of the "discourses" of the ancien régime, such as Nation or *patrie*, could be said to have been firmed up in the context of Revolutionary politics into specific ideologies, as alternative applications or meanings of the discourses were discarded, becoming outmoded or dangerous. Here again there is a sense of a language to some extent manipulating its user, so that people were obliged to adopt certain ideological positions and abandon others. Thirdly, there is the notion of political language as a rhetorical strategy. Here the emphasis is much more on a writer or speaker deliberately constructing a particular argument, though the choice of words is still confined to an available repertoire of terms currently in use, and the argument has to be constructed according to the accepted rhetorical structure of the time. So the same words will still be used, such as Nation, virtue, or *patrie* for example, for these were the currently accepted terms, with a set of culturally accepted significances. But when one sees a language in terms of its rhetorical strategy the emphasis is more on the writer, and on the choices that have been made. Why has this particular word been used, what were the intentions of the author? What was their political background, their context, their choices? One must bear in mind that in practice, these three aspects, discourse, ideology, and rhetorical strategy, tend to shade into one another. Thus, a strategic rhetorical argument that is successful may well later be firmed up into a conscious ideology.[41] Discourses, ideologies and rhetorical strategies are all apparent in the intellectual origins of the Revolution. Heretofore the standard meaning of politics had been interpreted as the exclusive business of the king and his appointed ministers. But by 1789 there was a whole repertoire of words in existence that was readily available for use in political polemic by a wide section of new participants in the public arena. These words provided a common language and culture by means of which politics might be understood and contested as a matter of public concern. The participants who used this language extended through a wide range of literate society – from drafters of the *cahiers de doléances* to the elite of ancien régime society within the Assembly of Notables.[42] These participants by no means agreed on the kind of political model they wanted to see for their nation, but they now had a common language with which to debate the matter. Thus, nobles who found themselves potentially excluded from the election process to the Estates General in Artois were moved to expostulate indignantly, "What's the point of being noble if one is no longer a citizen?"[43]

THE POLITICS OF VIRTUE

One word that was central to eighteenth-century political culture, wherein it featured simultaneously as a discourse, as an ideology and as a rhetorical strategy, was virtue.[44] Political virtue meant the abnegation of self-interest in order to devote oneself to the public good. In the early eighteenth century there were three competing political discourses of virtue. Each of these was used to sustain very different sources of political authority. The first of these was the discourse of virtuous kingship. Here virtue was attached to one individual, the king, who was depicted as the sole conduit for that virtue necessary to ensure the wellbeing of his people. The second discourse was that of noble virtue. Here virtue was attached to an elite group, the nobility, whose high birth, military prowess, and superior valor were said to provide the necessary skills to make them the primary functionaries of the state. The third discourse was that of civic virtue, a theme with its roots in the classical republics of Greece and Rome. Here virtue was much more widely dispersed through society: all citizens could lay claim to it, and through their virtue they might make a case for their political rights. To these three discourses a fourth was added from about the mid-century: the discourse of natural virtue. Like civic virtue it tended to support an egalitarian political view, but here the argument was based more on shared sentiments that ensured that all people might care for their fellows and be drawn to the public good through their sympathy and desire to ensure the happiness of their fellow citizens. Virtue could thus be enlisted to support widely differing sources of political authority. From about the middle of the century the discourse of civic and egalitarian virtue began to predominate ever more strongly over its alternatives, deriving its justification partly from the classical republican tradition, but partly also from the notion of natural innate virtue which could be accessible to all, regardless of social status. Even kingly virtues began to be described more in terms of civic and natural virtues than the traditional exclusively royal ones: kings and dauphins (notably Louis XVI's father) were depicted more in terms of their civic sense of duty, their philanthropy (*bienfaisance*), and their sympathy and concern for their subjects than in terms of exclusively royal virtues. In the case of Louis XV, even his staunchest supporters often referred to the extent to which he fell short of these virtues. On the other hand, there was a concerted attempt to portray Louis XVI as a citizen king, a man of virtue and *bienfaisance*. In some ways this appeared to offer a more positive view of monarchy, and to emphasize its more humane and approachable face. But it also meant that the grounds of royal legitimacy were perceptibly shifting. Louis XVI was increasingly presented in terms of his civic and natural virtues, but these were qualities to which his own subjects might equally lay claim. What then remained of the sacred aura of kingship when a king could be judged as a man like other men, even by his supporters? The danger was that the king might subsequently be judged to have failed in these necessary virtues.[45] In the case of Louis XVI such a judgement was most strongly articulated through the attacks on his queen, Marie-Antoinette, who was depicted as a source of vice, of pro-Austrian sympathy, and of female guile, operating at the heart of the French monarchy and subverting its virtue.[46]

The rhetoric of virtue can be traced through an immense variety of sources. As well as featuring in the classic texts of the *philosophes*, it can be found in texts as diverse as journals, treatises, sermons, novels, essays written for academy prizes, conduct books, memoirs, and scurrilous literature. It indicates how widely we must cast our nets in seeking out the intellectual origins of the Revolution. It is also very evident that the idea of virtue was deliberately and strategically manipulated: it served as part of a rhetorical strategy that could be enlisted to justify a whole range of political arguments and positions. For example, it could be deployed in the justificatory remonstrances of the noble magistrates of the parlements as they claimed to be acting in the best interests of the nation, in the tradition of virtuous magistrates. It could be invoked as an attribute of the politically ambitious duc d'Orléans as his advocates sought to build up his political credentials in the years leading up to the outbreak of the Revolution, portraying him as a true man of virtue, dedicated to the public good and, by implication, a more altruistic and politically moral man than his cousin, Louis. Virtue could also be used to justify the validity of public opinion: people who wanted to give their views on current events sought legitimacy through the concept of civic virtue. They presented themselves as virtuous citizens, whose moral concern for the wellbeing of the country gave credibility and the weight of moral force to their arguments. Most significantly of all, virtue could be used to justify political rights for citizens.[47] Their virtue gave them a right to political representation, for, it could be argued, there was more genuine virtue amongst the poor and uncorrupted sections of society than amongst the nobility which ranked status according to birth and hereditary status above intrinsic merit. It was this last rhetorical use of virtue – as a justification for political participation – that hardened into an ideology (a consciously held belief that was used to justify a particular political position) in the context of the Revolution itself.

François Furet depicted 1789 as the moment of the invention of a new "political discourse": one that conflated politics and morality.[48] He argued that this juxtaposition of politics and morality was both novel and inherently unstable and that these very instabilities led directly to the Revolutionary Terror. For Furet, this language determined the course of the Revolution, But the relationship between ideas and revolution was more complex than this. Far from the conflation of morality and politics being a new (and intrinsically revolutionary) idea in 1789, the argument that politics should be about virtue was a long-established feature of much of eighteenth-century thought. Nor did this argument appear only in the mouths of future Terrorists: it was used across a wide spectrum of reformers, radicals, and polemicists, and they used it strategically to pursue a range of arguments. Between 1789 and 1793, the language of virtue did indeed develop into an ideology that would be used to justify Terror, but this was an altogether more complex and less deterministic process than that outlined by Furet, one in which the political context of those years, not least the impact of war and civil war, must be taken into account.

The example of the language of political virtue is not intended to imply that the intellectual origins of the Revolution lay primarily in the idea of virtue. Certainly it was important, but so were other ideas, amongst which, as we have seen, were such key concepts as *patrie*, despotism, privilege, citizen and Nation. My point is that in understanding how the concept of virtue was taken up and applied in specific polemical contexts we may be able to suggest a methodology for understanding the appropriation of other key concepts in the political lexicon.[49] The revolutionary potential of the rhetoric of virtue was available long before the advent of that momentous year of 1789, but it remained only a potential until it was fired in the crucible of Revolutionary politics. By 1793 it had become a cornerstone of Revolutionary – and Terrorist – ideology.[50] Nonetheless, in some ways the roots of the concept retained very strong intellectual links with eighteenth-century thought and this is true of the other important concepts. Perhaps the single most important link was the idea that politics was about morality even more than about democracy. Eighteenth-century thinkers had used this kind of argument as a way of critiquing ancien-régime politics rather than as any kind of actual policy. In the hands of the Jacobins, in the context of the desperate political context of the Year II, the intellectual assumptions of the eighteenth century were hardened into ideological truths to be literally applied. The Revolution is too diverse to be reduced to any one set of ideological objectives, but in the minds of some of its leading figures it was about, first and foremost, the project of making the people of France into virtuous citizens, and to understand what they meant by that we have to look back into the context of eighteenth-century ideas.

6. The Religious Origins of the French Revolution, 1560–1791

DALE VAN KLEY

Summary

Starting with Henry of Navarre's reconciliation with Leaguer Paris by his conversion to Roman Catholicism in 1593 and ending with Louis XVI's alienation from revolutionary Paris by his fidelity to Roman Catholicism in 1791, this chapter sets out to explore this paradox in the long run and in religious terms. The principal argument is that, after successfully reinventing itself as a sacred and absolute authority safely above the religious fray of the sixteenth-century wars of religion, the Bourbon monarchy set about undoing itself by embroiling itself in another religious conflict – the Jansenist controversy – this one within Catholicism and largely of its own making. One result was the "desacralization" of a monarchy that, while usually attributed to the French Enlightenment, in this argument assumes a place alongside a militantly anticlerical enlightenment as both products of the Jansenist controversy. Another result was a reenactment of the sixteenth-century wars of religion in memory, words and warrants, not only reproducing some of their divisions within Catholicism but also reviving their theories of limited or "constitutional" monarchy long obscured during the apogee of absolutism, and which fed into the prerevolutionary debate. And while Henry IV might once have hoped that a distinctly French or Gallican Catholic Church would eventually reunite French protestants and Catholics, his successors' policy of aligning the monarchy with the papacy allowed persecuted Jansenists to redefine the church in ever more "constitutional" terms, and, in alliance with the judicial milieu and "public opinion," rhetorically to pit the *patrie* against monarchical, papal, and episcopal "despotism." The stage was thus set whereby the National Assembly imposed a "civil constitution" on the Church that, added to the one imposed on the king, led to the parting of the paths between Louis XVI and Paris.

INTRODUCTION

Henry IV never said, "Paris is worth a Mass" although he may have acted as if it were. This saying attributed to him emanates from contemporary Catholic critics unconvinced by the authenticity of the new king's conversion from Calvinism to Catholicism, a conversion now regarded as sincere.[1] But whether sincere or not, it still remains unlikely that Henry of Navarre could ever have entered a fervently Catholic Paris and made good his claim to the throne of France had he not adopted the confession of the overwhelming majority of his subjects. Although, as king, Henry IV soon issued the Edict of Nantes granting religious toleration and a separate estate to his former co-religionists, he also upheld the right of public worship to the French Catholic Church everywhere and even took a few of the initial steps toward the recatholicization of his realm that pointed distantly in the direction of the revocation of the Edict of Nantes by his grandson Louis XIV in 1685. Merely taken for granted until then, Henry's choice of 1593 was to confirm that the French monarchy could never be other than Catholic. By the time Henry IV fell to an ultra-Catholic assassin's assault in 1610, the king's Catholic confessional identity had become one of the fundamental laws of the French realm.

Nearly two centuries after Henry IV acted as though Paris was worth a Mass, another French king acted as though the Mass might well be worth Paris. This monarch was Louis XVI who, like his ancestor Henry, found himself king of a religiously divided nation and saddled with a religious choice to make. In this case the division ran between French Catholics and through the Gallican (that is, French Catholic) Church, pitting those Catholic clergymen who had accepted and sworn to uphold the revolutionary National Assembly's radical reform of their Church – the so-called Civil Constitution of the Clergy – against those who refused it. This division deepened after the papacy condemned the Civil Constitution in the spring of 1791, making it harder for those Catholics who had accepted it to continue to be Catholics and supporters of the Revolution too.

The Most Christian King himself fully embodied this tension. Although he had earlier promulgated the Civil Constitution, the papal condemnation clarified his conscience, concluding that he could not take communion from his "constitutional" parish priest. But this time Parisians acted a lot less Catholic than they had in 1594: when Louis XVI tried to leave the Tuileries Palace for nearby Saint-Cloud in April 1791 in order to take Easter communion from an "orthodox" or non-juring priest, a hostile crowd prevented him from doing so. So bound up with Catholicity was Louis XVI's concept of French kingship that this incident was an important factor – perhaps the decisive factor – in his fateful attempt to flee France on June 21, 1791 for the safety of the eastern border, only to be recognized and arrested at Varennes.[2] The road to Varennes ultimately led to the king's final falling out with an ever more radical Revolution and his execution in January 1793.

Thus did "absolute" monarchy and Catholicity rise and go down together in France. While the alliance between them remained constant, what obviously varied from the end of the sixteenth century to the end of the eighteenth was the attitude toward both of a good many of the monarchy's "subjects" doubling as the church's lay "faithful." For the intervening two centuries had gradually transformed the realm's "subjects" into "citizens" who had come to think that the last word in matters of both Church and State belonged by rights to them.

What accounts for this seismic shift in attitudes toward religion and political power as well as in the relation between them over the course of two centuries? The textbook answer is of course the secularization of mentalities for which the shorthand is the "Enlightenment." Yet, while far from untrue, this answer begs the question because the Enlightenment in France was not quite like any other in Europe or America, being unique in the degree of its anticlericalism and hostility to revealed religion. The nature of the French Enlightenment thus calls for an explanation in turn, one that cannot bypass developments between the sixteenth and eighteenth centuries. One of these developments is religious, and may be introduced by any number of characteristic cross-roads like the conversion of Henry IV or Louis XVI's decision to try to flee France.

Another such crossroad conveniently lies midway between the two others, this one in 1693, about a quarter century before an "Enlightenment" took recognizable form in France but another quarter century after France had again become divided along religious lines. As in 1791, the issue in 1693 divided Catholics from each other and ran through the Gallican Church, pitting a majority who sided with the papacy and certain of its doctrinal decisions against a "Jansenist" minority who rejected these decisions and yet persisted in viewing themselves as both better Catholics and Frenchmen than their opponents were. Jansenists effectively combined their identities as Catholics and Frenchmen by arguing that the Pope's judgments were not infallible unless unanimously accepted by the Gallican Church. Jansenists could thus also claim to be very Gallican – in other words, very French – by appealing to the historic rights or "liberties" of the Gallican Church, which had long prided itself on adhering to what it regarded as the pristine "constitution" of the Catholic Church which had vested ultimate authority, not in the papacy, but in the whole Church assembled in general councils. In 1791, revolutionary "patriots" who wished to be good Catholics too would argue no differently than did Jansenists in 1693.

What happened in 1693 is that Louis XIV acceded to Pope Innocent XI's request that he disavow these Gallican "liberties," even though he himself had strong-armed the Gallican clergy into proclaiming them in its general assembly only a decade earlier, in 1682. If he disavowed this declaration in 1693, he did so in part in order better to proceed against Jansenists, whom he suspected of being crypto-Calvinists and closet republicans and who thereafter joined Protestants as the most persecuted people in ancien-régime France.

Although perhaps not irreversible at the time, Louis XIV's decision nonetheless became so toward the end of his reign in 1713 when he solicited and obtained a papal bull called *Unigenitus* that censored tenets of Gallicanism along with Jansenist doctrines condemned earlier. Becoming a symbol both of "absolute" royal power and "infallible" papal authority, this bull set the propapal Bourbon monarchy on a collision course with a portion of its clergy, its royal judges and even Parisian "public opinion." At the same time that the Enlightenment of Voltaire and Montesquieu was taking shape in eighteenth-century France, this public would grow ever more sympathetic to "Jansenists" and more hostile to their chief enemies, the Jesuits, who since Henry IV had become so influential in the making of royal religious policy. Still pro-Jansenist though on a trajectory ending in the rejection of revealed religion in general, this hostility would become poignantly apparent on the occasion of the royal judges' trial and dissolution of the Jesuits and their society in defiance of the king's known will in the years around 1762.

From 1593 to 1791 by way of 1693, 1713 and 1762 are five telltale chronological markers in a trajectory from an era of religious revolutions to a self-consciously irreligious revolution by way of religion itself. The pages that follow are devoted to explaining and connecting these points along a line making up some of the religious origins of the French Revolution.

RELIGION, RELIGIOUS ORIGINS, AND ROYAL RELIGION

The argument that a revolution that eventually turned against Christianity had religious origins is nothing if not counterintuitive, calling for an initial word or two by way of apologetic explanation. One possibly helpful consideration is that a "revolution" with paradoxically religious origins and secularizing consequences was far from new in 1789, seeing that the Protestant Dissenting tradition played a major role in the almost simultaneous American Revolution and its disestablishment of religion at the national level, and that Puritanism had similarly destroyed the Anglican establishment and dealt deadly blows to a quasi-sacral monarchy during the Great Rebellion from 1640 to 1660 in England a century and a half before. To be sure, the French Revolution is different in that its idea of "revolution" is itself more revolutionary and that it eventually abandoned the goal of reforming Christianity in favor of trying to abolish it entirely.[3] Yet that only gave both anticlerical revolutionaries and Catholic counterrevolutionaries equal if opposite motives for obscuring any religious origins the Revolution may have had – a bias inherited by both "liberal" and "conservative" historians of the Revolution throughout the following century. Such origins are therefore best viewed from a distance, the best perspective being from well before the Revolution. Hence the chronological scope of this argument must include the entire ancien régime from the sixteenth-century wars of religion to Louis XVI's flight to Varennes.

By "origins" is meant long-term "causes" plus their changes over time, with no implication that the Revolution can be fully explained by these or any other origins. By "religion" is meant a way of finding final meaning in temporal experience with reference to a "reality" outside of and transcending it, including such external expressions as rituals and institutions as well as sources of revelation and confessions and commentaries based upon them. It goes without saying that religion, thus defined, interacts in countless ways with other more "horizontal" facets of experience without being reducible to any or all of them, and that the line between religion and what is called "ideology" is often a very thin one, especially in the eighteenth century which witnessed a seismic tilting from one toward the other.[4] The religions at issue are the well-known ones of Calvinist Protestantism plus varieties of Catholicism, principally "devout" and "Jansenist." By "religious origins" finally is meant just that, with no implication that the Revolution did not have other origins, including economic and social ones.

If religions could exist in total isolation there would be no reason for them to contain – much less spell out – any ideological or political implications. But of course they exist in no such vacuum but rather find and define themselves in a social-political matrix. In old-regime Europe the most pertinent such matrix was the confessional state. The confessional state is what took the place of the medieval ideal of a seamless Catholic Christendom when, after both the Protestant and Catholic reformations and more than a century of intermittent religious conflict, the Treaty of Westphalia in 1648 retroactively ratified the fact of religious diversity and the Religious Peace of Augsburg's formula of *cujus regio, ejus religio* ("whosoever reign, his religion"), with, however, the proviso that no future royal conversions could alter the confessional status of their domains. Thereafter each state and dynasty sought to give itself legitimacy by replacing the universal Catholic church with an established confessional Church that, even if "Catholic," acted as a state or dynastic Church as well.

The well-nigh unanimously accepted assumption that underlay this arrangement was that political unity presupposed religious unity and that obedience to secular law would be impossible to enforce without the concurrent moral suasion of the inner conscience. The consequence was that confessional conformity to these ecclesiastical establishments was everywhere the equivalent of today's "citizenship," and that failure to conform was everywhere visited with penalties ranging from the physical expulsion of no fewer than thirty thousand Protestants from the Archbishopric of Salzburg as late as 1731 to the comparatively benign civil disabilities put up with by Catholics in the Dutch Republic. In Europe's dynastic monarchies the situation of religious minorities tended to deteriorate in the course of the seventeenth century along with the rise of royal claims to "absolute" power, claims that were never more absolute than in the policing of the religious conscience. And, despite the slow but steady growth of religious toleration in many parts of Europe during the succeeding century of "lights," religious dissent continued widely to be viewed as the most dangerous form of political dissent. This assumption tended to be self-fulfilling, with the subversive potential of religious dissent varying more or less directly in proportion to the pressure exerted to suppress it.

The French monarchy did not differ in kind from other European states in point of any of these generalities. What was perhaps peculiar to France was the degree to which the Catholicism that this monarchy defended had become inseparably entwined in the religious identity of this monarchy, or what has been called the "royal religion" in France. Unlike the English monarchy, the Capetian monarchy had been unable to take for granted the political unity vouchsafed to his successors by William's conquest and protected by England's island status, and had had to build up France by extending the royal domain fief by feudal fief, each retaining its own laws and franchises. What unity there was depended on loyalty to the dynasty and the affective charge of its symbolism, both of which depended on religion as inseparable supports.

Building on Germanic, late imperial, and Christian precedents, the comparatively weak Capetians stored up sanctity in occasional alliance with the papacy and added a whole array of accoutrements to their religious armor, such as the miraculous power to heal scrofula and the myth of the supernatural origin of the holy oil used to consecrate French kings at Reims. As it took form in the thirteenth century, the royal coronation and consecration ritual brought some of these elements together, added the (otherwise uniquely clerical) prerogative of communing in both bread and wine, and gained "national" credence as a kind of eighth sacrament.[5]

By the time the Capetian monarchy's turn came to do battle with the papacy, the king's position as head of the Gallican Church and the mystical body of France was such that Philip the Fair could count on the loyalty of "his" bishops as well as his lay vassals in his conflicts with Pope Boniface VIII. And when, during the Hundred Years' War, the French realm and monarchy seemed in peril of their lives, "royal religion" had penetrated deeply enough that a peasant girl from Lorraine led by divine "voices" played a crucial role in the resurrection of both, culminating in the coronation of Charles VII at Reims in 1430.

Any attempt to deny that "royal religion" thus defined ever put down any roots in the popular imagination must dispose of the counter-evidence of Joan of Arc. If, moreover, the Capetian monarchy possessed a religious identity with popular purchase in the middle of the fifteenth century, it is implausible to suppose that it had disappeared without a trace when the Valois successors of the direct Capetian line found themselves challenged by Protestant would-be reformers a century or so later. This challenge was to result in a period of religious civil war that threatened both the monarchy and the royal religion that was its buttress. The same civil war also generated very opposed conceptions of monarchy that, after being driven underground during the rise of absolutism and the long reign of Louis XIV, were to reappear in "enlightened" form to play a role in the political polarization of the declining ancien régime and even during the early years of the French Revolution.

1594 AND THE CONVERSION OF HENRY OF NAVARRE

Although the newly converted Henry of Navarre was able to buttress his claim to the kingship with a coronation and consecration, he had to make do with the cathedral of Chartres and holy oil attributed to Saint Martin of Tours because Reims, along with its cathedral and Holy Vial, was still under the control of the Holy Union, better known as the "Catholic League." This religious and paramilitary organization had seized this city along with many others including Paris in genuinely popular revolutionary risings shortly before the assassination of Henry III at the hands of a zealous monk in 1589. In 1594 Reims as well as Paris continued to hold out against Henry IV on the grounds that he was a doubly relapsed and excommunicated heretic, and as such a would-be tyrant with no legitimate claim to the throne. For in Protestant and Catholic casuistry alike, the public profession of "heresy" by a crowned head of state was the most flagrant form of tyranny, endangering as it did the eternal destiny of the realm's Christian subjects and therefore justifying resistance to it to one degree or another. It was only after Henry IV contrived to deprive Catholic resistance of the crucial premise in this argument as well as to win over Paris that he was able to negotiate the end of the remaining Leaguer resistance – and with it 32 years of intermittent religious warfare.

To ask whether Henry of Navarre could have become Henry IV of France as a Calvinist is to ask if as such he could have been anointed by Catholic bishops, taken Catholic communion, sworn to expunge France of all heresies and then have touched and miraculously healed various victims of the king's disease. The question, in other words, is not whether Calvinism was compatible with monarchy in some form – it was – but whether it was compatible with the form that the French monarchy had assumed by the sixteenth century, and the answer is "no." This monarchy would have had to undergo a drastic reformation of its own were it to have become compatible with a Christianity and Church as "reformed" as the form that Protestantism took in France.[6]

Calvinism denied that miracles had occurred since the apostolic age; the monarchy possessed the gift of miracles. Calvinism ridiculed the veneration of relics; the French monarchy derived its own gift of healing in part from the relics of Saint Marcoul. Calvinism opposed the entire concept of sainthood; the French monarch had produced a saint (Louis IX) and had derived legitimacy from association with Saint Denis. Calvin criminalized the adoration of visual images and his iconoclastic followers took care to smash them, while the French monarchy ritually lived and died on a diet of images, which were tightly intertwined with those that adorned the cathedral windows and exterior porches. Even that Renaissance and neo-imperial tendency of the French "new monarchy" to become more "absolute" was adversely implicated by the (all too notorious) Calvinist emphasis on divine predestination and the attendant denial of human free will, since what was supposed to be "absolute" was above all the king's "will" to create new law without his subjects' consent as opposed to upholding their diverse rights as defined by traditional notions of justice and law.[7]

At the center of this implicit incompatibility was an acutely heightened sense of divine transcendence that, while not unique to Calvinism in the sixteenth century, found its clearest expression in the conception of God's unique "majesty." The concept was laden with political implication in historical context, since Calvin denied that "majesty" was attributable to anyone or anything other than God alone at precisely the time that "His Majesty" was becoming a part of the official title of the King of France.[8] To be sure, French Calvinism's largely potential opposition to sacral kingship and absolute monarchy in the making did not become entirely actual until it reacted to the St Bartholomew's Day Massacre in the form of theories of contractual government and justifications for armed resistance, some of which like the *Vindiciae contra Tyrannos* remain classics in the history of pre-Lockian political thought. But action at ground level hardly waited for high theory, since the Huguenots had begun the religious wars in response to a mini-massacre in Champagne with the revolutionary seizure of municipal governments in 1562, proceeding to wage seven more distinguishable wars punctuated by compromise peaces until Henry's conquest of Paris in 1594. Nor had all high theory waited for Saint Bartholomew's Day to find expression, since François Hotman's *Francogallia*, which argued that Valois "tyranny" was an illegitimate deviation from an original Frankish-Gallic "constitution" subordinating king to the "nation," lay in manuscript well before that massacre.

It is true that Huguenots tended to abandon these justifications for resistance to "tyrants" as soon as "their" leader, namely Henry of Navarre, found himself next in line for the throne, and that the clerical apologists for the Catholic League adopted these same Huguenot arguments when their turn came to seize whole cities and take the field against "tyrants" in their own estimation, first against the feckless Henry III and then against the "heretical" Henry of Navarre. This mind-boggling turnaround has given rise to much cynical historiography about "real" human interests as opposed to ideological smokescreens. But if the line of argument advanced here has merit, then the similarity of ideological justifications is quite superficial, while the religious reasons for resistance to the monarchy by the two sides are very real and really different. For where the Huguenots perceived a royal religion in competition with the "honor" due to the divine "majesty" alone and a king overdue for demotion to human scale, zealous Catholic Leaguers perceived a royal religion that was not producing on its promises and a king who, all too human, was failing to be a saint. The problem that the Catholic League had with sacral monarchy lay less with the ideal than with the degree to which royal reality fell short of sacral standards.

The Catholic League's political threat to the monarchy may be profitably compared to the late-antique heresy of Donatism, which held that priests who had apostatized during periods of anti-Christian persecution could not validly administer the Church's sacraments including the sacrament of baptism. The "orthodox" position championed by St Augustine maintained that the Holy Church was no less the Church if represented by priests unworthy of it, with the result that its sacraments "worked" even if administered by such priests so long as they were duly ordained and orthodox believers. Similarly, the "political Donatism" of ultra-Catholic religious sensibility tended to declare open season on kings who were unworthy of the sacral kingship they were supposed to incarnate although not quarreling with the desirability of such an incarnation itself. While the justification for armed resistance to "tyrants" as spelled out by League preachers and theologians like Jean Boucher and Guillaume Rose might be lifted wholesale from the works of Huguenot publicists, the spirit that informed these arguments was anything but the same.[9]

Nor for that matter were the arguments always the same, since League justifications tended to reserve a crucial role for the papacy and the sentence of excommunication in determining at what point a legitimate prince had become a tyrant as well as the range of actors who might take the field against him. And more typically than in Huguenot pamphlets, the kind of action envisioned was political assassination, a vision acted upon often enough. Late sixteenth- and early seventeenth-century Europe is littered with the bodies of prone princes; Henry IV sustained no fewer than twenty attempts on his life, most emanating from the same quarters, before François Ravaillac finally felled him with a dagger in a narrow Paris street in 1610.

By that time neither the French monarchy nor the unity of the realm was any longer in danger, the Protestant presence having been contained, ultra-Catholic passions having cooled, and the king having produced an heir. But it had come close to a mortal blow for a reputedly immortal monarchy, caught in the middle of a 30-year joust between equally zealous if opposite religious combatants during a period of weakness for the dynasty. Long before the royal funeral cortege carried Henry's body to Saint-Denis in the last ceremony that distinguished between immortal Crown and mortal incumbent, royal jurists and panegyrists were at work putting the body royal together again.[10]

1693 AND THE ROYAL RETREAT FROM CONCILIAR GALLICANISM

When Henry IV's grandson, Louis XIV, found himself at the height of his power in 1693, he had persecuted much of the remaining French Protestant population into flight, found himself at war with Europe's chief Protestant states, and was competing with the papacy for the title of leading defender of the Catholic faith. If he was ready to surrender the Gallican Church's traditional "liberties" to the papacy's pride in 1693, it was in part because he thought that the monarchy did not need them any more. He no longer had the same reasons to fear the papacy as had Henry IV. So formidable had the Sun King's power become both at home and in Europe that "absolute monarchy" in the seventeenth century had no better personification than he.

That assumes of course that "absolute monarchy" existed as a distinguishable phase in the history of European monarchy – a big assumption, given the contrary grain of present historiography.[11] So what if anything was uniquely "absolute" about absolute monarchy? And what was its relation to the Gallican "liberties" in France? It is time to analyze some problematic terms.

Although the Sun King's writ undoubtedly extended farther at home than had Henry IV's, the term "absolute" as used here refers to the claims made by the monarchy rather than to any real increment in power. One of the claims new to the late French seventeenth century was the contention that no "higher" obligation might ever untie the knot of obedience owed by subjects to their sovereign, and that the king owed no account of his conduct except to God alone. This included the Catholic Church as well as even the king's highest lay subjects who might advise him or remonstrate with him via the regular hierarchical conduits but not constrain him in a "constitutional" way.

As it happens, this claim was also the newest addition to the Gallican "liberties." When first put forward as a proposition by the commoner or Third-Estate delegation to the Estates General in 1614, it bore the marks of a reaction to the still-recent assassination of Henry IV and to the whole experience of the religious civil wars when Protestants and Catholics alike felt entitled to resist the king on constitutional and religious grounds. If the regency government refused to enshrine this proposition as law at that time, it was partly due to opposition by the Catholic clergy who deemed it a threat to the newly fundamental law requiring the king to be a Catholic. But on the occasion of his most serious run-in with the papacy over his regalian rights in hitherto exempt dioceses, Louis XIV pressured his whole clergy into proclaiming this new Gallican "liberty" along with the older ones while convoked in a special session of its General Assembly in 1682.[12] When the Sun King disavowed this Gallican declaration 11 years later, his retreat hardly compromised this new "absolutist" article.

What the Sun King was ready to part with were the medieval conciliar tenets of Gallicanism that, though reaffirmed in 1682, stood in tension with the principle of the king's accountability to God alone. If, as these tenets held, the whole Church assembled in general council was superior to the Pope, and if any part of the Church had a right to reject papal judgments until the whole had been heard from, then similar conclusions seemed to follow about the whole of France as assembled in the Estates General in relation to the king. As Pope Innocent XI less than innocently pointed out to Louis XIV's ambassador in Rome, "if councils were superior to the popes whose power comes from God, then the Estates General would have leave to press the same claim against kings."[13]

Nor did these political conclusions remain merely implied, since late-medieval Sorbonne theologian–philosophers like John Major and Jacques Almain had long spelled them out: namely, that in the State as in the Church the whole community possessed what would later be called "sovereignty" and only delegated its use to a "chief" who might be deposed in case of abuse. Far from original, both Calvinist and League publicists had drawn freely from these Gallican sources along with Roman ones in the sixteenth century. The French monarchy hence became less comfortable with these tenets in proportion as its own claims to power were becoming less limited and more "absolute."

In addition to the new Gallican article redefining "divine-right" as temporal unaccountability, the full armor of absolutist doctrine drew liberally from the sixteenth-century jurist Jean Bodin's treatise entitled *The Six Books of the Republic*, which characterized "sovereignty" not only as "absolute" but as "indivisible" and "perpetual" as well. Bodin's emphasis on indivisibility had the effect of countering any case in favor of "mixed" government or "balanced" powers on the confusing English model as well as associating the monarchy with the unity of the Trinity. And the emphasis on perpetuity helped the monarchy both to eliminate the few remaining elements in the coronation–consecration ritual that suggested that the king reigned by virtue of election and to enshrine the principle of automatic blood-right dynastic succession from king to nearest relative in the male line.

Although practice never kept pace with theory – the monarchy remained very constrained in practice to the end of the ancien régime – high theory was essential in justifying those real gains that royal power registered over the course of the seventeenth and eighteenth centuries. These gains included putting the Estates General "on ice" after its penultimate meeting in 1614, an indefinite prorogation of all but the most indispensable provincial estates, and the permanent imposition of royal commissioners called *intendants* on older corporate bodies of officers in order to manage the collection of direct taxes. However, the parlements could not be similarly dispensed with and emerged as the institutional foci of the revolt known as the Fronde that lasted from 1648 to 1652. Louis XIV effectively muzzled them for most of his reign by means of good political management and an edict that allowed the magistrates to remonstrate against royal acts of legislation only after they had obediently registered them as law.[14]

Absolutist high theory also took on a life of its own, in which it went hand in hand with a deification of the monarchy by its propagandists and apologists, going well beyond the christological analogies regnant before the religious civil wars. While the new royalist first Gallican article was meant to immunize the king against religiously motivated resistance to the royal will, the properly religious aspect of French absolutism regarded monarchical majesty as a lesser incarnation or reflection of divine majesty and made it into an object of veneration in its own right. And while the late-medieval new monarchy had invented and ritualized the juristic distinction between the immortal Crown and the mortal incumbent, the post-Reformation monarchy violated this distinction, conflating the two in the royal court ceremony of Louis XIV at Versailles that publicized his private life and privatized his public life.[15] In France the monarchy assumed a very positive religious identity and demanded interior as well as exterior adhesion.[16]

That this religious identity was still bound up with Catholicism rather than the neo-paganism suggested by Louis XIV's sobriquet of "Sun King" became apparent in royal policy toward "unorthodox" religious dissidence of all kinds. The long-term logic of this policy consisted in relentless revenge against the remnants of the confessional combatants and threats to the monarchy during its trial by fire in the sixteenth century.

First in line of fire was the million-strong Huguenot community that, deprived of their strong places by Louis XIII in 1629, suffered an attrition of the toleration vouchsafed them by the Edict of Nantes from the time Louis XIV took the reins of government until he revoked the edict in 1685. This edict of revocation sent half of this population into flight to Protestant states surrounding France while transforming those who stayed into persecuted non-persons. It also created a Huguenot Diaspora ringing Louis XIV's France that was to play a role in the marketing of the Enlightenment as well as in the spread of anti-absolutist thought, some of it salvaged from Huguenot sources. A lesser target was the remains of the Catholic League in the form of the *parti dévot*. Already a casualty of Cardinal Richelieu's bellicose anti-Habsburg foreign policy in 1630, a similarly mystical and pacific religious orientation recrystallized toward the end of the century as a court faction around the dauphin's tutor Archbishop Fénelon of Cambrai, only to run afoul of Louis XIV who exiled him from court in 1697.

Coming in the wake of 1693, Fénelon's fall from royal grace is a further chapter in Louis XIV's retreat from traditional Gallicanism because it occurred in connection with a papal condemnation solicited by Louis XIV and imposed by him upon the Gallican Clergy and an unenthusiastic Paris parlement. The same assertion of royal Gallicanism at the expense of traditional Gallicanism colors the royal edicts of 1695 and 1698 that proposed to end the threat of "anarchy" represented by parish priests – in the sixteenth century the League's most eloquent voices – by subjecting them as never before to the authority of bishops ever more rutted in the role as agents of royal religious policy. Legislative symbols of Louis-Quatorzian absolutism, these two edicts undermined the traditional Gallican liberties in that, in the thought of their late-medieval theologians, these had once contained a separate niche for parish priests conceived as direct bearers of Christ's authority. As it happens, by 1695 the Parisian parish clergy also bristled with Jansenists who, with the Paris parlement's judges and barristers, had become the chief defenders of the conciliar tenets of Gallicanism.

If Louis XIV was willing to sacrifice the conciliar aspects of Gallicanism to the papacy in the 1690s, it was not mainly in order to secure the papacy's cooperation against Fénelon who sought no cover from Gallicanism, much less against the Huguenots to whom the Gallican liberties did not apply. Rather, it was in order to obtain the papacy's help in his pursuit of Jansenists who were already looking for cover from these liberties in response to two major papal judgments against them, and never more clearly so than in a popular devotional book called *Moral Reflections on the New Testament* by the Oratorian Father Pasquier Quesnel. Although the 1690s witnessed no major royal act or papal bull against Jansenists, Louis XIV had already been long at work on their case, one that was to lead to the destruction of the convent of Port-Royal in 1709 and the papal condemnation of Quesnel's book in the bull *Unigenitus* in 1713. Yet another symbol of Bourbon absolutism, that bull was in turn to result in a religious and political conflict that would result in the undoing of sacral absolutism, making the French eighteenth century a century of *Unigenitus* as much as of "lights."

1713 AND THE BULL *UNIGENITUS*

Fulminated by Pope Clement XI, the constitution or bull *Unigenitus* condemned 101 propositions extracted from Quesnel's devotional hand-book, qualifying them globally rather than individually with some 22 different condemnatory "notes" ranging from merely "offensive to pious ears" to plainly "heretical." The bull represents the apex of a series of papal condemnations of Jansenism that began with *In eminenti* in 1643 and ended with *Autorem fidei* against the Acts of the Synod of Pistoia in 1794. Because it mixed typically Jansenist doctrinal tenets condemned earlier with propositions enunciating a radically Gallican conception of the Church, the bull's effect was further to confound the cause of Jansenism with that of Gallicanism, as well as to solidify a growing alliance between Jansenists and the Paris parlement. By the time Louis XV's first minister Cardinal Fleury forced the Paris parlement to register the bull as a law of both State and Church in 1730, all three – Jansenism, Gallicanism, and the cause of the parlement of Paris – had become part and parcel of the "Jansenist" side of the Jansenist controversy in France.

As it takes two to tango, the other side of the Jansenist controversy was made up of Jesuits and those clerics and religious orders that shared the Jesuit point of view. In his polemical restatement of St Augustine's doctrine of divine grace entitled *Augustinus*, Cornelius Jansen targeted not the fifth-century monk Pelagius and his followers, against whom Augustine had done battle, but the mid-seventeenth-century Jesuits accused by Jansen of reviving the Pelagian "heresy." In Jansen's view, the Jesuits' neo-Pelagianism consisted in maximizing the extent of "fallen" humanity's residual freedom and goodness and in minimizing the amount of divine help or "grace" needed to overcome "sin." Against these "devout humanistic" tendencies, Jansen and his followers set out to revive Augustine's Catholic theology of grace and to rescue it from its heretical appropriation by Protestants. Along the way, however, they came to stress, as had Calvinists, human dependence on a divine grace "efficacious" enough to liberate the will from its propensity to sin as well as God's prerogative of deciding who was – and was not – to become a member of the "elect" by receiving this grace.[17]

The Jesuits responded by inventing the pejorative "Jansenist", and accusing "Jansenists" of dressing up Calvinist heresy in Catholic clothing. Whereupon Jansenists widened the battlefront to include the Jesuits' allegedly elastic moral teaching and criminally accommodating conduct in the confessional, to which Jesuits retorted that the penitential rigorism practiced by Jansenist confessors would produce only despair, alienating Catholics from the sacraments altogether. Much in the conflict replayed the Reformation one between Catholics and Protestants. If anything, Jansenist religious sensibility actually accentuated the Calvinist contrasts between the grandeur of human nature before the Fall and the misery of the human condition thereafter, the unique majesty of God and unworthiness of all below it, and the absence of any neutral ground between acts motivated by grace on the one side and "concupiscent" self-interest on the other.

Jansenists were nonetheless not crypto-Calvinists but genuinely Augustinian Catholics. Although in time Jansenists like Calvinists came to stress the lay reading of Scripture in vernacular translation and to develop a distaste for certain aspects of externalized popular devotion such as rosaries, their emphasis on divine grace remained compatible with "good works" and distant from the Protestant doctrine of justification by faith alone. In contrast to Calvinism's easier acclimation to a "disenchanted" world, the Jansenist quest for salvation bore a fearful and ascetic caste, while the belief in ongoing miracles remained alive and well, above all in the miracle of the Mass.

Which is also to say that, unlike the Protestant–Catholic schism, the Jansenist controversy started and stayed within the Catholic Church. That it persisted in regarding itself as Catholic despite papal condemnations enabled Jansenism to deflect these anathemas and to use all the defensive devices available to French Catholics, most particularly the appeal to Gallican liberties. While Jansen's own "Jansenism" remained a clerical and professorial presence in his Flemish homeland, his French friend and collaborator, the abbé de Saint-Cyran, disseminated a more practically oriented spirituality that spread first to the convent of Port-Royal-des-Champs near Paris where he became spiritual director and then, via its abbess, to the influential Arnauld family and from there to the Sorbonne.

The erudite and elite character of this spirituality also helped it find a home among the Benedictines of Saint-Maur and in Pierre de Bérulle's Oratory, a congregation of secular priests devoted to the enhancement of the parish clergy. For it was above all the parish clergy and lay judicial milieu that became the carriers of the movement. France is the only Catholic state where Jansenism put down significant lay bourgeois and even popular urban roots; by the end of the first quarter of the century of lights, whole parishes in Paris as well as in some other northern cities had become "Jansenist" redoubts. Indeed, one historian has even made the Jansenist controversy essential to the formation of the identity of the Parisian bourgeoisie.[18] For the process of purging Paris's parishes of their many Jansenist priests challenged that bourgeoisie's temporal control over these parishes, polititicizing them in the process, while the monarchy's offensive against the spate of miraculous cures and "convulsions" in the parish of Saint-Médard in the late 1720s and 1730s around the tombstone of a deceased opponent of *Unigenitus* further popularized the politicization, notably in quarters such as Saint-Marcel that would later provide the Revolution with so many of its *sans culottes*.[19]

But a reformist movement within the Gallican Church was not by itself a formula for the century-and-a-half-long fratricide that began to occur in the 1640s. Nor does the cause lie entirely in the tension between Bourbon sacral absolutism and the Jansenist denigration of concupiscent majesties. Similar though it was to that of Calvinism, this tension was far more passive and implicit in the Jansenist case. When, late in the eighteenth century, Jansenism spread to Austria, the Italian states, and Spain, it struck up alliances with monarchies at least as absolute as the French one in a common front against the papal curia and its jurisdictional pretensions. But those monarchies had not undergone the ordeal of the French religious wars, nor, in consequence, had their "absolute" authority come to depend on sacrosanctity to quite the Bourbon degree. The most distinctive features of the Bourbon monarchy were its strong religious charge and – hence the intensity and duration of the Jansenist conflict in France – its capacity to transform religious dissent into a challenge to "absolute" authority.

Left entirely to its own devices, the papacy might well not have gone much beyond its first major pronouncement against "Jansenism" in 1653, singling out five propositions for censure without attributing them to Jansen or his book. Yet even that statement came at the demand of the young Louis XIV's first minister Cardinal Mazarin, suspicious of Jansenist complicity in the Fronde and spurred on by Jesuits and their allies in the secular clergy and Sorbonne.[20] A fateful step was taken in 1661 when Mazarin obtained from the papacy a new bull attributing these propositions to Jansen's book and then prevailed upon the Gallican clergy to adopt an oath of adhesion to this bull, requiring the oath of all ecclesiastical benefice holders. Reformulated on its own authority by the papacy in turn in 1665, the Formulary of Alexander VII became a cross for the consciences of those who would not sign it for the remainder of the seventeenth and the entire eighteenth century, beginning with the sisters of Port-Royal and the likes of Arnauld and Quesnel who soon followed Huguenots into exile in the Netherlands.

The decade-long "peace" of Clement IX negotiated between this Pope and Louis XIV in 1669 brought these exiled Jansenists temporarily back to France and enabled the sisters of Port-Royal to calm their qualms by signing the formula with reservations.[21] But then came renewed persecution and still more papal condemnations culminating in the destruction of Port-Royal and the bull *Unigenitus*, again promulgated under pressure from Louis XIV. So set was Louis XIV on obtaining this bull that he promised Clement XI that he would enforce it in France, Gallican liberties or no.

But in 1713 the king had only two more years to live; not even the Sun King's day was eternal. And if *Unigenitus* was to be yet another cross for Jansenists, it was to be a cross for the French monarchy as well. As for Jansenists, *Unigenitus*, unlike previous papal condemnations, unquestionably censored word for word sentences extracted from Quesnel's devotional treatise, making it impossible for Jansenists to argue that the condemnation fell on propositions to which nobody really adhered. Augustinian "truth" seemed roundly condemned by the bull, even in the opinion of the Paris parlement's advocate general who proposed to deposit the bull in the law court's registry as an "eternal monument to the fallibility of the pope."[22] And as for the monarchy, Clement XI not unreasonably took Louis's promise as an invitation to condemn some Gallican as well as Jansenist propositions from Quesnel's book, for the fusion of Jansenism with aspects of Gallicanism was already well under way, even before the advent of *Unigenitus*. But that made the bull even more unacceptable to numbers of French clergy, to say nothing of the Paris parlement, jealous guardian that it was of the traditional – that is, conciliar – Gallican inheritance, enabling the judges to be more Gallican than the king. To be sure, in the two years remaining to him, Louis XIV was able to bludgeon a majority of the clergy into accepting the bull, albeit with added explanations, and the parlement into registering it, although with qualifications. But his death, followed by a vacillatory regency government, gave rise to a crescendo of protestation culminating in 1717 with a formal appeal of *Unigenitus* to a future general or ecumenical council lodged by four Jansenist bishops and adhered to by the majority of Parisian clergy headed by the Archbishop of Paris.

While transforming French Jansenists into formal "appellants" to the higher authority of a council, the appeal as such had nowhere to go, unsupported as it was by either the monarchy, the majority of the Gallican clergy, or any other segment of Catholic Christendom. At best it functioned as a public "witness" to what Jansenists regarded as the "truth" during a period they perceived as one of general apostasy on the part of the Catholic magisterium.[23] The appeal nonetheless further recommended the movement to the Paris parlement, which was the only institution where the appellate principle still maintained any purchase and which also, by 1720, numbered enough Jansenists in its midst to constitute a "party" of sorts.[24]

This endearment was reciprocal. For after the Cardinal de Fleury's rise to power in 1726 the monarchy resumed a policy of persecution toward Jansenists, while the Paris parlement, supported by some provincial parlements, proved to be Jansenism's only reliable institutional source of support.[25] Jansenist theologians as well as barristers thus not unnaturally looked to the parlement's putatively constitutional rights to resist the royal will for a measure of protection, emerging as the most articulate publicists in their defense. Beginning with the "right" to "register" new royal legislative initiatives, these rights had meanwhile taken on a new lease on life in 1715 when the regency government restored the parlement's right to remonstrate against such initiatives before rather than after the act of registration, thereby reversing Louis XIV's edict of 1673 promulgated in reaction to the Fronde.

Although this constitutionalism, like Gallicanism, long antedated the appearance of Jansenism and played a real role in the Fronde, Jansenist publicists so inflected the articulation of this constitutionalism as to make it hard to distinguish the two, "figuring" the parlement in the role of minority mouthpiece of constitutional "truth" in an age of advancing "despotism," just as appellants voiced the truth in an age of general apostasy. In the longer run, this constitutionalism felt the effect of the principle of the appeal and conciliarism, giving birth to an even more radical strain of Jansenist political thought that featured the nation as represented by the Estate General as superior to the monarchy, just as the Church as assembled in a general council was superior to the Pope. And as Jansenism gradually lost its champions among bishops and found itself reduced to lay and priestly effectives, this same conciliarism further legitimized a radically Gallican version of the Church that, precociously condemned in *Unigenitus*, vested infallibility in the whole Church alone, giving a voice in the articulation of dogma not only to parish priests but also to laymen as "witnesses" to the "truth." Thus, in the longer run, the royal and episcopal policy of the persecution of the Jansenists gave rise to a set of arguments limiting both monarchy and episcopacy that, while not always precisely the same as those put forward by Huguenot and Leaguer publicists in an earlier religious conflict, revived and passed on their principal thrust, as the many citations of the work of François Hotman attest. They also conveyed a common conciliar and constitutionalist inheritance to an eighteenth century conceptually prepared to restate them in far more sweeping terms.[26]

In the shorter run, the kind of appeal that was of most practical value for appellants and parlements alike was the appeal *comme d'abus*, the judicial procedure that allowed the royal courts to annul or reform both

actions and judgments by bishops and church courts on appeal in case
of error or "abuse." It was this "appeal" that enabled the parlements
sometimes to intervene on behalf of hard-pressed appellant priests inter-
dicted by their bishops or dying Jansenists publicly refused the last sacraments of the viaticum and extreme unction. In doing so, the parlement
claimed to be enforcing a sacral monarchy's (and outside bishop's) rights
of judicial oversight over all external or public aspects of the Gallican
Church, even against the king's express wishes if need be – and that was
often the case. For that was another aspect of Gallicanism, especially as
interpreted by the king's courts: the right of the state to exercise super-
vision over the administration of the Gallican Church including what
that Church regarded as its most "spiritual" functions. It goes without
saying that Jansenists enthusiastically justified claims that served them in
such good stead. Not the least paradoxical feature of eighteenth-century
Jansenism is its capacity to justify state "absolutism" in relation to the
Church even while it was developing ever more antiabsolutist visions of
the constitutions internal to both Church and State. This was a paradox
that would resurface during the French Revolution in the form of the
Civil Constitution of the Clergy.

But as the monarchy chose bishops for their opposition to Jansenism
and support for *Unigenitus*, the Gallican Church hierarchy grew corre-
spondingly restive under the restraints of this version of Gallicanism.
And the defense of this papal bull of course also aligned them on the side
of the infallible papal authority that had fulminated it as well as against
what passed for or called itself "Gallican." The result was an equal if
opposite paradox: a Gallican episcopacy that grew ever less Gallican and
more propapal or ultramontane as the century of *Unigenitus* went on.
Unigenitus had become a symbol of royal as well as papal authority, it is
true, so that these bishops defended the Bourbon throne in the same
breath as they defended the papal altar. But the authority of the throne
was not the same as that of the state as propounded by the judges and
barristers of the Paris parlement. And the bishops' strident insistence on
the necessary union of throne and altar made it clear enough that they
would take the side of the altar against the throne in the event of any
disunity between the two – as in fact they increasingly did after the king's
council began to try to navigate between the shoals of episcopacy and
magistracy during the crisis-fraught decades of the 1750s and 1760s.

By this time the side of the Jesuits, an ever-more ultramontane episcopacy, and a coterie at court had once again come to be called the *parti
dévot*, while Jansenists never ceased to be accused of crypto-Calvinism

and, truth to tell, were becoming a bit more Protestant-like in certain respects.[27] While this polarized situation obviously recalled the dilemma of the monarchy during the sixteenth-century civil wars of religion, it also curiously anticipated that of Louis XVI as he tried to react to the ecclesiastical legislation of the National Assembly in 1791. For, in contrast to the sixteenth-century religious civil wars which had resulted in the reinforcement of royal Gallicanism, a resacralized monarchy, and a closer union between the king's two bodies, the effect of the conflict over *Unigenitus* was to align fragments of the Gallican heritage against each other, to drive a wedge between the king's person and the state, and ultimately to desacralize the monarchy forever. The irony is that a sacral absolutism that had justified itself by its capacity to make itself an object of devotion above the confessional fray came undone by another religious conflict largely of its own making.

1762 AND THE SUPPRESSION OF THE JESUITS

But the paradoxes of a Gallicanism at loggerheads with the Gallican bishops and the cause of a supposedly monarchical "constitution" at odds with the monarch himself did not wait until 1791 to become flagrant. For both staged a full dress rehearsal in the years around 1762 when the parlements of France led by that of Paris seized the occasion of the monarchy's fiscal discomfiture during the Seven Years' War to dissolve the Society of Jesus in France.

France was of course far from alone among Catholic monarchies in taking it out on the Jesuits in this period, having been beaten to the punch by Portugal in 1759 and then followed by Spain, Parma, and Naples in 1767. Whereupon all of these Bourbon powers led by Spain enforced an anti-Jesuitical "family pact" at the expense of Pope Clement XIV who finally abolished the entire society under strong pressure in 1773. But while everywhere else the monarchs or their ministers took the initiative with the compliance of the vast majority of their bishops, in France it was the parlements that took the field from "below" against the wishes of a majority of pro-Jesuit bishops as well as the Pope, forcing the hand of a reluctant Louis XV to put the royal imprimatur on what they had done in the form of a royal edict in 1764. This incongruously un-Gallican alignment of forces in France thus perpetuated and solidified a pattern that had set in during the Jansenist controversy, especially since 1713. And while in the rest of Catholic Europe the expulsions of the

Jesuits were the cause of no little religious controversy in their wake, importing French religious polarization where there had been none before, in France the end of the society was the result and last chapter of a long religious and political polarization for which the conflict between Jansenists and Jesuits stands as shorthand.[28] For in France the suppression of the Jesuits definitely represented the revenge of the Jansenists, making it possible to perceive in the stones falling on the Jesuits' heads the debris from the demolished abbey of Port-Royal.

It is true that no amount of plotting and planning on the part of the parlementary *parti janséniste* could have set the perfect anti-Jesuit trap: namely, the bankruptcy of the mission in the French West Indies plus the astonishing decision by the French Jesuits to appeal to the Paris parlement a series of adverse decisions on the matter by the consular courts. But from the moment in 1760 that the Jansenist barrister Charlemagne Lalourcé took over the legal direction of the case of the bankrupt creditors and advised them to proceed against the entire society in France rather than against the mission alone, the conduct of the case against the Jesuits remained mainly in the hands of Jansenist judges and barristers, at least where the Paris parlement was concerned.

Once the Jesuits had taken the bait by allowing the case to go to the Paris parlement, it was but a short step for the judges to demand to see and examine the society's constitutions to which all parties had appealed but which, like the decrees of the Council of Trent, had never acquired a legal status in Gallican France. The Paris parlement led by its *parti janséniste* then cleverly circumvented a royal edict designed to save the society by reforming it along Gallican lines. Aided by the intervention of the provincial parlements, which this royal edict ironically forced into action, as well as abetted by Rome's refusal to accept any of the reforms proposed, the parlement was able to bring its own procedure against the Jesuits to a conclusion in 1762. When in November 1764 Louis XV belatedly issued a royal declaration dissolving the society in France while allowing former Jesuits to remain there as "particulars," it was clear that he was only salvaging the principle of royal authority that had been repeatedly flouted over the previous three years.

If being allowed to remain in France as individual "citizens" was in an obvious sense a more moderate treatment than the bodily expulsions sustained by the Jesuits in Spain and Portugal, what happened to the society was in a conceptual sense far more radical in France. For here the secular courts took it upon themselves to dissolve a religious order along with, in effect, the religious vows that defined the Jesuits as regulars.

(When a first edition of the Normandy parlement's printed judgment disingenuously acknowledged that vows were being abolished, the Paris parlement swiftly had it corrected with the formula that it was only the exterior "form" of these vows that was at issue.) The case in favor of the structural dissolution of the society was in part protonationalist or "patriotic": that the special vows sworn to a "foreign" power in the form of the papacy made the society's constitutions incompatible with the fundamental laws of Gallican France. It was not possible, maintained a French pamphleteer in 1774, to give the society a "patriotic spirit"; to the extent that its members were "faithful to their vows, they were not to their country."[29] Along with the sequestration of Jesuit property on the grounds that it had been on loan to the Jesuits by the nation all along, both the "reality" and the rhetoric of the trial of the Jesuits uncannily anticipate the ecclesiastical reforms of the National Assembly, which would need to look no further for arguments in 1790 in order to dissolve all contemplative religious orders along with the clergy as a propertied corps.

If the Gallican case against the Jesuit constitutions anticipated the radical "national" Gallicanism of the Civil Constitution of the Clergy, then the "constitutionalist" case against these same constitutions foreshadowed that of 1789. For fundamental to that case was the contention that the unlimited power given by these constitutions to the Jesuits' general made the notion of Jesuit constitutions close to a contradiction in terms and the society a veritable "monarchy or rather a universal despotism."[30] Elaborated in a four-volume Jansenist-inspired "general history" of the society that shortly preceded and largely informed the parlements' procedure against the Jesuits, the charge that the Society of Jesus was structurally "despotic" and therefore incompatible with the constitution of the monarchy reverberated throughout the trials in all the provincial parlements while becoming a commonplace in the accompanying pamphlet literature. "Such as the Turk is under the law of his Emperor, such as the Negro is under the domination of his slaveholder, such is the Jesuit," charged one anonymous author, "under the scepter of the Sovereign monk."[31] And since the constitutional restraints that distinguished monarchy from "despotism" consisted largely in the rights of registration exercised by the parlements that increasingly justified its resistance to the royal "will" by appealing to that of the "Nation," the "despotism" that the parlements condemned in the form of the Society of Jesus was surely closer to absolute monarchy as it was understood by Louis XV.

While elsewhere it was the monarchs who tried the Jesuits, here it was the trial of the Jesuits that was also in some sense the trial of the monarchy. And while, in permitting, the parlements to destroy the Jesuits, Louis XV reluctantly allowed them to define the monarchy as well as royal religious policy, his grandson Louis XVI would later try to run away from a yet more radically "constitutionalized" redefinition of both.

However unfortunate for the Jesuits, the period of Jansenist revenge narrowly defined was short-lived enough. In retrospect, the suppression of the Jesuits in France was the one of the last battles in a hundred years' war of words and warrants for arrests in which French Jansenists gave far less than they took. During the contentious 40-year period from 1725 to 1765 when the anti-Jansenist alliance of monarchy, Jesuits and pro-*Unigenitus* bishops had been able to do its worst, it had emptied its quivers of 40,000 to 50,000 *lettres de cachet*, replaced Protestants with Jansenists as the single most numerous habitués of the Bastille, repeatedly purged the priesthood, the Sorbonne, and any number of other colleges, seminaries, and university faculties both in Paris and the provinces, while doing as much to religious orders and congregations for men and women alike, suspending the constitutions of some and entirely dispersing others. Nor did laypeople escape the crossfire. In the most unedifying phase of the conflict on the eve of the suppression of the Jesuits, dying laymen and women joined appellant priests as targets of persecution in the form of the public refusal of the sacraments of the viaticum and extreme unction. It was not really until this period that Jansenists were able to turn the tide with the legal assistance from the parlements and – another structural anticipation of the revolutionary division of the clergy – manage to harry priests who obeyed their ecclesiastical rather than temporal superiors temporarily out of the land. The Paris parlement's victory in the refusal of sacraments controversy in 1757 was a prelude to their successful offensive against the Jesuits in the 1760s.

In retrospect, the vindication of the Jansenist cause in the suppression of the Jesuits proved in some sense to be its undoing. While the trial still filled the Palace of Justice's courtyard and galleries with a delirious "public" that also devoured the pamphlets and the parlement's printed sentences against the society, it was to be the last *affaire* capable of galvanizing Parisian "public opinion" apropos of a discernibly Jansenist cause. By destroying the enemies who had come close to defining them, French Jansenists in some sense destroyed themselves as a visible force in the public space. By the time the trial of the Jesuits was over, Voltaire had already successfully mobilized the "public" in favor of a Protestant victim of "religious fanaticism" more generally, while his friend and fellow philosophe Jean Le Rond d'Alembert could plausibly write that it was really "philosophy" that had judged the Jesuits in France, relegating Jansenism to the role of "solicitor."[32] The succeeding decades were to witness a series of judicial *causes célèbres* that, although freely drawing on the constitutional themes and rhetoric of anti-despotism forged in the heat of the Jansenist controversy, mobilized "public opinion" on behalf of quite different and more "Enlightened" causes.[33] And shortly after the event, from 1771 until the end of the reign of Louis XV, Chancellor René-Nicolas Maupeou purged and reformed the parlements in what was widely regarded as a constitutional coup d'état, seriously weakening them as constitutional barriers and bringing back no few ex-Jesuits and exiled anti-Jansenist and sacrament-refusing priests to positions of power.

Yet the very same developments that seem on first reading to be evidence of the waning power of religion and religious controversy in France can simultaneously be read as testifying to their structuring influence over the political culture of the declining ancien régime as well as of the divisions of the Revolution to come. If, as is certain, the French eighteenth century was one of *philosophes* and their "lights" as well as of Jansenists and *Unigenitus*, it makes a difference that in France these lights shone most brightly during a period of increasing rather than decreasing religious conflict. While elsewhere in Europe the cause of "lights" also took shape in reaction to the memory of Reformation-era religious warfare, for French *philosophes* this warfare was an ever-present reality, as the many Jansenists and Jesuits who people Voltaire's philosophical stories attest.

Hence the tripartite division of Jansenist, Jesuit and *philosophe* in France as opposed to the pattern elsewhere in Catholic Europe where what passed as "Jansenist" merged imperceptibly into the cause of "lights." Hence also, in large part, the anti-clerical – in moods, even anti-Christian – character of the French Enlightenment in comparison to the other far softer hues of "lights." This trait would resurface as "dechristianization" during the most radical phase of the French Revolution, in large measure in reaction to the renewal of religious conflict in the form of the division over the Civil Constitution of the Clergy.

But the relation between the Jansenist controversy and the French Enlightenment is politically more positive than merely to have given rise to Voltaire's famous campaign against "superstition," "fanaticism," and the "infamous thing." For when, with the end of the Jesuits, the Jansenist cause sacrificed its galvanizing scapegoat, and political conflict began to assume a more secular cast, *philosophes* found at hand a pair of proto-political–ideological "parties" or formations of religious origin that had already advanced opposing positions on the virtues and vices of absolute or "despotic" authority, on the national or divine origin of sovereignty, and on the legitimate place of corporate orders and religion as a whole within the state. Like hermit crabs, they could begin to make themselves at home and fill out these formations or parties, except that they could also conceptually remodel them as well as enlarge them along the way.[34]

Thus, when in 1771 Chancellor Maupeou perpetrated his anti-parlementary coup, the resultant political controversy displayed many continuities with the preceding *Unigenitus*-related controversies, with Jansenists still orchestrating the lion's share of the "patriotic" protest against ministerial "despotism." Yet here was a controversy of interest to would-be "Enlighteners" who weighed into it on either side, helping to transform the *parti janséniste* into the constitutionalist "patriot party" and the *parti dévot* into a defense of Enlightened if undivided authority. With some alteration, these were also the "parties" and positions that were to inaugurate the prerevolutionary debate on the occasion of the fiscal crisis of the monarchy in 1787.[35]

The political contest into which *philosophes* began to invest themselves more directly in the 1770s was moreover one that had been transformed over the century by the coming of age of "public opinion."[36] If, in the fifteen or so years remaining to the ancien régime, the self-anointed "party of [philosophical] reason" was to prove more adept at shaping and directing public opinion than what remained of the Jansenist interest, the politics of public opinion as such had been largely a Jansenist creation. For Jansenists had pioneered this kind of politics from the time in 1656 when, Antoine Arnauld having lost his case in the Sorbonne, Pascal launched his *Provincial Letters* against the Jesuits, to the time in 1728 when the appellants, having lost their case in the century's only provincial council that ever met in France, launched the clandestine weekly *Ecclesiastical News* and laid their case directly before the "Public . . . all other Tribunals having been closed to them."[37] By the time the *philosophes* directly entered the fray, the monarchy itself had taken to pleading its case before the bar of public opinion, sponsoring about a hundred pamphlets including several by

Voltaire in defense of Maupeou's reforms and in criticism of what was said to be a self-interested and only apparently patriotic "aristocracy."

That is also to say that this absolute sacral monarchy did not emerge unscathed from this hundred years' religious war of words and warrants. If one religious war had given rise to the combination of absolute and sacral monarchy, another of its own making had largely taken it apart in its very own terms. As for the integrity of the "absolute" half of the identity, just about all of its Louis-Quatorzian absolutist monuments had crumbled in the course of the controversy. Besides the privileged place of the Jesuit preacher and confessor at the royal court, this inventory includes the Edict of 1672 curtailing the parlements' right of remonstrance, the 1682 Gallican Declaration wedding the new and old "liberties," the Edict of 1695 protecting ecclesiastical jurisdiction from the parlementary appeal *comme d'abus*, the Declaration of 1730 making *Unigenitus* a law of Church and State – even the Edict of Fontainebleau revoking the Edict of Nantes in 1685. For even Huguenots began to enjoy more de facto toleration after the parlementary victory in the refusal of sacraments controversy in 1757.

As for the sacral side of royal identity, it could hardly have survived the confessional crossfire of the middle of the century, especially after royal religious policy began to tack in the 1750s and 1760s. For while Jansenists, picking up the Huguenot mantle, continued to sacralize the constitutional state at the expense of the king's mortal body, a reborn *parti dévot* began to subject the notorious sexual shortcomings of Louis XV's mortal body to a scurrilous rhetorical barrage that ceded nothing to the one earlier directed against Henry III. And, looking forward, the attacks described by Robert Darnton directed against Louis XVI's supposed impotence and Marie-Antoinette's putative promiscuity only continued in a more secularized vein what began to happen in the 1750s.[38] However much filial affection that the French may have felt toward Louis XVI when he convoked the Estates General in 1788, it was not the awe befitting the king so well celebrated by Bishop Bossuet in "words drawn from Scripture itself."[39] Historians who deny that any desacralization of the monarchy took place in eighteenth-century France seem implicitly to be arguing that, given the chance, Frenchmen would have gladly transformed the monarchy by the grace of God into one by the will of the Nation at any point from 1715 to 1789.[40] To the contrary, it took nothing less than a quasi-religious war under the glare of a century of lights to bring them around to that point.

1791 AND THE FLIGHT TO VARENNES

This time the damage done to sacral monarchy by religion itself turned out to be structural and permanent. That is, the damage done was hardly amenable to reparation in exclusively religious terms. For, given the conceptual possibilities open to the eighteenth century that had been unavailable to the sixteenth, the cost of indulging in something as sordid as a refusal-of-sacraments showdown under the high noon of the French Enlightenment was to have desacralized not only the monarchy but also the sacraments themselves, at least for an important portion of the urban and especially Parisian opinion. When, at the climax of the refusal-of-sacraments controversy, an unbalanced, unemployed, and only technically literate domestic servant "touched" King Louis XV with the blade of a penknife in January 1757, not only did he blasphemously reverse the meaning of the "royal touch" but also articulated his motivation in globally anticlerical – even antisacramental – terms.[41]

Unlike at the end of the sixteenth century, therefore, the road to a redefined monarchy lay only in a literally lay direction, toward terms of "utility" and as the first servant of a sacred *patria* and constitutional state. By reluctantly letting the parlements have their way in pursuit of the Jesuits as well as in the refusal-of-sacraments conflict, even Louis XV chose to remain King of France rather than the first servant of *Unigenitus* or the Jesuits. That his successor was confusedly aware of the choice that lay before the monarchy, as well as how he would decide if he absolutely had to, is suggested by his refusal to take his new "philosophical" controller general Anne-Robert Turgot's advice to transfer the scene of the coronation–consecration ceremony to Paris from Reims and to forgo the oath to rid the realm of heretics.

Like *Unigenitus*, the Civil Constitution of the Clergy was to become the cross of clergy and monarchy alike, while reversing the roles of persecutor and persecuted. Not, to be sure, in the sense of simply reversing *Unigenitus*, for it was not a uniquely Jansenist-inspired ecclesiastical reform. While Jansenists took the lead in justifying it, and although it enforced episcopal residence, instituted clerical elections, nearly nullified papal influence, suppressed uncanonical benefices, restored diocesan synods, and disallowed oaths like the formula of Alexander VII – all of these provisions to Jansenist liking – it also contained numbers of provisions quite alien to Jansenism. And although such measures as the abolition of all contemplative orders, the surgical reduction in the number of dioceses, the complete destruction of the clergy as a corporate order, and the enfranchisement of all "active" citizens as electors of the clergy undoubtedly sat better with deputies of a more "philosophical" cast, the legislation was if anything even less satisfactory to the self-anointedly "Enlightened" community than it was to the Jansenist one. The Civil Constitution thus refracted rather than reflected prerevolutionary religious divisions, dividing the revolutionary "Nation" in new and unpredictable ways.

Above all the Civil Constitution was radically Gallican. That radical Gallicanism consisted above all in the National Assembly's conviction that the sovereign "nation" could take the king's place at the head of the Gallican Church and, as "outside bishop," impose a set of drastic reforms on its own secular authority without any formal involvement or concurrence of the Catholic Church as "spiritual" authority whether in the form of council or papacy. It was that pretension that constituted yet another cross for many Catholic consciences, including even some Jansenist ones. The Civil Constitution is nonetheless a product of Jansenism in the indirect sense that the Gallicanism at work in its making was one that had gone through the wringers of the Jansenist controversy and had come out entirely one-dimensional, refining independent "spiritual" authority into something so ethereal as to be neither here nor there, and flattening out the rest under the jurisdiction of the state. The public justifications for the Civil Constitution therefore differed in no way from earlier Jansenist ones in defense of the Paris parlement's right to intervene in the refusal of sacraments controversy or to dissolve the Jesuits in France, however obviously wider the scope of the National Assembly's ecclesiastical reforms.

But while this radically royal strand in the Civil Constitution's Gallicanism was enough to divide French Catholics against each other, it would not by itself have sufficed to incur papal anathemas if it had come from divine-right royalty rather than from the sovereign authority of the Nation "below." Along with its democratization of the structure of the Church itself, the national source of its authority is what chiefly distinguished the Civil Constitution of the Clergy from the almost equally drastic ecclesiastical legislation of Louis XVI's brother-in-law Joseph II, the Habsburg Holy Roman Emperor, which however never incurred papal censure. An aura of inevitability therefore hangs about Pius VI's condemnation of the Civil Constitution of the Clergy, a degree of probability at least as strong as the papal condemnation of the conciliar tenets of Gallicanism as revived by Jansenism. For not even more moderate ecclesiastical reforms of purely Jansenist inspiration would have escaped papal censure if, similarly emanating from "below," they had contented themselves with instituting clerical elections by clergy and people and reforming the governance of the Church along collegial and deliberative lines. Like Clement XI who used the occasion of *Unigenitus* to condemn the conciliar aspects of Gallicanism as well as Jansenism, so Pius VI was unwilling to condemn the Erastian Gallicanism of the Civil Constitution in the brief *Cum Aliquantum* without also anathematizing the thesis of national sovereignty that authorized and underlay it.[42]

By converting to Catholicism while trying to win Paris in 1593, Henry of Navarre was putting behind him not only the Calvinist Protestantism of his mother but also the "monarchomach" theories vesting ultimate sovereignty in the entire political community with which the Protestant cause had become linked. Unlike his immediate predecessors, Henry IV never convened the realm's Estates General, consigning them to an early death after their penultimate meeting in the wake of his own death in 1610. Yet by choosing Catholicism over Calvinism there can be no doubt that Henry of Navarre was implementing the will of the vast majority of his Catholic subjects, in particular that of his Parisian ones.

By contrast, Louis XVI's choice in favor of refractory Catholicism in 1791 carried with it a set of very different consequences. To be sure, in attempting to flee France on June 21 he was, like Henry IV, also rejecting the thesis of national sovereignty that, in the form of a written constitution, had shackled the royal will to that of a self-anointed National Assembly arisen from the Estates General which he himself had convened. But in linking, as had also Henry IV, this rejection to a choice for a certain kind of Catholicism, Louis XVI was not clearly following the "real" will of the vast majority of his subjects – and even less that of the Parisian citizens who had successfully prevented him from taking mass from a refractory or propapal priest a month or so before. For in the intervening two centuries the monarchy's own religious identity had been one of the causes of religious controversies within French Catholicism itself, a controversy that had come to recapitulate some of the divisions that had earlier separated Catholicism from Protestantism. As a result, a royal choice for a pointedly propapal Catholicism in 1791 had come to be perceived as a choice against a more national Catholicism and indeed France herself. And as a further result, divergent paths between an "Enlightened" France and Catholicism *tout court* had already opened up. In choosing as he did, Louis XVI insured that those paths would diverge much more widely and sooner than they might otherwise have done.

7. The Contested Image: Stage, Canvas, and the Origins of the French Revolution

MARK LEDBURY

Summary

Both the ancien régime and the Revolution are now being explored more intensively by scholars as cultural entities, since both regimes employed specific visual and theatrical rhetoric to sustain their legitimacy and their politics. Well aware of such approaches by historians, Mark Ledbury's very interdisciplinary essay draws on his own investigation of the complexities of genre in the period, and his researches on Greuze and David. It explores some precise examples, in theatre and painting, of the processes of "idealization" (the use of the stage and canvas to project fantasies of society as reportage of preexisting fact), and of "desacralization" (the eroding of the sacredness of institutions vital to the ancien régime). It also explores how various genres of painting and drama in the1760s, 1770s, and 1780s might be understood as reflecting of the confusions, contests, and tensions of the late ancien régime. Nevertheless, the interpretation of artistic productions cannot be limited simply to broader cultural influences, and the essay also argues for the importance of identifying the aesthetic processes at work in paintings and dramas of the era. Their forms coopt popular culture as well as rework elite culture, and we are encouraged to see the political significance of these aesthetic processes. In this approach we see why the conceptualizing of the "public sphere" is so vital to the "cultural explanation" of the Revolution.

Why write about the relationship of the arts to the origins of the French Revolution? Until quite recently, the answer to this question would not have been obvious. There is a deeply engrained tradition in history writing that considers the arts, broadly understood, as nothing but the froth on the waves of social change, change whose currents are always directed by broader political and economic forces. For some historians, mostly seeking causal explanation for the social fact of the Revolution, trends in the arts bear at best a tangential relationship to profound revolutionary upheaval, and tend to be regarded as irrelevant except insofar as they might serve as *symptoms* to highlight the growing confidence of a particular class or to illustrate a preexisting social fact. Furthermore, for many historians there is simply no adequate empirical evidence to demonstrate any causal relationship between the individual products of the cultural sphere of the pre-Revolutionary period and the broader events and processes of the French Revolution. Unlike drought, economic hardship, tax imposition, or food shortage, and unlike specific and widely circulated documents such as Necker's *Compte rendu au roi* or the *Declaration of the Rights of Man*, the effect of cultural productions such as paintings or plays can seem beyond the reach of verifiable empirical analysis – simply too contingent to stand themselves as *causes* of agitation, uprising or revolution.

Historical scepticism about the importance of cultural production to social change has also been based on a belief that painting, theater, and literature were essentially an elite concern, touching only a small minority of the French population and remote from popular culture. Painting in particular can be seen as part of the Paris-centred economy of luxury, and thus an irrelevance for the vast majority, grappling with problems of subsistence, justice, and social order. The ticket prices at the *Comédie-Française* were mostly beyond the means of the urban poor, and the debates and disputes which dominated it seemed more like intellectual parlour games than matters of pressing political relevance or even presentiments of revolution.

This empirically and socially based scepticism persisted while the social (often Marxist-derived) model of pre-Revolutionary origins held a tight grip on frameworks of understanding. But in recent years, as part of a shift away from purely social explanations of the French Revolution, which others in this book have discussed, historians have begun to think again about the importance of "culture" understood broadly as the spectrum ranging across literature, drama, the visual arts (from painting to the popular print), costume, decoration, even habit and ritual. This has led historians to reinvestigate a wide variety of material, including pictures and plays, seeing them as indications and representations of ideas, ideals, and dreams which might be of relevance to our understanding of how and why the French Revolution happened. Historians are not alone: the earlier model of disinterested connoisseurial scholarship and patrician disdain for the social context that once characterized the discipline of art history has now been replaced by much more historically and socially aware frameworks.[1] There is now a significant overlap of scholarly enquiry between social, political, and cultural historians from various disciplines, which means that today's students of the French Revolution can learn much from the art history and literature shelves.

THE CULTURAL SPHERE AND THE ORIGINS OF THE REVOLUTION

In some ways, the new emphasis on the cultural sphere in our understanding of the origins of the French Revolution is logical. In the past 30 years, the French absolute monarchy that was overthrown by the Revolution has itself come to be understood as underpinned by performance and spectacle. Scholars from a variety of points of view have examined with rigor and originality the place of representations and performances (dramatic, visual, rhetorical and political) in the culture of the Court, especially during and after the reign of Louis XIV. Recent work has pointed to the ways in which the system of absolutism might be understood as a sphere of representations, where form, protocol, hierarchy, and ritual, as well as rhetoric and self-representation, played crucial roles.[2] The conduct of war and diplomacy, and the administrative organization of the state, still maintain their relevance to historians, but now we also examine how the regime defined itself by, amongst other things, triumphal entries, the *lit de justice*, garden design, coronations, announcements of births, and the daily rituals of the Court, as well as theatrical tragedy and grand schemes of historical and mythological painting. These formed a language of spectacle, in which appearance and performance became crucial signifiers of power, rank, and hierarchy.[3] If we accept this line of argument, that absolutist politics in their French form were, in part at least, a "theatrical–spectacular" phenomenon, a culture of representations, we can see that the cultural realm might become a particularly interesting place to explore challenges, tensions, and modulations that led to the demise of that regime.

At the same time, current historians of the Revolution have paid more attention than the generations before them to the crucial role of festivals, symbolism, dress, and other codes of behavior and ritual to the Revolutionary process. As the idea of identity-formation has assumed greater importance – how groups of people with a stake in the Revolution (Jacobins, *sans-culottes*, counterrevolutionaries in the Vendée, etc.) defined themselves, asserted their communal ties and allegiances, understood themselves – historians have turned to costume, visual representation, and the expressive arts for clues. It is unsurprising that in seeking the origins of revolutions, historians have increasingly looked to changes in the complex pattern of cultural representation in the last years of the ancien régime for an understanding of the formation and importance of this Revolutionary cultural sphere.[4]

In this chapter I shall point to a few of the ways that the sphere of cultural representation (visual art and drama, principally) might be seen as a useful place to explore Revolutionary origins and understand pre-Revolutionary and Revolutionary changes:

- I argue that representations of all kinds, whether scenes of everyday life, portraits of powerful people, grand-scale paintings of events, or caricatures, might be seen not merely as depictions, but in fact as *actors* in the political processes that lead to Revolution;
- I show how art and drama provided spaces for alternate ways of thinking about society and politics, about people's relationship to power and people's relationships to each other. Following on from this, I focus on aesthetic quarrels and disputes, seeing them as a kind of acting out in culture of more general tensions and debates about the state of the nation which occurred in the latter half of the eighteenth century in France.

BEYOND DESCRIBING – ART, IDEAS, AND IDEALS

No representation in art or literature can be viewed as innocent, transparent, or neutral. A picture of a peasant interior, for example, cannot be seen as a faithful depiction of preexisting material or social conditions; it must be investigated according to the history of such representations in art, in the context of its contemporary public, and in relation to other representations of such interiors in literature, theater, music, and the other arts. Greuze's painting of 1761, known as *The Village Betrothal* or *The Marriage Contract* (Illustration 7.1), is one of the most

Illustration 7.1 *Jean-Baptiste Greuze*, The Village Betrothal *(oil on canvas, 92 × 117 cm, 1761: Louvre, Paris)*
Photo: RMN/ART RESOURCE.

renowned representations of a rustic interior in later eighteenth-century France. The painting shows a group of people gathered in a modest domestic space, involved in a family moment of exchange and a legal ceremony. The seemingly realistic appearance of the slightly rough and worn surfaces of the floorboards, walls, and furniture, and the attention to details of costume and accessory seem to hint at a kind of *reportage* of a real incident and it is tempting to explore this image as a "representation" of an event. But we must resist this temptation. This painting belongs to a *tradition* which is sometimes known as "genre painting," one which takes as its subject the depiction of scenes of domestic life often of the middling sort or the labouring classes, urban or rural, one which flourished in the seventeenth century in the low countries, and which gained new popularity in the later eighteenth century in France.[5] Greuze was aware of these traditions as he created the scene, just as he was aware of the repertoire of symbolic and formal languages of art, which prompted him to paint a hen and her chicks in the left foreground and thereby symbolize the relationship between the mother and her daughter, and the future role of the bride. Other traditions and examples may have led him to create a triangular (or pyramidal) composition linking all his figures, a structure which is common to the grandest paintings of history and mythology and the popular print.[6] In this sense, it is not a transparent representation of a social scene at all, but a carefully crafted, one might even say staged, picture. In the context of pre-Revolutionary history, once we recognize that this picture is a construction rather than an illustration, we must investigate *why* it was constructed as it was, and what impact its display might have had. Ultimately we may realise that it does not so much describe a scene as *assert* ideas and even ideals.

The first and obvious thing to note is that Greuze depicts a serious, solemn scene, not the drinking, dancing, or merrymaking surrounding a wedding that might have featured in paintings of this type a century before. This is a clear reference to the new status accorded to common folk which artists and writers were beginning to advocate. Greuze's peasants are exemplary peasants, two loving, generous, sincere, responsible, and law-abiding families of the "upper peasantry" or modest provincial bourgeoisie, coming together in a morally uplifting moment of union and happy exchange. These anonymous people, the picture asserts, can provide all the emotional drama, seriousness, and moral lessons that previously might have been learned through the tales of "great men," heroes, and kings. The peasant and the lowly bourgeois are not now the figures of comedy but of serious drama. In Greuze's painting his perfectly joined families are also a model of modesty, respect, and probity. There is modesty in the subtle, nervous gestures of mother and daughter, modesty in the lack of extravagance of the purse which symbolizes the dowry, modesty in the sober-toned clothing and footwear. There is respect in the deference of the posture and glance of the bridegroom towards his father-in-law, and probity as well as generosity in the father-in-law's overseeing of this crucial operation of good family order. The very lack of extravagance is vital: Greuze has made a spectacle out of virtue and decorum, one which challenges the culture of spectacular adornment, luxury, dubious sexual conduct, and fiscal extravagance which had been reflected in the genre painting of the previous generation, and was already in the early 1760s starting to be criticized by the new rhetoric of virtue.

Although pictured in a rural milieu, the characters in Greuze's painting resemble the perfectly worthy mercantile citizens of Michel-Jean Sedaine's near contemporary *Le Philosophe sans le savoir* (written in 1761 and 1762 but performed in 1765). This was the most successful of the new type of dramas which emerged on the French stage at mid-century and which were much contested, much debated, and encountered much resistance of an institutional, political, and aesthetic nature.[7] Diderot's blueprint for a theater of virtue, in which new situations and emotive spectacle could be created from the "conditions" of the lives of ordinary people, was a fundamental development in the history of modern drama. Diderot's theatrical aesthetic was one designed to question and contest the conventions of the traditional court stage to allow the theatrical representation of the anonymous family and the domestic sphere to become the space for articulation of new moral and political imperatives.[8] Although Diderot's own plays on this new model did not meet with universal critical or popular acclaim,[9] Sedaine's *Le Philosophe sans le savoir* made a resounding success of this new kind of drama of civic life. Sedaine in it created a paradigm of probity, philosophic virtue, and enlightened paternity in the character of his protagonist Vanderk, and then forced him into a terrible dilemma by the device of his son's virtuously intentioned but misguided entanglement in a duel. Nowhere in the play (except in the title) does Sedaine actually use the word *philosophe* but instead he accumulates examples of Vanderk's exemplarity: his financial and domestic probity is highlighted – most notably in a scene in which he prepares his daughter's wedding feast, (I, iv) in conjunction with Antoine, his servant, aide, and confidant, who is given enormous importance in the drama, and whose role Sedaine himself used to act in private performances of the drama.[10] Vanderk makes outspoken comments on the benefits of commercial cosmopolitanism (II, v) and advises his daughter, Victorine, on decorum. Sedaine balances his didacticism with humour and spectacle, but there can be no doubting the care and deliberateness with which he establishes a familial circle of virtue as a kind of *tableau*. Like Greuze, he constructs a careful and idealized image of domestic virtue, while maintaining or seeking to maintain a fiction of a preexisting reality into which the audience is "peering."

An uncertainty of status pervades Sedaine's drama and characterizes the central figures; the identity of Vanderk, the main protagonist, is never clarified or satisfactorily explained. This uncertainty, together with the repeated use of disguises and misunderstandings and the virtue inherent in the servant figure, Antoine, all seem to point to a strong advocacy of human mutuality, what we might perceive as an ideological move not to show "antagonism," but a vision of universality, founded on a discreet confusion, even hybridization of "*états*." Along with this goes an insistence on viewing received social hierarchies as contingent "prejudices," thus clearing the way for imagining a different order, one based on innate virtue, on a sense of a wider humanity. For modern sensibilities this may seem rather weak and nebulous as a political message, but enlightened universalism was a rather radical proposition in the context of the hierarchical understandings of rank and worth which were so much a feature of ancien-régime culture. No less than Brutus (to whom Sedaine compares his protagonist in a preface to one of the sections of the play censored by the authorities), Vanderk is an *exemplum*, an example and model of virtue. This was, undoubtedly, political theater, and Sedaine's success emboldened others, including Beaumarchais and Louis-Sébastien Mercier, who wrote several of these "citizen dramas." Mercier went on to compose a radical theatrical reform pamphlet, *Du théâtre*, in 1773, published in outright opposition to the *Comédie-Française* and in the wake of the parlement disputes, which established a clear relationship between theatrical reform and political reform.[11]

The new ideals of fatherhood, motherhood, charity, self-sacrificial virtue, as well as breast-feeding, filial duty, domestic economy, and many of the other themes beloved of the *philosophes* certainly found their way into visual and dramatic culture and became a fixture after the 1760s.[12] In our own time, when bourgeois morality has triumphed and when such morality is often seen as deeply conservative and oppressive, it is difficult to appreciate just how far the spectacular envisioning of the virtuous, modest, and well-run home and altruistic acts was a radical step. It implicitly critiqued habits associated with corruption at Court, provided an alternative to the "over-sophisticated" and selfish lifestyle of the wealthy, and thus contributed vitally to the development of that discourse of radical virtue which was such a trademark of Revolutionary politics. The arts envisioned ideals, and it was this envisioning quality, rather than any reportage function, which made them so powerful.

THE PUBLIC SPHERE AND CULTURE

Historians might legitimately ask how Greuze's painting or Sedaine's drama could possibly have imprinted the ideas and ideals they promoted on the minds and imaginations of their time if they were simply painted for a private individual or given in private performance. We know that Greuze's patrons were often aristocratic and that Sedaine's dramas were favorites in some noble circles, and this might tempt us to reject any possible oppositional resonance to these works.[13] Yet the reason we can discuss the impact of a painting or drama is because the history of their creation and display links them to the newly developing public sphere of later eighteenth-century France. Recent accounts of the later eighteenth century and the Revolution owe some kind of debt to a crucial concept, which emerged from work in political theory: the notion of the "public sphere" (*Öffentlichkeit*) as elaborated by Jürgen Habermas. Although Habermas's hypotheses and conclusions have often been disputed, the theorization of a bourgeois public sphere demonstrably in development in the pre-Revolutionary years has proved useful to historians exploring links between society, politics, and culture.[14] The public sphere might be described as a real or virtual space of debate, discussion, and contest, a space created by the rapid growth in pamphlet journalism, newspaper and journal circulation, and the mushrooming of public forums for aesthetic, philosophical and political engagement (the multiplication of theaters, the increasing size, scope, and popularity of exhibitions of painting, the proliferation of informal gatherings of intellectuals, etc.).[15] Whereas Habermas and Roger Chartier in their evocation of a public sphere of exchange of opinions and ideas placed their central emphasis on the importance of the diffusion of print and reading, others more recently have insisted that signs of crucial transferences of power in the pre-Revolutionary epoch can be fruitfully explored through analysis of image and performance.[16]

In the case of painting, sculpture, and engraving, the principal public cultural space was the *Salon carré* of the Louvre, the location of the biennial public art exhibitions organized by the *Académie royale de peinture et de sculpture*, in which members of the Academy would show their work, and which was frequented by large numbers of Parisians[17] (see Illustration 7.2). Greuze's painting was part of a spectacular public event lasting six weeks or more, in front of which people could gather and exchange views, opinions, and observations. In this sense the painting was just the starting point, the spark which ignited discussion, as is partially revealed in the genre of discourse that these exhibitions spawned: art criticism. This new kind of writing came about as observers started to respond to the paintings, commenting on their merits and faults in pamphlets (often published anonymously and hawked outside the exhibition) and a proliferating range of journals. In these commentaries, the picture often served to prompt a more wide-ranging, philosophical, often satirical and sometimes overtly political discussion; these pamphlets circulated in ever greater numbers, being avidly read by nervous administrators and curious artists, as well as visitors to the *Salon*.[18] It is significant that at this moment art belonged in the public realm and was open to free scrutiny. The *Salon* and the discourses and spin-offs it fostered (including the circulation of engraved reproductions of paintings of later eighteenth-century France) means that paintings can be analyzed as part of that wider explosion in public culture so vital to our understanding of the growth of revolutionary sentiment.

Theater had always been a prominent part of this public culture and the new dramatic genres pioneered by Diderot, Sedaine, and others are not just to be seen as part of literary history, but as experiments which challenged the traditional role of theater as upholder of the values of the Court and nobility. They were also fuel for public debate, and even catalysts for institutional reform – it is not coincidental that it was writers of new genres of drama, including Sedaine, Beaumarchais, and Mercier, who most powerfully advocated reform of theatrical institutions, new rights for authors, and other changes which challenged the world of state-run theater in later eighteenth-century France. Theater was the space of energetic, argumentative gatherings, especially in the standing room or *parterre*, where the wits and advocates and enemies of new plays would gather. The *parterre* has been seen by some as a model for the tensions and the possibilities of the public sphere.[19] Here, after all, was a space of instant feedback, (in the shape of more or less witty repartee) but also a place where cabals could gather, and often did, to argue and

Illustration 7.2 *Gabriel de Saint-Aubin*, Vue du Salon du Louvre en 1753 *(engraving, reproduced from E. Dacier,* Gabriel de Saint Aubin, *2 vols., Paris, 1929: author's collection)*

militate against plays and plots or actors and actresses. And in the case of Beaumarchais's *Marriage of Figaro*, a drama which has been the subject of much debate recently about whether or not its brilliant sallies, diatribes, and mockeries add up to a coherent pre-Revolutionary politics, it could almost be said that its major importance was precisely as a catalyst for debate and opinion, and Beaumarchais was a brilliant manipulator of the public sphere: his drama, on which "everyone has an opinion," spawned imitations, songs, parodies, jokes, and arguments which made it resonate far beyond the words contained in its text.[20]

Only by understanding the *Salon* and the *parterre* as a space where people began to formulate a political as well as an aesthetic discourse, where the aesthetic and the political were intertwined in debate, can we understand how Jacques-Louis David's *Oath of the Horatii* (see Illustration 7.3) has come to be viewed as a politically charged painting. This was a piece commissioned by the king's arts administration, the *Bâtiments du roi*, the product of a state-sponsored program engineered by its director, the comte D'Angiviller, to raise the cultural status of France through a revival of large-scale heroic painting of ancient history, mythology, and epic, a genre known as history painting). This was seen as the most elevated form of painting, the one which reflected the goals of the regime. Like tragedy on stage, it was to be the highest form of painterly expression and would serve the needs of the king and the nation. However, once thrust into the public domain of the *Salon*, David's painting was transformed – appealing to a different crowd, a politically sensitive, even oppositional one. The subject matter was not intrinsically radical, and was well known to French audiences through Corneille's *Horace* (over a century old by then) and through the much-circulated sourcebook of Roman history, Plutarch's *Lives*.

However, it was the way David treated the subject matter that distinguished this picture from others and attracted a group of "dissident critics."[21] In the 1760s Greuze had created a spectacular, seductive language of virtue, presenting an example of domestic good management and happy togetherness of families in a virtuosic way stressing harmony, naturalness, and fluidity, in handling as well as subject matter. David's painting presented a very different scenario, stressing tensions, conflicts, muscularity, violence, and the necessary cruelties of military combat, using severe architectural forms, echoed by uncompromising stiffness in the male figures and contrasted with a lifeless fluidity in the female figures. By this time, the language of virtue was oppositional – not implicitly but explicitly opposing itself to the frivolities, luxuries, and flippancy

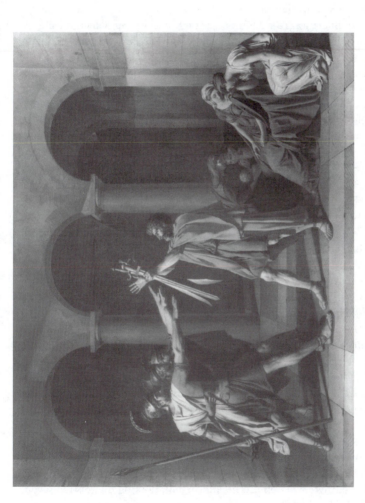

Illustration 7.3 *Jacques-Louis David*, The Oath of the Horatii *(oil on canvas, 330 × 425 cm, 1785: Louvre, Paris)*

Photo: RMN/ART RESOURCE.

of current culture. Where Greuze's *Village Betrothal* had been fluid and crowded with figures and details, David's picture was deliberately sparse, spare, even stiff. Tradition was used somewhat aggressively too: David had returned to Rome to finish the picture, and displayed it there first, sending it late to the Parisian Salon. Rather than integrate the sculptural, architectural, and literary learning that he had gained during his Italian studies into his picture in subtle and pleasing ways, as he might have been expected to by his academic mentors, he exceeded the stipulations on canvas size, chose a moment not previously depicted by any writer or artist, and foregrounded the "classicizing" elements of his picture, not in smooth ways but in troubling ones.

The *Oath of the Horatii* shows the three Horatii brothers swearing to fight to the death as champions for Rome against the Curatii brothers, as their father hands them their swords. David ensures that the spectators are also reminded that the brothers are bound by ties of love to the Curatii family, and so this noble gesture of patriotic volunteering is also a deadly one which will cleave family bonds and create conflicts of multiple kinds between love and patriotic duty. This alone gave the subject something new and vital, as David refigured the terrible beauties of Corneille on canvas, but it was the vigour, muscularity, stark contrasts, and severe stylistic bravado of the picture which seemed to enthuse "radical" critics and disconcert conservative ones. It appears to be a disciplined picture, which should have gladdened the hearts of the administrators who had been encouraging their new generation of artists to inject vitality into French history painting by imitation of the antique. Yet on closer inspection there is something troubling and overemphatic about the geometries – whether of the architecture of the columns, or of the insistent triangular structures formed out of the slightly overstretched legs of the brothers standing rather improbably and nebulously together, and the lifelessly drooping women on the extreme right or the startling but slightly incorrect positioning of the three hands and the three swords. Voids play an important part here too: the gloom of the background; the strange lack of domestic detail which makes the location uncertain. This is an interior space and it appears to be a family space, yet there is no object, no adornment, nothing that distracts from the immediate human drama. It was the creation of a vocabulary clearly derived from ancient art and sculpture, but at the same time uncanny, "incorrect," and intense, that created the impression of emotional immediacy, frontality, and immediacy. This starkness, an excited and muscular assertion of virtue, and a lack of compromise was noted by some observers as a sign of values associated with notions of patriotism and radical virtue – and thus opposition to frivolity and excess – and this is what has allowed historians to link it with the radicalization of the public sphere taking place in the 1780s, in the wake of scandals like the Kornmann affair.

The absence of decorative detail, and the starkness of the setting, also helped David emphasize what has been called "the eloquent body" in the *Oath of the Horatii*, and this stark gestural and corporeal eloquence might be seen as itself a harbinger of the ways in which the Revolution sought to embody (give bodily form to) their values and ideals during the Revolution. It was artists who could provide corporeal distillations of virtue or patriotism through the various languages of the visual – the combination of formal and compositional allusion to antique ideals and the emotional intensity of the frozen "tableau" of pathos, recognition or revelation. This particular combination would be a staple of Revolutionary political rhetoric, and during the years 1789–94, David was asked on many occasions to articulate in paint, in morally edifying and emotionally affecting ways, the stakes of the Revolutionary effort. The depiction of the Revolutionary body in portraits of slain martyrs for the Revolution, in work such as David's *The Last Breath of Marat* (1793, Musées Royaux, Bruxelles) or *Death of Bara* (1794, Musée Calvet, Avignon), produced at moments of significant political pressure and functioning for political purpose, use an emotive, compressed, and intensified language of the body to crystallize a sense of struggle, loyalty, and revolutionary identity.[22]

THE POLITICS OF CULTURE

In finding political resonance in the aesthetic disputes around the *Oath of the Horatii*, historians reveal how writing about the arts and writing about politics slide into one another. But this painting was by no means an isolated example of this slippage from the aesthetic to the political. Historians of other forms of culture have proposed similarly political readings of ostensibly aesthetic debates in the culture wars of the latter half of the eighteenth century in France. The *querelle des bouffons*, for example, which divided the intellectual and musical establishment in France during the 1750s, is no longer seen simply as a dispute about musical genre, but as a precursor of the debates about national identity, patriotism, and even liberty so crucial to Revolutionary consciousness.

In 1752 the Paris Opera invited a company of Italian singers for a residence, to perform Italian-style opera buffa, including Pergolese's *Serva Padrona*. This Italian music seemed pleasing, graceful, and natural, and made the "establishment" French model of music theater, the *tragédie en musique*, seem dull and dated. Jean-Jacques Rousseau, composer as well as philosopher and the author of some of the most influential music articles for the *Encyclopédie*, was the most fervent and high profile "pro-Italian." Rousseau's stance earned him the fury of many, and he was burned in effigy at the Opéra by musicians who feared that the Italians would put them out of a job. The controversy threatened to lead to imprisonment for Rousseau but, more pertinently here, there was a concerted effort by government-hired hack writers to denigrate the "*philosophes*" and their views, in pamphlets and satires. Scholars have identified patterns of similarity between this controversy and key political and theological debates, such as those over Voltaire's views on religion, or the Parliaments' opposition to papal bulls on Jansenism. Culture was a space where views could be expressed more vehemently, and with less danger of arrest, while at the same time the subliminal messages of a more overtly contestatory, even political nature could easily be read.[23]

PICTURING MONARCHY

Another productive area in the search for clues as to the importance of the visual in understanding pre-Revolutionary tensions is the way that royal figures, and by extension the *idea* of monarchy, was represented in the latter half of the eighteenth century. One useful line has been to explore how kingship is visualised in royal portraiture and iconography.[24] I will focus on three examples of the representation of royalty from many which have drawn the attention of scholars of the visual and the dramatic.

Representations of Henri IV and the uses of his image in the art and drama of the later years of the ancien régime supply some evidence of the process of "desacralization" (a progressive erosion of the seemingly god-given and even divine qualities that the monarchy had sought to assert for itself) which Dale Van Kley and Roger Chartier have highlighted as a key phenomenon of the pre-Revolutionary period.[25] A version of this fabled king, whose myth, founded on a simplicity and "poule au pot" populism contrasted sharply with the rhetoric of Louis XV, appeared on stage, lost in the woods, stripped of entourage, but virtuous, concerned, and just, in Sedaine's 1762 *opéra comique*, *Le Roi et le fermier*, and in a different guise in Charles Collé's near-contemporary *La Partie de chasse de Henri IV* (1764). These portrayals suggest how understandings of the shortcomings and corruptions of the court were to be perceived, and the very fact of representation of the king without entourage, without spectacle, without splendour, might be seen as an indication of an attack on the entire rhetoric of royal spectacularity. Appearing toward the end of the unsuccessful Seven Years' War, these were strikingly different and non-martial models of kingship, designed, in the face of military defeat, to remodel what ideal kingship might be. Both Sedaine and Collé worked within the censorship regimes and the carefully controlled theatrical scene of their day, and neither presented an attack on royal injustice or court extravagance in overt terms, although Sedaine's play certainly contained thinly veiled criticism of the court. They did, however, demystify royalty. Sedaine's aim was not in any ostensible way subversive or anti-monarchic and, in bringing the king into the humble living room of the forester and into the domestic conversations and jokes of a family, his intention was to show the innate goodness and sense of justice of the king. However, in a culture that linked display and power, this very "domestication of majesty," to use Schama's term,[26] the monarch, his representation, devoid of any trappings of splendor, in a spartan domestic setting, in a dialogue of ironic confusion assumes its own meaning, and might be analyzed as part of a process of erosion of aura.

Sedaine's play reached the stage, stripped of explicit references to Henri IV and his ministers and thus less sensitive for existing regimes who right up to the Revolution were to suffer by comparison with the perceived "good king" or "people's king." It was condoned by the authorities who perhaps realized the need to give monarchy a new, softer image. Collé's *La Partie de chasse d'Henri IV*, though performed in noble and court settings in the early 1760s, was effectively blocked from theatrical performance in Paris, and not performed on the public stage until after the death of Louis XV. The fate of the two dramas in some ways points to the crucial tensions in the reigns of Louis XV and Louis XVI – the agendas of the *philosophes*, the pressures of the public sphere, provoked a wavering between majesty and domesticity, between the need to maintain all the pomp, authority, and dignity of a complex and long-established code of royal representation, and the attempt to propagandize the monarchy according to the new ideals of family togetherness, sentiment, and benevolent virtue.

The second example, from a later moment and in a different medium, is François-Guillaume Menageot's *The Death of Leonardo da Vinci in the Arms of François I* (1781) (see Illustration 7.4). This picture, the runaway success of the Salon exhibition of 1781, was a state commission designed, perhaps, as an allegory of enlightened royal patronage. Yet at its center was a scene which owed its vocabulary as much to the tender leave-takings of Greuze as to the heroic model of Poussin's *Death of Germanicus*. In it, another well-regarded king, François I, was represented in what can only be described as an intimate and emotional moment, leaning as tenderly as one of Greuze's young sons over the bearded and patriarchal figure of Leonardo da Vinci, who, as the title of the painting in the Salon guide made clear, could be regarded as *"l'homme le plus universel de son siècle."* Here the artist is the hero, the universal man, and the king, however virtuous, noble, and concerned, plays a (literally) supporting role. Not that of the glorious monarch or father of the people, but one more akin to that played by the figures of dutiful sons, nurses, and mothers from the genre images of previous Salons such as Greuze's *Filial Piety* from 1763. Ostensibly this image is a positive, virtuous one of generous support and magnanimity, but in the process the king has lost primacy, being decentralized (if not desacralized),and while the painting was intended to be an allegory of the beneficent art patronage of the French monarchy, the result seemed (oddly) to place the monarch in a no-man's-land – neither the well-loved paterfamilias, nor the splendid military hero.[27]

Another telling hesitation surrounding a royal portrait occurred in the Salon of 1787, during a period of increased political and social tensions, around the time of the Assembly of Notables furore, and during the exile of the Paris parlement. In 1785 a young Swedish artist, Adolf-Ulrich Wertmüller, had displayed an unsuccessful portrait of the by-now-deeply unpopular queen, Marie-Antoinette, strolling in Versailles – it had been seen as inappropriate by many hostile commentators and failed miserably to make the Queen seem human. Elizabeth-Louise Vigée-Lebrun, who had become one of the favorite royal portraitists and would paint 30 portraits of the queen in the ten years before her execution, was that commissioned to complete a portrait of *Marie-Antoinette and her Children* (see Illustration 7.5). However, the turbulent conditions of 1787 led the administration initially to withhold the portrait from the Salon, for fear that it might provoke "the outrage of an excited populace," before finally displaying it for fear that its absence would provoke "really offensive suspicions."[28] This incident reveals the bind in which the monarchy found itself – it was dangerous to display itself, and

Illustration 7.4 *François-Guillaume Ménageot,* The Death of Leonardo da Vinci in the Arms of François I *(oil on canvas, 278 × 357 cm, 1781: Musée de l'hôtel de Ville, Amboise)*

Illustration 7.5 *Elizabeth-Louise Vigée-Lebrun,* Marie-Antoinette and her Children *(oil on canvas, 264×208 cm, 1787: Musée National du Chateau, Versailles)*

dangerous to hide from display – and demonstrates the extent to which the power of the critical public had grown and the authority of the monarchy had waned, and how such tensions crystallized in the visual image. The picture divided and still divides critics, but it was clear that Vigée-Lebrun's considerable skills had been enlisted to make the queen the object both of attachment (her daughter looks admiringly at her while caressing her, as the object of tender filial devotion) and of admiration (the viewer is supposed to admire her calm connectedness and control as she delicately controls her distracted youngest son and holds him close on her knee, unafraid of intimate contact but dignified and maternal). Those "happy mothers" and dutiful breastfeeding matriarchs who had been staples of the print culture which supported the reformers' aggressive use of dutiful motherhood had effectively set the agenda here, whatever the references to Rubens and to nativity scenes. However, Vigée-Lebrun was also careful to tug at heartstrings by having the eldest son point to the empty crib of the recently deceased princess Sophie, so that the queen is represented as stoically grieving as well as skilfully maternal, deserving sympathy and compassion. The portrait works in a pregnant void; relies on an absence rather than insisting on spectacular presence. In the end, this is a reactive not an assertive portrait, demonstrating the ways in which royalty was forced to give a different image of itself, one which emphasized not glory but restrained sensibility and virtue, but also allowing us to probe tensions in its mixed registers and in the checkered history of its display.

This portrait cannot be fully explained without an excursus into an entirely different register of visual material, an extreme form of desacralization which has attracted much attention among historians of pre-Revolutionary culture: pornography and bodily satire. The circulation of erotic pleasures of voyeurism via the print market, clandestine books, and the staging of "erotic" dramas and parades in the pre-Revolutionary decades has already been the subject of many studies.[29] It is clear that Marie-Antoinette was the centre of many pornographic tales of incest, lesbianism, and nymphomania.[30] Pornography could also ridicule and destabilize institutions such as the Church, which found its official image distorted and parodied in the most cruel and crude of ways, caught up in a complex economy of lubricity. Robert Darnton observes:

> We consider *Du contrat social* political history and the *Histoire de Dom B* . . . pornography. But the bookmen of the eighteenth-century lumped them together as "philosophical books": If we try to look at their material in their way, the seemingly self-evident distinction between pornography and philosophy begins to break down.[31]

Thus, we might ask if the *Histoire de Dom B* . . . and *Thérèse Philosophe* might be seen as part of a continuum with the "ideas" literature of later eighteenth-century France, and treated as significant actors in challenging preexisting images of authority.[32] Given the pervasiveness of the pornographic in pre-Revolutionary culture, we do have to engage with the significance and resonance of the pornographic mode. We might want to see pornography as the *"revers de la médaille"* (other side of the coin) of the effort to promote what is outlined above as the "virtuous ideal," and the attempt by the monarchy to subscribe to these values. If one branch of visual culture was idealizing, heroicizing, a virtuous body, embodying ideals and inscribing beliefs, another, opposite branch, pornography, relentlessly used configurations of the sexualized body (of the wayward, oversexed priest or lesbian queen, for example) to pillory the Church, court, and other figures of authority. In the *Histoire de Dom B . . .* readers and viewers could see, explicitly presented, the spectacle of a priest engaged in acts of violent buggery. Pornography is not just about the process of desacralization; it is an active degradation of existing "models" of authority, by submitting their incorporated, fantasized bodies to relentless repeated obscenity. And Marie-Antoinette's body was also submitted to this treatment in print – in works penned and illustrated in the late 1780s.[33]

FIGHTING OVER THE BODY

Whatever else it may be, pornography is a discourse of the body. In the current post-Foucauldian and, more anecdotally, body-obsessed climate, it is perhaps not surprising that the body as a disputed site, as a carrier of symbolic meaning, of semiotic force, has become a fertile focus for an understanding of power and politics in the late ancien régime and Revolution. Historians have increasingly had to look to the field of representation – on stage, on canvas, in taverns, at festivals, and in dress and ephemeral images (on bills, coinage, etc.), to chart the way the body is depicted, signified, and understood. Historians are also more drawn to those ways and spaces in which the Revolution acted *on* the body. It is the execution of the king, rather than his trial, which is the focus of Lynn Hunt's *Family Romance of the French Revolution* This scrutiny of the body in culture relies on a belief in representation and the creation of images as in some way an agent as well as a symptom. In other words, the body is *formed* in images, not just depicted. The "battle of the bodies" between an official, decorous, maternal body in official representations of Marie-Antoinette, and a lewd, explicit, sexualized and out-of-control body in pornographic or other unofficial images is a major focal point of a battle to bolster or discredit the very concept of absolute monarchy. Such battles over bodies would also characterize Revolutionary politics, as different moments brought different and competing ideas about how to represent France (the "Hercules or Marianne" dilemma explored by Lynn Hunt).

Pornography is one complex variant on what might be called distorting or anti-ideal cultural languages, which also include caricature (so vital a part of English visual culture), proverbs, slang, the fair, popular humor, and the whole spectrum of what we now call popular festive culture. It is difficult to recover this culture, except in fragments, but we can detect traces of it in more official cultures, because a number of artists, including Mercier, Sedaine, and Greuze, were acutely attuned to the energies and the creative possibilities of popular custom, proverbial wisdom, and ludic and commercial habits and tried to incorporate them in their works.[34] Where it might be most interesting to historians is where it mixes with, inflects, and even clashes with other "levels" of cultural discourse, and the spirit of carnival can be found in the most unlikely places in the late ancien-régime public sphere. Bernadette Fort and others have noted that the Salon critics of the later 1770s and 1780s adopted the forms of parody, mockery, and satire associated with popular theater and with carnival in their discussions of paintings. Indeed, we find that many of the Salon pamphleteers were not stern advocates of a Rousseauist politics of virtue but instead drew on the techniques of popular festive celebration and protest.[35] Fort's attention was on the specific mix of genres in Salon criticism, and the re-creation in print not of high literary debate but of the language and tone of the marketplace and the carnival square.[36] Antimonarchical pornography too, with its sexual inversions and subversions, its fondness for buggery, incest, and lesbianism, might be seen as an attempt to point to a moral world turned upside down, and thus an attack on existing orders and proprieties which drew some of its energy from the license and spirit of inversion expressed in carnival. Greuze was a keen observer of popular custom, and a witty, sometimes ludic interpreter of the proverbial. His *Village Betrothal* draws on some of the compositional strategies of the popular print. In this fusing of different registers, in the use of languages of popular culture along with those of elite culture, might we assert that the aesthetic realm acts as a kind of avatar, a presentiment in culture of a wider social phenomenon? Might the mixture of elements from opposing registers of the dramatic be seen to prefigure a wider acknowledgment in political rhetoric of the interdependence of the socially "high" and "low"? Certainly, reconciling elite and popular rhetoric, elite and popular conceptions of the political, and elite and popular desires and grievances, and trying to establish "common" cause, would be a major preoccupation of Revolutionary leadership and a major source of Revolutionary tensions.

DAVID'S *THE TRIUMPH OF THE FRENCH PEOPLE* (1794)

To draw together the threads of this chapter, I turn to an analysis of a complex piece of Revolutionary visual culture designed by David to be part of a music–drama spectacle.

One of David's political projects, conceived in 1793–4, was a design for a stage curtain, now called *The Triumph of the French People* (see Illustration 7.6). It was probably designed for a Revolutionary pageant play by Gabriel Bouquier, a painter and deputy to the convention, (and P. L. Moline) called *The Meeting of the Tenth of August or the Inauguration of the French Republic*.

Examining this drawing, it is clear how it relates its Revolutionary message (the trampling of royalty and feudalism by liberty and equality) through a complex of symbols, personifications and devices that David learned through his training as a painter in a particular neoclassical tradition. When asked to make the events of the Revolution clear, to commemorate them, David draws on several distinct registers. The physical characteristics of the chariot, and the frieze-like, processional disposition of the figures seem to come from his experience of, and interest in, the sarcophagi and funerary monuments of the ancient world, which he had studied in Rome. The use of such disposition was deliberately designed to chime with the spectacles and the processions which David had been masterminding for the Revolutionary government throughout the preceding year to commemorate anniversaries, ideas, or people.[37] Yet it was not simply the disposition of figures that drew on the ancients; indeed, this image is incomprehensible without the understanding of the syncretism of ancient and modern heroism and struggle which was part of the political and visual language of the Revolution. A chariot is led in procession by two muscular male figures, one naked and with the tight curls of classical statuary, one clothed and with the flowing locks of the energized *sans-culotte*, who with swords menace the prostrate figure – not a portrait of Louis XVI but an allegorical figure of the monarchy, his crown toppling, revealing a bald head. They are spurred

Illustration 7.6 *Jacques-Louis David,* The Triumph of the French People *(ink, brush, and brown wash, 32.7 × 72 cm, 1793: Musée Carnavalet, Paris)* © Photothèque des Musées de la ville de Paris (ou PMVP)/Cliché.

on by an avenging angel, or winged victory, armed with a spear, above. The chariot behind them is pulled by two oxen and ridden by the giant and muscular figure of Hercules, representing the French people, armed with his club, and holding aloft a Phrygian cap. The chariot is preceded by a group of figures who had become models and who had been part of the vocabulary of the visual artists of the pre-Revolutionary generation: Cornélie, the Mother of the Gracchi, painted by, among others, Angelika Kauffman in 1785 (Virginia Museum of Fine Arts); Junius Brutus, holding the decree condemning his sons to death, most memorably depicted by David himself but also by a series of painters throughout Europe; William Tell, his musculature emphasized so that he has the stature of an ancient athlete to match his heroic status, holding his young son in his arms;[38] Marat, showing his wound, and emerging out of the frieze to face us frontally, in a gesture of rhetorical revelation; and Lepelletier. In the background are other recent martyrs, Châlier and Gasparin.[39]

What can this image tell us, as historians? Very little, some would argue, especially since this design was for a project that never came to fruition, thanks to the intervention of the fast moving world of contingent, real, politics, as the fall of Robespierre prevented the performance for which this curtain design was made. Yet considered as "evidence," it might be argued that the mixture of the violent, the processional, the allegorical, the contemporary and the ancient in this image are conveniently emblematic of many aspects of the political universe of this period of the Revolution's history, with its need for martyrs, its pressing violence, its heroicization of the violence of the *sans-culottes*, its appeal to emotional identification, its insistence on sacrifice and the need to suffer for the greater good of the nascent Republic. The visual rhetoric of this image was constructed out of elements familiar to the visual culture of later eighteenth-century, and might not have been imaginable without it. However, David's sources are wide and diverse. The figure of Hercules, as Lynn Hunt has shown, was developed as a Revolutionary symbol out of a combination of classical mythology and more native, popular "giant" traditions, exemplified by Pantagruel and Gargantua.[40] The figure of Marat, kneeling and tearing at his wound, owes something to figures of grieving and despairing parents, a feature of the visual arts of the pre-Revolutionary decades, and the emotionally charged dramas of Sedaine and Mercier, among others.[41] The very presence of children in David's design (Cornélie's "treasures," and William Tell's son and near-victim) points to the by then well-established topos of virtuous parenthood which had been given a major boost in the visual register by

Greuze three decades earlier and by the stage and literary fictions of the *Encyclopédistes*.

Perhaps most importantly, David's central motif, the triumphal cart trampling the enemy, is one with which he probably became familiar precisely, even ironically, through the saturation of the visual sphere in Bourbon France with images of heroic kingship. Any number of seventeenth-century examples might be found, but a good one is the almanac image, *The Magnificent Triumph* from 1658, which features Louis XIV, having conquered his passions, conquering his enemies.[42] It too features a chariot, an accompanying angel, personified qualities, and the trampling of enemies. Are we to conclude that images of triumph, and of procession, could not resist drawing on a vocabulary fashioned by Bourbon kings, even when the message was so resolutely republican? Or might we speculate that David (and other artists and writers) deliberately, and with a kind of vigor and relish, used the visual vocabulary of kingship against itself, in an ironic and even carnivalesque way, to use Bakhtin's terms? Is there not something of a turning-upside-down of the world in this deliberate reversal of the expected position of the king in this image? In the language of Revolutionary self-representation, the spectacular body of the Bourbon kings continues to be a presence, but it is a mocked and jeered one. Continuing our understanding of the register of popular imagery, perhaps the cattle (above and beyond their connotation of brute strength and their association with ancient ritual) were to resonate with a rural, popular cultural symbolism as beasts of burden, with all their force and might (and contrasting with the aristocratic horse).

It seems possible to suggest that the power of this image as persuasive fictional representation relies on its combination of the intellectual complexity and resonance of ancient culture, with the immediacy, energy, and even the violence of the popular processional mode so vital to Revolutionary spectacle. Further, it might be claimed that contingent but intense images like these function politically, forging visual alliances and even a visual rhetoric which is both didactic and utopian, alive with contemporary reference but steeped in an intellectual culture of allusion.

However, and here we turn full circle, this picture, like so much of Revolutionary visual culture, was part of an "incomplete project" to give the events, processes, and ideas of the Revolution visual form. Like the vast and extraordinarily ambitious memorialization, which was David's *Oath of the Tennis Court* (1791–2, Versailles) it ultimately failed to see the light of day and remained a plan, a sketch, an idea, in some sense a fantasy.[43] Some might conclude from this that there was always a lack of fit between the cultural sphere and the murky human realities and rhythms of cause and effect, action and reaction at the centre of the Revolutionary process. Others might also note that confused military allegories, clumsy "imitations of the ancient" and creakingly wooden dramas created during the Revolution *far* outnumber the eloquent and complex works of art or theater perfectly in tune with Revolutionary ideology. Yet others, the most conservative cultural historians, might even argue that the Revolution arrives in the cultural sphere as an unforeseen and disruptive, even tragic event, ending the enlightened regimes of the *Bâtiments du Roi*, which had done so much to boost new ideas and tendencies in the arts, and destroying the networks of patronage and commission that had sustained artists and writers.

However, I hope to have demonstrated, through some concrete examples, for how long before the Revolution the sphere of the visual and the theatrical had been slipping from royal grip, and to demonstrate that a continuum can be established between products of the French cultural sphere of the latter half of the eighteenth century and Revolutionary culture more generally. I have also suggested that the most complex and resonant cultural productions do have the capacity to illuminate processes that are perhaps more nebulous and slippery than, for example, economic flows of supply and demand, shortage and inflation, but which we are beginning to see as crucial to a wider understanding of the process of Revolutionary change in France. In the emergent public sphere, visual and dramatic representation could serve to erode an old corporeal code, an old mode of spectatorship, and stage and canvas could become the space of embodiment for values such as virtue and patriotism or cosmopolitanism or probity, making the ideals and the fantasies of a progressive generation present and setting out a vision of possibilities as well as a critique of the present.

8. The Pamphlet Debate over the Organization of the Estates General

KENNETH MARGERISON

Summary

The public sphere is vital to Kenneth Margerison's chapter on the pamphlet debate. His careful analysis of the pamphlet literature published in the months preceding the convocation of the Estates General informs his interpretation of events at Versailles in the summer of 1789. He argues that the largely aristocratic Society of Thirty's well-known publication campaign calling for a doubled Third Estate and vote by head in the Estates General was designed to bring the Third Estate into an alliance with the privileged orders to combat ministerial despotism. The abbé Sieyès, who distrusted the aristocratic leadership of the society, rejected such an alliance in his famous pamphlet, *What Is the Third Estate?* Disputing the conventional assessment of this pamphlet's importance, Margerison argues that it had little impact on public opinion, which had come by early 1789 to accept the necessity of a union of the three orders in the Estates General. Furthermore, the success of Sieyès's motion that created the National Assembly in June 1789 did not result, as historians usually contend, in a victory establishing the political dominance of the Third Estate. Instead, the formation of the National Assembly, after a brief but fraught period of tension, led directly to the common deliberations sought by the unionist nobility who emerged as important leaders in the body. By emphasizing the efforts of the leaders of the Society of Thirty and their allies to create a basis for cooperation among the three orders, Margerison's analysis challenges not only Georges Lefebvre's classic description of events in the summer of 1789 as a struggle between the Third Estate and the nobility but also the more recent interpretations of François

Furet and Keith Baker, who have emphasized the influence of Sieyès
on the development of the Revolutionary concept of sovereignty.

The organization of the Estates General dominated political discussion
in the public sphere from September 1788 until the Estates General met
in May 1789. Once convened, the elected deputies continued to debate
the form of the Estates General until the Third Estate declared itself to
be the National Assembly on June 17, 1789. Historians, following the
lead of the great French historian Georges Lefebvre, have traditionally
explained the controversy as one in which the Third Estate, determined
to achieve proper representation in the Estates General, openly challenged the political position of the nobility.[1] First through pamphlets and
later through its actions in the Estates General, the Third Estate pressed
its demands until it achieved victory with the creation of the National
Assembly. By the 1960s Lefebvre's Marxist interpretation of the origins
of the Revolution as a class struggle between the Third Estate and the
nobility began to come under a variety of attacks, but an alternative
explanation of the origins of the Revolution and the political controversies surrounding it only started to appear in the 1980s as historians investigated the political culture of the old regime.[2]

    This political culture was characterized by a bitter contest between
the king and his ministers on the one hand and the magistrates of the
Paris parlement on the other. The ministers, naturally, wished to maintain and even expand royal authority. Since the 1750s, the parlementary
magistrates had repeatedly claimed to protect the liberties of the nation
through the preservation of the ancient, historical constitution of France
and the privileges associated with it. By the late 1780s the struggle
between these antagonists was conducted in the public sphere where
each side published pamphlets to justify its political position before the
court of public opinion. After the king promised to convene the representative assembly of the nation, the Estates General, both the ministry
and the parlement hoped to gain control of this institution to further
their political goals.

    When the Estates General had last met in 1614, the three orders of
the realm (clergy, nobility, and commons or Third Estate) had assembled in their respective chambers, each represented by roughly the same
number of deputies. Each Estate voted separately, and agreement of all
three chambers was required for recommendations to be forwarded to
the king. Organized in this fashion, any one of the orders could in effect

veto proposals passed by the other two. If the ministry wished to introduce any measures which threatened the privileges of the clergy or the nobility, such as the new taxes proposed at the first Assembly of Notables in 1787, one or both of these Estates could easily block the passage of such legislation. However, if the balance of power in the Estates General could be somehow shifted to the Third Estate, which presumably would support a government reform program based on the reduction of privilege, the ministry might be able to turn the meeting of the assembly to the king's advantage.

Loménie de Brienne, the king's principal minister, issued a decree on July 5, 1788 indicating that the government indeed had plans for reforming the Estates General. The decree authorized government officials and scholars to investigate the nature of past meetings of the assembly and suggested that the proper balance between the three Estates might require altering the form of the assembly.[3] With this clever ploy Brienne hoped to win the support of public opinion, which demanded a meeting of the Estates General, while providing a rationale for the government to organize the assembly in some form other than that of 1614. Perhaps an earlier meeting of the Estates General would provide a model with increased representation for the Third Estate. On September 25 the newly restored Paris parlement, reading Brienne's decree as a ministerial scheme to undermine the ancient constitution and gain control of the Estates General, insisted that the assembly must be organized as it had been in 1614. Responding to the parlement's counterattack, Jacques Necker, who had replaced Brienne in the ministry, announced that he would reconvene the Assembly of Notables in November 1788 to discuss the proper organization of the Estates General. Naturally, he hoped this meeting would lead to a reversal of the parlement's decision regarding the 1614 form of the assembly and result in greater representation for the Third Estate. These maneuvers of the ministry and the Paris parlement laid the foundation for the pamphlet debate over the form of the Estates General.

The ultimate goal of both camps was to win, through the pamphlets they sponsored, the support of public opinion.[4] The language of the debate was not novel, and knowledgeable readers of this literature quickly recognized that the arguments on both sides were the same ones used earlier in the Jansenist controversy of the 1750s and the Maupeou crisis of the 1770s. The ministerial pamphleteers utilized the language of royal absolutism to make the government's case. According to them, the king exercised his sovereign power to promote the interests of the entire nation, especially those of the Third Estate, while the parlement simply worked to defend the privileges of the few. The parlementary writers, primarily barristers who formed the core of the patriot party which had emerged during the Maupeou era, relied on the well-developed language of parlementary constitutionalism. Their publications argued that the magistrates acted only to protect the liberties of the nation from the despotic intentions of the ministry.[5]

Keith Baker, one of the principal contributors to our current understanding of the use of language in eighteenth-century politics, has argued that political authority is based on controlling the language of political discourse. Any society in which public opinion plays a role will ultimately only sanction government actions that seem to flow from this generally accepted political language. In periods of turmoil, a contest develops between two or more competing political discourses, with governmental authority ultimately determined by the discourse which emerges victorious. The French Revolution, in Baker's view, was one of those periods where the adoption of a new language of politics was followed by dramatic changes in the nature of government.[6] In 1788 such a contest between the languages of royal absolutism and parlementary constitutionalism was in full swing. Each side believed that the winner would control the Estates General.

One of the principal issues of the debate was the historical nature of the Estates General. An axiom of the parlementary discourse was the obligation of the Paris parlement to protect the constitution from the despotic intentions of the ministers. Parlementary writers, drawing from histories of France written earlier in the century, produced numerous pamphlets in the autumn of 1788 reminding readers of the nature of this constitution, the necessity of organizing the Estates General in three equal chambers, and the role of the Nation's representatives in sanctioning taxes and limiting royal authority. For its part, the ministry's position was bolstered by pamphleteers arguing that the history of the Estates General yielded no consistent pattern of organization or function. According to one author, the principal lesson to be learned from this history was "that we lack a real, fundamental and immutable constitution," a conclusion that would presumably leave the ministry free to organize the Estates General in any manner it pleased.[7]

Beyond the historical reality of the Estates General, the parlementary writers revived the issue of the general will of the nation, which had first appeared in the political literature of the Maupeou era. Both Rousseau and the Jansenists had insisted on the authority of a unanimous general will, and the language of the parlementary pamphlets of 1788 reflected a belief that the will of a despotic monarch could only be effectively countered by the unanimous will of the nation.[8] According to the parlementary writers, this general will was expressed through the constitutionally sanctioned Estates General, which had required since 1355 the unanimous agreement of the three Estates for the implementation of new taxes or any other legislation. Furthermore, as a practical matter, little could be done to halt the despotism of the royal ministers if the three orders meeting in the Estates General could not agree on a political program with which to oppose the government's plans. The abbé Mably in the 1760s had made this abundantly clear in his *Observations on the History of France.* Mably had described the early medieval assemblies under Charlemagne as democratic bodies composed of members of the three orders of the realm who "represented the will of the nation," and worked together for the common good. But later the kings of France began to encourage division between the orders so that they could dominate the assemblies and prevent them from carrying out the will of the nation.

This necessary unity between the three Estates described by Mably, however, was severely threatened by the parlementary insistence on the 1614 form of the Estates General. Writers on the ministerial payroll worked hard to convince public opinion that the parlement's "secret motive," in calling for the 1614 form was to limit the representation of the Third Estate so that the magistrates could dominate the deliberations of the assembly. One such pamphleteer, Simon-Nicholas-Henri Linguet, urged the Third Estate to "[r]ise up against the clergy, the nobility, and the magistrature," which wanted to deny the Third its rights.[9] Parlementary authors responded to this campaign by warning the public that these publications were merely the work of ministerial hacks who had been hired to sow "the murderous poison of discord" between the Estates. These writers urged members of the Third Estate to remember the lessons of disunity that Mably had presented in his history and to unite with the privileged orders to thwart the progress of despotism.

Parlementary pamphleteers claimed that the nobility, in an effort to create a union with the Third, were willing to make a patriotic sacrifice of their tax privileges. However, the insistence on the 1614 form of the Estates General, which seemed to relegate the Third Estate to a subordinate role, cast doubt on the parlement's desire to create a union in which the Third Estate would be an equal partner. A number of pamphlets that did not seem to be the work of the ministry began to make insistent demands that the deputation of the Third Estate be increased in size. One notable publication, *Petition of Citizens Residing in Paris*, by the soon-to-be-famous Dr Joseph-Ignace Guillotin, was placed in the offices of notaries where it could be signed by those demanding increased representation of the Third Estate. Numerous municipal bodies also issued published demands for a larger deputation of the Third Estate in the Estates General.

Astute observers in the parlementary camp quickly realized that the demand for the 1614 form could easily scuttle the patriot program in the face of hostile public opinion. Among those was Adrien Duport, a magistrate in the Paris parlement and long-time supporter of parlementary constitutionalism. On the eve of the meeting of the reconvened Assembly of Notables, Duport organized a political club, later known as the Society of Thirty, to devise a strategy to revive the popularity of the patriot position.[10] The membership of the society consisted primarily of magistrates from the Paris parlement and members of some of the great noble families of France. A few distinguished commoners also took part in the discussions. The dilemma for the patriots assembled at Duport's was how to structure a program that would fulfill the goals of parlementary constitutionalism and simultaneously win the support of public opinion. They desperately wanted to use the opportunity of the meeting of the Estates General to revive the ancient constitution, and they recognized that they had to involve the Third Estate in this project to be successful.

In these circumstances, the recent political events in the province of Dauphiné provided them with what appeared to be the ideal formula for success. During the summer of 1788 members of the Dauphiné elite led by Jean-Joseph Mounier, a local magistrate from the Third Estate, called for the reestablishment of the long-dormant provincial estates of Dauphiné. Mounier's plan demanded doubling the representation of the Third Estate and requiring the deputies to meet and vote as a body in a single chamber. This proposed organizational scheme of the Dauphiné estates, commonly referred to as a doubled Third Estate with a vote by head, provided the deputies of the Third Estate with an influence equal to that of the privileged orders. Ultimately the Brienne government agreed to the plan. Upon achieving success, the comte de Virieu, one of Mounier's allies, asserted in his pamphlet, *Spirit of the Actions of the Three Orders of Dauphiné*, that the goal of the movement had been to create a union of the three orders capable of thwarting the schemes of the despotic ministers. The union, as Virieu described it, was a product of the generosity of the nobility, who had agreed both to sacrifice their tax privileges and to increase the political influence of the Third to cement the alliance between the orders. The result was the creation in Dauphiné of "a union, a harmony, unknown in ten generations," and a constitution which could serve as a model for the nation.

Dauphiné provided the leaders of the Society of Thirty with an organizational plan for the Estates General. The Dauphiné model established increased political influence for the Third Estate, but it also recognized the legitimate right of the clergy and nobility to half the deputies in the provincial estates and the extraordinary political influence such representation provided. The model advocated the abandonment of tax privilege, but it emphasized the maintenance of most other privileges so important to the noble and clerical estates. Once these compromises had been effected, the Third Estate of Dauphiné had willingly joined with the patriotic nobility to defend the ancient constitution and liberty against the despotic plans of the ministry. This was the kind of union of orders that Duport and his allies hoped to put into place on a national scale, and they turned to Guy-Jean-Baptiste Target to present their proposal in a series of pamphlets entitled *The Estates General Convoked by Louis XVI.*

As a parlementary barrister, veteran pamphleteer, and experienced opponent of the ministry extending back to the Maupeou era, Target seemed the perfect candidate to provide the language that would bridge the divide between the forces of parlementary constitutionalism and the supporters of increased representation for the Third Estate. In his pamphlet he undercut the argument that the 1614 form of the Estates General provided a constitutional model for the assembly. He backed this assertion with historical evidence that many meetings of the Estates General before 1561 had been characterized by a doubled Third Estate and a vote by head. In addition, Target stressed the importance of creating unity among the orders of the nation in order to counter successfully the schemes of the ministry. This union would come through the creation of a doubled Third Estate and a vote by head which would establish "the equality of force" between the Estates. Decrees accepted by the united orders in the Estates General and the king would become "the expression of the general will and the most eminent act of sovereignty." Thus Target's series of pamphlets, which appeared between October and December 1788, established that organizing the Estates General with a doubled Third Estate and vote by head would not violate the historic constitution of France, would establish the long-sought sovereignty of the general will, and would provide the necessary union between the orders to thwart the nefarious schemes of the ministry. In short, Target's program conformed to the political language of the parlementary constitutionalists while meeting the demands for the Third Estate's increased representation and influence.

That many in the camp of the parlementary constitutionalists did not accept this program reveals much about the political culture of France on the eve of the Revolution. The problem with the plan was that the results would be similar, if not identical, to those sought by the ministry which also wanted, based on the language of its pamphleteers, to increase the influence of the Third in the Estates General. Although Target's credentials as a patriot were impeccable, how could anyone be sure that the Third Estate, granted a doubled representation and vote by head even with the support of the nobility, would still not be seduced by ministerial operatives. The only certain guarantee against ministerial interference in the deliberations of the Estates General was to maintain the 1614 form where the patriots among the nobility could be certain of exercising a veto over any legislation. Not surprisingly then, Target's pamphlet met with stiff resistance after its distribution by members of the Society of Thirty at the Assembly of Notables. Parlementary pamphlets vehemently countering Target's historical accounts quickly appeared to shore up the claim that the 1614 form was in fact the historic and constitutional form of the Estates General, and the Assembly of Notables meeting in November 1788 refused to adopt any changes in the organization of the Estates General.

In a further complication of the issues, the princes of the blood, the male relatives of the king, followed the decision of the Notables with the publication of their infamous *Mémoire des Princes*. This pamphlet, signed by most of the princes with the exceptions of the comte de Provence and the duc d'Orléans, quickly distinguished itself as one of the most vigorously denounced publications to appear before the French Revolution. The princes, who often did not support royal policy, not only refused to consider any alteration in the form of the Estates General but also condemned as inflammatory the pamphlet literature which had attacked noble privilege. But even more significantly, by implying that demands for reform reflected insubordination on the part of the Third Estate, the princes seemed to confirm the ministerial charge that the nobility cared for little beyond the protection of its privileges. The *Mémoire des Princes* stimulated the publication of numerous counterattacks, which condemned the tone of the publication and charged the princes with fomenting division between the orders.

Although the leaders of the Society of Thirty had strong links to the Paris parlement, they had created a program and a language distinct from the old patriot party of the Maupeou era. Their goal of integrating the Third Estate into the antiministerial party broadened their program making it both more representative of the population and more national in scope. Although much of what they advocated was compatible with the language of parlementary constitutionalism, in developing their program they had in effect created the new political discourse of national constitutionalism. Supporters of this program formed the new national, as opposed to the old patriot, party. During the autumn of 1788, Duport's society sponsored a number of publications that developed this new political language. Although the subject matter and arguments of these pamphlets were often quite distinct, they all called for increased representation of the Third Estate, the creation of a union of orders, and government by the general will. Because the goals of the Society of Thirty have not been clearly understood, historians have often assumed that all publications calling simply for a doubled Third Estate and vote by head were sponsored by this club.[11] In fact, only about twelve titles published in the autumn of 1788 advocated the club's program.[12] Nevertheless, the influence of the society on public opinion was great, as we shall see below.

Necker, the king's principal minister, was naturally troubled by the Notables' insistence that the 1614 form be preserved. If the Estates General were organized in this manner, the government would be faced with an assembly dominated by the privileged orders. However, if he urged Louis XVI to convene the Estates General with a doubled Third Estate and a vote by head, he would almost certainly be accused of violating the ancient forms of the constitution. The privileged orders might refuse, as the *Mémoire des Princes* had threatened, to participate in such a corrupted body, dooming the government's plans to increase tax revenues. In these circumstances, Necker decided to pursue a middle course and recommend to the king that the Estates General be convened simply with a doubled Third Estate. Louis accepted this proposal on December 27, 1788, and Necker immediately organized a publication campaign to win the approval of public opinion for this decision.

To make his case to the public, Necker arranged for the printing and distribution of two documents, *Result of the King's Council of State* and *Report*

Made to the King. The first of these merely announced that the king had agreed to a doubled Third Estate in the next Estates General, but the document made no mention of how the orders would vote. In the accompanying *Report* Necker provided the rationale he had presented to the king for increasing the representation of the Third Estate. Here Necker wanted to reassure the privileged classes that the ancient constitution would be preserved and that the three orders would deliberate and vote separately in the Estates General unless all three orders unanimously agreed to common deliberations. But he also sought to win favor with the supporters of increased representation of the Third Estate by arguing that the ministry hoped that the orders would deliberate in common "in affairs where their interest is absolutely equal," or if a deadlock developed as a result of the traditional vote by order. He even asserted that the Third Estate, "when it is unanimous and when it conforms to the general principles of equity," could speak for the nation and bind the actions of the monarch.

The king's decision and, even more importantly, Necker's *Report* revitalized the debate in the public sphere concerning the organization of the Estates General, and led to an expansion of the contested issues. Naturally, a number of ministerially sponsored pamphlets praising the decision and Necker's *Report* quickly appeared. These publications tried to demonstrate that the decision fulfilled the goals of all political factions since it both maintained the constitutional form of the Estates General while allowing for possible modifications if circumstances warranted. Nevertheless, parlementary writers, ever wary of ministerial initiatives, weighed into the discussion with a condemnation of the decision which they said threatened the constitution. Supporters of the increased representation of the Third Estate expressed skepticism that the nobility, under Necker's plan, would ever agree to common deliberations. Thus, instead of rallying public opinion to the side of the government, Necker's *Report* only further stimulated the ideological debates in the public sphere.

Both Necker's plan and that of the Society of Thirty relied on convincing the privileged orders that common deliberations in the Estates General were necessary for the well-being of the nation. Was there no way in which the Third Estate could influence its own fate? The answer appeared to be no until the abbé Sieyès published *What Is the Third Estate?* This famous pamphlet, reputed to be the most influential publication in the months preceding the meeting of the Estates General, presented a novel argument that empowered the Third Estate to seize the political initiative by itself and break the deadlock over the form of the Estates General.

Sieyès was part of a small group of men who attended meetings of the Society of Thirty but did not share the political ideology of the great majority of its members. Although they too were associated with the national party, these individuals were attracted to the rational reform proposals of the physiocrats, the eighteenth-century French economic reformers. Two of these men, Pierre-Louis Lacretelle and Pierre-Louis Roederer, published pamphlets in 1788 that had urged the establishment of an assembly where deputies, empowered to speak for the general will, would be elected without regard to estate.

Like Lacretelle and Roederer, Sieyès had also begun developing proposals for a rationally organized representative assembly during the autumn of 1788, but his ideas did not fully mature until he wrote *What Is the Third Estate?* which appeared in early February 1789. Sieyès's underlying premise was his famous dictum that the Third Estate is the Nation. The implications of this assertion in the context of the political language of pre-Revolutionary France were momentous. If the Third Estate alone comprised the Nation, then the clergy and nobility had no right to representation in the assembly of the Nation. They were to be denied this right, according to Sieyès, because of the privileges they possessed, which separated them from the body of citizens living under common laws. The representative assembly of the nation must work for the general interest, and, since the privileged classes were "by definition enemies of the common order," they could "be neither electors nor elected as long as their odious privileges endure."

Sieyès's concept of representation directly challenged not only the defenders of the traditional Estates General but also the reformers in the Society of Thirty who sought a union of the three orders. Sieyès bluntly condemned efforts to unite the orders: "the deputies of the clergy and the nobility have nothing in common with the national representation," so that "no alliance is possible between the three orders at the Estates General." The very concept of an Estates General was anathema to proper representation of the nation; therefore, the deputies of the Third Estate should refuse to accept vote by order or by head. Sieyès argued that vote by head would only result in an "equality of influence between the privileged and nonprivileged," whereas only the deputies of the Third Estate "could speak without error in the name of the entire nation."

Sieyès offered two means by which the Third Estate could seize the initiative in the Estates General and create a truly representative national assembly. The first was for the deputies of the Third to refuse to cooperate with the privileged orders in the Estates General and simply to declare themselves to be the national assembly. The second was for the Third to call for an extraordinary assembly of the Nation to determine the proper form of its representative body and to suspend its activities in the Estates General until its demands were met. In either case, the Third Estate would act as the representatives of the Nation, refuse to cooperate with the other orders or bend to the will of the monarch, and refuse to vote by order or by head.

To contemporaries, Sieyès's conception of the Nation was truly startling. No other writer had dared to suggest that privilege and citizenship were incompatible. Yet Sieyès had insisted that the privileged could not be part of the Nation and implied that, once the Nation could legislate for itself through a national assembly, privilege would be eliminated. Furthermore, Sieyès had indicated that the Nation could will whatever it pleased, in a manner suggested by Rousseau's theory of the general will. This will could not be limited by ancient traditions, privileges, or the will of the monarch. While other writers of the national party had insisted on the authority of the general will of the nation, they had always indicated that there were limits on this will. Target and other national constitutionalists had implied that ancient traditions could not simply be ignored and insisted that the king played a role in the development of the general will. Sieyès, however, asserted the full authority of this will and its ability to cast aside the distinctions between citizens.

Historians have long believed that *What Is the Third Estate?* was influential in shaping public opinion on the eve of the Estates General of 1789.[13] Not only did this pamphlet express a profound logic and startling conclusions, but events in the Estates General in June of 1789, where the Third Estate declared itself to be the National Assembly, seemed to confirm that Sieyès's words had tremendous influence on the deputies. Contemporaries were equally impressed with the pamphlet. Immediately after its appearance, the bookseller Siméon-Prosper Hardy wrote in his private journal that *What Is the Third Estate?* was "the work of a man endowed with true genius." Since the pamphlet appeared in three editions in the spring of 1789, it is fair to assume that it was read by a reasonably wide audience.

Nevertheless, considerable evidence exists to indicate that public opinion, while perhaps impressed with Sieyès's work, was little convinced that its proposals were pertinent to the political situation in the spring of 1789. Hardy himself, who had a clear understanding of Sieyès's argument and accepted the "just consequences" of his principles, remained firmly committed to the program of a doubled Third Estate and a vote by head sponsored by the Society of Thirty. Three publications offered tepid refutations of Sieyès's argument, a very meager challenge when compared to the vigorous responses generated by other controversial pamphlets like those authored by Target and the princes of the blood. Furthermore, among 638 politically important pamphlets published between January 1 and May 6, 1789 only eight demonstrate any influence by *What Is the Third Estate?* Even so, while these pamphlets argued that the Third Estate had the right to legislate for the nation, most of them asserted that this would be possible only if the privileged orders refused common deliberations in the Estates General. In fact, only two pamphlets adopted Sieyès's argument that the Third Estate accept neither vote by head nor vote by order and that it insist on assuming the legislative power of the Nation by itself.[14]

Readers were not receptive to *What Is the Third Estate?* in early 1789. The political language of the era had conditioned the public to believe that a union of orders was necessary for the successful operation of the Estates General. Politically knowledgeable individuals could not imagine the Third Estate refusing to cooperate with the privileged orders if vote by head was instituted. Public opinion had come to accept the desirability of union and, clearly, circumstances had not yet reached the point where all-out war between the orders seemed a wise course.

During the early months of 1789, despite Sieyès's warnings, support for the creation of a union of orders seemed to grow. The Necker government, which until late 1788 had been paying writers to levy fierce verbal attacks on its opponents, came to realize that it had to foster some sort of cooperation between the orders if the Estates General, voting by order or by head, were to accomplish anything. Dauphiné provided the obvious model for creating harmonious relations between the estates, and the ministry formed a plan to encourage the orders to meet and vote in common in the *bailliage* assemblies where the deputies to the Estates General were to be elected. Thus in early 1789 a number of ministerial writers, especially the Norman barrister Jacques-Guillaume Thouret, began to advocate the practice of common deliberations in the *bailliage* assemblies. The result of such common deliberations, Thouret argued in his *Advice of Several Good Citizens of All the Orders,* would be the establishment of the "union and concord of the citizens." Seemingly unable to develop a coordinated strategy, however, the ministry proceeded to issue electoral decrees insisting that the orders meet separately. Further complicating any effort to encourage common deliberations, the decrees also limited the total number of electors from the Third Estate so that the privileged orders would have the majority of electors in every *bailliage*. Even if common deliberations could be arranged, the Third Estate would likely refuse to participate since they would be consistently outvoted by the privileged electors.

The Society of Thirty was also determined to encourage common deliberations in the *bailliage* assemblies, despite the impediments created by the electoral decrees. The club published a pamphlet by Target which assured the electors that the decrees were not so restrictive as to prohibit common deliberations or any necessary adjustment in the size of the delegation of the Third Estate. Target also published an *Instruction* which described how the assemblies were to be organized for common deliberation, and suggested the items to be included in the *cahier*, the grievance list that was to accompany the deputies to the Estates General. Once the *bailliage* was organized, the *Instruction* urged the electors to insist that the Estates General "destroy all the causes of division among the orders." This was to be accomplished by drafting a *cahier* which demanded the elimination of tax privileges while simultaneously assuring the clergy and nobility that their other privileges, especially their seigneurial rights, remained sacrosanct. In addition Target urged each *bailliage* to demand vote by head in the Estates General, the establishment of a constitution, the drafting of a declaration of the rights of the nation, and the recognition of the authority of the general will. This last requirement distinguished Target's plan from that of the ministerial writer Thouret, who insisted that sovereignty lay with the monarch.

Target's *Instruction* elevated to a new level the Society of Thirty's efforts to influence public opinion. Because of the impending elections to the Estates General, the public now extended far beyond the Parisian elite which had been the primary target of so much previous publishing activity. Influencing the elections to the Estates General required molding opinion in as many of the nation's *bailliages* as possible. The Viroflay Society, an association of important noblemen sympathetic to Duport's political program, assisted in this effort by printing Target's pamphlet in enormous quantities and distributing it throughout France. Despite this effort, no *bailliage* assembly in France seems to have met in the manner Target suggested.

The goals of the ministry and the Society of Thirty were seriously challenged in March 1789 with the appearance of a curious publication consisting of the *Instructions* of the duc d'Orléans, coupled with the abbé Sieyès's *Deliberations to be Undertaken in the Bailliage Assemblies.* The duc d'Orléans, a prince of the blood and the richest man in France, was widely believed to have a political agenda considerably at odds with that of the monarch.[15] Although his *Instructions* were only vaguely supportive of the Third Estate, the inclusion of Sieyès's pamphlet provided the entire publication with the aura of an Olympian statement on behalf of the rights of the Nation. The potential impact of the brochure was increased when the duc arranged to have an estimated 100,000 copies, a truly gargantuan press run by eighteenth-century standards, distributed throughout France. The pamphlet certainly made an impression on the public. The bookseller Hardy wrote in his journal that Sieyès's *Deliberations* had "produced an astonishing sensation," and a number of publications soon appeared both praising and condemning the work, a response that *What Is the Third Estate?* never achieved.

In the *Deliberations*, Sieyès continued his attack on the political program designed to create a union of orders, but he significantly altered his suggestions for the conduct of the Third in the Estates General. Regarding the upcoming *bailliage* assemblies, Sieyès ridiculed the campaign to bring about common deliberations of the orders. He belittled Necker's presumed interest in encouraging such deliberations, which could hardly take place given the directives of the royal electoral decrees. As he had argued in *What Is the Third Estate?*, Sieyès insisted that even with numbers equal to the privileged orders, the Third Estate would not have an influence in the *bailliage* assemblies equal to its importance to society. A similar situation would exist in the Estates General if the orders met in common. But unlike in *What Is the Third Estate?*, where he argued that the Third Estate should refuse to vote by head or order in the Estates General, Sieyès now implied that the Third should vote by order.

Why the dramatic about-face? *What Is the Third Estate?* had failed to ignite public opinion, and there seemed to be growing support for a union of orders which was advocated by some of the greatest nobility in France and, now, the Necker government. If something like Target's plan was actually adopted, the result would be the maintenance of most privilege and the continuation of the three estates. Fear of this outcome appears to have led Sieyès to form a tacit alliance with the duc d'Orléans. Orléans, alone among the nobility of France, possessed the political independence and the funds to finance a counterattack on the Society of Thirty and the ministry. Since the public seemed to lack enthusiasm for his earlier demand that the Third Estate refuse to cooperate with the nobility, Sieyès now suggested that the Third Estate cooperate with the privileged orders to achieve the destruction of despotism, but retain separate deliberations in the Estates General. In this manner the Third Estate would appear cooperative yet maintain its independence and the ability to veto unacceptable proposals of the privileged orders. Sieyès did not abandon his claim that the Third Estate was in fact the Nation nor his goals of achieving the destruction of privilege and the creation of an assembly elected without regard to order. He now argued, however, that the necessary reforms would somehow emerge over time in the deliberations of the traditionally organized Estates General. In effect, Sieyès had been forced to alter his political program because the public had come to believe that a union of orders on some basis had to be created in the forthcoming Estates General. However, Sieyès's message, despite its wide distribution, does not seem to have led any *bailliages* to demand that the Third Estate deliberate by order.

When the Estates General convened at Versailles in early May 1789, the Necker government and a substantial number of deputies from all three estates favored the establishment of a union of orders to be achieved through common deliberations. Eighteen members of the Society of Thirty had been elected deputies to the nobility, and they were joined by the noble delegation from Dauphiné. The Third Estate included such well-known pamphleteers and supporters of union as Target, Mounier, and Thouret. In addition to a few bishops, a large number of parish priests among the clergy also wished to establish vote by head. However, opponents of union dominated the nobility which refused as a body to join the Third Estate in common deliberations. Within the Third Estate, Sieyès, who had been elected as a deputy from Paris, was well known for his ideological opposition to union.[16]

From the outset, the debates within the chamber of the Third Estate, or the commons as it came to be called, were between the ideological foes who had emerged during the pamphlet wars of the preceding months. The issue at hand was the Third's course of action, given the noble refusal to accept vote by head. The advocates of a union of orders in the Third Estate led by Target and Mounier worked to keep their colleagues from making demands that would prevent the nobility and the clergy from voluntarily accepting a vote by head and joining the Third Estate in deliberations. However, the fiery Breton deputies, who had engaged in a bitter battle with the nobility over representation in the provincial estates of Brittany, were not inclined to compromise. These individuals insisted from the beginning that the privileged accept common deliberations or be barred from the assembly of the Nation. Upon his arrival at Versailles, Sieyès allied with the Bretons because of their distrust of a union of orders, even though their demands left open the possibility of common deliberations, something Sieyès strongly opposed.

Pursuing the creation of a union of orders that seemed to have the support of public opinion, Mounier and Target had been able to hold a majority in the commons for the first month of the Estates General. Simultaneously, members of the Society of Thirty and supporters of the Dauphiné reform, who were serving as deputies of the nobility and the clergy, worked hard to convince their orders to accept common deliberations. However by mid-June, when the conciliatory attitude of the Third and the efforts of the unionists in the privileged estates had failed to move the nobility, Sieyès and the Bretons were able to carry the day. Sieyès introduced a motion that would, in effect, transform the Third Estate into the National Assembly. Mounier, Target, and about one hundred others in the Third Estate were convinced that this radical step, which indicated that the deputies from the nobility and the clergy played no role in representing the nation, would forever close the door on the creation of a union of the three orders. Instead of developing a united front of all Frenchmen to establish liberty and constitutional government while battling the forces of despotism, the nation would now experience open warfare between the three orders. On this basis Mounier and Target valiantly tried to turn the tide against Sieyès's motion, but the intransigence of the nobility seemed to offer the frustrated deputies in the Third no other choice. On June 17, the Third Estate declared itself to be the National Assembly of France but did not bar the deputies of the privileged orders from joining it at any time.

Historians have often described the events of June 17, 1789 as the Third Estate's first step in seizing political power from the monarch and the privileged orders.[17] On June 20 the Third Estate took the famous Tennis Court Oath in which it pledged not to disband until it had created a constitution for the nation. It refused to vacate the meeting hall after Louis XVI's Royal Session of June 23, despite explicit orders from the monarch to do so. The Third's victory was complete when Louis XVI ordered the other estates to join the Third in common deliberations on June 27. The Third Estate, under Sieyès's impulsion, had in fact established itself as the Nation.

Or had it? During the month of June many of the clerical deputies, who were parish priests from the Third Estate, indicated that they were at the point of joining the deliberations of the commons. And on June 22 a majority of the clergy voluntarily joined the Third. Within the noble chamber an estimated ninety-five of the three hundred deputies were sympathetic to common deliberations. Forty-seven of these noblemen voluntarily joined the commons on June 25 and promised that the others would appear in a few days. When these deputies from the privileged orders entered the National Assembly, they were greeted by an outpouring of joy on the part of the deputies of the Third Estate. In fact, Sieyès's motion, far from excluding the privileged from the National Assembly, had actually broken the constraints that had prevented those noble and clerical deputies who favored a union of orders from joining the Third Estate. Most of the deputies of the Third had likewise sought a union of orders and had only voted for Sieyès's motion because no other alternative presented itself. These deputies, who clearly did not believe that the Third Estate by itself formed the Nation, were, therefore, very relieved when the clerical and noble deputies voluntarily joined the Third. When Louis XVI ordered the remaining clerical and noble deputies to join the National Assembly on June 27, he was merely acknowledging that a union of orders had already been established.

In the newly formed National Assembly the privileged deputies composed half the membership of the body. This configuration reduced the influence of the radical element of the Third Estate and increased the authority of the noble deputies from the Society of Thirty, most notably Duport and Lafayette. Likewise, the new configuration helped restore the leadership of Mounier, Target, and other unionists in the Third Estate. To solidify their position, these men believed it necessary to make the union of orders a reality and to eliminate any suspicions that the privileged were not committed to establishing the general good of the Nation. But the very nature of privilege itself made this commitment uncertain.

In Target's model *cahier* distributed throughout France in the spring of 1789, the Society of Thirty had suggested that the nobility sacrifice their tax privileges but argued that seigneurial rights, which were property, must be maintained. However, the growing sentiment favoring the creation of a declaration of rights on the American model, and the peasant uprising known as the Great Fear, made Target's formula unacceptable by the summer of 1789. In a brilliant move, the noble deputies from the Society of Thirty formulated a plan whereby certain noblemen would voluntarily cede their seigneurial privileges in an effort to stop the peasant uprising, clear the way for drafting a declaration of rights, and demonstrate the willingness of the nobility to make sacrifices for the general good of the nation. The plan was taken to the Breton Club, where the most radical deputies of the Third Estate enthusiastically endorsed it. That the nobility expected compensation for the sacrifice of their rights raised no objections since virtually all the deputies were firm believers in the sanctity of property. The plan was carried out on the night of August 4 when two members of the Society of Thirty, the vicomte de Noailles and the duc d'Aiguillon, the greatest owner of seigneurial rights among the nobility, offered to sacrifice these privileges in the interest of establishing the equality of the rights of Frenchmen and ending the peasant uprising. This offer created a patriotic fervor in the assembly that led to the complete abolition of privilege by the end of the session; deputies from all estates expressed their belief that a union of orders had now truly been established.[18]

The night of August 4 solidified the leadership of Duport, the founder of the Society of Thirty, and his allies from all three estates. These men then proceeded to play a major role in the drafting of the Declaration of the Rights of Man and the Citizen. They forged a coalition that crafted a compromise in the form of the suspensive veto on the knotty constitutional question of the king's right to sanction legislation. After September 1789 Duport and other noble deputies exercised tremendous influence in the assembly in conjunction with like-minded leaders such as Barnave from the Third Estate. At the same time the influence of Sieyès diminished significantly.

The Estates General of 1789 was the culmination of the long eighteenth-century political contest between the French monarchy and the Paris parlement. The ideological disputes between these contestants, far from dissipating by the late 1780s, had actually increased and continued during the months preceding the opening ceremonies of the assembly at Versailles. As the language of the pamphlet literature of 1788–9 demonstrates, even the goals of the Dauphiné reformers and the Society of Thirty were a variant of the parlementary constitutionalism that had been developing since mid-century. Sieyès's pamphlet *What Is the Third Estate?* developed the only truly revolutionary language to appear before the convening of the Estates General, and even he had to make a considerable retreat from this position in his *Deliberations* and actions in the assembly.

The events that transpired in the Estates General must be understood to have taken place within the context of the ideological contest, revealed in the pre-Revolutionary pamphlet literature which preceded them. Sieyès and possibly the Bretons may have believed that the Nation, in the guise of the Third Estate, was taking political control of France after the momentous declaration of June 17. The other deputies in the commons and many in the privileged orders as well, however, understood the National Assembly created that day to be a meeting of the representatives of the Nation composed of the three orders. This interpretation of events is vastly different from that proposed by Georges Lefebvre. Instead of an assembly dominated by the Third Estate, the leadership actually consisted of a coalition of individuals from the three orders. The patriotic nobility were strongly represented in the most powerful positions and committed to achieving reform supported by representatives from the three orders. Once the unionist leadership had gained control of the National Assembly, the issues under discussion quickly moved beyond the question of representation which had dominated public attention since September 1788. At that point the concept of a union of orders ceased to be important, and reform, removed from the shackles of privilege, took on a life of its own. Even though many in the clergy and nobility ultimately turned their backs on this reform, the work of the National Assembly continued to be guided by individuals from each of the former three estates, a profound legacy of the political program of the Society of Thirty.

9. Peasants and their Grievances

JOHN MARKOFF

Summary

John Markoff's work makes several contributions to debates about the origins of the Revolution. To begin with the evidence: first, in exploring a systematic national sample of villagers' own statements of the grievances, he is able to clarify just what it is that France's rural people were demanding as France slid into revolution; secondly, in exploring the subsequent patterns of rural insurrection, he is able to show how the forms and targets of peasant actions changed in the unfolding situation. This permits looking in new ways at processes unfolding on different timescales. By being able to trace rural action on a month-by-month and even (in some of his work) day-by-day basis, he provides new documentation on just what was happening in the short run. He argues that an important part of what made the French Revolution what it was occurred as rural people shifted towards attacking the rural lords, which had an enormous impact on the entire course of Revolutionary politics. In addition, by showing the ways in which peasant actions in 1789 were growing out of their increasing challenges to local elites in a variety of arenas, he strongly suggests that such a middle-run notion as "pre-Revolution" needs to be expanded. Historians have generally designated as the "pre-Revolution" the growing crisis among France's regional and national elites out of which the fateful and fatal decision to convene the Estates General emerged. But Markoff's work suggests that the concept of "pre-Revolution" probably should also include the growing challenges to seigneurial authority in the legal arena and certainly should include the increasing tempo of semi-insurrectionary challenge that some have noted in the wake of the great food riots of the 1770s. There appears to be a growing tension in rural France in the late ancien régime that needs a great deal more attention from historians.

239

INTRODUCTION

The great majority of the French people who lived during the years of revolution were peasants, and historians have formed the most diverse views of the part those peasants played. For Albert Soboul, France's peasants were a major source of radicalism: "The peasant and popular revolution was at the very heart of the bourgeois revolution and carried it steadily forward."[1] Georges Lefebvre identifies the target of the peasants' revolutionary actions: "Against the aristocracy the peasants had far more substantial grievances than the people of the cities, and it is natural, therefore, that they took it upon themselves to deal the blow by which the aristocracy was laid low."[2] Rather than a social class whose grievances drove the Revolution forward, George Taylor urges us to see peasant "docility."[3] Donald Sutherland's portrait, however, suggests neither docility nor radicalization: "In the end, therefore, the vast weight of ancient peasant France imposed itself upon the government at the expense of many of the ideals of 1789."[4] Four distinguished historians in so few words manage to express so many differences. The peasants are one of the engines of revolution and the peasants are the major brake on revolution. The peasants are active and the peasants are docile. The peasants act on their own behalf and the peasants act together with the urban popular classes to move the bourgeoisie's revolution forward.

The diversity of their actions makes it easy to understand how historians have characterized the impact of the peasants on the Revolution in so many different ways. Peasants engaged in organized, collective actions to secure food, to destroy the lords' documents, to drive away the tax collectors, to support a favored priest and make life miserable for a detested one, to rescue a fellow villager from the hands of the authorities, to defend a roadside cross from an urban National Guard unit, to burn the records on which military conscription would be based, to gain access to land, to seek higher wages, and many less dramatic actions as well.[5]

To understand the peasant role(s) in bringing on the Revolution, we need to consider the *threats* confronting them, their *resources* for defending themselves, their *opportunities* for advancing their cause, and their *wishes and hopes* that informed actions. Throughout we need to keep in focus the diversity of the French countryside and to distinguish long-standing contexts from the rapidly changing circumstances of the crises of the late 1780s. The delineation of threats, resources, opportunities, and wishes are perennial subjects for scholarly debate about the central participants in revolutions[6] – and neither the French Revolution nor its peasant component is an exception. But with regard to the wishes of the country people, scholars of the French Revolution are in the fortunate position of having an unparalleled source in the form of documents in which France's villagers told us what they wanted. We shall therefore begin with their expressed wishes, and we shall keep these wishes in mind as we turn to threats, resources, and opportunities.

GRIEVANCES

The Estates General promised for May 1789 was to be constituted by a multistep process. French villagers were to elect representatives who would meet with representatives of the nearby towns to choose the Third Estate's deputies. At every step of the process, the assembly that elected them might provide deputies with a *cahier de doléances* (a statement of grievances) and many of these assemblies were actually required to provide such a statement.[7] It was probably the case that almost every rural community in France produced a written statement of its views at the beginning of the great upheaval.[8] So something on the order of forty thousand rural communities gave their deputies such documents, many of which have survived. Scholars of other, similarly great, revolutionary upheavals have to try to infer the wishes of country people (often, as in France, the majority) from police reports, judicial records, statements by revolutionary ministers who claim to speak for them, journalists both sympathetic and hostile, frightened statements by those under attack, songs, engravings, and other troublesome sources. France's historians have all those sorts of sources, to be sure, but they also have the words written down all over France at the behest of the villagers themselves. If modern historians disagree, it is not because an absence of sources reduces them to speculation.

We must remember two important things about these documents: first, they are public documents, and second, they are the documents of communities. They are not simply collections of the complaints of individuals that someone pasted together but are collective acts produced to get results (and to avoid unpleasant reactions by angry authorities). This means that people who carried little clout in village life (the poor more often than the rich), or who were barred from participating by the official rules (all children and most women other than widows), are not going to be those whose wishes are reflected in the texts. It means additionally that things the community found it difficult to

Table 9.1   *Percentage of all grievances in parish grievance lists that concern claims on income*

Type of claim on income	
Taxation	32
Seigneurial regime	10
Clerical exactions	4
Total	46
(*N*)	(*27,742*)

Source: Adapted from Markoff, *Abolition of Feudalism*, Table 2.2.

agree on were likely to be avoided. It also means that things they might agree on, but judged imprudent to put on paper, were also likely to be avoided. With these considerations in mind, we can attack the historical challenge of the grievances of the peasantry at the beginning of the great upheaval in the most direct way possible: we can listen to what they have told us themselves.

Let us ask which were the areas of French life most likely to figure for discussion on the peasants' lists of grievances.[9] We see in Table 9.1 two very important things: first, the claims of others upon them were a very important part of their world – taxation, the seigneurial regime, and clerical exactions taken together amount to nearly half of all peasant grievances (and this table does not take into account such other burdens as conscription or the fees of legal professionals, both much resented in the countryside); secondly, the burdens most under discussion were those imposed by the state. As burdensome as the claims of the lord or the various payments made to the Church may have been, taxation occupies a weightier place in the grievance lists of the spring. To put this all into proper context, we need to step back from the way they formulated their grievances to examine what these burdens were, why they were so weighty, and how they weighed differently on peasants in very different situations from one another.

THREATS TO PEASANT INCOME

Something between a quarter and two-fifths of French farmland was "owned" by peasants – if by owned we mean the rights to work the land, profit from its yield, sell it if one wished, and pass it on to one's heirs. Since many rural families held some of their land, one might think of France, especially in comparison to much of Europe, as a country of peasant smallholders. (Perhaps a million people were "serfs," which implied some significant restriction on being able to sell one's land.)[10] But even very approximate, simple figures like these threaten to mislead us for two reasons. First of all, like much else about the peasantry, this rough effort at generalization amalgamates a sprinkling of good evidence from different areas that clearly demonstrate extreme differences from place to place. According to one survey of this research, for example, around Toulouse only about one-fifth of land was under peasant ownership, but in Pyrenean Béarn 98 percent was.[11] But second, and even more important to understanding the situation of France's country people, modern notions of ownership are conceptually misleading because rights over that parcel of land were shared with others. Before the Revolution not only would the state claim its taxes, but there would probably be a lord claiming various rights and the Church its dues as well. A peasant family's rights over land would very likely be constrained, moreover, by the collective rights of the local peasant community. Let us look more closely at these various claims.

Landownership did not and does not confer absolute rights to do whatever one wishes with one's property nor on one's property. In all twenty-first century states, for example, even on their own property people are subject to the criminal statutes of states and can kill people only under very limited circumstances (although your right to shoot people dead at your doorstep is not quite so limited in Paris, Texas as in Paris, France). In addition, their rights to sell or to bequeath may be subject to state regulation and limitation (there might be a sales or inheritance tax, for example).

The state was an important part of the world of eighteenth-century peasants, too, but so were a number of other institutions that are far less familiar in the twenty-first century (in large part because of the Revolution). First of all, by virtue of lying within the territory subject to a lord's seigneurial rights (the *seigneurie*) peasants might have any of a wide variety of obligations and any of a wide variety of limitations on their property rights.

Lords might have claims to a variety of regular payments in cash or kind, the former often rather light, the latter frequently a very large portion of the crop. Lords might have claims to large payments when land was transferred by sale or inheritance. Lords might have claims to compulsory peasant labor, deeply resented although often quite light compared to such obligations in eastern Europe. (State claims to labor on roads had tended to push aside lords' labor claims.) Lords might have a variety of rights to economically significant monopolies. Peasants might have to grind their grain in the lord's mill, bake their bread in the lord's oven, extract the juice of their grapes with the lord's winepress, and mate their female pigs with the lord's males. Like all protected monopolies, such practices could get very expensive. Lords might lease the mill at quite a high price – after all the miller got a captive clientele – and the miller charged quite high rates in turn.

Lords might have a monopoly on the right to hunt or to fish, and such rights could be supplemented by a monopoly on the right to carry weapons. This not only deprived some peasants of an opportunity to add some protein to their diets, but it could leave them vulnerable to a variety of animal nuisances, which might on occasion still include wolves. Adding insult to injury, lords might have the right, denied peasants, to raise their own rabbits or pigeons, or to stock a fishpond. Even when customary law restricted, in principle, the way the lord carried on the hunt, kept the rabbits or pigeons, or constructed the ponds, it was difficult for peasants to get those laws enforced and protect their fields.

Lords might have the right to collect a toll on the local roads and a fee on the local ferry – and it was not always easy for a peasant community to get the lord to live up to what was often, in customary law, a corresponding obligation to maintain the road and provide a reliable ferry service. Lords might be able to interpose themselves in place of the buyer in a peasant land sale, or to seize peasant land for nonpayment of some of the other rights.

Many of these rights were lucrative and many reminded lord and peasant alike that one was high, the other base – reminders reinforced by rights to symbolic deference. The lord's family might have a preferred bench in the local church, beneath whose floor the lord's ancestors lay buried, and the local priest might honor the lord's ceremonial occasions (the birth of children, for example). The lord's château was more than just a house, even more than just a large house, for it might carry emblems of status denied the peasant – a weather vane, a coat of arms, and architectural reminders of a military past (perhaps fictive). Such turrets might be wholly ornamental, if the château dated from recent centuries since royal cannon had long since made real turrets outmoded.

And some lords exercised their right to erect a gallows, no longer operational now that the royal courts had taken over the power to try people for life and death, but a striking reminder of where power was lodged nonetheless. When that archcritic of backwards foolishness, Voltaire, having become famous, acquired a *seigneurie* he acquired along with it the right to his own gallows.[12] Like that decorative gallows, the lord's court was sometimes a symbol of power, and a reminder of a bygone age, but if it was moribund in places, elsewhere it was an active institution.

Seigneurial claims could be seconded by ecclesiastical ones. A portion of the crop might be owed in the form of the tithe, nominally in support of the work of the parish priest but often enough paid to a monastery or other clerical body. The community of Bazus near Toulouse, for example, complained that their tithes went to "the *abbé* d'Aurillac who has never appeared in this parish and has never performed charitable works for the needy poor."[13] Even villagers who might tolerate payments for priestly services could deeply resent the tithe if the priest got little; and they might resent the practice of collecting still other fees for baptisms, marriages, and funerals on top of the tithe. Moreover, it was not always easy for peasants, lawyers, or even twenty-first-century historians to disentangle the seigneurial obligations from the ecclesiastical ones. A monastery or other ecclesiastical corporation might in fact be the local lord in some places, because there was no requirement that a lord be an individual or that a lord not be a clerical person or corporation. A payment to a lord of a portion of the crop and a payment to a monastery of a portion of the crop might have some profoundly different meaning to a legal theorist, but peasants in Burgundy who called the lord's portion "the devil's tithe" saw a considerable resemblance.[14] (And occasionally a lay lord had somewhere in the past actually gotten the right to collect the tithe, a circumstance not made more palatable to those who had to pay it by the legalese of "infeudated tithe.")

In addition to peasant proprietorship being constrained by lord and Church, rural communities exercised rights that limited the ownership claims of individuals. There might be rules about the time and method of planting or harvesting, the pasturing of animals, access to commonly held land, rights to fence one's one property. Historians have had a considerable, long-running, and generally inconclusive debate on precisely which peasants benefited the most from such collective institutions. In one view, it was the poorer members of the village community who benefited. A variety of communal practices, for example, provided something for the animals of those whose own plots were inadequate – animals might be able to graze on common field or forest, or on land whose owner was obliged to leave some land fallow and unfenced, or on the post-harvest stubble guaranteed by restrictions on harvesting tools. In a diametrically opposed view, it was the better-off peasants whose own resources put them in a position to take advantage of communal property – if, for example, you did not even own any animals, what use were collective grazing rights? While the matter remains unresolved, it does point to the existence of divisions within rural communities.[15]

The extent of peasant well-being varied considerably. A majority of peasant families owned less than 5 hectares, which in many parts of France was about the minimum needed to live from one's own land. Many peasant families, therefore, had to have some members who brought in extra income – and in some parts of France very many families had very many members doing something other than working their own land. A small number constituted a significant peasant elite and leased large tracts of land, subleasing them in smaller plots or hiring laborers for wages. Such tenant-farmer entrepreneurs might also lease from the local lord the collection of seigneurial rights. But most peasants were far less prosperous. Some would work as laborers on nearby land; others traveled as seasonal workers, often for months on end; many young girls worked in town as servants, and men from rocky hill country came to town to work with stone in the construction trades; in some places, especially in the south, many worked someone else's land for a share of the crops; and large numbers worked in rural industrial trades, especially weaving and spinning. For some families these were supplements, and for some the major source of family income. In places like Normandy a very large number of rural families were extremely dependent on extra-agricultural sources of employment. By such expedients many were scraping by, but a poor harvest, an energetic lawyer hired by a demanding lord, a new tax, an extension of the tithe to some untraditional crop, or a family illness could easily have a terrible impact.

Some did not even scrape by. The countryside, even in an average year, relentlessly generated those who could not make a go of it, and every city was full of country people looking for work. An early death for a family member might easily spell the difference between more or less managing and ruin. Desperate rural poverty and its fallout in the form of traveling work-seekers, begging and criminality – all difficult to distinguish from one another – made the fear of criminal strangers a commonplace, and made such fears and the reality that underpinned them multiply radically in hard times.[16]

Family security was not only a question of securing income, but of being able to purchase those necessities not secured by one's own labor on one's own land. Several generations of historians were of the view that the population increase – now estimated at growing from about 21.5 million in 1700 to 28.6 million toward the beginning of the Revolution[17] – accounted for downward pressure on wages, rising land-lessness and shrinking family landholdings. Recent research by economic historians suggests a more vigorous French economy than used to be thought, and wages may have been more or less stable after mid-century, rather than in decline.[18] To an older picture of a tradition-encrusted "immobile village" must be added a new picture of rural entrepreneurs "quick in using the opportunities and challenges that came their way."[19] But even this recent, less dark picture demonstrates how precarious was the existence of large numbers of rural families. For example, a recent national estimate of the relationship of wages to food prices over the course of the eighteenth century suggests that standards of living were stagnant at best, and maybe grimmer than that.[20] Any rural family dependent on the wages of some of its members was in for a struggle. Times of scarcity in which grain, flour, and bread prices all rose radically might offer opportunities to those with marketable surpluses of grain, but they were acutely hazardous to the rural majority who, like the town dwellers, needed to purchase essentials.

But peasant income was challenged beyond the relationship of income and prices, since the state, the lord, and the Church might have claims on a part of that income. Historians are in general agreement that the great antitax insurrections of the seventeenth century produced not only bloody repression but also a shift into the more subtle form of indirect taxation. Such taxes tended to be doubly indirect in fact: they were assessed on transactions of many sorts, making them at once pervasive, hard to evade, and profoundly regressive; and many of them were collected not by state employees but by a vast bureaucratic apparatus whose control was leased to a corporation of financiers, the "tax farmers" ("the state's leeches," "vermin," "a plague," according to villagers near Rouen[21]). The grievance lists reveal these indirect taxes to be particularly loathed.

The antipathy inspired by taxation led historians for a very long time to think of the tax burden of the French as unusually heavy, growing heavier, and unusually skewed toward poorer people. To the extent that more recently we have been able to develop national data, however, we can be highly confident that over much of the eighteenth century, the British, on average, paid about double what the French did; it is even likely (but less certain) that it was British taxation that was the more skewed towards poorer people.[22] It is probably not the measurable burden on France's peasants that generated their hostility, but their sense of a system permeated by arbitrary assessment, privileged exemption, personal profit, and devoted to expenditures from which they drew inadequate benefit and over which they had no voice.

Historians are in a good deal less agreement on the weightiness of seigneurial rights and ecclesiastical exactions. They varied so much from region to region, from village to village, and even from one peasant plot to another that the degree to which they weighed on the peasants and the degree to which they were a major part of the income of the lords (as opposed to such other important sources of income as the lords' commercial exploitation of their own crops, herds, and forests, or their return from investments in commerce, government office, or manufacturing) have been difficult to generalize about with confidence. Historians have been struggling for two centuries to put together a compelling national portrait that takes account of this immense variation, but this has proven very difficult.

Some historians, moreover, see evidence that commercial opportunities in the developing national and international markets, combined with the economic challenge to provide suitable resources to their heirs in a century of population growth, was leading France's lords to be more stringent in collecting their dues from the peasants than in the past (or hiring lawyers to concoct new rights) as well as doing their best to enlarge their own properties by forcing peasants to sell out. Although several generations of historians have spoken of a "feudal reaction" others remain less convinced.[23]

Although the nature and extent of the claims of state, lord, and Church all varied enormously across France, since they all laid claim to the same limited peasant income, there probably was a tendency for the three kinds of claim to be in competition. Claudine Wolikow captures this in suggesting that light taxes in Burgundy went hand in hand with heavy seigneurial claims, while Norman peasants whose lords took little paid much to the state, and southern peasants whose lords took little paid a good deal to the Church, and so forth.[24]

TRADITIONS OF RESISTANCE

France's villagers not only differed in the nature and extent of the burdens represented by state, lord, and Church as well as the never-altogether-absent threat of hunger, but in their traditions of attempting to lighten these burdens. Resistance might range from the surreptitious and individual actions of concealment (of grain from a tithe-collector, of a son's true age when conscription threatened), to clandestine networks of evasion (in smuggling goods past tax collectors), to collective challenges in the legal arena (in the form of communally supported lawsuits), to collective and semi-insurrectionary substitutions of direct action for failed authority (as in many food riots). Among these practices the open, collective, and flagrantly illegal actions were the riskiest in light of the possibility of severe, repressive countermeasures, and they also – and perhaps one should say "therefore" – were often carried out with the support of overt or tacit allies. Such allies might include the local priest at whose church many an action was planned, the lawyer who pressed a case in court (especially in challenges to lords), and the independent courts challenging administrative action or inaction (notably around food supply and price).

I will sketch with broad strokes some of the important traditions of contestation. Military expenditures were a major strain on Europe's rival states for a very long time and a major source of rising taxation. The seventeenth century was an especially violent moment, as large-scale interstate warfare (much of it involving religious conflict) intersected widespread rebellion (much of it likewise having a significant religious dimension). Hunger played its part as well: increasing and sometimes impoverished populations collided with states' rising taxation and landowners' more stringent exactions to produce still more social explosion. In France the result was a series of great rebellions in which taxation was a major target. Although the French countryside became, once again, more or less pacified, intermittent, smaller-scale tax rebellions remained a major form of peasant collective action. The particulars of these antitax actions varied considerably since there were many different taxes; the weight of these taxes varied greatly from one region to another; and the mechanism of collection varied a good deal. In addition to a large number of small-scale semi-insurrectionary challenges, the great tax diversity stimulated a tenacious clandestine tax-evading network.

Consider as an example the salt tax, which was, as we saw above, extremely widely detested. Its weight was far from uniform. Let us look at northwest France. According to Jacques Necker (who, having served as France's chief tax official, should know) the going price for salt in Artois in 1780 was a low seven to eight livres per minot while in Brittany, free of the tax, it went for an almost insignificant one livre ten sous to three livres. If you went from Artois to Normandy along a coastal route you would find salt at thirteen livres and local people were allowed to get their salt from seawater. But in inland Normandy, one of the "provinces of the Great Salt Tax," the price rose to 54 livres and in neighboring Picardy, south of Artois, from 57 to 59.[25] Around such steep price differences, active smuggling networks formed and large numbers of people were able to earn their living moving contraband salt past the authorities. Some 23,000 people were employed trying to police the borders of Brittany, and failed consistently, despite arresting some 6,600 children from smuggler families in an average year at the southeast corner of Brittany alone.[26]

The extreme variety of taxes on alcoholic beverages, the taxes collected by national and town governments on entering goods, and the numerous customs barriers – some part of the tax system, but others in the hands of individual lords – all encouraged smuggling as well. The resentments generated by these numerous, varying taxes on goods of various kinds – none more part of the fabric of daily existence than salt – and the well-established networks of lawbreakers seem to have been the nucleus from which many of the tax rebellions of the revolutionary period sprang. In northwest France, the clear majority of the Revolution's rural antitax actions took place within a few kilometers of the boundaries between places that were taxed at such very different levels.[27]

In the course of the eighteenth century, urban and rural people alike refined the techniques of a second form of struggle, known in summary to historians as the "food riot." These were attempts to obtain food at acceptable prices, particularly grain, flour, or bread. Country people became adept at staging blockages of grain transportation routes and invading urban market places to coerce sellers into providing their goods at what the crowd held a proper price.[28] In times of scarcity, government officials vacillated between trying to assure affordable provisions for major towns (often by buying grain and then releasing it on the market) and trying to let market forces operate, thereby managing to implicate itself in the minds of the frightened in the very scarcities it hoped to remedy.[29] Since such crises could bring threatened town dweller and threatened villager alike into rebellious action, state agents were very wary. The greatest wave of insurrectionary action in the decades preceding the collapse of the ancien régime, in fact, was the Flour War of 1775, in which governmental support for liberalization of the grain trade was derailed by scarcity-induced widespread popular actions.

Since price rises were profoundly threatening to those without enough land to be producing a surplus, while creating windfalls for those who did, they were probably divisive moments within village communities; since those growing something other than grain were especially vulnerable, hardship was unevenly distributed across the map of France; and since those near roads had the opportunity to attack grain shipments, traditions of mobilization did not coincide with the locales experiencing the greatest hardships. A region like Normandy, where large numbers of rural people had been shifting out of agriculture into textiles and along whose waterways grain traveled towards Paris, was particularly vulnerable, which may explain why Normandy was especially prone to food riots throughout the century, as well as during the Revolution.[30]

Participation in invading a marketplace and setting prices gave the sensation of filling in for derelict authority and provided a powerful if fleeting experience of self-rule. This may have provided an experiential frame of reference for radical conceptions of popular sovereignty that emerged down the line in revolutionary rhetoric. A sense of legitimacy was sometimes imparted to such actions by local officials favoring social peace over new economic theory and by magistrates sometimes spoiling for yet another fight with overweening ministers.

Even in poor years there tended to be grain right after harvest and therefore over the half-century before the Revolution, insurrections tended to rise from a winter low to a summer high.[31] One nervous deputy to the Estates-General wrote his brother in 1790: "I've always feared June and July."[32] His fears were well grounded: beginning in 1789, the French Revolution was to see the largest wave of food riots in French history and probably in European history;[33] they were rising as the grievance lists were being written in the spring and continued to rise into the summer, and they were especially concentrated in the rural hinterlands of large towns through which some good roads ran.

Nonetheless, there is precious little about the price and availability of food in the grievance lists. What we probably have to picture is the incapacity of many villages to arrive at a united position on these questions, unlike their considerable agreement on taxation, seigneurial rights, and clerical exactions.

While the lion's share of the eighteenth-century's small-scale rebellions were about taxes and food (and we shall look at some confirmatory figures shortly), no account of peasant burdens and resistance could neglect the demands of lord and Church. Mitigating these demands was the aim of a well-established repertoire of resistance. Peasants concealed the extent of the harvest so that lord and Church got lower payments in kind. They pretended, plausibly enough, not to understand all the complex payments they owed. Threatening letters, menacing looks, and the occasional act of arson or thievery may have intimidated some lords. And there is some evidence that as the eighteenth century advanced, peasant communities were increasingly likely to enter the legal arena and challenge some new form of the tithe here and some lord's claim there. When the new Revolutionary *département* of Pas-de-Calais did a study of legal actions between lords and communities, it learned that among the 772 communities for which we have the data, no fewer than 184 had such contests.[34]

These legal actions brought peasant communities into contact with attorneys. France's law schools were turning out graduates as never before[35] and it may be that some of these increasingly numerous lawyers kept an eye out for new kinds of clients. This peasant–lawyer encounter may have been a very important connection; indeed, one in which peasants learned to connect their everyday experience of the pervasive seigneurial system with nationally understood legal principles, and attorneys learned a great deal about rural circumstances. This is very likely part of what sparked the tenacity with which French peasants used the courts to resist lord and Church, and even to launch counterattacks.[36] And the conversations between peasant clients and their legal agents as well as the lawyers' written briefs and oral pleadings were probably one of the very important places in which an antiseigneurial discourse was being forged.[37] So peasants found some ideological support for their quarrels with the claims of Church and lord in working with legal professionals eager to make a name for themselves on behalf of an enlightened cause.

The French state could sometimes supply allies against the lords as well. Although at the centers of state power the advanced economic champions of individualistic conceptions of property rights got a hearing, out in the village where taxes had to be collected in practice, some local officials readily saw how much easier it would be to collect from a community, rather than a bunch of individuals, and from a community secure in its communal property at that. So at least in some places government officials encouraged the legal actions of peasant communities against lords.[38] (Other local officials fought communal rights.[39])

If one may speak of a local geography of peasant–lord contention, pride of place would probably go to forest, pasture, and commons (to some extent overlapping categories). These were all places in which growing opportunities for enterprising lords conflicted with the peasants' economic safety net. Lords and communities often had ambiguously demarcated claims on such places, not a problem when their value was marginal. A forest might be a place where all community members had the right to pick up what had fallen to the ground and where animals could freely graze but they might also be places lords claimed to own; the village commons might be where all peasants could graze their animals but lords might have some right to seize some customarily set portion, should they choose. In the eighteenth century, demand for wood rose steeply: growing urban populations expanded the markets for fuel and construction; royal attempts to match England on the seas promoted shipbuilding as well as trying to prevent others from destroying forests; ironmaking and other industrial production enlarged the fuel market. A single 74-gun warship needed 2800 oaks and in the 1780s the navy had almost four dozen built, and other ships besides.[40] With the price of wood rising steeply, enterprising lords might press their claims more strongly – and be resisted more strongly by both enterprising peasants who sought the same opportunity and desperate peasants who faced ruin if they had to buy their fuel in the marketplace. And we might say much the same of pasture: for example, rising urban demand for meat and military demand for leather was leading some lords to try to rent out their rights to a portion of common pasture to commercial stockraisers, a practice whose dubious basis in customary law could easily encourage a lawyer and a village clientele to try the legal route to resistance. Uncertainty over who had what rights over which plot of land were pervasive enough that one recent economic historian has seen in this uncertainty a major barrier to economic growth – whether you were a lord or a peasant, you wouldn't invest much in land that a court might say you had no right to.[41]

But such conflicts generated clandestine resistance as well: taking wood in the dead of night, killing the lords' livestock. And then there was the open, collective land invasion in which the bold simply occupied a field and destroyed new fencing, generally claiming to be taking back what the lord had illicitly usurped.[42]

One especially institutionalized contest developed around the lords' monopolies on hunting and arms-bearing. Peasants developed poaching into a fine art, in which you had not only to bag the game but also to evade the lords' hired guards. This cat-and-mouse of game wardens and poachers took place within a particularly complex field of social struggle.

Well-off commoner landowners might also hunt, perhaps hoping for some splendid game for dinner, but also in refusal of the claims of the lord down the road to be the only one around with hunting rights. And the local lords themselves, should their property happen to lie within the zones set aside for the king's own hunting claims, would find that they themselves could only hunt on what they liked to think of as their land by defying royal prerogatives. So peasant poachers operated against a background of complex rules and multifaceted defiance of rules.

As for the illicit use of firearms, the expanded size of armies virtually guaranteed that weapons found their way into the villages, and created yet another intermittent zone of struggle as the thinly stretched rural police mounted occasional raids hoping, in vain, to get such weapons out of the hands of peasants. In this conflict government officials hoping to disarm potential troublemakers were allied with lords hoping to preserve the status honor of being the only civilians allowed to display weaponry.[43]

In addition to collective challenge in the legal arena and surreptitious acts of concealment and defiance, there were collective, illegal, and even semi-insurrectionary confrontations. The large insurrections of the seventeenth century had been put down, mostly by force, but also to some extent by shifting taxation into the wide variety of taxes on everyday acts from the purchase of alcohol to the registration of a legal document. Such taxes were far easier to assess than taxes on crop yields or land values that sensible peasants would be sure to falsify. The open, collective, confrontational, and sometimes violent challenges of the eighteenth century operated on a lesser scale: a smallish group, from a single village (at most a few neighboring communities), making trouble for a day (or at most two or three). These events were highly integrated into the fabric of rural life. They were, for example, often organized on Sunday after Mass, an event that brought the community together. Sunday was by far the most common day for riots through the entire period.[44]

Let us examine some of the results of a large-scale French data collection project that identifies the forms of popular involvement in conflict between 1661 and the spring of 1789.[45] In Table 9.2, we compare three decades that span the beginning of the eighteenth century with the last three decades before the Revolution. These figures do not distinguish urban and rural participation; however, they are a pretty good rough guide to the changing patterns of rural contestation in part because about two-thirds of the events are rural, and in part because some of the urban events had rural participants as country people invaded a market

Table 9.2 *The changing forms of eighteenth-century conflict (%)*

Form of conflict	1690–1720	1760–1789
Antitax resistance: efforts to prevent the collection of taxes, including attacks on officials, burning of offices and their records, wrecking of checkpoints	31.3	14.3
Food riots: efforts to secure food at affordable prices, including invasion of markets, blocking grain shipments, coerced sales, intimidating bakers, demanding official intervention	23.5	32.3
Clashes with military, police, or judicial authorities: a miscellany of battles with authority not fitting other rubrics, including conflict over fines, property seizures, and conscription	19.2	15.3
Religious troubles: clashes of Catholics and Protestants, conflicts over management of parish affairs, conflicts over religious practice	7.3	0.9
Antiseigneurial actions: destruction of enclosures, damaging trees, filling in ditches, violence against seigneurial agents	5.7	7.2
Labor conflict: strikes over wages	3.1	5.9
(*N*)	(*776*)	(*2021*)

Source: Computed from data in Guy Lemarchand, "Troubles populaires au XVIIIe siècle et conscience de classe: Une préface a la Révolution française," *AHRF*, no. 279 (1990), pp. 32–48.

or attacked a tax office. To point up the elements of change in the century before the Revolution, the forms of conflict are in descending order of frequency at the beginning of the century.

Antitax conflict and food riots head the list at the beginning of the eighteenth century and were running strong in the last decades before the Revolution, but antitax actions were a less likely form of conflict late in the century, and food riots more likely, having become in fact the most common form of conflict. A miscellany of clashes with national and local authority, police, military, and judicial, was also running strong. Religious troubles were a small but still notable component of social conflict at the beginning of the period but had almost completely died off on the eve of Revolution.

Only after considering all these do we arrive at the distinctly minor category of antiseigneurial actions. To be sure they are on the rise at the end of the ancien régime, but that rise leaves them still far behind food riots and antitax resistance. Nonetheless, even this limited increase, particularly when taken in conjunction with communal challenges to lords in the judicial arena, suggests that historians' (debated) conception of a seigneurial "feudal reaction" needs to be joined by a more intensive scrutiny of a peasant "antifeudal reaction."[46] Finally, labor conflict, largely over wages, is still small, although also heading up.

In noting the variety of forms of conflict, and recalling the variety of peasant circumstances, let us not neglect one last striking element. The total number of these small-scale clashes was way, way up at the end of the ancien régime compared to the early eighteenth century, more than two-and-one-half times as frequent. Small in scale many of these events undoubtedly were, but in their growing frequency they are telling us something very important about the increasing capacity and will of the people of the countryside to challenge authority.

While some common targets of peasant action probably tended to unite a fairly broad spectrum of villagers, others were probably quite divisive. Taxation united. Earlier generations of historians pictured a peasantry up against a financially strapped state desperately tightening the screws as a privileged elite kept taxes off themselves. In light of the great diversity of taxes whose patterns of privileged exemption differed greatly, the omnipresent regional differences, and the continued governmental tinkering with allocation and collection, we probably should confess a good deal more uncertainty about generalizing, and renew our research on who was paying how much.[47] But what is fairly clear is that the numerous taxes collected on transactions injured those with something to sell, to transport, and to buy alike. And landowners owing a large cut to the state were likely to take a tougher position on the wage demands of the landless, so taxation troubled the better-off and their laborers alike.

On the other hand, the increasingly numerous actions aimed at securing food at affordable prices were very likely far more divisive, since those with marketable surpluses might be benefiting from the very shortages that frightened and enraged those with less land. One of the keenest students of the evolution of French subsistence conflicts writes that by the 1760s "[t]hese disorders brought together agricultural laborers and small- and medium-holders against the large holders of grain."[48]

That so many different kinds of collective action were carried on for so long tells us that many parts of France had strong traditions of local organization. In much of northern France the intermingled properties of individual proprietors were unfenced and communal rules regulated times of planting, agricultural technology, and the grazing patterns of animals. Sometimes the lord had a considerable say in these decisions (a lord might have the right to be the first to harvest grapes, for example, thereby having a marketing advantage, or the right to set the harvest date), but often a strong community organization played a major role. In other places, especially in parts of the south, rural communities could be almost little republics, with a lot to say about internal allocation of taxes or other claims on income. In all such places, peasant communities would have officially recognized forms of organization.[49] These organizations might differ considerably in how oligarchic they were and in the extent of their authority, but they provided a vehicle for mounting legal challenges to state, lord or Church, and perhaps a framework for mounting insurrectionary action as well.

But models of organized planning for collective actions could be drawn on for the creation of unofficial, ad hoc bodies for local contestation, too, like the 98 residents of one southwestern village who deliberated before a notary as they challenged the tithe demanded by a religious body in 1780. That such organizations were fairly commonplace is suggested by the existence of a label ("syndicates of individuals").[50]

If official village assemblies, ad hoc organizations, or Sunday's coming together for church services all provided vehicles for a broad spectrum of villagers to thrash out legal and illegal modes of collective action, France's villagers also had some experience in organizing for collective disputes within the rural community itself. Rural wage laborers were often recruited in gangs, especially if they were seasonal workers whose foreignness might be reinforced by linguistic distinctiveness. Work-gang chiefs, often country people with some experience away from the village acquired in town or military service, recruited the gangs and supervised their work. But these chiefs could also come together to organize actions to challenge the terms of employment, thereby developing a lot of experience in coordinating with one another, in getting the laborers to act in concert, and in judging the most propitious moments for such action (moments of labor shortage, especially when harvest or planting had to be done soon, were probably particularly favorable).[51]

And then there were the thoroughly illegal networks engaged in smuggling salt, alcohol, tobacco, manufactured goods, and so forth past tax collection authorities. The enduring existence of such practices implied entire clandestine networks linking buyers and sellers, along which information as well as contraband would move.

   We may think of these as the major traditions of collective action in the French countryside at the moment of Revolution. Yet the pattern of rural insurrection in the Revolutionary years was to diverge notably from the past. While subsistence fears and tax grievances played their part, the most striking aspect of French villagers' insurrectionary actions was the intensity of their campaign against the lords. France's villagers challenged the new government until the seigneurial system was abolished. So vivid, in fact, has been the image of an antiseigneurial uprising that the great twentieth-century medieval historian Marc Bloch commented that whenever we now think about feudalism "[i]n the background there is always a reflection of the firing of châteaux during the burning summer of '89'."[52] To understand this burning summer better, we need another look at the grievances of the spring.

PEASANTS COMPLAIN ABOUT THE DEMANDS OF LORD, CHURCH, AND STATE

The great variety of seigneurial rights explains the great variety one finds in the grievance lists. Consider, for example, a single very interesting institution, the seigneurial courts. Historians have made clear that in some places these were somnolent institutions, hardly functioning at all, entirely superseded by the royal courts, and not merely because the royal courts were successfully encroaching on formerly localized power, but because the lords were unenthusiastic about bearing the expense and were delighted at the prospect of being rid of the responsibility. In other places, however, the courts were very much alive as the lowest level of the judicial system, the place peasants might go to in search of settling their own disputes and providing some resolution far cheaper than the costs of legal action in the more distant royal courts. And in still other places the seigneurial courts seem to have been virtually the linchpin of the entire complex of seigneurial rights, providing the lord with the capacity to coerce peasant conformity to all the rest.[53] So one fine piece of research in the Toulouse region convincingly finds their courts to be "a key institution in the maintenance of the noble's interests in general and of the seigniorial system in particular,"[54] and another fine study of 55 seigneurial courts not very far away finds it quite rare that the courts enforced payment of dues (although they did protect hunting rights).[55]

Faced with their own, local experience, the assemblies drew up very different sorts of grievances. The northeastern village of Dolving calls for abolition when it insists that "under such justice the people can never be anything but a hopeless victim of the most disastrous rapacity and pillage."[56] But other assemblies propose mechanisms for reforming the courts so that the people will not be hopeless victims. In Champagne, the village of Bucey-en-Othe would have lords barred from bringing cases involving themselves or their land, would secure judicial independence by making court officials irremovable (unless duly convicted of embezzlement), would require a court to have its full complement of officials so that it could function properly, and would require proper physical facilities, such as a usable courtroom and jail.[57] About one-third of parish assemblies discussing seigneurial courts acted like Bucey-en-Othe and proposed reforms, not abolition.[58]

This is unusual among peasant attitudes toward seigneurial rights, and it is also deeply revealing. In general, rural communities were not asking that seigneurial rights be reformed, but that they be ended. We can see this clearly in Table 9.3.

Very few villages call for any aspect of taxation, ecclesiastical exactions, or seigneurial rights to continue unchanged. But not much below half of all grievances about taxation call for reform or for replacing some element of the tax system with something else, a far less common proposal with regard to the seigneurial rights. Inversely, not much below

Table 9.3 *Grievances to maintain, replace, reform, or abolish some aspect of seigneurial rights, ecclesiastical exactions, and taxation in the parish grievance lists (%)*

Action demanded	Seigneurial rights	Ecclesiastical exactions	Taxation
Maintain substantially unaltered	1	0	1
Replace	2	0	4
Reform	15	23	42
Abolish with compensation	9	1	0
Abolish without compensation	36	42	24
(*N*)	(*2174*)	(*357*)	(*6032*)

Source: Adapted from Markoff, *Abolition of Feudalism*, Table 3.1.

half of all grievances about seigneurial rights are for their abolition
(although sometimes with compensation to be paid to the lord), something advocated only about half as often with regard to taxation. In
other words, taxation is preeminently an arena for reform, seigneurial
rights for abolition. Ecclesiastical dues lie somewhere in between, but
closer to seigneurial rights than to taxation.

Now what makes these burdens so different? Let us note that not a
single parish grievance list that I have seen demands the abolition pure
and simple of all taxes, while some 18 percent of those discussing "the
seigneurial regime in general" do precisely that. There is much evidence
that however much particular taxes might be detested, however unfair it
seemed that some, especially nobles (along with towns, some provinces,
and the Church) did not seem to be paying their fair share, and however
heavy the burden, villagers felt that there were desired services to be
funded out of taxation – road repairs, arresting murderers, provision for
the destitute, education, policing the scales used by merchants, enforcing
legal agreements, and many other things that many villagers would not
want to do without.

Consider for a moment that tax on legal transactions which we saw
to have occasioned so many complaints. Among the many parish assemblies with something to say, 27 percent wanted their abolition but 63
percent wanted them reformed or replaced. As we hear the peasants of
Beaulieu-en-Argonne discuss the most important such tax, the *droit de
contrôle*, we can readily see why:

> For the *contrôle*, we ask a fixed and invariable schedule of rates that may
> not be extended at the whim of clerks; that these agents do not contin-
> ually harass poor people who do not know what taxes one demands of
> them and who therefore are subject to fines; that the *contrôle* is surely
> necessary to establish the date of contracts; that this tax be moderate
> and that other taxes not be added on; that, from time to time, there be
> displayed an announcement of the taxes to which one is subject, so that
> an accidental slip of memory not be punished as fraud.[59]

Summarily put, taxes paid for some valued services – although there
could be fierce anger over whether all taxes did so; over whether the
peasants paid more than their fair share, especially in light of noble privilege; over whether the benefits went where they ought; over whether tax
officials managed to make great personal rewards out of their control of
the funds; and much else besides.

By contrast, the seigneurial rights, on the whole, were a burden for which there was little in return. But when village communities did see some valuable service at stake they might favor reforming particular seigneurial rights, which is why one third wanted a reformed, not an abolished, seigneurial administration of justice. If you could just get rid of the abuses, there was something to be said for locally administered and inexpensive justice. If you could only stop the lords trampling the peasants' fields and shooting the peasants' interfering dogs, if you could be assured that the lords would not only hunt when it suited them but took it as a duty to kill wolves, if the penalties for peasant infraction were clearly known, then perhaps the lords' hunting rights could be kept, after all (about 15 percent of parish assemblies were advocating a reformed right to hunt, in fact).[60] As for payments due the Church, peasants could clearly distinguish the tithe, intended for support of the valued work of the local priest, and other fees, which seemed superfluous. But they also readily recognized the frequency with which the tithe in practice went for other purposes, as well as what they held to be inequities and arbitrariness in its allocation and collection. Thus village assemblies were far less likely to demand the outright abolition of the tithe than of other ecclesiastical exactions. The Norman village of Equemauville, for example, calls for an end to some of their tithes and insists that a portion "be divided among priests with responsibilities but no revenues – for the honor of religion and the happiness of humanity."[61] But no peasant communities wanted the tithe maintained in its present form (see Table 9.4).

In the first spring of Revolution, peasants were making distinctions among their various burdens. The claims of the lords may have been more detested, but taxation got the lion's share of attention, and to a very large degree what village France proposed was not the abolition of

Table 9.4 *Parish grievance lists with demands to maintain, reform, or abolish the tithe and other ecclesiastical exactions (%)*

Action demanded	Tithe	Other ecclesiastical exactions
Reform	39	6
Abolish	29	80
Maintain	0	2
(*N*)	(*102*)	(*95*)

Source: Adapted from Markoff, *Abolition of Feudalism*, Table 3.10.

the state and its tax collection system, but its reform: it should be fairer, it should be more efficient, its weight should be less, it should be more predictable. The elite debates about taxation, so important to the very convening of the Estates General, encouraged the villagers to take up taxation in their own statements. The prospect of significant tax reform through the Estates General, indeed, may have seemed to many communities a good deal more promising at that moment than the prospects of antitax insurrectionary mobilizations. Thus many peasant communities formulated large numbers of reformist demands about taxation within a legal framework and far fewer launched the sorts of insurrectionary actions about taxes that a simple extrapolation from their own rebellious traditions would indicate. A similar extrapolation would have suggested relatively few antiseigneurial insurrections, and, at first, antiseigneurial actions were indeed far less common than distur-bances around subsistence questions. And, as we have seen, seigneurial rights were taken up far less often in the grievance lists than taxation. But when they were addressed the tone is more bitter, extreme, and unyield-ing – indicating something of the potential for an antiseigneurial campaign in village France should circumstances prove propitious.

ECONOMIC CRISIS, POLITICAL OPPORTUNITY, AND REVOLUTIONARY ACTION IN THE FRENCH COUNTRYSIDE

In light of the foregoing, it would be foolish to search for *the* role played by France's peasants in the origins of the Revolution, and even more foolish to search for *the* role in making the Revolution what it came to be. It is not for nothing that a leading historian of rural France speaks of "twenty contrasting peasantries."[62] France's country people variously planted grains but other crops as well; owned land, sharecropped, and worked for wages; owed different mixes of taxes, seigneurial rights, and ecclesiastical dues; had different traditions of collective action; lived in villages and in separated farmsteads; were involved to different degrees in rural industrial production; were more or less literate. A village was likely to agree on some courses of action against external targets but was also likely to have internal divisions. So it is not surprising that France's villagers played many different parts in the Revolution. But to understand their roles in the crisis of 1789, we need to start by listening to what they told us when they put their grievances on paper. We need to start with hardship.

We have asserted that for a considerable number of those who lived in the countryside, a growing economy did not significantly mitigate the difficult struggle for existence. This assured a large number of rural families who were barely making do and a steady supply of paupers who had failed to do so, strong incentives for communities to challenge lords' questionable claims to pasture and forest, plenty of motivation for the daring or desperate to hunt and fish illegally or to set their children to smuggling highly taxed commodities past checkpoints, and no shortage of participants in food riots.

The severe economic hardships of the 1780s amplified all of these trends profoundly. Families in wine country were already strapped for economic resources as the result of a severe price fall in that cash crop in the late 1770s. Rural industrial employment weakened seriously from English competition in the 1780s, profoundly exacerbated by an Anglo-French trade treaty of 1786 that dismantled protectionist barriers to textile imports. In places where rural industry was a significant supplement to agricultural incomes, let alone for those many families who had completely gone over to domestic weaving, the result was catastrophe. So it was with more limited resources than usual that many rural families faced the disastrous harvest of 1788. Cash crops, animal fodder, subsistence plots all failed. As the price of bread began to rise so did the trajectory of food riots.

And country people were coming to turn to other targets as well. To understand this we need to add an element of hope, of opportunity, as well as other threats into the picture. The elections for the Estates General were a central element in turning peasant action in new directions. The social conflicts in the French countryside played little direct role in the political crisis of the upper reaches of wealth and power out of which the decision to convene an Estates General was made. Although, as we have seen, the intensity of collective rural contestation had risen since the 1760s, it is understandable that historians have generally applied the expression "pre-Revolution" exclusively to the conflicts among the elites, for no one has yet produced any evidence of any great elite awareness of the mounting frequency of these small-scale village clashes. The economic disasters of the late 1780s, however, had dramatically visible results. Not only were food riots in the ascendant from the summer of 1788 on, but the flood of impoverished country people, the bands of beggars and the threat of criminality, never terribly well contained by the ancien régime's inadequate poor relief and inadequate police repression, were now much exacerbated.

The pervasive visible rural impoverishment of the moment did enter the awareness of the elite contestants in the great political crisis, as shown by the Third Estate propagandists' depiction of those country people staggering under the weight of the privileged. Such images of passive peasant suffering served as a metaphor for the Third Estate in the struggles surrounding the Estates General. Such images seemed to say: "We, the skilled and educated commoners, like the peasants, bear the awful burden of privilege. Is it not time for us to throw off this weight?"[63]

If elite propaganda could depict the peasants as ground down by social privilege, not just suffering from harvest failure, and do so sympathetically, small wonder that by the spring of 1789, rural communities were beginning to organize to attack the lords. The elections for the Estates General took place that spring, and the villagers assembled to draw up their grievances. It was not, as we saw, the food issues that dominated their documents – these would have been divisive within those very villages. But they could agree on a sweeping critique of taxation, which moreover was plainly at the center of the elite debates.

They were also beginning to discover the extent to which the Third Estate's leadership had its own critique of seigneurialism, as Third Estate and nobility competed for the allegiance of the countryside. Publicists circulated model grievance lists hoping to persuade France's 40,000 rural communities to support their causes. Nobles in Brittany attempted to reach the country people by circulating literature in Breton;[64] to the south, one official expressed shock that Third-Estate activists were circulating pamphlets in Provençal to "address the peasants and workers in their usual language in order to get them to take an interest in present affairs."[65]

To the very general hope for change represented by the Estates General was added the impact of the great flood of information now reaching villagers about the thinking of the elites and the sorts of change that might now be possible. Where the elites were most bitterly at loggerheads, as in Brittany, peasant mobilization was especially vigorous at an early stage; and where elite debates were inclined to address the issues surrounding "feudalism" as in Provence, peasants were earlier than elsewhere beginning to target the lords.[66]

Following the elections, as the frequency of peasants engaging in collective actions mounted, so did the propensity of those actions to target the seigneurial regime (as shown in the first two rows of Table 9.5). And the character of antiseigneurial actions changed, too (as Table

Table 9.5 *Insurrectionary events in the French countryside, June 1, 1788–August 11, 1789: frequency of events, percentage of antiseigneurial events, and selected characteristics of antiseigneurial events*

	June 1, 1788– February 28, 1789	March 1, 1789– June 30, 1789	July 1, 1789– August 11, 1789
Number of events per day	0.5	3.0	29.4
Antiseigneurial events as a percentage of all events	12	25	31
Antiseigneurial events with selected characteristics (%):			
Land invasions	31	10	9
Forest use asserted	25	2	4
Hunting; seizing or killing lord's pigeons, rabbits, fish; destroying dovecotes, warrens, ponds	44	48	5
Coerced renunciation of rights	0	9	8
Documents seized or destroyed	0	6	29
Château attacked or entered	0	20	67
Château seriously damaged	0	4	32

Source: Adapted from Markoff, *Abolition of Feudalism*, Tables 8.2 and 8.3.

9.5 also shows). From the summer of 1788 up into the winter of 1789, villagers were continuing in more dramatic form to challenge the same aspects of the seigneurial regime that they had been pursuing in legal actions or individual rule-breaking for decades. Instead of going to court to debate who owned the fields, pastures, and forests, and instead of surreptitious poaching or furtive slaughter of the lords' detested pigeons and rabbits, now collectively and in the light of day a rural community marched onto the contested terrain, hunted, and seized or slaughtered pigeons and rabbits. From the spring electoral period into the early summer, villagers were beginning to coerce the lords into renouncing their rights as well as seizing or destroying the documents with which the lords could demonstrate their claims. Lords might be dragged outside their homes and terrified into a renunciation, sometimes transcribed formally by a notary (whose own participation might be less than willing). Or villagers might break in to hunt for the lord's papers. In the course of such actions the château might be damaged (especially likely if the lord resisted). By the summer, coerced renunciations and seizure of documents were more strongly emphasized. The château was a target more often than not and fairly likely to be severely damaged.

The continuing food riots and rising attacks on seigneurialism, the swarms of hungry beggars and desperate thieves, the news of violent clashes in town and country, the fears of aristocratic countermeasures, the tensions surrounding the Estates General and its transmutation into the National Assembly, and the disintegration of assured authority – this rush of events generated both great hope and great anxiety. With summer's ripening grain at stake, it didn't take much to generate rumors of invaders coming for revenge, coming to attack the lords, coming to defend the lords, coming to destroy the crops. Such rumors spread fast and far and enormous waves of panicky mobilization ensued, some in flight before imagined foes, some in heroic attempts to repel those foes. This Great Fear[67] and the tremendous crescendo of peasant actions as a whole peaked in late July but remained at an exceedingly high level for the next week or so.

With a bit of delay, the deputies at the National Assembly would have been getting news of all this turmoil. At eight in the morning of August 4, for example, most of the deputies from Alpine Dauphiné were gathered for a reading of letters from home urging swift action since "the disorders already committed are less frightening than those that some are trying to commit."[68] That evening, aided mightily by the previous day's election as the Assembly's presiding officer of a man of what would soon be known as "the left,"[69] a group of deputies set in motion their plan to regain the initiative by pushing forward a plan for limited rural reforms by way of damage control. The evening did not go as planned and far more radical notions were soon under discussion. The upshot, after a turbulent week's debate, was a declaration that "The National Assembly destroys the feudal regime in its entirety."[70] Some seigneurial rights were slated for immediate abolition; others were to be maintained pending the development of mechanisms by which peasants would be permitted to buy their freedom.

Far from ending the upheaval in the Revolutionary countryside, however, this declaration only marked a moment in a long, tumultuous struggle. France's peasants continued to engage in insurrectionary actions, and for the next several years were to make their struggle against the lords their most common form of defiance of the authorities. But we must not forget the multifaceted character of the French countryside. Down the road, the peasants were central participants in counterrevolution as well. As for the new Revolutionary legislators, their own positions could not be very well represented by an image of a passively suffering peasant as they faced the challenges of coping with very real and highly active real-life peasants. But these are other stories.

10. From the Estates General to the National Assembly, May 5–August 4, 1789

MICHAEL FITZSIMMONS

Summary

This chapter focuses not upon the complex politics of the various groups in the Estates General, which is an enormous task still in need of research, but upon the processes. The Estates General has traditionally been viewed as an inherently revolutionary body, with the members of the Third Estate having arrived inspired by the abbé Sieyès and ready to undertake bold reforms. In fact, the deputies of the Third Estate arrived in Versailles hoping for guidance from the Crown at the opening of the Estates General, and when such direction did not occur they followed a moderate course of action. Indeed, during the first weeks of the Estates General, the majority of deputies of the Third Estate resisted the counsel of Sieyès and the Bretons, and his influence began to emerge only after weeks of stalemate. Even after the transformation of the Estates General into the National Assembly, during the initial period of which deputies continued to sit by order, the men of the National Assembly pursued only a moderate program of reform. The first product of its deliberations, a report by its Committee of the Constitution on July 27, was exceedingly modest in scope, disappointing many contemporaries. Just over a week later, however, the meeting of the night of August 4 completely transformed the scope of the agenda of the National Assembly, as the meeting resulted in the sudden and unanticipated dismantling of French ancien-régime society. In its aftermath, the National Assembly had to reconstruct the French polity in its entirety, but this total restructuring had been thrust upon the Assembly by the meeting of the night of August 4. Ultimately, then, the extraordinary changes instituted by the National Assembly were less a product of pamphlet debates prior to the meeting of the Estates General than they were the outcome of the course of events after the Estates General opened.

> The Commons have in their chamber almost all the talents of the nation; they are firm and bold, yet moderate. There is indeed among them a number of very hot headed members; but those of most influence are cool, temperate, and sagacious. Every step of their house has been marked with caution and wisdom.
>
> Thomas Jefferson to James Madison, June 18, 1789

The opening of the Estates General in May, 1789, after a hiatus of 175 years, represented the culmination of a remarkable process that had begun two years earlier with the failure of the Assembly of Notables. The outcome of the meeting of the Assembly of Notables became the catalyst for a passionate debate on political reform in which the Paris parlement took a leading role. The quiescent reaction of the Paris parlement to its suspension by the Crown in May, 1788 – it was the only parlement to comply – shifted the momentum of events from Paris to the provinces during the summer of 1788.

Provincial resistance led to a recall of the parlements, but soon after, in September 1788, the Paris parlement effectively excluded itself from continued involvement in the movement for reform when it ruled that the Estates General should follow the forms and procedures of the Estates General of 1614. In addition, because of its enormous size, elections to the Estates General for the city of Paris were governed by a separate set of regulations, and the elections had not yet been completed when the Estates General began. As a result, when the Estates General opened, early leaders and styles of leadership in the body would be drawn from the provinces.

In the months that preceded the opening of the Estates General, two locales had distinguished themselves as potential examples to emulate: Dauphiné and Brittany. Ultimately, Dauphiné became the symbol of noble–Third-Estate cooperation and rising above privilege in the greater interest of the nation, whereas Brittany became the model of noble–Third-Estate confrontation and noble adhesion to privilege over the greater interest of the nation.

During much of the summer of 1788 two issues had competed as major matters of concern – the problem of privilege, which had arisen out of the failure of the Assembly of Notables, and despotism, stemming from the dissolution of the parlements. The month of August, 1788, however, served to clarify what had been concurrent and, in many respects, contending issues. On August 8 the Crown set a date of May 1, 1789 for the meeting of the Estates General. On August 16 the Crown suspended interest payments on the debt, which represented bankruptcy. These two events resolved the competition between the issues of privilege and despotism. With a date set for the convening of the Estates General and the declaration of bankruptcy, despotism was no longer a critical issue.

Instead, privilege emerged as the primary concern, for bankruptcy not only weakened the Crown, but also eradicated doubts concerning the existence or magnitude of the fiscal crisis. With the critical condition of state finances manifestly apparent, the fiscal privileges of the clergy and the nobility clearly emerged as the principal issue to be resolved at the Estates General. This, in turn, served to discredit altogether the ancien-régime model of the Estates General, with vote by order. Indeed, the contradistinction between the self-evident financial needs of the state and the fiscal privileges of the clergy and nobility set up a clear antithesis between them – fiscal privilege and the nation became mutually exclusive categories.

Furthermore, with the convocation of the Estates General no longer in doubt, the composition and procedure of that body now assumed extraordinary importance. Because the task of regeneration, as contemporaries termed it, was so eventful, and because the fiscal privileges of the clergy and nobility was the decisive issue to be decided, the method of voting by order, which effectively gave the first two orders a veto over reform, was not acceptable. In fact, the issue of the composition and procedure for the Estates General blended into the dichotomy between privilege and the nation, thereby superseding the narrower focus of fiscal privilege.

As the controversy on the Estates General began, the position of the Crown was unclear, and the Crown remained passive even after the meeting of the Estates General began. It had inaugurated the debate on July 5, 1788 – before its announcement of the convening of the Estates General – when it solicited ideas about the manner in which the Estates General should be constituted.

The uncertain stance of the Crown allowed each opposing side to believe, until the opening of the Estates General, that the Crown might side with it. In fact, on the one hand, with the perception that the Crown had struggled unsuccessfully against privilege during the Assembly of Notables, it could be viewed as a victim of privilege; on the other hand, as the source and guarantor of privilege, and the perceived ally of what was increasingly called the "privileged orders," the Crown could equally be seen as deeply implicated in the system of privilege.

The solicitation of ideas about the manner in which the Estates General should be constituted, suggesting that all possibilities were open, imparted a great sense of weight and fervor to the debate. One scholar has argued, in fact, that the unestablished position of the Crown represented a deliberate effort to encourage division in society. Because it could no longer postpone the convocation of the Estates General, the Crown sought to generate controversy over its composition and procedure in order to weaken the body and to render its actions of minor consequence.[1]

Whether intended by the Crown or not, the controversy continued unabated. It was in this context, on September 25, 1788, that the Paris parlement ruled that the Estates General should follow the forms of 1614 – deliberating and voting by order. Although it has been argued that that decision marked an effort by the parlement to provide orderliness to the debate by asserting what it believed were established principles,[2] it was certainly not perceived in such a manner by contemporaries. To many, it appeared instead to be a selfish and reactionary effort to control the Estates General, and it caused all of the popularity that the parlement had heretofore won to disappear instantly. Indeed, although it later made an unsuccessful effort to regain its popularity by amending its pronouncement, the parlement never again played a major role in events. The Crown also reconvened the Assembly of Notables in November, 1788, in order to solicit its opinion on the matter. In December, 1788 the Notables likewise ruled that the Estates General should follow the forms of 1614.

These pronouncements gave added impetus to the debate on privilege and expanded it to include political as well as fiscal privilege. They also served to sharpen the antithesis between privilege and the nation more clearly than ever. After the second meeting of the Assembly of Notables, one pamphleteer summarized the situation in the following terms:

Twice the king has gathered [them] around himself to consult on the interests of the throne and the nation: what did the Notables do in 1787? They defended their interests against the throne. What did the

Notables do in 1788? They defended their privileges against the nation.[3]

On December 27, 1788 the Crown authorized double representation for the Third Estate, but said nothing about the method of deliberation or voting. During the following month, it promulgated electoral regulations for the Estates General, but still did not address the issues of deliberation or voting. As a result, the controversy continued. Indeed, a Parisian bookseller wrote to his brother early in 1789 that hundreds of pamphlets concerning the Estates General appeared weekly,[4] and the fervor of the debate concerning the Estates General has been documented by a study of the holdings of the Bibliothèque nationale. Whereas there were 217 pamphlets published in 1787, and 819 in 1788, after the Crown authorized the debate on the form of the Estates General, in 1789 3305 pamphlets appeared – the largest single number for any year between 1787 and 1799.[5]

During the late winter of 1789, inhabitants of villages, towns, and cities across France gathered to draft *cahiers* and to elect deputies. In each locale the orders met separately, but in many places the delegations exchanged formal greetings. In several areas, the renunciation of fiscal privileges by the nobility generated a sense of goodwill, obscuring deeper political differences, but the issues of deliberation and voting seemed to be matters that should more properly be settled at the Estates General itself. The Third Estate of Château-Thierry, for example, instructed its deputies to bring to the Estates General "the good sense that will overcome obstacles that initially seem insurmountable" and reminded them that "they are not dispatched toward enemies whom they ought to face audaciously and proudly, but toward citizens with whom they are going to deal with the peace and happiness of the nation."[6]

In Brittany, however, the nobility refused to send representatives to the Estates General because the Estates of Brittany would not elect the deputies. In January, 1789 there had been a violent clash in Rennes orchestrated by the nobility against members of the Third Estate demanding a greater political role in the Estates of Brittany, embittering relations between the two groups. Months of discord followed in the province, and the decision by the Breton nobility in April, 1789 to refuse to send delegates to the Estates General made them a symbol of selfish adhesion to privilege and led the Breton delegation to be the most relentlessly hostile to the nobility when the Estates General opened. In Dauphiné, during January, 1789, the elections took a different course, although there was some tension between the clergy and the nobility on the one side and the Third Estate on the other. Not only did the Dauphinois elect their deputies in a relatively harmonious fashion, they also mandated that their delegates could not participate in the meeting of the Estates General unless the three estates met in common and voted by head.

The deputies from Brittany and Dauphiné arrived at Versailles aware of the fact that political developments in their respective provinces had attracted the attention of the nation. Each deputation was equally convinced that its example was the correct one for the Estates General and that the other represented the primary competing model.

The Estates General opened on May 5, 1789. Meeting for the first time in 175 years, the occasion had an unfamiliar air, and deputies were hoping to receive a sense of clarity and purpose from the Crown at its opening. It was, in fact, a moment when the power and prestige of the Crown was at its zenith. As one contemporary later noted, no one would have dared to begin the Estates General with direct disobedience of the king; if Louis had ordered meeting in common and vote by head, he would have won over the Third Estate, and if he had ordered the separation of chambers, he would have had the clergy and the nobility behind him.[7]

Instead, in an error of enormous magnitude, the Crown did neither. Indeed, after the enormous hopes raised during the spring by the convening of the Estates General, its opening was anticlimactic. The ceremony that officially opened the Estates General, which emphasized the distinction of orders and denigrated the Third Estate, annoyed several Third-Estate deputies. The king gave a short, conventional speech that did not mention procedure. Barentin, the Keeper of the Seals, spoke next, but his remarks were virtually inaudible because of his weak voice. Then it was the turn of Necker, who had been heavily applauded by the Third Estate when he arrived for the ceremony. He presented a long, technical analysis of the financial situation, but he tired after approximately a half hour, and the remaining two and one-half hours of his presentation were read by an assistant. As one observer noted, even the most intrepid partisans of Necker were soon fatigued by the speech,[8] and the sense of disappointment among the three orders at the conclusion of the ceremony was palpable.

The failure of the Crown to prepare a program deprived it of the ability to influence events. Consequently, the next day both the nobility and the Third Estate sought to seize the initiative through the issue of verification of credentials. The nobility and the clergy convened in their respective chambers, whereas the Third Estate met in the common meeting room to await the other two orders.

In the chamber of the nobility, despite a plea by a liberal noble that the current circumstances called for unity and goodwill among the orders, and despite a statement by the Dauphinois delegation that it could deliberate only in common with the other two orders, the deputies of the nobility sought to impose deliberation and vote by order. By a large majority, the deputies of the nobility quickly voted to constitute themselves as an order and to verify the credentials of members separately.

The clergy also met separately in its chamber, although its members stopped short of formally constituting themselves as an order. The Third Estate sent a delegation to the chamber of the clergy to propose that the verification of credentials of members be performed in common. The clergy temporized, professing its respect for the Third Estate and its desire to establish harmony among the orders. The clergy instead proposed the naming of commissioners from each order to attempt to forge an agreement on the proposition put forward by the Third Estate.

The deputies of the Third Estate sought to dictate deliberation in common and vote by head, and had distinct advantages over the clergy and the nobility. Its members believed unanimously in vote by head, giving the Third Estate a greater unity of purpose than the other two orders, which were sharply divided on the issue. In addition, the Third Estate benefited from the fact that it met in the common assembly hall, with its sessions open to the public, whereas the clergy and nobility met in their respective chambers in closed session. The openness of its meetings reinforced the notion that the Third Estate represented the nation, whereas the clergy and nobility were perceived as more concerned with their special interests.

Indeed, the belief that it represented the nation also reinforced the unity and cohesion of the Third Estate. The strength that this ideal gave to the Third Estate is evident in a letter from the deputy François Ménard de la Groye to his wife during the early days of the Estates General. Ménard de la Groye, who was an unassuming man of moderate views, wrote that the issue to be decided was whether the clergy and the nobility would submit to the Nation or whether the Nation would submit to them.[9]

The mutually exclusive positions of the nobility and the Third Estate quickly plunged the Estates General into a deadlock, and when it became clear that neither of the other orders would join them, the deputies of the Third Estate had to decide upon a course of action. Although Third Estate deputies believed deeply that they represented the nation, most also believed that they should not act abruptly. In the initial debates on how to respond to the failure of the clergy and nobility to join them, two contrasting approaches emerged. One course, advocated by Jean-Paul Rabaut de Saint-Etienne, from Languedoc, and seconded by Jean-Joseph Mounier, the best-known member of the Dauphinois delegation at the opening of the Estates General, sought to explore all efforts to bring about an agreement with the other two orders before undertaking any independent actions. To this end, Rabaut argued for participation by the Third Estate in the conciliatory conferences proposed by the clergy.

The Breton deputation put forward an alternative program. With Isaac-Guy-Marie Le Chapelier as their principal spokesman, the Bretons argued that the Third Estate should issue a single invitation to the other two orders to verify credentials in common. If the other two orders failed to respond, then the Third Estate should immediately move forward on its own. The Breton deputies asserted that participation in the conciliatory conferences would distract the Third Estate from its objectives.

The debate once again reflected the contrasting manners of the two most influential delegations within the Third Estate at the beginning of the Estates General. Because Paris had been the object of a separate set of electoral regulations, the election of its deputies to the Estates General was still underway when the Estates General opened, so it did not have a deputation present. This absence opened the way for the Dauphinois and Breton deputies to lead the way. Whereas the Dauphinois delegation was small and worked unobtrusively, the Breton deputation was the largest in the Third Estate when the Estates General began, and it openly sought to advance its agenda. Their aggressiveness and violent language, however, generated alarm and resentment among other deputies and prevented the Bretons from achieving the degree of influence that they had hoped to have at the Estates General.[10]

On May 18 the Third Estate decided to participate in the conciliatory conferences, but, ironically, the conferences served to transform the situation at the Estates General from a general stalemate among the three orders into a more direct confrontation between the nobility and the Third Estate. Deputies of both the nobility and the Third Estate found the position of the clergy equivocal and regarded the clergy as virtually irrelevant.

The conferences clearly revealed the depth of misunderstanding among the orders, and especially between the nobility and the Third Estate. Just as the Third Estate had not sought the abolition of orders during the period preceding the opening of the Estates General, so, too, the deputies of the Third Estate at Versailles did not seek to abolish orders altogether but only to accomplish deliberation in common and vote by head. Pursuant to this stance, before the conciliatory conferences opened, the Third Estate renamed itself "the commons," a carefully-chosen designation that reflected the limited goals of the Third Estate. Renaming itself "the commons" was a political tactic intended solely to overturn vote by order, which was implicit in the term Third Estate. But even as it sought to overturn vote by order, the adoption of the appellation "the commons" preserved separate honorific social distinctions.

Members of the nobility, however, viewed the action of the Third Estate not merely as an effort to overthrow vote by order, but as an attempt to eradicate orders altogether. As a result, a majority of the nobility staunchly opposed the position of the Third Estate, including its adoption of the term "the commons." In fact, in an effort to enforce vote by order, the nobility linked a renunciation of its fiscal privileges with the maintenance of vote by order at the Estates General, thereby negating whatever positive effect the relinquishment may have had.

Nevertheless, as the renunciation of their fiscal privileges reveals, one must recognize that the adhesion of the majority of the nobility to vote by order went beyond self-interest or defense of privilege. The overwhelming majority of noble deputies at the Estates General believed deeply that vote by order was a fundamental component of the constitution, providing a balance among the orders that a single chamber would not. In yielding their fiscal privileges, then, they regarded themselves as addressing the financial crisis and assuming their share of the fiscal burden, but their allegiance to vote by order reflected the view that it was a vital issue of constitutional import. The gravity of the issue is evident in the *cahiers* of the nobility – according to one study, 41 percent of noble *cahiers* favored vote by order whereas only 8 percent unambiguously favored vote by head.[11]

The conferences opened contentiously on May 23 and broke down after only a few days. But during the evening of May 28, as the conferences were about to be abandoned, Louis sent a letter to each of the three orders asking that the conciliatory conferences be continued under the auspices of the Keeper of the Seals. On the eve of the new conferences, however, the nobility decisively reaffirmed its commitment to deliberation by order, apparently foreclosing the key issue that the commons had presumed to be an object of negotiation. Consequently, on this occasion, the question of whether or not to participate in the conferences was much more vigorously debated in the commons. Ultimately, however, the commons did not want to place itself in the position of defying the monarch, and agreed to participate. But once again, after several days of discord and heated exchanges concerning the term "the commons," the second set of conciliatory conferences collapsed on June 9.

By this time, public interest in the Estates General had become intense, as Arthur Young, who was visiting Paris, observed. On June 8 he wrote that Paris was utterly absorbed by events at the Estates General and that "not a word of anything else talked of." The next day Young was astonished at the activity in pamphlet shops, noting that "nineteen-twentieths of these productions are in favor of liberty, and commonly violent against the clergy and nobility."[12] The frustration and impatience of the commons was strengthening as well. On May 31, early during the second set of conciliatory conferences, the deputy Nicolas-Jacques Camusat de Belombre lamented that what he already termed "the national assembly," which had been called to regenerate the kingdom, was mired in inaction. Similarly, François Ménard de la Groye wrote to his wife on June 2 about his anger at having been meeting for a month and having accomplished nothing.[13] Deputies were clearly anxious to move beyond conflicts over procedure and even terminology – the second round of conciliatory conferences collapsed partially because the nobility disputed the use of the term "the commons" – and to deal with the issues for which they had been summoned.

It was only at this juncture, after the failure of all attempts at conciliation, that the commons began to contemplate taking action without the clergy and nobility. Indeed, it was only in the aftermath of the failure of the conferences that the influence of the abbé Sieyès began to emerge. Under his prodding, the commons began to consider representing itself as the nation without the clergy and the nobility. On June 10, he proposed a motion under which the other two orders would be summoned to the common room to verify credentials in common. If they failed to respond, verification would be carried out without them. The hardening of opinion that had occurred among the commons is apparent in the vote on Sieyès's motion. Whereas only 64 deputies had opposed participation in the first set of conciliatory conferences, and only 70 had opposed participation in the second set, on June 10, after the collapse of the second round, 493 deputies voted to move ahead without the clergy and nobility, and only 41 voted to pursue further efforts at conciliation.[14]

On June 13, in response to the invitation of the commons, three *curés* entered the common room to have their credentials verified. Identifying themselves as "members of the order of the clergy from the province of Poitou" and asserting that they sought to establish peace and harmony "among the orders," they were seated, after the verification of their credentials, in a separate section designated for the clergy – a clear indication of the intent of the commons to maintain orders except for deliberation and voting. During the following days other *curés* entered the commons room.

On June 17, the commons adopted Sieyes's motion and assumed the title of National Assembly, rejecting quantitative formulations that would possibly have excluded the upper clergy and nobility.[15] This was a revolutionary measure, transforming a traditionally consultative body into a deliberative, policy-making one, presaging the assertion of national sovereignty. Without question, it represents the beginning of what we have come to think of as the French Revolution. At the same time, however, it conformed to the traditional system of estates and orders, saying nothing about merging or abolishing orders. Indeed, the critical reference to orders, which stated "representation being one and indivisible, none of the deputies, in whatever order or rank he may be chosen, has the right to exercise his duties separately from the Assembly," clearly envisaged the distinction of orders as long as they met in a single assembly. It is evident that the goal of the commons continued to be simply deliberation in common and vote by head.

The assumption of the title of National Assembly by the commons alarmed the nobility and finally led the Crown to take action.[16] Louis had personally been unconcerned with the action of the commons – he reportedly said of the Third Estate renaming itself the National Assembly that "it is only a phrase"[17] – but there was a deep split at the Court, with several key ministers, not including Necker, advocating that the king intervene in the proceedings at the Estates General. In addition, Marie-Antoinette, who had originally favored the cause of the Third Estate, now opposed it, as did Louis's brothers, the comte de Provence and especially the comte d'Artois. Furthermore, after the death of the dauphin, Louis's eldest son, on June 3, Louis withdrew to Marly on June 14, temporarily isolating him from his ministers and giving greater access and influence to the royal family.[18] They prevailed, and Louis decided to hold a royal session in which he would decree that both deliberation and vote would be by order.

On June 20, when deputies of the National Assembly went to the room in which they had been meeting, they found it closed and guarded by soldiers, ostensibly for refurbishing in preparation for the royal session on June 23. Concerned that the deployment of soldiers signified that the Crown was seeking to dissolve the National Assembly, deputies moved to a nearby tennis court where they vowed not to disband until they had given France a constitution. Not only did the Tennis Court Oath reinforce the unity and resolve of deputies, but also, by tacitly asserting that France did not have a constitution, it weakened the constitutional arguments later used by Louis to justify deliberation and vote by order during the royal session.

Indeed, at the royal session on June 23 Louis offered a program that in all likelihood would have been acceptable had it been put forward when the Estates General opened.[19] But after weeks of stalemate, and after the actions of June 17 and June 20, which the monarch explicitly annulled during the royal session, and without Necker's support, it was incongruous and inadequate. Although Louis imperiously commanded that deliberation and vote be done by order, the commons remained in the chamber and refused all demands to disband.

The following day, June 24, the clergy met separately as an order, but at the conclusion of the meeting a majority of its members went over to the National Assembly. Those who crossed over, however, continued to sit as an order within the National Assembly and were not seeking to combine themselves with the commons.[20] For example, when Jean-Baptiste Dumouchel, the rector of the University of Paris and a deputy for the clergy, joined the National Assembly, he explicitly stated that he had come to join the majority of his order, the interests, rights, and prerogatives of which, he asserted, he would never cease to uphold. At this juncture, the chamber of the nobility also began to experience defections as some of its deputies joined the National Assembly. On June 25, 47 noble deputies entered and, like the clergy, were seated together in a section designated for their order.[21] Like those members of the clergy who had joined, the noble deputies who entered the National Assembly did so primarily in an effort to break the stalemate, which was in its eighth week.[22]

Implicitly acknowledging the failure of the royal session, on June 27, with preparations to dissolve the body underway, Louis, without using the term National Assembly, wrote to the recalcitrant members of the clergy and the nobility to ask that they join "the other two orders." In a transparent effort to hinder the National Assembly, Louis did not ask that they recognize vote by head and specifically stated that even after joining the other two orders they did not have to participate in deliberations until they had received new instructions from their constituents – a process that in some instances could have taken weeks. After an extraordinarily emotional meeting between Louis and the presidents of the clergy and the nobility to confirm the monarch's wishes, late during the afternoon of June 27 a minority of the clergy and the majority of the nobility entered the National Assembly. Their entry raised the hopes of deputies already there and produced festivities in both Versailles and Paris – in fact, the Assembly decided to adjourn for two days in order to allow celebration of the event.

During the days between June 27 and June 30, however, many of the recalcitrant deputies, particularly among the nobility, held meetings to discuss measures to impede the proceedings of the National Assembly. Although the Crown thwarted some of the more extreme measures, most of the recalcitrant deputies entered the National Assembly refusing to acknowledge in any manner vote by head rather than by order.

Two examples illustrate the perspective of some of the more intractable noble deputies who had now entered the National Assembly. On May 28, on the eve of the second set of conciliatory conferences, Jean-Joseph de Châteauneuf-Randon, marquis d'Apichier, had written a letter in which he had disparaged the notions of goodwill, peace, and concord advanced by the commons as it pursued deliberation in common and vote by head and asserted that the nobility would remain in its chamber. On June 29, he wrote to a noble acquaintance that the creation of the National Assembly would forever change the French monarchy and that in centuries to come it would be seen as inconceivable that a revolution of this magnitude could occur with so little resistance from the clergy, nobility or the Crown. Referring to vote by head, he wrote that it was his intention to oppose everything that would be decided in this manner in this assembly. He also intended to resign, asking the nobility of Geraudon, which he represented, to allow someone else to carry out the task, because the new deputy would surely do it better.[23]

The baron de Lupé, from Auch, refused to enter the National Assembly and went instead to the chamber of the nobility, where he sat alone for several hours each day. When the room was subsequently closed, he paced the hallway outside of the National Assembly, and never entered it.[24] Although both of these deputies left the National Assembly during the autumn of 1789, their outlook illustrates the difficulties faced by the National Assembly as it struggled to come together and to forge a sense of purpose.

Indeed, although the union of the three orders was the object of local celebrations and was hailed throughout France, in reality it did little to resolve the stalemate for, as a *sui generis* entity, the National Assembly had little sense of identity or purpose during its early existence. The lack of common purpose became immediately apparent at its first joint meeting on June 30. The meeting was scheduled to begin at 9:00 A.M., but the minority of the clergy and the majority of the nobility did not arrive until 11:00 A.M. In what was presumed to be a prearranged strategy, many of these deputies attempted to maintain vote by order by claiming that they could not deliberate in common without receiving new powers from their constituents, which would have impeded the operation of the Assembly for several weeks. After allowing dozens of such protests to be read, a deputy convinced the Assembly to cut them off by arguing that men whose credentials had not yet been verified did not have the right to lodge protests with a body to which they did not yet belong. The incident made deputies aware of the problem of imperative mandates – binding instructions given to deputies – as an issue that would have to be addressed quickly.

The fissures in the Assembly became glaringly apparent on July 2, when the cardinal de La Rochefoucault, speaking for the minority of the clergy, sought to reserve the right of the clergy to continue to meet and to vote separately as an order. Although he limited his claims only to matters affecting the Church, the action, which threatened to reverse the formation of the National Assembly, produced an uproar in the body. The next evening, a majority of the nobility reassembled separately as an order and drew up a similar declaration. In addition, members of these two groups boycotted meetings of the subcommittees of the National Assembly during the evening in order to meet separately as an order, and the group of nobles soon withdrew from the National Assembly altogether. On July 4, in the first voice vote by head since June 30, a substantial number of noble and clerical deputies refused to participate – most either sat in silence when their name was called or left the hall just before it was to be called.

Despite such obstructions, the National Assembly moved ahead, largely completing the verification of credentials during early July. On July 7 the Assembly took up the matter of imperative mandates because, in another effort to retard the work of the National Assembly, several clerical and noble deputies had again raised the issue. With their credentials now verified, several deputies argued that they were *mandataires*, strictly bound by an imperative mandate to carry out the directions of those who had elected them, which in many cases had specified vote by order. On July 8 the Assembly resolved the matter by abolishing imperative mandates, although a great deal of confusion surrounded the vote.[25]

The rejection of imperative mandates represented a critically important step for the National Assembly. Not only did it endow the Assembly with an independence that could serve as the basis for its own sense of identity, it also established the conditions that made it legally possible for the momentous meeting of the night of August 4 to take place, although the latter aspect could not, of course, have possibly been foreseen at the time. Although the decision has been relatively overlooked, members of the Assembly regarded it as one of the most significant acts that occurred during the initial period of the Revolution. One clerical deputy, in fact, believed that the rejection of imperative mandates marked the real transition from the Estates General to the National Assembly.[26]

On July 14 the National Assembly elected a Committee of the Constitution to expedite the drafting of a constitution. It is again indicative of the primacy of achieving vote by head and the continuing distinction of orders practiced by the Assembly that members were not chosen at large, but strictly in accordance with orders – two from the clergy, two from the nobility, and four from the commons.

The election of the committee was all but overshadowed by the popular rising in Paris, which initiated popular participation in the Revolution. On the very day that the price of bread reached its highest point, and amidst fear of a counterrevolutionary coup presaged by the dismissal of Necker, the people of Paris intervened to ensure that hopes for reform were not destroyed. The taking of the Bastille established that the population of Paris would have a share in the Revolution, which would no longer be limited to debates in the National Assembly about a constitution. The more immediate effect of the Parisian rising, however, was to secure the ascendancy of the National Assembly over the Crown.[27] One deputy, in fact, asserted that had the rising lasted one more day Louis would have lost his throne, and Thomas Jefferson similarly characterized Louis's recognition of the outcome of events in Paris as a "surrender at discretion."[28] Even though it represented an unambiguous victory over the Crown, however, the rising did little to instill any sense of cohesion or identity in the National Assembly. The insurrection did lead the noble deputies who had withdrawn from the Assembly to return and to agree to vote by head, but on this occasion, in contrast to their initial entry on June 30, they were not warmly received – they were now an object of resentment.

At the time of its creation, the Committee of the Constitution had been given a mandate to draft a plan for the new constitution and to present it to the Assembly – in essence, it was to act as a steering committee for the Assembly. It is illustrative of how limited the task of drafting a constitution was perceived to be that on July 24, only ten days after the formation of the committee, a member of the National Assembly proposed that the committee be required to present a report on its work immediately. Other deputies supported the motion, and the Assembly decided that the committee should have to present an account of its work on the following Monday, July 27. The Assembly also stipulated that the committee condense its program into a form that would allow for discussion of it.

The July 27 presentation of the Committee of the Constitution is of particular interest because it reveals how limited the initial aspirations of the National Assembly were. Jean-Baptiste-Marie Champion de Cicé, the archbishop of Bordeaux, began the presentation by summarizing the deliberations of the committee. He stated that the committee had believed itself obligated to take account of the views of constituents as expressed in the *cahiers*, on which Stanislas-Marie-Adelaïde, comte de Clermont-Tonnerre would report immediately afterward. Champion de Cicé presented the first chapter of the constitution, dealing with the principles of French government. He concluded by asking deputies to submit ideas on such issues as administrative organization, judicial power, public education, the military, and the legislature, with particular emphasis upon the last.

Clermont-Tonnerre then delivered his report summarizing the *cahiers* on the question of a constitution. He observed that although the *cahiers* were unanimous in their desire to see a regeneration of the kingdom, they were divided on the extent of regeneration. Some simply asked for a reform of abuses and a repair of the "existing constitution," whereas others desired a new constitution. After summarizing the contents of some *cahiers* on selected questions, Clermont-Tonnerre put forward two sets of propositions, one consisting of accepted principles and the other comprised of questions arising from the lack of uniformity among the *cahiers*. Among the latter issues – issues that the Assembly would have to decide – were whether or not laws would be submitted to sovereign courts for registration and whether *lettres de cachet* would be abolished or merely modified.

The presentation by the Committee of the Constitution offers particular insight into the outlook and objectives of the National Assembly during its first weeks. It is notable, for example, that clerical and noble members of the committee played the leading role, representing yet another effort to reassure members of these two orders that the commons was not seeking to take control – the commoner member, Mounier, spoke last. Furthermore, although the committee recognized the latitude provided by the decision to abrogate imperative mandates, it intended to adhere as closely as possible to the *cahiers*. The committee was so conventional that it did not rule out the possibility of seating by various forms of orders in future legislatures. The readiness of the Assembly to maintain traditional – and, in the case of the *lettres de cachet*, one of the worst – attributes of the kingdom is apparent. Under such a standard of prescriptive tradition, it is clear that alterations to the basic physiognomy of the state would have been of a limited character. Because the *cahiers* had been concerned especially with greater equality of taxation, and because the clergy and nobility had already yielded on this matter, the fiscal system clearly would have been amended. Beyond that, however, it is equally clear that the fundamental privileged, corporate structure of the polity would have remained largely undisturbed.

The program outlined on July 27 produced little reaction in the country. One contemporary wrote to a friend that the report was scarcely innovative in its proposals and would leave the monarch in an extremely favorable position.[29] Another noted that it was clear that the commons sought to grant the king the greatest authority and most extensive powers in everything that did not curtail the freedom of people, adding that in fact the king lacked nothing.[30]

Just over a week later, however, the agenda of the National Assembly expanded exponentially as a result of the historic meeting of the night of August 4, 1789, which led the National Assembly to remake the French nation virtually in its entirety, including the abolition of orders. Unsettled by reports of rural unrest that seemed to indicate that much of France was engulfed by violence, a group of deputies sought to formulate a strategy to defuse it. Not wanting to employ force against the peasantry, which would have engendered hostility toward the Assembly and strengthened the position of the Crown, the deputies devised an alternate plan.[31]

Recognizing that seigneurial obligations were at the heart of peasant discontent, they worked out a plan whereby one of the largest landowners in France, the duc d'Aiguillon, would surrender seigneurial rights in return for a long-term monetary reimbursement. In addition, they planned to introduce it during an evening session, which many of the noble deputies usually did not attend. After the meeting of the night of August 4 began, however, before the duc d'Aiguillon was given the floor to speak, a lesser, landless noble, the vicomte de Noailles, who had apparently gained some knowledge of the plan, rose and offered ideas similar to those that the duc d'Aiguillon had been slated to present. It was a confused moment but, perplexed and flustered, the duc d'Aiguillon gave his approval to the propositions advanced by the vicomte de Noailles and offered some of his own. Their proposals were general and nonspecific, but essentially sought to suppress seigneurial dues in return for a cash redemption. The duc d'Aiguillon suggested a sum equal to 30 times the annual value of each obligation, but stated that the Assembly should ultimately determine the rate.

However contrived in origin and clumsy in execution, the relinquishments electrified deputies and produced a round of hearty applause that in turn generated a strong wave of emotion within the National Assembly. In a development that could not possibly have been anticipated, other deputies began spontaneously to offer relinquishments of their own, sparking a comprehensive abandonment of privilege that went on for several hours. Deputies from all three orders and from different parts of the kingdom became caught up in the moment, lining up at the podium to yield privileges of every sort. The renunciations cascaded in an astounding fashion, with each pronouncement seemingly more startling than the one that had preceded it. The tithe, hunting rights, seigneurial courts, venality of office, and provincial and municipal privileges, among others – all were given up. One deputy observed that everyone searched his pockets for sacrifices to make.[32]

In a moment of political theater during the meeting, the delegations of Brittany and Dauphiné came together on the floor to renounce jointly the privileges of their respective provinces.[33] It clearly symbolized the end of their rivalry – a rivalry that had existed even before the opening of the Estates General – and signified that there would no longer be competing models of operation within the National Assembly, but only the new path opened by the meeting of the night of August 4, 1789.

The meeting of the night of August 4 baffled contemporaries – even

deputies who experienced it admitted that they had difficulty communi-
cating what had occurred to those who were not there[34] – and has
generally puzzled historians ever since. But to a body that had initially
been stalemated for several weeks and then hindered by adhesion to
privilege and prerogative, operating in an atmosphere fraught with fear
and tension, the largely unanticipated actions of the vicomte de Noailles
and the duc d'Aiguillon struck a responsive chord and moved the
Assembly, leading other deputies to emulate them.

Without question, there were many motives that propelled the renunciations that were made during the meeting, including fear, generosity,
enthusiasm, spite, and political theater. In the final analysis, however,
the motives matter much less than the outcome: at the end of the meeting the structure and spirit of the French polity had been utterly
destroyed, mandating a complete reconstruction. Furthermore, the
assumption of the task of reconstructing French society provided the
National Assembly with the sense of purpose and identity that had
heretofore been lacking.

The meeting made it possible to forge what might be called a functional consensus. It was not a consensus based on shared values or
ideas, but adherence to a program that presented the Assembly with a
way out of stalemate and drift – the renunciations formed the starting
point from which the quest for reform could begin. Indeed, in the aftermath of August 4, a body that during the previous three months had
achieved very little proceeded during the next 24 months to remake the
French polity in its entirety.[35] Deputies grew into the role thrust upon
them and enacted an astonishing series of measures – reforming the
Church, abolishing nobility, suppressing the parlements and craft
guilds, doing away with provinces and replacing them with departments, and many others.[36] The degree of success that they achieved,
particularly with respect to reform of the Church, is still a matter of
debate, but if the accomplishments of the Assembly are open to question, the basis from which they proceeded is not – the meeting of the
night of August 4.[37]

To be sure, within a few weeks of the meeting of August 4, sharp
differences of opinion arose over the extent of reform, but these disputes
centered on how to refashion French society in the aftermath of the
eradication of privilege – the Assembly never contemplated returning to
a system of privilege in any sphere. Although the mood within the
Assembly would at times become vitriolic during the next two years,
disagreement by members of the clergy and nobility, which before the

meeting of August 4 had often been perceived as selfish and obstruc-
tionist, was legitimized by the relinquishments made during the meeting.

It has been a matter of interpretive difference whether the stalemate at
the Estates General and the evolution of that body into the National
Assembly was an outcome brought about primarily by noble intransigence or by aggressiveness on the part of the Third Estate. Although this
dichotomy seeks to frame and understand events, and this essay has
worked somewhat within that context, it is also what the French call *une
question mal posée* (a badly-posed question). Its greatest shortcoming is that
it fails to take into account the role that the course of events itself played
in the outcome – a progression set in motion by the lack of a royal
program at the opening of the Estates General.

The convening of the Estates General in 1789 was the first meeting of
that body in 175 years, and the unfamiliarity of the situation intensified
the desire for guidance at its opening. Initially, the belief in deliberation
in common and vote by head – a conviction that had formed before the
Estates General opened – gave unity and cohesion to the Third Estate. At
the same time, however, the Third Estate spent several weeks seeking to
accommodate as much as possible the concerns of the nobility as it
pursued the objectives of deliberation in common and vote by head.
During that time the members of the commons began to coalesce and to
gain confidence as they worked together. The increase in confidence is
evident in the contrasting responses of May 29 and June 23. On May 29,
despite their sense of dismay with the nobility and a reluctance to enter
into further negotiations, they did so because they did not want to defy
the wishes of the king – wishes that had been expressed indirectly in a
letter. Just three and a half weeks later, however, the commons directly
defied the king – rejecting a program personally enunciated by the
monarch during the royal session. It was the virtual vacuum in which the
commons had operated for seven weeks that had enabled it to gain confidence and to advance to the position that it took.

One other element of the virtual vacuum present at the outset of the
Estates General merits attention. From the beginning, the Third Estate
was far more unified than either the clergy or nobility, allowing for
greater perseverance in its position. Consequently, as public pressure
mounted – by early June one noble deputy genuinely feared that civil
war was imminent[38] – the resolve of the clergy and nobility eroded more
quickly, enabling the commons to prevail. Again, however, the sense of
unity became decisive only because of the absence of a royal program.

Ultimately, then, to whatever degree noble intransigence or aggressiveness by the Third Estate came into play at the Estates General, it was the direct result of the lack of royal guidance for several weeks. Whether that inaction possibly represented a continuation of royal strategy to weaken the Estates General through disagreement cannot be ascertained but, rather than weakening the Estates General, it allowed events to slip beyond the control of the Crown.

The Estates General/National Assembly is a body that has become synonymous with boldness and revolutionary change, but it is somewhat ironic that it should have achieved that reputation. All of its members had arrived seeking guidance from the Crown, and, even after the conflicting positions of the nobility and the commons had produced a deadlock, for several weeks the latter was conciliatory in its dealings with the other two orders. Indeed, even the adoption of the term National Assembly was designed to accommodate the clergy and nobility within its ranks, and for weeks after its formation the National Assembly continued to sit by order.

Again, it should be noted that the formation of the National Assembly in June, 1789 should not in any way be overlooked or underestimated. Through that action, the commons converted a traditionally consultative body into a deliberative, policy-making one, clearly signifying the appropriation of national sovereignty. To the extent that the creation of the National Assembly departed from centuries of tradition and observance, it was unquestionably the Revolutionary moment.

At the same time, however, during the next several weeks the Assembly operated in a tentative and uncertain fashion. Its first major offering, the report of the Committee of the Constitution on July 27, was utterly conventional, even timid. It refused to condemn outright *lettres de cachet* and, to the degree that it left open the possibility of submitting laws to sovereign courts for registration, it appeared willing to dilute or share sovereignty. It is little wonder that many contemporaries were disappointed in it.

The attack on the Bastille on July 14, 1789, and the peasant disturbances in the same month, give the Revolution its reputation for the violent destruction of the regime. The rising in Paris in July clearly established popular participation in the French Revolution, but it actually sought merely to save the National Assembly, which was itself committed at this time only to modest and incremental reform. Instead, the notion of revolution as an agent of bold and extraordinary change – an ideal with which the French Revolution became indelibly associated –

stems directly from the meeting of the night of August 4. During that night the men of the National Assembly overturned an entire society and ultimately sought to replace it with a new, more equitable structure – replacing privilege as the governing principle of the polity with that of laws common to all.

As a result, the French Revolution altogether redefined the concept of revolution. Until 1789, revolution had been understood to be an effort to return to an earlier golden mean. The very term implied a reversion – or revolving – back to a fixed point in the past, correcting the degeneration of institutions brought about by time or circumstance. The French Revolution, however, produced an entirely new conception of revolution as a force for transformation and renewal, and – it merits reiteration – this new understanding, which has remained in place ever since, is rooted in the meeting of the night of August 4, 1789.

In order to understand the Estates General/National Assembly, one should not simply read backward through events nor extrapolate material from pamphlets to impute a Revolutionary impulse from the outset – one must appreciate the role that unforeseen circumstances and contingency played in the outcome. The French Revolution became an event of world-historical significance due largely to the assertion by the deputies of the National Assembly of the right of a people to break with tradition and to remake society in accordance with what it perceived to be its own values and interests. Such an assertion, however, would not have been made in May, 1789, when deputies arrived at the Estates General expecting guidance from the Crown. The Revolutionary ideal did not emerge, like Athena from the head of Zeus, fully grown from the mind of deputies at the opening of the Estates General, but developed in stages.

Glossary

absolute monarchy   Form of legitimate monarchy in which the king's sovereignty was not shared and was absolved from restrictions, but which also respected the laws of the realm and rights of subjects, for whom he was the ultimate arbiter in law. Undivided sovereignty did not mean unlimited power, for the restrictions were many and the sphere of legitimate activity circumscribed by tradition, although extent of royal prerogative was hazy especially in wartime.

absolutism   Term invented in 1820s, used anachronistically by historians to confuse themselves and students about the nature of "absolute monarchy"; tendency in ministerial and royal thinking toward a more authoritarian exercise of power.

aides   Wide variety of indirect taxes, mostly on drink, levied by the state.

ancien régime (old regime in the sense of former regime)   Term invented by French Revolutionaries to refer to the preceding regime, long used by historians to refer to the kind of social, economic and political system that prevailed in France from the early sixteenth century up to 1789.

annuel   Annual tax of one-sixtieth of the value of an office, also called the *paulette*, first levied in 1604.

appel comme d'abus   Appeal to the Paris parlement against an abuse of ecclesiastical jurisdiction, over which the parlement had superiority as a defense against papal or the French Church's encroachments on French independence.

Assembly of Notables   Consultative assembly convened by the king in 1626 then February–May, 1787, composed of leading nobles, magistrates, clerics and office-holders from the upper ranks of the Third Estate. With a traditional membership it was hard to "pack" with Calonne's supporters in 1787.

bailliage   Bailiwick: royal judicial circumscription, dating from the twelfth century, with court in the first instance and appeal for relatively minor cases, and headed by a *bailli* similar to a seneschal.

Bastille   Huge medieval fortress on the eastern edge of Paris, a prison and symbol of despotism, but with a small garrison and a handful of prisoners only.

bourgeoisie   Those members of the upper echelons of rural and urban society sufficiently well-off not to work with their hands and possessed of privileges.

cahiers de doléances   Statements of grievances drawn up by electors for the Estates General. The surviving primary *cahiers* from the approximately 44,000 rural communes of France provide an extraordinary guide to the concerns of ordinary Frenchmen in 1789. The *cahiers* of the nobility, clergy, and trades, as well as secondary (amalgamated and redrafted) *cahiers* from the peasantry tended to be more radical and/or explicitly "political" than the peasants' *cahiers*, except on "feudalism."

capitation   Direct tax on all men, including the privileged, except the clergy, instituted in 1695 and levied until 1699, and renewed with many variations and privileged exemptions from 1701.

chambre de justice   Special financial court designed to claw back the gains of financiers from 1661–4 and 1716, a strategy no longer compatible with maintaining credit by the 1780s.

champart   Tax in kind due to the seigneur, averaging one-twelfth of produce.

Chancellor   Head of the judiciary in the kingdom, chief minister advising on legal issues in council. Usually also held the office of Keeper of the Seals.

Civil Constitution of the Clergy   Radical redefining in June, 1790 of the dioceses and relationship of the French Church to the new state, it made the clergy into salaried employees of the state, introduced elections for bishops and priests, and distanced the Church from the Papacy. Only seven bishops and about half the clergy were prepared to swear an oath for this, thus creating a problem of nonjuring priests of suspect loyalty to the Revolution.

controller general   Royal minister responsible for royal (state) finances and for running several provinces. For constitutional reasons Necker had the same job under the title director general of finances.

cour des aides   Parisian and provincial "sovereign" court of appeal in most matters of taxation, that also registered fiscal measures.

Dauphin   The title given the heir presumptive to the throne.

despotism   Tyranny, form of monarchy with no respect for the laws and traditions, oppressive to subjects, as thought to be the case in the Orient. Degenerate form of absolute monarchy.

dixième   Royal direct tax levied from 1710 and then 1733 on wealth in land, offices, and manufactures – an addition to the *taille* as the privileged managed to pay a very reduced amount.

élection   Fiscal circumscription presided over by the official known as an *élu*, responsible for apportioning the taille and indirect taxes, and judging such matters.

émigrés   Those who fled France because they feared or did not support the Revolution. Mostly nobles and nonjuring priests.

Estates General   Consultative assembly of representatives from all three orders convoked infrequently by the king from the fourteenth century onwards in times of crisis, usually to persuade the French to pay "extraordinary" taxation which it was thought would not be considered legitimate without such consent. It last met before 1789 in 1614 and the royal policy with the delegates of divide and rule prevented it acquiring power in return for granting taxation.

Farmers General   Syndicate of 40 financiers who bought the right for six years to collect the taxes due from the five principal indirect taxes in most of France except in those provinces with provincial estates. A full-scale administration, it made its profits from the difference between the sum it advanced for its lease of the taxes, and what it actually collected. The privatization of part of the tax system provided ready money for the state and maintained a class of wealthy financiers to call on in times of need. A powerful vested interest preventing tax reform.

fermier   Leaseholder responsible for collecting seigneurial dues for his own profit.

Frondes   Civil wars in France from 1648 to 1653 over policy during the Regency, involving parlements, princes and higher nobility or *grands*, against the royal army and especially Mazarin.

gabelles   Taxes on salt levies in many but not all provinces.

Gallicanism   Doctrine of defending the independence of French royal council, parlements and ecclesiastical jurisdictions against encroachments by the papacy. Each body tended to define it in its own interests.

General Farm   Lease in 13 provinces of the principal indirect taxes, for which the Farmers General advance the funds.

généralité   Large fiscal circumscription which by 1680 had become the seat of intendancies, with a bureau of finances and several *élections*.

intendant   Royal commissary now permanently based in each *généralité* or administrative region, empowered to oversee financial or military affairs in the provinces, with a major administrative role. Traditionally regarded with suspicion by the local elites fearful for their own powers.

Jansenism   A reformist current in Catholicism that was rigorist, austere, and condemned by the papacy in 1713 (Bull *Unigenitus*) and persecuted in France from the 1650s to the 1750s with the result that Jansenist opposition became increasingly active, strategically inventive, and successful. Jesuits were their archenemies.

Keeper of the Seals Revocable ministerial office usually joined to that of chancellor, as head of the judiciary, but when a chancellor was in exile (with an irrevocable office) as in the 1780s, he fulfilled both roles in practice.

lettre de cachet Letter with royal seal containing royal command or punishment by exile or imprisonment, emanating from the personal authority of the king without ratification in council. Became symbolic of "despotic" government by 1780s.

liberty The older definition was a recognized legal exemption from an obligation, thus a privilege or exemption from some obligation – not our idea of natural rights. The Enlightenment definition was of a natural right in a more positive sense of right to do something unless explicitly forbidden.

lit de justice Highly ceremonial and imposing session of the parlement at which the king in person, as formal (or indeed fountain-) head of the judicial system, after hearing the views of his magistrates, personally decreed the registration of an edict. Theoretically the last word, but determined magistrates found ways of undermining its efficacy.

livre Money of account, comprising 20 sous, and each sou 12 deniers, as in £.s.d. Worth about one-third of a US dollar at the time.

Maupeou coup The highly controversial "reform" of the judicial system in 1771, beginning with exiling of the Parisian parlementaires by *lettres de cachet*, was designed to break the recalcitrance of the courts to ministerial wishes and legislation. Registered in a *lit de justice* on April 13, 1771, it involved dividing the jurisdiction of the Paris parlement up between itself plus six new superior councils of smaller jurisdictional regions, with intendants as First President; remodeling smaller parlements in most provinces; suppressing venality of judicial office in the new courts; establishing free access to justice. A significant step in the creation of an image of a despotic monarchy.

May Edicts (May 8, 1788) Lamoignon's reform of the judiciary in 1788. Forty-seven *grands bailliages* were established for most appeal cases, leaving the parlements with jurisdiction over the privileged only, with a *cour plénière* (plenary court) to register legistation; criminal procedure was reformed, torture abolished, and numerous overlapping jurisdictions rationalized. Strongly opposed by the parlements and their supporters.

minister Often, but not always or necessarily, a secretary of state with entry to the royal council of state in which policy was made.

ministerial despotism   Acts of "despotism" promoted by a minister misleading or "surprising" the monarch against his better judgment or without his knowledge.

National Assembly   Name adopted on June 17, 1789 by the Third Estate, seeing itself as virtually the complete nation (in contrast to the "privileged" orders of nobles and clergy), designed to break the deadlock in the Estates General, and confirmed by the king on June 27. Also known later as the Constituent Assembly, it lasted until September 1791.

noblesse d'épée   Nobility of the sword, military nobility.

noblesse de robe   Nobility associated with the judicial profession.

octrois   Urban sales taxes.

officier   An official or officeholder in the royal administration, who had inherited or bought his "venal" office and received *gages* as interest on the price of the office but no real salary, so not a modern bureaucrat. Often stubbornly resistant to change and with local loyalties in conflict with those towards royal policies.

parlement   Sovereign, that is final, court of appeal with wide powers of *police*; the Paris parlement had jurisdiction over 40 percent of the realm; other parlements existed in 12 other provinces.

parti dévôt   Partisans of a Catholic foreign and domestic policy at court, very anti-Jansenist in the 1750s–1760s.

parti janséniste   Jansenist party: strongly Jansenist clerics, magistrates and lawyers, and parish notables (all in small numbers), some of whom were very well organized and maintained an illegal newspaper, the *Ecclesiastical News*, who attempted to defend Jansenism after the condemnatory Bull *Unigenitus*, through legal appeals to public opinion, to the parlements, and to a hoped-for General Assembly of the French Church, against persecution from the ecclesiastical hierarchy supported by the royal ministry.

parti national   National party: body of opinion that in 1788 regarded sovereignty as lying with the nation, which was composed essentially of commoners, but which was not against monarchy as the form of government.

parti patriote   Patriot party: label given either to the individuals who stirred up public opinion, or more usually and generally to the "body of opinion" (*parti*) which formed that ideological opposition, against ministerial despotism in the form of Maupeou or Loménie de Brienne and their policies, employing from 1771 much of the rhetoric and strategies developed by the *parti janséniste* earlier. The appeal to "patriotism" legitimized intervention in the theoretically forbidden political sphere of the absolute monarchy.

pays d'élection   Provinces whose royal administrative and fiscal area was composed of an *élection*, a medieval fiscal area that was under the direct control of the royal administration, thus different from and less independent than a *pays d'état*.

pays d'état   Provinces with assemblies representing the three estates, which exercised financial and general administration, they generally were territories that were acquired by France after the Middle Ages, with independent traditions. Most important of more than a dozen were Languedoc, Provence, and Brittany. Dauphiné had lost its estates in the seventeenth century.

police   Concept that combines our separate ideas of justice and administration.

privilège   Right or privilege, in the sense of an exemption or freedom from a general imposition or restriction; a social distinction. Privilege is a fundamental concept in the ancien régime.

Provincial Assemblies   Necker set up a new model of estates in Berry in 1778, to allocate taxation and involve the population in government. Their wider institution was proposed in 1787, implemented in 1788, with double representation for the Third Estate but to be presided over by that agent of the ministry, the intendant.

Provincial Estates   Body with powers of taxation and administration or *police* composed of representatives of the three orders (clergy, nobles, and Third Estate). They dated back to institutions before their regions' incorporation into the French Kingdom and continued to thrive in the provinces of Languedoc and Brittany, and existed in several smaller provinces. Those of Dauphiné were abolished in 1628.

rente   Annual return on an investment; the investment itself, often in the form of a life annuity or a loan to the municipality, clergy or provincial estate.

Royal Session   Term from the Middle Ages used by the government for the session of parlement on November 19, 1787 at which the king was present for registration of legislation and loans, but the session was intended to be less offensive (and just as effective as) a *lit de justice*. Louis inadvertently transformed it into the latter when challenged by the duc d'Orléans.

secretary of state   High noble of the robe or sword who had a government department or "ministry" under his control: war, the marine, foreign affairs, the king's household. Each one also administered several provinces, with the household minister having Paris. Not necessarily a minister with entry to council of state.

seigneur   Lord, lay or clerical, noble or bourgeois, possessing rights and privileges of feudal origin.

taille   Tithe, the most important royal direct tax, either a hearth tax or a land tax, levied on "common" persons or lands, depending on the region. It dated from 1439 and its proceeds were used as collateral for the extensive royal borrowing in wartime.

Tennis Court Oath   On June 20, 1789 the deputies of the Third Estate, thinking the estates were about to be closed when their usual large venue was closed by soldiers to prepare for the royal session of June 23, swore an oath in a nearby tennis-court building to give France a constitution.

Third Estate / Tiers État   The formal order or grouping of or representatives of all who were not either nobility or clergy. In terms of deputies it meant in practice members of the middle classes, thus excluding the peasants and artisans who formed the bulk of the order.

venality of office   Offices, both royal and corporative, were acquired by inheritance or purchase as property, so royal and corporate officials were "venal" and resistant to modifications in their role. Fundamental principle of functions throughout society, except for a few royal officials with special commissions like intendants (who had nevertheless bought offices as masters of requests).

Political Chronology

1702	War of Spanish Succession begins.
1713	Papal Bull *Unigenitus* condemning 101 propositions that it associated with Jansenism.
	Treaties of Utrecht bring War of Spanish Succession to a close.
1715	Death of Louis XIV. Louis XV becomes king at 5 years old with Philippe d'Orléans as regent. Debt at 2000 million *livres*.
	Parlement regains authority.
1716–20	John Law, Scottish financier in France, sets up a bank then the "Mississippi Company," eventually controlling foreign trade, issuing shares then paper money.
1718	*Polysynodie*, or system of aristocratic governing councils, essayed unsuccessfully.
1720–1	"Mississippi Bubble": Law made controller general, bank become statebank, huge speculation in Mississippi Co. (India Company now) shares led to crash, and discredited idea of paper money until 1780s.
1721–4	Inflation and "Visa" to remedy financial situation.
1723	The regent Philippe d'Orléans dies.
1725	*Cinquantième* (one-fiftieth) property tax introduced; abandoned in 1727.
1726	Cardinal de Fleury becomes first minister.
1730	Bull *Unigenitus* made a law of Church and State.
1730–2	Intense quarrel between ministry and reluctant Paris parlement over legal status of Bull *Unigenitus*, made into a law of state in 1730.
1733	*Dixième* tax introduced during War of the Polish Succession 1733–7.
1734	Voltaire's *Lettres philosophiques*.
1740–7	War of Austrian Succession.
1743	Cardinal de Fleury dies, Louis governs without a "first minister."
1748	Montesquieu's *The Spirit of The Laws*; Toussaint's *Les Moeurs*.

1749	Machault introduces *vingtième* tax, general property tax even on Church lands.
1750	*Encyclopédie* begins publication, with *Preliminary Discourse*; volumes follow from 1751.
1751–7	Crises with parlement over refusal of sacraments to Jansenists.
1753	Le Paige's *Lettres sur . . . les parlements*; parlement makes *Grandes remontrances* to king.
1753–4	Refusal of sacraments affair; Paris parlement transferred to Bourges.
1756–63	Seven Years' War.
1757	Damiens "touches" Louis XV with penknife, investigation, trial, execution.
1758	Choiseul most influential minister replacing Bernis (1757–8).
1761	Rousseau's *La Nouvelle Héloïse*.
1762	Rousseau's *Emile* and *The Social Contract*; Jansenists succeed in orchestrating judgment in parlement against Jesuit order in France.
1763	Controller general Bertin's tax edicts.
1764–5	Controller general L'Averdy's municipal reforms with elections.
1766	*Séance de la Flagellation*: Louis XV reprimands parlements.
1768	L'Averdy dismissed.
1770	Parlement tries d'Aiguillon, king revokes case, parlement protests, Choiseul exiled in December.
1771	"Maupeou coup" as Chancellor "reforms" judiciary, exiling magistrates, abolishing venality in parlements, creating new Plenary Courts.
	Controller general Terray abolishes L'Averdy's municipal reforms to reestablish venality.
1771–4	Bitter pamphlet debate between supporters of parlements and those of ministry (far fewer).
1774	
May	Death of Louis XV; accession of Louis XVI aged 20, who retains existing ministers Maupeou, Terray, and d'Aiguillon, but Maurepas becomes his mentor.
June	Vergennes replaces d'Aiguillon as foreign secretary.
Aug.	Miromesnil replaces Maupeou, Turgot replaces Terray.
Nov.	Recall of parlements.

1775

Apr.–May   Flour War.

1776

May   Turgot dismissed after reforms (Six Edicts) generated underhand opposition via Miromesnil; Turgot's *Memoir on Municipalities*.

1777

June   Necker appointed "Director General of Finances."

1778   France enters American War of Independence.

1781

Feb.   Necker's *Compte rendu* give impression of sound financial state even in wartime.

May   Necker resigns, replaced by Joly de Fleury.

Nov.   Maurepas dies.

1782   French naval defeat at Battle of the Saints.

3rd *vingtième* registered to run until 1791.

Choderlos de Laclos's *Dangerous Liaisons*.

1783

Jan.   Peace preliminaries signed with Britain. Vergennes dominant minister in government.

Mar.   Joly de Fleury replaced by d'Ormesson.

Aug.   D'Ormesson warns king of need to restructure finances by 1787.

Oct.   D'Ormesson defeated by General Farmers when "reforming" their lease.

Nov.   Calonne becomes controller general; Breteuil gets Maison du Roi ministry thanks to influence of queen.

1784   Beaumarchais's *Marriage of Figaro*.

1784–5   France mediates successfully Austro-Dutch dispute over Austrian attempt to open Scheldt river to navigation.

1785

Aug.   Diamond Necklace Affair begins.

Nov.   Franco-Dutch Treaty of Fontainebleau.

1786

May   Rohan acquitted by parlement, he is exiled by the king.

Aug. 20   Louis XVI agrees to convene Assembly of Notables in 1787.

Sept. 26   Anglo-French trade treaty (Eden Treaty) reduces duties on imported manufactured British goods to France with British lowering tariffs on French wine and spirits.

Sept.–Dec.	Calonne's projects discussed in *comité*.
Dec. 29	King announces convocation of Assembly to his Council.

1787

Feb. 13	Death of Vergennes.
Feb. 22	Assembly of 144 Notables meets.
Apr. 1	*Avertissement* read from pulpits to arouse popular support.
Apr. 8	Royal attempt to save projects in Assembly by Calonne's dismissal and Miromesnil's replacement by Lamoignon.
May	Loménie de Brienne appointed *chef du conseil royal*; Notables reject revised plans and are dismissed; provincial assemblies announced in closing speech.
June–Aug.	Brienne attempts to register measures in Paris parlement.
July 16	Parlement calls for Estates General.
July 26	Remonstrances include this appeal for Estates General.
Aug. 6	*Lit de justice* to register taxes and reforms.
Aug. 7	Parlement declares forced registration nul.
Aug. 15	Parlement transferred to Troyes.
Sept.	France powerless to intervene in Holland invaded by Anglo-Prussian forces, serious setback to France. Negotiations with parlement.
Sept. 28	Parlement recalled to Paris.
Nov.	The new provincial assemblies convened.
Nov. 19	Royal session at Paris parlement to register 420-million-livre loan over five years, but Estates General to meet within five years. Parlement later declares registration illegal.
Nov. 20	Duc d'Orléans exiled to his château; Fréteau and Sabathier imprisoned by *lettres de cachet*.
Nov. 26	Parlement begins long campaign for recall of its magistrates and against *lettres de cachet*.
Dec. 8	Parlement makes respectful representations claiming "justice" from king. Rebuffed.
Dec. 1787–Apr. 1788	Provincial parlements express opposition to royal session and its consequences.

1788

Jan. 17	Deputation from Paris parlement to Versailles with its judgment against *lettres de cachet*. Rebuffed.

Mar. 13	Paris parlement presents remonstrances against *lettres de cachet*, invoking public liberty as a right and return of its three members.
Apr. 13	Paris parlement remonstrance in favour of free registration of laws (a delayed response to forced registration of November 19).
Apr. 17	Royal reply accuses them of wanting "an aristocracy of magistrates."
May 3	Paris parlement lists "Fundamental laws."
May 5–6	Arrest of two magistrates inside *palais de justice*.
May 8	May Edicts: Lamoignon's coup against parlements establishing a Plenary Court for registering legislation and reducing their jurisdiction by creating new *grand bailliage* appeal courts.
May 15	Extraordinary Assembly of Clergy (May 5–June 5) presented remonstrances calling for Estates General soon and thereafter periodically, on principle of subjects' consent to taxation.
May–June	Resistance to May Edicts in several provinces with parlements, based upon provincial liberties against despotism.
June 7	"Day of Tiles" in Grenoble in support of Grenoble parlement.
June 14	Meeting of Notables from Grenoble from all three orders supports parlement and calls for reestablishment of provincial estates.
July 5	Ministry invites opinions on future composition of Estates General.
July 21	Meeting in Vizille near Grenoble in Dauphiné of moderate nobles, clergy and Third Estate of the province.
Aug. 8	Council decision to convoke Estates General published; Pamphlet campaign begins in earnest over nature and form of estates.
Aug. 16	Debt crisis: Treasury payments suspended.
Aug. 25	Loménie de Brienne resigns.
Aug. 26	Necker recalled.
Sept.	Lamoignon replaced by reactionary Barentin; recall of parlements.
Sept. 25	Paris parlement announces Estates General to meet according to forms of 1614.

Nov. 3–12	Second Assembly of Notables for issue of forms Estates General should take, especially on taxation and voting. Six of seven bureaux against voting by head but for voting by estates.
Dec. 5	Paris parlement supports double representation for Third Estate to regain favour.
Dec. 12	Memorandum of the Princes of the Blood.
Dec. 27	"Result of the Council" decrees doubling of Third Estate representation in Estates General.

1789

Jan.–Mar.	Urban bread riots.
Jan. 24	Electoral rules for Estates General.
Jan. 27	Anti-noble riot in Rennes.
Feb.	Sieyès publishes *What Is the Third Estate?*
Mar.–Apr.	Elections to Estates General and *cahiers* drawn up; some provincial riots and pillaging.
Apr. 27–8	Réveillon riots in Paris: crowd sacks wallpaper manufacturer's factory.
Apr. 30	Radically minded Breton deputies meet in "Breton Club" in Versailles, joined by other radicals later.
May 5	Opening of the Estates General in Versailles.
May 19	Newspapers permitted to print record of debates: effectively freedom of the press.
June 17	Third Estate declares itself a "National Assembly."
June 20	Tennis Court Oath.
June 23	Royal Session at which Louis XVI proposes reforms no longer sufficient to the moment.
June 24–5	Most clergy and 47 nobles join Third Estate.
June 27	Louis orders all deputies to meet in common; also calls up army units to near Paris.
July 6	National Assembly appoints a constitutional committee.
July 11	Dismissal of Necker.
July 12	Reactionary "Ministry of a Hundred Hours" with Breteuil. Paris revolts.
July 14	Fall of the Bastille.
July 15	First emigration; recall of Necker.
July 17	King visits Paris.
July 22	Lynching of Foulon and Berthier.
July 20–Aug.	"Great Fear" begins and spreads amongst peasantry, bringing widespread attacks on châteaux against

records of feudal dues. Municipal revolutions; bourgeois militia formed.

Aug. 4	Night: abolition of feudalism and privileges.
Aug. 26	Declaration of Rights of Man and of the Citizen.
Sept. 10	National Assembly rejects proposal for a bicameral legislature.
Sept. 11	Suspensive veto accorded to king.
Oct. 5-6	March to Versailles by women, and royal family taken to Paris.
Nov. 2	Church property nationalized.
Dec. 19	First *assignats* issued (paper money guaranteed on former Church property).

1790

June 19	Abolition of Nobility.
July 12	Civil Constitution of the Clergy.
July 14	First *Fête de la Fédération.*

1791

Mar. 10	Pope condemns Civil Constitution.
Apr. 18	St Cloud affair: king prevented from leaving Paris to take communion from nonjuring priest.
June 20–1	King's flight to Varennes and capture.
June 25	King returns unpopular to Paris.
July 14	Second *Fête de la Fédération.*
July 17	Massacre at the Champ-de-Mars.
Sept. 14	King accepts slightly modified constitution.
Sept. 30	End of Constituent Assembly.

Abbreviations

AHR	*American Historical Review*
AHRF	*Annales historiques de la Révolution française*
AMWS	*Annual Meeting of the Western Society for French History. Proceedings*
Annales ESC	*Annales. Économies. Sociétés. Civilisations*
BJRL	*Bulletin of John Rylands Library*
EcHR	*Economic History Review*
ECS	*Eighteenth-Century Studies*
EHR	*English Historical Review*
FH	*French History*
FHS	*French Historical Studies*
HEI	*History of European Ideas*
HJ	*Historical Journal*
JEcH	*Journal of Economic History*
JMH	*Journal of Modern History*
P&P	*Past and Present*
RH	*Revue historique*
RHMC	*Revue d'histoire moderne et contemporaine*
SVEC	*Studies on Voltaire and the Eighteenth Century*
TRHS	*Transactions of the Royal Historical Society*

Notes

Introduction THE ORIGINS OF THE FRENCH REVOLUTION IN FOCUS
Peter Robert Campbell

Acknowledgment

To attempt an interpretation of the origins of the Revolution in a single long chapter is a tall order. The author could not have done it without the support, encouragement and critical acumen of Mark Bryant, Joël Félix, Michael Fitzsimmons, John Hardman, Tom Kaiser, Marisa Linton, Kenneth Margerison, John Markoff, and Dale Van Kley, and wishes to thank them.

1. A. Cobban, "Historians and the Causes of the French Revolution," in Cobban, *Aspects of the French Revolution* (London, 1969); P. Geyl, "French Historians for and against the Revolution," in Geyl, *Encounters in History* (London, 1963), pp. 115–87.

2. W. Doyle, *The Origins of the French Revolution* (Oxford, 1980); G. Ellis, "The 'Marxist Interpretation' of the French Revolution," EHR, 93 (1978), pp. 353–76.

3. For recent French interpretations, see S. L. Kaplan, *Farewell Revolution. The Historians' Feud, France 1789/1989* (New York, 1995) and two amongst several good review articles, S. Desan, "What's after Political Culture? Recent French Revolutionary Historiography," FHS, 23, 1 (2000), pp. 163–96 and J. Popkin, "Not Over After All: The French Revolution's Third Century," JMH, 74 (2002), pp. 801–21. FHS, 16 (1990) has useful important forums: the first is a debate between W. Doyle and M. Vovelle on the Revolution's origins, pp. 743 ff; the second is a discussion of the work of F. Furet, including contributions from C. Langlois, D. Bien, and D. Sutherland, with the last word being left to Furet himself, all pp. 766 ff.

4. R. Chartier, drawing on Foucault, in Chartier, *The Cultural Origins of the French Revolution* (Durham, NC, 1991).

5. This problem was neatly sidestepped by Furet who argued that the unfolding of the Revolution was inherent in the ideologies of 1789, but this argument in turn depends upon a certain idea of what the crucial ideologies were (for him it was Sieyès's expression of Rousseau's version of popular sovereignty) and upon a philosophy of history that sees it moving forward through the inherent contradictions in discourses – a sort of neo-Hegelian view. People get reduced to actors or mouthpieces of discourses.

6. H. Gough, *The Terror in the French Revolution* (Basingstoke, 1998) surveys the debate.

7. For example, could Darnton's Grub Street revolutionaries, as the outsiders they were, have influenced the fall of the ancien régime, or is his argument better addressed to the question of how the Revolution after 1789 was

influenced by radicals embittered by their experience of the previous regime? See R. Darnton, "The High Enlightenment and the Low Life of Literature," P&P (1971), reprinted in D. Johnson, ed., *French Society and the Revolution* (London, 1976).

8. Indeed neither the bourgeoisie nor capitalism was very modern in 1789: G. V. Taylor, "Types of Capitalism in Eighteenth-Century France," EHR, 79 (1964), pp. 478–97.

9. How can Furet credibly say that nothing resembled the France of Louis XVI so much as the France of Louis Philippe?

10. See Alice Gérard, *La Révolution française, mythes et interprétations 1789–1970*, (Paris, 1970) and especially A. Cobban, *The Myth of the French Revolution* (London, 1955) reprinted in Cobban, *Aspects of the French Revolution* (London, 1969).

11. G. Lefebvre, *The Coming of the French Revolution*, trans. by R. R. Palmer (New York, 1947).

12. The problem of the intensive standoff between nobles and bourgeois in the Estates General of 1789 could be explained by the fact that many of those nobles elected in 1789 were more conservative than the noble *cahiers* in general (which as Markoff shows were themselves more conservative than bourgeois ones) and were subject to factional alignments pushing them rightwards under the influence of d'Epresmesnil and the Artois faction; and by the prominence of vehemently anti-noble Breton deputies rather than the Dauphinois delegation. On the notables, M. Reinhard, "Élite et noblesse dans la seconde moitié du XVIIIe siècle," RHMC, 3 (1956) in English in B. and E. G. Barber, eds, *European Social Class: Stability and Change* (New York, 1965), pp. 91–110.

13. "Absolute sovereignty of the people," one might say. His most important precursors seem to be the nineteenth-century liberals who saw the revolution as establishing a state that undermined individual liberty, and J. L. Talmon, *The Origins of Totalitarian Democracy* (London, 1952), and, for his sense that the immediate project was doomed to failure but would succeed gradually in the long run, Edmond Burke. He was of course vehemently against Marxist interpretations: see F. Furet, *Interpreting the French Revolution*, trans. by E. Forster (Cambridge, 1981).

14. L. Stone, *The Causes of the English Revolution* (London, 1972), ch. 1 on theories.

15. J. Markoff, "Revolutions, Sociology of", in N. Smelser and P. Baltes, *International Encyclopedia of the Social and Behavioral Sciences* (Oxford, 2002), 20, pp. 13310–14.

16. See, for example, E. Hernassi introducing a special issue on revolution in *Comparative Studies in Society and History*, 1976.

17. G. V. Taylor, "Non-Capitalist Wealth and the Origins of the French Revolution," AHR, 72 (1966–7), pp. 469–96, p. 491. That, however, is not the argument of this Introduction.

18. Furet famously wrote that "The Revolution replaced the conflict of interests for power with a competition of discourses for the appropriation of legitimacy," Furet, *Interpreting the French Revolution*, p. 49.

19. See, for example, P. M. Jones introducing his selections in *The French Revolution in Social and Political Perspective* (London, 1996), pp. 5–6.

20. A. Cobban, "The Age of the Democratic Revolution," in his *France since the Revolution* (London, 1970).

21. R. R. Palmer, *The Age of Democratic Revolutions*, 2 vols (Princeton, NJ, 1959–64).

22. T. Skocpol, *States and Social Revolutions* (Cambridge, 1979). See the critical response by W. H. Sewell, "Ideologies and Social Revolutions: Reflections on the French Case," JMH, 57 (1985), pp. 57–85.

23. B. Stone, *The Genesis of the French Revolution* (Cambridge, 1994).

24. J. A. Goldstone, *Revolution and Rebellion in the Early Modern World* (Berkeley, CA and London, 1991). For cogent criticism, see L. Stone, "The Revolution over the Revolution," review, *New York Review of Books*, June 11, 1992 and reply by Goldstone, April 22, 1993, and E. Berenson, "The Social Interpretation of the French Revolution," in N. R. Keddie, ed., *Debating Revolutions* (New York and London, 1995), pp. 85–111. Goldstone's more recent work suggests a greater stress on state structures.

25. K. M. Baker, *Inventing the French Revolution* (Cambridge, 1990), p. 27.

26. And thus scholars fall like Marx into writing history as teleology, taking a single modern element like democracy or republicanism that matured in the future, and, by blowing up these first unsuccessful glimmerings and taking them out of context, infer that that was what the Revolution was "about." This is another variant on the reification argument mentioned above.

27. On the general crisis, see T. Aston, ed., *Crisis in Europe, 1560–1660* (London, 1967) and R. Forster and J. P. Greene, eds, *Preconditions of Revolution in Early Modern Europe* (Baltimore, MD, 1970). For the additional argument that the state was constantly in a precarious balance requiring deft political management to prevent an inherent tendency to conflict that could threaten collapse, see P. R. Campbell, *Power and Politics in Old Regime France* (London, 1996), Conclusion.

28. Alain Rey, *Révolution. Histoire d'un mot* (Paris, 1989).

29. J. Markoff has worked on this idea. See his *The Abolition of Feudalism Peasants, Lords and Legislators in the French Revolution* (University Park, PA, 1996) for index references to "momentous time" at which people took decisions, and A. Stinchcombe, "Revolutions and Building New Governments", *Annual Review of Political Science*, 2 (1999), pp. 49–73.

30. Although the *pays d'états* tended to be around the periphery, their existence conditioned and limited the scope for government reforms and centralization, preventing uniformity.

31. D. Dessert, *Argent, pouvoir et société au grand siècle* (Paris, 1984). In the eighteenth century other creditors joined the system, notably the "Protestant bank": see H. Lüthy, *La Banque protestante en France*, 2 vols (Paris 1959–61), summarized by J. Bouvier in R. Hatton, ed., *Louis XIV and Absolutism* (London, 1976), pp. 263–80. Lüthy does not think they played as important a part as "the real managers of the kingdom's money, the financial directors of the king and court, the high finance officials, the Farmers General, the treasurers for war and navy and the financiers of the high nobility" (p. 277). See also J. C. Riley, "Dutch Investment in France, 1781–1787," JEcH (1973), pp. 732–60.

32. R. Mettam, *Power and Faction in Louis XIV's France* (Oxford, 1988); P. R. Campbell, *The Ancien Régime in France* (London, 1988); N. Henshall, *The Myth of Absolutism* (London, 1992); F.-X. Emmanuelli, *Un mythe de l'abolutisme bourbonien: L'Intendance du milieu du XVIIe siècle à la fin du XVIIIe siècle* (Aix-en-Provence, 1981).

It therefore follows that in terms of centralization, the French Revolution was perhaps a much more radical break with the past than Tocqueville suggested.

33. On the seventeenth-century state, see J. Collins, *The State in Early Modern France* (Cambridge, 1995). On the continued existence of seventeenth-century governance in the period after Louis XIV see Campbell, *Power and Politics*; J. Swann, *Provincial Power & Absolute Monarchy: The Estates General of Burgundy, 1661–1790* (Cambridge, 2003).

34. On conceptualizing the seventeenth-century monarchy, see esp. E. L. Asher, *The Resistance to the Maritime Classes. The Survival of Feudalism in the France of Colbert*, (Berkeley, CA, 1960); W. Beik, *Absolutism and Society in Seventeenth-Century France* (Cambridge, 1985); Dessert, *Argent, pouvoir et société*; A. N. Hamscher, *The Parlement of Paris after the Fronde, 1653–1673* (Pittsburgh, PA, 1976); S. Kettering, *Patrons, Brokers and Clients in Seventeenth-Century France* (New York, 1986); J. R. Major, *Representative Government in Early Modern France* (New Haven, CT, 1980); Mettam, *Power and Faction*; A. L. Moote, "The French Crown versus its Judicial and Financial Officials, 1615–83," JMH (1962), pp. 146–60 and J. Vicens Vives, "The Administrative Structure of the State in the Sixteenth and Seventeenth Centuries," in H. J. Cohn, ed., *Government in Reformation Europe* (London, 1971), pp. 58–87, an important attack on Mousnier and Hartung. See also D. Richet, "La Monarchie au travail sur elle-même?", in K. Baker, ed., *The Political Culture of the Old Regime*, Oxford 1987, pp. 25–40 and *La France moderne. L'Esprit des institutions* (Paris, 1973).

35. D. Bien, "Office, Corps and a System of State Credit: The Uses of Privilege under the Ancien Régime," in Baker, ed., *The Political Culture of the Old Regime*, vol. 1, pp. 89–114; Dessert, *Argent, pouvoir et société*; G. T. Matthews, *The Royal General Farms in Eighteenth-Century France* (New York, 1958).

36. J. B. Wood, "The Decline of the Nobility in Sixteenth and Early Seventeenth Century France: Myth or Reality?," JMH, 48 (suppl.) (1976), pp. 1–30.

37. W. Doyle, "Was there an Aristocratic Reaction in Pre-revolutionary France?," P&P, 57 (1972), pp. 97–122, reprinted in Johnson, *French Society and the Revolution*, pp. 3–28.

38. Most explicitly made by F. L. Ford, *Robe and Sword. The Regrouping of the French Aristocracy after Louis XIV* (Cambridge, MA, 1953).

39. W. Doyle, *Venality: The Sale of Offices in Eighteenth-Century France* (Oxford, 1996).

40. R. Darnton, "Trends in Radical Propaganda on the Eve of the French Revolution" (DPhil, Oxford, 1964); S. Maza, *Private Lives and Public Affairs: The Causes Célèbres of Pre-Revolutionary Paris* (Berkeley, CA, 1993); on virtuous citizenship see M. Linton, *The Politics of Virtue in Enlightenment France* (Basingstoke, 2001) For the contrary argument that there was no self-conscious bourgeoisie, see D. Garrioch, *The Formation of the Parisian Bourgeoisie, 1690–1830* (Cambridge, MA, 1996), p. 1, and S. Maza, *The Myth of the French Bourgeoisie. An Essay on the Social Imaginary, 1750–1850* (Harvard, 2003).

41. See C. Lucas, "Nobles, Bourgeois and the Origins of the French Revolution," originally P&P, 60 (1973), reprinted in Johnson, *French Society and the Revolution*, pp. 88–131.

42. On L'Averdy see J. Félix, *Finances et politique au siècle des lumières: Le ministère de Laverdy, 1763–1768* (Paris, 1999); Turgot's "Memoir on the Municipalities" is

in English in K. M. Baker, ed., *Readings in Western Civilization, 7, The Old Regime and the French Revolution* (Chicago and London, 1987), pp. 97–118.

43. See G. Shapiro and J. Markoff, *Revolutionary Demands. A Content Analysis of the Cahiers de Doléances of 1789* (Stanford, CA, 1998); also R. Chartier's revealing comparison of demands in 1614 and 1789 in "De 1614 à 1789: Le Déplacement des attentes," in R. Chartier and D. Richet, eds, *Représentation et vouloir politiques: Autour des Etats-généraux de 1614* (Paris 1982). On the composition of the *cahiers*, R. Chartier, "From words to texts. The *cahiers de doléances* of 1789," in Chartier, *The Cultural Uses of Print*, trans. by L. Cochrane (Princeton, NJ, 1987), pp. 110–44. The most complete long-term perspective is provided by J. Nicolas, *La Rébellion française. Mouvements populaires et conscience sociale 1661–1789* (Paris, 2002).

44. E. Teall, "The Seigneur of Renaissance France: Advocate or Oppressor?", JMH, 37 (1965), pp. 131–50.

45. R. Forster "The 'world' between Seigneur and Peasant," *Studies in Eighteenth Century Culture*, 5, pp. 401–21.

46. On the poor see O. Hufton, *The Poor of Eighteenth-Century France* (Oxford, 1974).

47. On the police, see A. Williams, *The Police of Paris, 1718–89* (Baton Rouge, LA, 1979), and on provisioning, S. J. Kaplan, *Provisioning Paris. Merchants and Millers in the Grain and Flour Trade during the Eighteenth Century* (Ithaca, NY, 1984).

48. F. Crouzet, *Britain Ascendant: Comparative Studies in Franco-British Economic History* (Cambridge, 1990).

49. J. Riley, *The Seven Years War and the Old Regime in France: The Economic and Financial Toll* (Princeton, NJ, 1986); Félix, *Finances et politique*.

50. On patriotism see E. Dziembowski, *Un nouveau patriotisme français, 1750–70: La France face à la puissance anglaise à l'époque de la guerre de Sept Ans* (Oxford, 1998) and, for a different view, namely patriotism as a legitimizing rhetoric, see P. R. Campbell, "Patriotism in old regime France," forthcoming.

51. D. Roche, *France in the Enlightenment* (Cambridge, MA, 1998); D. Mornet, *Les Origines intellectuelles de la Révolution française* (Paris, 1933).

52. R. Darnton, *The Literary Underground of the Old Régime* (Cambridge, MA, 1982) and R. Darnton, and D. Roche, eds, *Revolution in Print. The Press in France, 1775–1800* (New York, 1989).

53. In addition to the work by D. Van Kley, *The Damiens Affair and the Unraveling of the Ancien Régime, 1750–70* (Princeton, NJ, 1984), see D. Bell, *The Cult of the Nation in France: Inventing Nationalism in France, 1680–1800* (New York, 2002).

54. D. K. Van Kley, *The Jansenists and the Expulsion of the Jesuits from France, 1757–65* (New Haven, CT, 1975), Conclusion, and D. Garrioch, *Neighbourhood and Community in Eighteenth-Century Paris, 1740–90* (Cambridge, 1986).

55. M. Sonenscher, *Work and Wages: Natural Law, Politics and the Eighteenth-Century French Trades* (Cambridge, 1989).

56. K. M. Baker, "Public Opinion as Political Invention," in Baker, *Inventing the French Revolution*; M. Ozouf, "Public Opinion at the End of the Old Regime," JMH, 60 (suppl. 1988), reprinted in T. C. W. Blanning, ed., *The Rise and Fall of the French Revolution* (Chicago, 1996), pp. 90–110.

57. The date 1788 is important, because the crisis of 1787–8 did more to politicize a generation of French subjects than all the previous evolution of consciousness put together.

58. D. Echeverria, *The Maupeou Revolution: A Study in the History of Libertarianism, France, 1770–4* (Baton Rouge, LA, 1985); K. M. Baker, ed., "The Maupeou Revolution: The Transformation of French Politics at the End of the Old Régime," *Historical Reflections/Réflexions historiques* special issue, 18 (1992).

59. Pidansat de Mairobert, *Memoirs of Madame du Barry*, ed. by E. Cruickshanks (London, 1956). See also T. Kaiser, "Madame de Pompadour and the Theaters of Power," FHS, 19 (1996), 1025–44. Also Linton, *Politics of Virtue*, ch. 5, "The Virtuous King."

60. D. Goodman, ed., *Marie Antoinette, Writings on the Body of the Queen* (New York, 2003).

61. R. Chagny, ed., *Aux origines provinciales de la Révolution* (Grenoble, 1990); A. Forrest, *Paris, the Provinces and the French Revolution* (London, 2004), ch. 3; M. Cubells, *Les Horizons de la liberté. Naissance de la révolution en Provence, 1787–9* (Aix-en-Provence, 1987); J. Egret, "The Origins of the Revolution in Brittany (1788–1789)," in J. Kaplow, ed., *New Perspectives on the French Revolution* (New York, 1965), pp. 136–52, and "The Pre-Revolution in Provence (1787–1789)," in Kaplow, *New Perspectives*, pp. 153–70.

62. B. Bonin, R. Chagny, G. Chianéa, V. Chomel, J. Godel, J. Solé, and G. Viallet, *Les Débuts de la Révolution française en Dauphiné* (Grenoble, 1988).

63. R. Dupuy, ed., *Aux origines idéologiques de la Révolution. Journaux et pamphlets à Rennes (1788–1789)* (Rennes, 2000).

64. On the consequences during the Estates General, see the excellent article by C. Kuhlmann, "The Influence of the Breton Deputation and the Breton Club in the Revolution (April–October. 1789)," in *University of Nebraska Studies*, 2 (Lincoln, NE, 1902) pp. 207–98.

65. Quotation from Popkin, "The French Revolution's Third Century," p. 806.

66. Comte de Caraman cited in Egret, "Prerevolution in Provence," p. 167.

67. Cubells, *Les Horizons de la liberté*, pp. 170–8.

68. F. Nussbaum, "American Tobacco and French Politics, 1783–1789," *Political Science Quarterly*, 40 (1925), pp. 497–516; Nussbaum, "The revolutionary Vergennes and Lafayette versus the Farmers General," JMH, 3 (1931), pp. 592–613.

69. A good brief summary is Forrest, *Paris, the Provinces and the French Revolution*, ch. 4, "The spread of popular revolution."

70. M. Sonenscher has explored the debate of the constitutional implications of various solutions to the debt problem: "The Nation's Debt and the Birth of the Modern Republic: The French Fiscal Deficit and the Politics of the Revolution of 1789," *History of Political Thought*, vol. 18, no. 1 (Spring 1997), pp. 64–103 and no. 2 (Summer 1997), pp. 267–325.

71. J. Hardman, ed., *The French Revolution Sourcebook* (London, 1999) p. 39.

72. Exile no longer meant political nullity, as Necker continued to have a faction.

73. J. Popkin, "Pamphlet Journalism at the End of the Old Régime," ECS, 22 (1989), pp. 351–67.

74. On the ministerial pamphlet campaign, see K. Margerison, *Pamphlets and Public Opinion* (West Lafayette, GA, 1998); D. K. Van Kley, "From the Lessons of History to Truths for all Times and All People: The Historical Origins of an

Anti-historical Declaration," ch. 2, in D. K. Van Kley, ed., *The French Idea of Freedom* (Stanford, CA, 1994); V. R. Gruder, "The Bourbon Monarchy: Reforms and Propaganda at the End of the Old Regime," in K. Baker, ed., *The French Revolution and the Creation of Modern Political Culture, I, The Political Culture of the Old Regime* (Oxford 1987), pp. 347–74.

75. G. Chaussinand-Nogaret, *The French Nobility in the Eighteenth Century. From Feudalism to Enlightenment*, trans. by W. Doyle (Cambridge, 1985); D. Wick, "The Court Nobility and the French Revolution," ECS, 13 (1979–80), pp. 263–84.

76. J. Egret, *The French Prerevolution* (Chicago, 1977).

77. B. Stone, *The French Parlements and the Crisis of the Old Régime* (Chapel Hill, NC, 1986); W. Doyle, *The Parlement of Bordeaux and the End of the Old Régime, 1771–90* (London, 1974).

78. G. Bossenga, *The Politics of Privilege: Old Regime and Revolution in Lille* (Cambridge, 1991); L. Hunt, *Revolution and Urban Politics in Provincial France. Troyes and Reims, 1786–90* (Stanford, CA, 1978).

79. R. W. Greenlaw, "Pamphlet Literature in France during the Period of the Aristocratic Revolt (1787–1788)," JMH, 29, 4, pp. 349–54. For over eleven hundred of the pamphlets, see D. K. Van Kley and J. Popkin, "The Pre-revolutionary Debate/Le Débat pré-révolutionnaire," in C. Lucas, ed., *The French Revolution Research Collection*, Section 5, "the Pre-revolutionary Debate" (Oxford, 1990), a microfiche collection now on line at the Bibliothèque nationale, France, via Gallica.

80. *Life and Letters of Mallet du Pan*, ed. by A. Sayous, 2 vols (London, 1852), 1, pp. 167–8.

81. G. V. Taylor, "Revolutionary and Non-Revolutionary Content in the Cahiers of 1789," *French Historical Studies*, 7 (1972), pp. 479–502.

82. T. Tackett, *Becoming a Revolutionary. The Deputies of the French National Assembly and the Emergence of a Revolutionary Culture, 1789–91* (Princeton, NJ, 1996) is excellent on this period.

83. J. Godechot, *The Taking of the Bastille, July 14 1789* (London, 1970); H. Lüsebrink and R. Reichardt, *The Bastille: A History of a Symbol of Despotism and Freedom* (Durham, NC, 1997); M. Cottret, *La Bastille à prendre. Histoire et mythes de la forteresse royale* (Paris, 1986).

1. THE FINANCIAL ORIGINS OF THE FRENCH REVOLUTION *Joël Félix*

1. Comment on Necker's demission published by M. F. A. de Lescure, *Correspondance secrète inédite sur Louis XVI, Marie-Antoinette, la cour et la ville de 1777 à 1792. Publiée d'après les manuscrits de la Bibliothèque Impériale de Saint-Petersbourg* (Paris, 1866), vol. 1, pp. 402–3.

2. By the end of his speech, Necker announced that his proposals would reduce the deficit from 160 to 56 million livres tournois,

3. For a survey of these issues see François Crouzet, *Britain Ascendant: Comparative Studies in Franco-British Economic History* (Cambridge, 1990), pp. 1–104, D. Weir, "Les Crises économiques et les origines de la Révolution française," *Annales ESC*, 1991, no. 4, pp. 917–47 and P. Butel, *L'Economie française au XVIIIe siècle* (Paris, 1993).

4. J. C. Riley, *The Seven Years' War and the Old Regime. The Economic and Financial Toll* (Princeton, NJ, 1987).

5. P. T. Hoffman, *Growth in a Traditional Society. The French Countryside, 1450–1815* (Princeton, NJ, 1996).

6. For a good summary of the literature on this subject see F. Crouzet, *La Grande Inflation. La monnaie en France de Louis XVI à Napoléon* (Paris, 1993), pp. 17–89. See also K. Norberg, "The French Fiscal Crisis of 1788 and the Financial Origins of the Revolution of 1789," in P. T. Hoffman and K. Norberg, eds, *Fiscal Crises, Liberty, and Representative Government, 1450–1789*, (Stanford, CA, 1994).

7. The deficit on the figure represents the difference between the ordinary revenue (taxes) and the total expenses which total both ordinary expenses (cost of government) and extraordinary expenses (war expenses). As this diagram shows, the deficit was systematically covered by extraordinary resources (extra-ordinary taxes, loans and cash advances).

8. On financing wars, see J. Riley, "French Finances, 1727–1768," *JMH* (1987), vol. 59, pp. 224–43 and T. Le Goff, "How to Finance an Eighteenth-Century War," in W. M. Ormrod, R. Bonney and M. Bonney, eds, *Crises, Revolutions and Self-Sustained Growth: Essays in European Fiscal History* (Stamford (England): 1999), pp. 377–413.

9. There were three main kind of loans: the *rentes perpétuelles* (long-term annuities), the *rentes viagères* (life-term annuities) and the *rentes héréditaires* (fixed-term annuities). The capital of the *rentes perpétuelles* was not redeemable; the capital of the *rentes viagères* redeemed itself on the death of the bearer; in the case of the *rentes héréditaires*, the bearer was paid both the interest and his investment which was fully refunded, usually in ten or twelve years.

10. M. Morineau, "Budget de l'état et gestion des finances royales en France au dix-huitième siècle," *RH*, 1980, t. 264, no. 536, pp. 289–336.

11. J. Félix, *Finances et politique au siècle des lumières. Le ministère L'Averdy, 1763–1768* (Paris, 1999).

12. P. Mathias and P. O'Brien, "Taxation in Britain and France, 1715–1810. A Comparison of the Social and Economic Incidence of Taxes Collected for the Central Governments," *Economic History*, vol. 5, no. 3 (Winter 1976), pp. 601–50.

13. M. Marion, *Machault d'Arnouville. Étude sur l'histoire du contrôle général des finances de 1749 à 1754* (Paris, 1891).

14. G. Chaussinand-Nogaret, *The French Nobility in the Eighteenth Century from Feudalism to Enlightenment*, trans. by William Doyle (Cambridge, 1985). For a good summary of these discussions, M. Kwass, *Privilege and the Politics of Taxation in Eighteenth-Century France* (Cambridge, 2000).

15. R. Bonney, "Le Secret de leurs familles: The Fiscal and Social Limits of Louis XIV's *dixième*," *FH*, 7 (1993), 383–416.

16. J. Félix, "Les Rapports financiers des contrôleurs généraux des finances: Deux rapports financiers de Bertin à Louis XV," *Études et Documents*, VII (1997), pp. 517–36.

17. By contrast to the views developed by Mathias and O'Brien in "Taxation in Britain and France, 1715–1810," which rely on inadequate and sometimes erroneous data of the French budget. One significant mistake is mentioned in

Félix, *Finances et politique*, pp. 36 passim. On the level of taxation in France see also Riley, "French Finances, 1727–1768."

18. The following graphs are based on the financial information published by Ambroise-Marie Arnould, *De la balance du commerce et des relations commerciales extérieures de la France, dans toutes les parties du globe, particulièrement à la fin du règne de Louis XIV, et au moment de la Révolution*, 3 vols (Paris, 1791), vol. 3.

19. Charles-Alexandre de Calonne, *Réponse de M. de Calonne à l'écrit de M. Necker, publié en avril 1787, contenant l'examen des comptes de la situation des finances tenus en 1774, 1776, 1781, 1783, & 1787, avec des observations sur les résultats de l'Assemblée des notables* (London, T. Spilsbury, 1788).

20. Ibid., pp. 174–5.

21. J. F. Bosher, *French Finances, 1770–1795 from Business to Bureaucracy* (Cambridge, 1970).

22. D. Weir, "Tontines, Public Finances and Revolution in France and England, 1688–1789," JEcH, vol. 49 (June 1989), pp. 95–124.

23. F.-R. Velde and D. R. Weir, "The Financial Market and Government Debt Policy in France, 1746–1793," JEcH, vol. 52 (March 1992), no.1, p. 3. On the policy of the late controllers general see also E. N. White, "Was There a Solution to the Ancient Regime's Financial Dilemma?," JEcH, vol 49 (1989), pp. 545–68 and F. Bayard, J. Félix and P. Hamon, *Dictionnaire des surintendants et des contrôleurs généraux des finances* (Paris, 2000).

24. J. Brewer, *The Sinews of Power: War, Money and the English State, 1683–1783* (London, 1989).

25. See Félix, *Finances et politique* and T. J. A. Le Goff, "Les caisses d'amortissement en France (1749–1783)," in *L'Administration des finances sous l'Ancien Régime* (Paris, 1997), pp. 177–93.

26. Jacques Necker, *De l'administration des finances de la France*, 3 vols (Paris, 1784), vol. 3, pp. 232–3.

27. R. D. Harris, *Necker, Reform Statesman of the Ancien Régime* (Berkeley, CA, 1978).

28. On the liberalization of the economy and its problems see Félix, *Finances et politique*; S. L. Kaplan, *Bread, Politics and Political Economy in the Reign of Louis XV*, 2 vols (The Hague, 1975) and *La Fin des corporations* (Paris, 2001); and P. Minard, *La Fortune du colbertisme: État et industrie dans la France des lumières* (Paris, 1998).

29. On political economy, reforms and public opinion see Félix, *Finances et politique*; Kaplan, *Bread, Politics and Political Economy*; Kwass, *Privilege and the Politics of Taxation*, as well as J.-C. Perrot, "Nouveautés: L'Économie politique et ses livres," in R. Chartier et H.-J. Martin, eds, *Histoire de l'édition française, le livre triomphant, 1660–1830* (Paris, 1990), pp. 298–328 and R. J. Ives, "Political Publicity and Political Economy in Eighteenth-Century France," FH, vol. 17, Issue 1 (March 2003), pp. 1–18.

30. G. Weulersse, *La Physiocratie à l'aube de la Révolution, 1781–1792*, Introduction, bibliographie et révision des textes par Corinne Butler (Paris, 1985); M. Sonenscher, "The Nation's Debt and the Birth of the Modern Republic: The French Fiscal Deficit and the Politics of the Revolution of 1789," *History of Political Thought*, vol. 18, no. 1 (Spring 1997), pp. 64–103 and no. 2 (Summer 1997), pp. 267–325.

2. DECISION-MAKING *John Hardman*

1. C. A. de Calonne (attrib.), *Lettre du Marquis de Caraccioli à M. d'Alembert* (1781), p. 15.
2. On tax-farming see G. T. Mathews, *The Royal General Farms in Eighteenth-Century France* (New York, 1958).
3. Castries, *Journal*, Archives de la Marine, ms. 182/7964, 2 vols., II, ff. 366 and 371.
4. Mercy-Argenteau, comte F.-C. de, *Correspondance secréte entre Marie-Thérèse et le comte de Mercy-Argenteau*, ed. by A. d'Arneth and M.-A. Geffroy, 3 vols (Paris, 1874–5), III, p. 36.
5. Calonne to d'Angiviller, late July 1787, AN 297 AP 3. 119 fo. 7
6. Castries, *Journal*, II, fo. 398.
7. A. Sorel, *Europe and the French Revolution: The Political Traditions of the Old Regime*, trans. and ed. by A. Cobban and J. W. Hunt (London, 1969), p. 244.
8. Castries, *Journal*, II, 341.
9. *Louis XVI and Vergennes: Correspondence, 1774–1787*, ed. and with an introduction by John Hardman and Munro Price (Oxford, 1998), pp. 43–4.
10. Ibid., p. 236.
11. Archives de Affaires Etrangères, C.P. Angleterre 526 fo. 49.
12. C. H. Van Tyne, "French Aid before the Alliance of 1778," AHR, 31 (1925), pp. 20–40.
13. J. Dull, *The French Navy and American Independence: A Study of Arms and Diplomacy, 1774–1787* (Princeton, NJ, 1975).
14. *Louis XVI and Vergennes, Correspondence*, p. 60.
15. For a fuller discussion of the Bavarian dimension, see ibid. pp. 64–6.
16. AN, K 164 carton 3, memorandum of Breteuil, 11 November 1784.
17. Castries, *Journal*, II, ff. 259–60.
18. "Objections et réponse" published by H. Glagau in *Reformversucke und Sturz des Absolutismus in Frankreich, 1744–1788* (Munich, 1908), p. 366.
19. Lefevre d'Amécourt, *Ministres de Louis XVI*, Bibliothèque nationale, Nouvelles acquisitions françaises, 22104, fo. 74.
20. B. Erdmannsdorfer, *Politische Correspondenz Karl Friedrichs von Baden 1783–1806* (Heidelberg, 1881), I, p. 273.
21. *L'Administration de l'agriculture au contrôle-générale des finances (1785–1787): procés-verbal et rapports*, ed. H. Pigemeau and A. de Foville (Paris, 1882), p. 371.
22. J.-F.-X. Droz, *Histoire du règne de Louis XVI* (Brussels, 1839), p. 355.
23. J. Bosher, *French Finances 1770–1795* (Cambridge, 1970), 178–96; R. D. Harris, *Necker: Reform Statesman of the Ancien Regime* (Berkeley, CA, 1979).
24. These have been published as an appendix in Glagau, *Reformversucke*.
25. Glagau, *Reformversucke*, p. 367.
26. Castries, *Journal*, I, fo. 334.
27. Castries, *Journal*, I, fo. 341.
28. Castries, *Journal*, I, fo. 335
29. AN, K 163 carton 8. no. 22.
30. Bibliothèque de l'Arsenal, Ms. 3978, p. 212.

31. AN, K 677 no. 111. Each secretary of state, for matters not grouped thematically by department, administered a bundle of provinces.

32. R. Lacour-Gayet, *Calonne* (Paris, 1963), pp. 176–77.

33. AN, K 163, carton 8. no. 7.

34. Dupont de Nemours, letter 246, in Erdmannsdorfer, *Politische Correspondenz*, I, p. 273.

3. THE PARIS PARLEMENT IN THE 1780S *Peter Robert Campbell*

1. The apparent contradictions within the monarchy are worth noting: the monarchy is limited but absolute, it is conservative but innovative. The ancien régime lived with these paradoxes by not discussing them openly.

2. F. L. Ford, *Robe and Sword: The Regrouping of the French Aristocracy after Louis XIV* (Cambridge, MA, 1953).

3. D. K. Van Kley, "New Wine in Old Wineskins: Continuity and Rupture in the Pamphlet Debate of the French Prerevolution," FHS, 17, 2 (1991), pp. 448–65.

4. There is an extended analysis of the *parti janséniste* and the 1730–2 crisis in P. R. Campbell, *Power and Politics in Old Regime France, 1720–1745* (London, 1996), Part 2; see also D. A. Bell, "Des stratégies d'opposition sous Louis XV: L'Affaire des avocats, 1730–31," *Histoire, économie et société*, 9, 4 (1990), pp. 567–90. For further discussion, see below, and ch. 6.

5. Motivation from Gallicanism and parlementary constitutionalism are the views of J. H. Shennan, *The Parlement of Paris* (London, 1968) and D. K. Van Kley in his several studies relating to the parlement.

6. J. Swann, *Politics and the Parlement of Paris under Louis XV, 1754–1774* (Cambridge, 1995).

7. It is worth noting that the interventionism of the Figurist religious beliefs of the Jansenists finds a strong echo in the patriotic language of the 1750s onwards, as it too stresses the need for intervention for secular reasons of good citizenship. See P. R. Campbell, "French Patriotism in the Old Regime," a forthcoming article.

8. The best and only study of the provincial courts for these years is J. Egret, *Louis XV et l'opposition parlementaire, 1715–1774* (Paris, 1970); chs 2–4.

9. N. Temple, ed., *The Road to 1789* (Cardiff, 1992), Doc. VII reproduces the king's "flagellation speech" in English and docs V and VI are from other important remonstrances in the 1750s.

10. On the Maupeou coup, see J. Rothney, *The Brittany Affair and the Crisis of the Ancien Régime* (Oxford, 1969); W. Doyle, "The Parlements of France and the Breakdown of the Old Regime," FHS, 6 (1970), pp. 415–58; Swann, *Politics and the Parliament of Paris*. Few historians now consider Maupeou a sincere reformer.

11. On the pamphlets, D. Echeverria, *The Maupeou Revolution: A Study in the History of Libertarianism, 1770–1774* (Baton Rouge, LA, 1985); D. K. Van Kley, "The Religious Origins of the Patriote and Ministerial Parties in Pre-revolutionary France: Controversy over the Chancellor's Constitutional Coup, 1771–1775," *Historical Reflections / Réflections historiques*, 18, 2 (1992), pp. 17–63.

12. The patriote pamphlets were republished by Pidansat de Mairobert, ed., *Les Efforts de la liberté et du patriotisme, contre le despotisme du Sr Maupeou, chancelier de France, ou recueil des écrits patriotiques publiés pendant le règne du chancelier Maupeou . . .*, 6 vols (Paris, 1775) and Mairobert, *Journal historique de la révolution opérée dans la constitution de la monarchie française par M. de Maupeou, chancelier de France*, 7 vols (London, 1776).

13. M. Antoine, *Louis XV* (Paris, 1989); A. Cobban, "The Parlements of France in the Eighteenth Century," *History*, 35 (1950), pp. 64–80, reprinted in Cobban, *Aspects of the French Revolution* (London, 1969).

14. Egret, *Louis XV et l'opposition parlementaire;* J. H. Shennan, *The Parlement of Paris* (London, 1998).

15. Doyle, *The Parlements of France*, Campbell, *Power and Politics*, and the influential study by A. N. Hamscher, *The Parlement of Paris after the Fronde, 1653–1673* (Pittsburgh, PA, 1976).

16. F. Bluche, *L'Origine des magistrats du Parlement de Paris au XVIIIe siècle (1715–1771)*, Paris, 1956); Bluche, *Les Magistrats du Parlement de Paris au XVIIIe siècle (1715–1771)* (Paris, 1960); J. Félix, *Les Magistrats du parlement de Paris, 1771–90* (Paris, 1990).

17. B. Stone, *The Parlement of Paris, 1774–1789* (Chapel Hill, NC, 1981).

18. J. Flammermont, ed., *Remontrances du parlement de Paris au XVIIIe siècle*, 3 vols (Paris, 1888–98); Fr. Olivier-Martin, *Les Parlements contre l'absolutisme traditionnel au XVIIIe siècle* (Paris, 1949–50, reprinted 1988).

19. Of these, L. A. Le Paige, *Lettres historiques sur les functions essentielles du parlement*, 2 vols (Amsterdam, 1753) was the most influential, contested by Voltaire and G. Bonnot de Mably, *Observations sur l'histoire de France*, in *Collection complète des Oeuvres de l'abbé de Mably* (Paris, 1794–5), vols 1–3. Voltaire did not believe a word of the ancient constitution argument: F. A. de Voltaire, *Histoire du Parlement de Paris* (n.p., 1769).

20. D. K. Van Kley, *The Damiens Affair and the Unravelling of the Ancien Régime 1750–1770* (Princeton, NJ, 1984); D. C. Joynes, "Parlements, Peers and the *Parti Janséniste*: The Refusal of Sacraments and the Revival of the Ancient Constitution in Eighteenth-Century France," *Western Society for French History: Proceedings* (1981), pp. 229–38; Joynes, "Jansenists and Ideologues; Opposition Theory in the Parlement of Paris, 1750–1775," PhD thesis (University of Chicago, 1981); J. Merrick, *The Desacralization of the French Monarchy in the Eighteenth Century* (Baton Rouge, LA, 1990); M. Cottret, *Jansénisme et lumières* (Paris, 1998).

21. J. M. J. Rogister, "The Crisis of 1753–4 in France and the Debate on the Nature of the Monarchy and of the Fundamantal Laws," *Studies Presented to the International Commission for the History of Representative and Parliamentary Institutions*, 59 (1977), pp. 105–20. This excellent article importantly shows how jurisdictional conflict led to constitutional statements.

22. On lawyers see D. A. Bell, *Lawyers and Citizens. The Making of a Political Elite in Old Regime France* (New York, 1994), M. Fitzsimmons, *The Parisian Order of Barristers in the French Revolution* (Cambridge, MA, 1987). A. Cocâtre-Zilgien, "Les Doctrines politiques des milieux parlementaires dans la seconde moitié du XVIIIe siècle, ou les avocats dans la bataille idéologique pré-révolutionnaire," *Annales de la Faculté de Droit et Sciences Économiques de Lille* (1963), pp. 29–154.

23. François-Joachim de Pierre de Bernis, *Memoirs and Letters of Cardinal de Bernis*, trans. by Katherine Prescott Wormeley, 2 vols (New York, 1901), pp. 247–8: "We see in what happened then [1732] the history of what has happened since; and what will always happen when the Court acts without a plan, without preparation, and without principles; it weakens, or at least it compromises royal authority by acts little reflected on by indecent retreats."

24. We might call this a new approach to institutional history in which the microhistory of events takes on new interpretative significance.

25. C-M. Talleyrand, *Mémoires du prince de Talleyrand-Périgord, 1754–1830*, ed. by duc de Broglie, 5 vols (Paris, 1891–2), vol 1, p. 94.

26. Bernis, *Memoirs*, pp. 269–70.

27. Even under Louis XIV this was the case: A. N. Hamscher, "Parlements and Litigants at the King's Councils during the Personal Rule of Louis XIV: The Example of Cassation," in M. P. Holt, ed., *Society and Institutions in Early Modern France* (London, 1991), pp. 190–222.

28. Bernis, *Memoirs*, pp. 249–50.

29. Bernis, *Memoirs*, p. 252.

30. Bernis, *Memoirs*, p. 252.

31. Bernis, *Memoirs*, pp. 250–1 and 256, writing before Maupeou!

32. J. Swann, "Parlement, Politics and the Parti Janséniste: The Grand Conseil Affair, 1755–1756," FH, 6 (1992), pp. 435–61.

33. Sénac de Meilhan, *Des principes et des causes de la Révolution en France* (Paris, 1987), p. 49.

34. Bernis, *Memoirs*, pp. 262–3.

35. The evidence they left has been used by Campbell, *Power and Politics*, for its relation to politics; by R. Darnton "An Early Information Society: News and Media in Eighteenth-Century Paris," AHR, 105 (2000), online at http://www.indiana.edu/~ahr/darnton/index.html, to trace places where ideas were exchanged; and most extensively by A. Farge, *Subversive Words: Public Opinion in Eighteenth-Century France* (Cambridge, 1994) in order to trace political awareness in the Parisian population.

36. The mismanagement of the court also created an "out group" of nobles deprived of honours and pensions they felt were their traditional due, and, as Wick shows, this fed into liberal noble opposition at the Estates General. See D. Wick, *A Conspiracy of Well-intentioned Men. The Society of Thirty and the French Revolution* (New York, 1987).

37. On the Diamond Necklace Affair, see A. Cobban, "The Affair of the Diamond Necklace," in Cobban, *Aspects*, ch. 4; S. Maza, "The Diamond Necklace Affair, 1785–6," in Maza, *Private Lives and Public Affairs: The Causes Célèbres of Prerevolutionary France* (Berkeley, CA, 1993); R. A. W. Browne, "The Diamond Necklace Affair Revisited: The Rohan Family and Court Politics," *Renaissance and Modern Studies*, 33 (1989), pp. 21–40; and M. Price, *Preserving the Monarchy* (Cambridge, 1995), ch. 7.

38. J. M. Augeard, *Mémoires secrets* (Paris, 1866), p. 154.

39. The decision for the Assembly of Notables is focused on by Hardman in his chapter in this volume.

40. Duke Étienne Denis Pasquier, *A History of my Time. Memoirs of Chancellor Pasquier Edited by the Duc d'Audiffret-Pasquier* [1789–1815], trans. by C. E. Roche, 3 vols (London & Boston, MA, 1893–94), vol. 1, p. 27.

41. "In 1787, nearly all those who were of some prominence in the peerage, nearly all those who with the magnificence of that high rank combined a cultured and distinguished mind, joined the ranks of the parlementary opposition. I cannot forget how powerfully the minds of the young magistrates were affected by the attraction of following such leaders." Pasquier, *Memoirs*, p. 28.

42. R. Bickart, *Les Parlements et la notion de souveraineté nationale au XVIIIe siècle* (Paris, 1932), pp. 249–51.

43. *Mémoires du comte de Ferrand*, ed. by V. de Broc (Paris, 1897), p. 11.

44. G.-M. Sallier, *Annales françaises, depuis le commencement du règne de Louis XVI, jusqu'aux Etats Généraux, 1774 à 1789* (2nd edn, Paris, 1813), pp 80–1.

45. Sallier, *Annales*, pp. 83–90.

46. Talleyrand says that the courts had no choice after the ministry's revolutionary step of calling Notables: *Mémoires*, I, p. 108.

47. Sallier, *Annales*, p. 93.

48. See on the period of the Notables through to the riots by the *basoche* after the exile of 15 August, Mallet du Pan's diary, in *Memoirs and Correspondence of Mallet du Pan*, trans and ed. by A. Sayous, 2 vols (London, 1852), I, pp. 140–50.

49. Sallier, *Annales*, pp. 100–5; Dorset to Camarthen, Dispatches from 20 Nov. 1787 to 13 Dec. 1787, in *Despatches from Paris, 1784–1790*, ed. by O. Browning, 2 vols (London, 1909–10), I (1784–87), pp. 265–74. These volumes are a useful source for these years in terms of diplomatic and public reaction to government actions.

50. Pasquier, *Memoirs*, p. 31.

51. Pasquier, *Memoirs*, p. 34.

52. *Journal de Target*, in P. Boullouche, *Un avocat au XVIIIe siècle* (Paris, 1893), pp. 47–53.

53. Flammermont, *Remontrances*, vol. 3, pp. 721–34.

54. Pasquier, *Memoirs*, p. 38.

55. For an eyewitness account of the Breton response, see A. F. Bertrand de Moleville, *Private Memoirs of A. F. Bertrand de Moleville, Minister of State, 1790–1791, Relative to the Last Year of the Reign of Louis XVI* (1797 trans.), ed. by G. K. Fortesque, 2 vols (Boston, 1909).

56. *Memoirs and Correspondence of Mallet du Pan, Illustrative of the French Revolution*, ed. by A. Sayous, 2 vols (London, 1852), vol. 1, pp. 153–4.

57. The best analysis of this provincial dimension, for Bordeaux, is W. Doyle, *The Parlement of Bordeaux and the End of the Old Regime, 1771–1790* (London, 1974), pp. 264–85; more generally, see B. Stone, *The French Parlements and the Crisis of the Old Régime* (Chapel Hill, NC, 1986).

58. N. Aston, *The End of an Elite. The French Bishops and the Coming of the French Revolution, 1786–90* (Oxford, 1992).

59. Stone, *Parlement of Paris*, p. 181.

60. *Le Despotisme des parlements, ou letter d'un anglois à un François* (London, 1789).

61. Note that there was much talk of bankruptcy, but that *banqueroute* in French meant a rescheduling of debts, not a complete failure to pay.

4. FROM SOCIAL TO CULTURAL HISTORY *William Scott*

1. J. Jaurès, *Histoire socialiste de la Révolution française*, new edn by A. Soboul in 7 vols (Paris, 1968–73). Jaurès, leader of the French Socialist party, was assassinated on July 31, 1914 for seeking strenuously to avoid war.

2. A. Mathiez, *The French Revolution* (London, 1928) and *La Vie chère et le mouvement social sous la Terreur* (Paris, 1927).

3. For a useful collection of Marx's dispersed assessments of the French Revolution, *Marx and the French Revolution*, ed. by F. Furet (Chicago, 1988). More generally, W. H. Shaw, *Marx's Theory of History* (Stanford, CA, 1978).

4. Of general works, G. Lefebvre, *The Coming of the French Revolution* (Princeton, NJ, 1947) and *The French Revolution. From its Origins to 1793* (New York, 1962); A. Soboul, *A Short History of the French Revolution* (Berkeley, CA, 1977), *Understanding the French Revolution* (London, 1988) and *The French Revolution* (London, 1989). Lefebvre's great work, of 1924, *Les Paysans du Nord* (reprinted Editori Laterza, Bari, 1959), had it been translated, would perhaps have dispelled crude critiques of "the social interpretation": but his *The Great Fear of 1789: Rural Panic in Revolutionary France* (London, 1973) should have done that. Soboul's *Les Sans-culottes parisiens en l'an II* (Paris, 1958) received an abridged translation by G. Lewis: *The Parisian Sans-culottes and the French Revolution, 1793–4* (Oxford, 1964).

5. Consult the 1999 edition of A. Cobban, *The Social Interpretation of the French Revolution* (Cambridge), with introduction by G. Lewis. Also, Cobban's article, "Political *versus* Social Interpretations," in his *Aspects of the French Revolution*, (London, 1971) pp. 260–9.

6. F. Furet, *Interpreting the French Revolution*, trans. by E. Forster (Cambridge, 1981). Furet's "disciples," P. Gueniffey, *La Politique de la Terreur* (Paris, 2000) and, especially, L. Boroumand, *La Guerre des principes* (Paris, 1999) reinforce the thrust, and narrowness, of the interpretation.

7. K. M. Baker, *Inventing the French Revolution* (Cambridge, 1990).

8. F Furet, *Revolutionary France, 1770–1880* (Oxford, 1992).

9. Tocqueville's classic *The Old Regime and the Revolution* has recently received an extremely thorough new edition, with much fascinating contextual material: F. Furet and F. Mélonio, eds (2 vols, Chicago, 1998).

10. P. R. Campbell, "Conspiracy and Political Practice from the Ancien Régime to the French Revolution," in B. Coward and J. Swann, eds, *Conspiracy in Early Modern Europe* (Chichester, 2004), pp. 197–213. A volume entitled *Conspiracy in the French Revolution*, edited by P. R. Campbell, T. Kaiser, and M. Linton, is forthcoming in 2006.

11. R. Darnton, *The Business of Enlightenment, A Publishing History of the "Encyclopédie", 1775–1800* (London, 1979). See also *The Literary Undergrowth of the Old Regime* (Cambridge, MA, 1982) and *The Great Cat Massacre* (London, 1984). Daniel Roche's magisterial *Le Siècle des lumières en province. Académies et académiciens français, 1680–1789*, 2 vols (Mouton, 1978) and his *France in the Enlightenment*, trans. by A. Goldhammer (Cambridge, MA, 1998). See also M. Vovelle, *Enlightenment Portraits*, (Chicago, 1997).

12. Much work on French commercial towns and merchants has not been translated. See, for surveys, W. Scott, "Commerce, Capitalism and the Political

Culture of the French Revolution," *Journal of European Ideas*, vol. 11 (1989), pp. 89–105 and "The Pursuit of 'Interests' in the French Revolution," FHS, 19, No. 3 (Spring 1996), pp. 811–51.

13. C. A. Bayly, *The Birth of the Modern World, 1780–1914* (Oxford, 2004) and E. Rothschild, *Economic Sentiments. Adam Smith, Condorcet and the Enlightenment* (Cambridge, MA, 2001).

14. See G. Chaussinand-Nogaret, *The French Nobility in the Eighteenth Century. From Feudalism to Enlightenment* (Cambridge, 1985), a work received particularly uncritically by "revisionist" historians.

15. A. de Baecque, *The Body Politic. Corporeal Metaphor in Revolutionary France, 1770–1800* (Stanford, CA, 1997); *French Caricature and the French Revolution, 1789–1799* (Grunwald Centre for the Graphic Arts, University of California, 1988); M. Vovelle, *Les Images de la Révolution française, images et récits, 1789–1799*, 5 vols (Paris, 1986).

16. Exploring this theme, P. Friedland, *Political Actors, Representative Bodies and Theatricality in the Age of the French Revolution* (Ithaca, NY, 2003).

17. Sonenscher, *Work and Wages.*

18. D. Outram, "Le Langage mâle de la vertu: Women and the Discourse of the French Revolution," in Peter Burke and Roy Porter, eds, *The Social History of Language* (Cambridge, 1987), pp. 120–35.

19. M. Linton, *The Politics of Virtue in Enlightenment France* (Basingstoke, 2001).

20. L. Hunt, ed., *The Invention of Pornography. Obscenity and the Origins of Modernity, 1500–1800* (New York, 1993) and, related, her edited volume, *Eroticism and the Body Politic* (Baltimore, MD, 1991). R. Darnton, *The Forbidden Bestsellers of Pre-Revolutionary France* (New York and London, 1996).

21. But see H.-J. Lüsebrink and R. Reichart, *The Bastille. A History of a Symbol of Despotism and Freedom* (Durhman, NC, 1997) and Mona Ozouf, *Festivals and the French Revolution* (Cambridge, MA, 1988).

22. Vovelle has written extensively on religious observance and iconography. Maurice Agulhon's *Marianne into Battle. Republican Imagery and Symbolism in France, 1789–1848* (Oxford, 1981) is a still-influential pioneering study.

23. G. Lefebvre, *The Great Fear of 1789* (London, 1973). This dramatic episode is reviewed in C. Ramsay, *The Ideology of the Great Fear: The Soissonnais in 1789* (Baltimore, MD, 1992).

24. Mikhail Bakhtin (1895–1975) explored the cruder, earthier aspects of popular culture, notably in festivals and carnival.

25. L. Hunt, *The Family Romance of the French Revolution* (Berkeley, CA, 1992).

26. Hippolyte Taine, *Les Origines de la France contemporaine*, vol. 1, *L'Ancien Régime* (Paris, 1876). Consult the extracts ed. by E. T Gargan, *The Origins of Contemporary France* (Chicago, 1974).

27. A. Farge, *Fragile Lives: Violence, Power and Solidarity in 18th-Century Paris* (Oxford, 1983) and *Subversive Words* (Oxford, 1994); C. Truant, *The Rites of Labor* (Ithaca, NY, 1994); C. Lucas, "The Crowd and Politics," in Lucas, ed, *The French Revolution and the Creation of Modern Political Culture*, vol. 2, *The Political Culture of the Revolution* (Oxford, 1988), pp. 259–85; and O. Hufton, *Women and the Limits of Citizenship in the French Revolution* (Toronto, 1992).

28. T. Tackett, *Becoming a Revolutionary. The Deputies of the French National Assembly and the Emergence of a Revolutionary Culture, 1789–1790* (Princeton, NJ, 1996).

29. T. Tackett, *Religion, Revolution and Regional Culture in Eighteenth-Century France. The Ecclesiastical Oath of 1791* (Princeton, NJ, 1986).

30. A new version of Georg Büchner's play, *Danton's Death* (1835), was edited by Howard Brenton (London, 1982). Andrzey Wajda's challenging film, *Danton*, appeared in 1983.

31. Theodor Adorno and Max Horkheimer, *Dialectic of Enlightenment* (London, 1979).

32. See, especially, M. Foucault, *Discipline and Punish* (New York, 1979).

33. H. Arendt, *On Revolution* (London, 1963) and C. Lefort, *Democracy and Political Theory* (Cambridge, 1988).

34. That the French Revolution retains a force to shock is clear from A. J. Mayer, *The Furies. Violence and Terror in the French and Russian Revolutions* (Princeton, NJ, 2000) and, especially, E. Sagan, *Citizens and Cannibals. The French Revolution, the Struggle for Modernity and the Origins of Ideological Terror* (Lanham, MD, 2001).

5. THE INTELLECTUAL ORIGINS OF THE FRENCH REVOLUTION
Marisa Linton

1. De Maistre, "Study on Sovereignty," in *The Works of Joseph de Maistre*, ed. and trans. by Jack Lively (New York, 1965), pp. 111–2.

2. R. Chartier, *The Cultural Origins of the French Revolution*, trans. by Lydia G. Cochrane (Durham, NC and London, 1991), p. 2. Chartier wrote: "attributing 'cultural origins' to the French Revolution does not by any means establish the Revolution's causes; rather, it pinpoints certain of the conditions that made it possible because it was conceivable."

3. D. Mornet, "Les Enseignements des bibliothèques privées (1750–80)," *Revue d'histoire littéraire*, xvii (1910), pp. 449–96. On the emotional response of Rousseau's readers, see R. Darnton, *The Great Cat Massacre and Other Episodes in French Cultural History* (Harmondsworth, 1984), ch. 6, "Readers Respond to Rousseau," pp. 209–49.

4. Marie-Jeanne Roland (née Philipon), *The Memoirs of Madame Roland*, ed. and trans. by Evelyn Shuckburgh (London, 1989), p. 217.

5. T. Tackett, *Becoming a Revolutionary: The Deputies of the French National Assembly and the Emergence of a Revolutionary Culture (1789–1790)* (Princeton, NJ, 1996), p. 65.

6. J. McDonald, *Rousseau and the French Revolution, 1762–1791* (London, 1965).

7. B. Manin, "Rousseau," in François Furet and Mona Ozouf, eds, *A Critical Dictionary of the French Revolution*, trans. by Arthur Goldhammer (Cambridge, MA,1989), p. 831.

8. D. Mornet, *Les Origines intellectuelles de la Révolution française, 1715–1787* (first pub., 1933; 3rd edn, Paris, 1938), pp. 1–2.

9. Ibid, pp. 2–3.

10. On the inspiration, but also the limitations, of Mornet's approach to the diffusion of ideas, see Chartier, *Cultural Origins*, ch. 1, esp. pp. 3–10; 15–19.

11. Ibid, p. 19.

12. Darnton first made this argument in "The High Enlightenment and the Low Life of Literatures," P&P, 1971, reprinted in D. Johnson (ed.), *French Society*

and the Revolution (London, 1976), though he has elaborated it subsequently. See, for example, the arguments of F. A. De Luna and L. Loft on the genesis of Brissot's radicalism, together with Darnton's responses and defence of his position in "Forum: Interpreting Brissot," FHS, 17 (1991), pp. 159–205.

13. R. Darnton, *The Forbidden Best-Sellers of Pre-Revolutionary France* (London, 1996), pp. 165–6, 216. See also Chartier, *Cultural Origins*, ch. 6, "A Desacralized King," pp. 111–35.

14. Darnton, *The Forbidden Best-Sellers of Pre-Revolutionary France*, Introduction, p. xix.

15. H. T. Mason, ed., *The Darnton Debate: Books and Revolution in the Eighteenth Century* (Oxford, 1998).

16. D. Gordon, "The Great Enlightenment Massacre," in Mason, *The Darnton Debate*, p. 148.

17. Chartier, *Cultural Origins*, p. 5.

18. J. Habermas, *The Structural Transformation of the Public Sphere: An Inquiry into a Category of Bourgeois Society*, trans. by Thomas Burger and Frederick Lawrence (Cambridge, MA, 1989).

19. Both citations in J. Hardman, *Louis XVI: The Silent King* (London, 2000), pp. 38 and 39.

20. Ibid.

21. Chartier, *Cultural Origins*, pp. 27–30.

22. This argument was first made by R. R. Palmer, *Catholics and Unbelievers in Eighteenth-Century France* (New York, 1961). Palmer showed that even Jesuits were not necessarily all that hostile to philosophic ideas. Nonetheless, many in the clergy continued to see the Enlightenment as a threat to stability and morality. On the intellectual counterattack to the Enlightenment amongst the clergy, see D. M. McMahon, *Enemies of the Enlightenment: The French Counter-Enlightenment and the Making of Modernity* (Oxford, 2001).

23. The phrase "common culture" to describe the collective body of ideas subscribed to by educated people of all classes is used by Darnton, *The Forbidden Best-Sellers of Pre-Revolutionary France*, p. 194.

24. Cited in P. France, *Diderot* (Oxford, 1983), p. 43. On the authorship of this article, and the influence upon it of the natural law theorists, as well as the extent to which Diderot went beyond them, see J. Lough, "The Article *Autorité Politique*," in Lough, *Essays on the Encyclopédie of Diderot and D'Alembert* (Oxford, 1968), pp. 424–62, esp. pp. 435–9. On reactions to the article, see Lough, pp. 440–62.

25. See Lough, pp. 450–1. On Diderot's – somewhat tactical – argument that the principles voiced in this article were in line with the principles of the parlement, see D. Echeverria, *The Maupeou Revolution: A Study in the History of Libertarianism, France, 1770–4* (Baton Rouge, LA, 1985), p. 229. For a more extended treatment of the politics of Jansenism and of the parlement see chs 3 and 6 of the present work: Peter Campbell, "The Paris Parlement in the 1780s"; and Dale Van Kley, "The Religious Origins of the French Revolution, 1560–1791."

26. See J. G. A Pocock, *The Machiavellian Moment: Florentine Political Thought and the Atlantic Republican Tradition* (Princeton, NJ, 1975); also Franco Venturi, *Utopia and Reform in the Enlightenment* (Cambridge, 1971), ch. 3, "From Montesquieu to Revolution," pp. 70–94.

27. On the impact of the American model in France, see Mornet, *Les Origines intellectuelles de la Révolution française*, pp. 389–99; also Denis Lacorne, *L'Invention de la république: Le Modèle américain* (Paris, 1991) esp. pp. 77–84.

28. On English republicanism's influence in France, see P. Gueniffey, *La Politique de la Terreur: Essai sur la Violence Révolutionnaire, 1789–1794* (Paris, 2000), pp. 43–9; J. Dédieu, *Montesquieu et la tradition politique anglaise en France* (Paris, 1909); and M. Sonenscher, *Work and Wages: Natural Law, Politics and the Eighteenth-Century French Trades* (Cambridge, 1989), pp. 333–41. On Mirabeau's English links, see J. Bénétruy, *L'Atelier de Mirabeau: Quatre proscrits génévois dans la tourmente révolutionnaire* (Paris, 1962).

29. See M. Foucault, *The Archaeology of Knowledge* (New York, 1972). For an alternative, more historically based approach to the applications of discourse theory, see his "Introduction: the State of the Art," in J. Pocock, *Virtue, Commerce and History* (Cambridge, 1985), pp. 7–34.

30. K. M. Baker, *Inventing the French Revolution* (Cambridge, 1990), pp. 12–27. On his use of "discourse" see especially pp. 15–16.

31. Ibid, p. 27.

32. On "nation" see D. A. Bell, *The Cult of the Nation in France: Inventing Nationalism, 1680–1800* (Cambridge, MA, 2001). On *"patrie"* see E. Dziembowski, "Un nouveau patriotisme français, 1750–1770, la France face à la puissance anglaise à l'époque de la guerre de Sept Ans," SVEC, 365 (Oxford, 1998); also the forthcoming article by Peter R. Campbell, provisionally entitled "Patriotism in Old Regime France." On "citizen" see Pierre Rétat, "The Evolution of the Citizen from the Ancien Régime to the Revolution," in R. Waldinger, P. Dawson, and I. Woloch, eds, *The French Revolution and the Meaning of Citizenship* (Westport, CT, 1993), pp. 3–15. On the discourse of anti-despotism as a means of attack on ministerial corruption, see J. M. Burney, "History, Despotism, Public Opinion and the Continuity of the Radical Attack on Monarchy in the French Revolution, 1787–1792," HEI, 17, 2/3 (1993), pp. 245–63. On "virtue" see M. Linton, *The Politics of Virtue in Enlightenment France* (Basingstoke, 2001).

33. The many influential writings by Van Kley on Jansenist thought as a means of critique of absolute authority are crystallized in D. Van Kley, *The Religious Origins of the French Revolution: From Calvin to the Civil Consitution, 1560–1791* (New Haven, CT, 1996).

34. See, above all, K. M. Baker, "A Classical Republican in Eighteenth-Century Bordeaux: Guillaume-Joseph Saige," in Baker, *Inventing the French Revolution*, pp. 128–52.

35. K. M. Baker, "Transformations of Classical Republicanism in Eighteenth-Century France," JMH, 73 (March 2001), pp. 32–53.

36. Recent historians who have, in different ways, argued for a return to a consideration of social factors in the history of the Revolution include: Jack R. Censer, "Social Twists and Linguistic Turns: Revolutionary Historiography a Decade After the Bicentennial," FHS, 22 (1999), pp. 139–67; Suzanne Desan, "What's After Political Culture? Recent French Revolutionary Historiography," FHS, 23, 1 (2000), pp. 163–96; and Jay M. Smith, "No More Language Games: Words, Beliefs, and the Political Culture of Early Modern France," AHR, 102 (December 1997), pp. 1413–40.

37. H. Chisick, "Public Opinion and Political Culture in France During the Second Half of the Eighteenth Century," EHR, 117, issue 470 (Feb. 2002), pp. 48–77.

38. Tackett, *Becoming a Revolutionary*, ch. 2, "A Revolution of the Mind?," esp. pp. 58–65.

39. Baker, *Inventing the French Revolution*, p. 305. See also Kates's account of Baker's and Furet's view of the relationship between ideology and Revolution – a perspective which Kates characterizes as "neo-conservative" – in the Introduction to G. Kates, ed., *The French Revolution: Recent Debates and New Controversies* (London, 1998), pp. 1–20.

40. On the changing meaning of the "Nation" from the 1740s to the Revolution, see Bell, *The Cult of the Nation*, esp. pp. 10–15.

41. This distinction owes much to the interpretive argument of Peter Campbell. See his forthcoming article on patriotism.

42. On the shared language of the Assembly of Notables, see Vivien R. Gruder, "Paths to Political Consciousness: The Assembly of Notables of 1787 and the 'Pre-Revolution' in France," FHS, 13, 3 (1984), pp. 323–55. On the adoption of this new language in the *cahiers* – chiefly in those passages that directly addressed the king, see the major study of the general *cahiers* of the nobility and the Third Estate by G. Shapiro and J. Markoff, *Revolutionary Demands: A Content Analysis of the Cahiers de Doléances of 1789* (Stanford, CA, 1998), pp. 369–76.

43. Cited in N. Hampson, "The Enlightenment and the Language of the French Nobility in 1789: The Case of Arras," in D. J, Mossop, G. E. Rodmell, and D. B. Wilson, eds, *Studies in the French Eighteenth Century Presented to John Lough* (Durham, NC, 1978), p. 85. Hampson shows how nobles in Artois used this form of language to protest at local rules which excluded them from the election process, admitting only "established nobles" (those with six generations of nobility and a *seigneurie de clocher*) to sit in the local estates. At stake was the struggle to control the elections to the Estates General. The excluded nobles invoked public opinion by publicizing their case in the *Affiches d'Artois*, and obtained the support of Necker. Hampson points out that once the excluded nobles were admitted to representation rights to the Estates General, they drafted a *cahier* demanding entrenchment of noble privilege, suggesting that their initial use of the rhetoric of citizenship had been a conscious and deliberate strategy to maneuver the political situation; ibid., pp. 90–1.

44. This argument is made at greater length in Linton, *The Politics of Virtue in Enlightenment France*.

45. On the changing depiction of kingly virtue, see Linton, *The Politics of Virtue in Enlightenment France*, ch. 5, "The Virtuous King: A Rhetoric Transfomed," pp. 129–52. This argument relates also to the debate on desacralization. For desacralization did not only emerge from clandestine *libelles* or hostile parlements whose overt intention was to criticize the monarchy. It could also be an unintended consequence of attempts by senior clerics and other apologists for the monarchy to depict Louis XVI as a citizen king, or a *bienfaisant* monarch, a portrayal that undermined the more traditional vision of the French monarchy as suffused with a sacred aura and quasi-mystical attributes.

46. This point is made extensively in the articles now collected in D. Goodman, ed. *Marie Antoinette, Writings on the Body of the Queen* (New York, 2003).

47. On the development of the concept of citizenship, see the articles in Waldinger, Dawson, and Woloch, *The French Revolution and the Meaning of Citizenship*. On the development of a language of political rights see Dale Van Kley, ed., *The French Idea of Freedom: The Old Regime and the Declaration of Rights of 1789* (Stanford, CA, 1994).

48. F. Furet, *Interpreting the French Revolution*, trans. by E. Forster (Cambridge, 1981), p. 26.

49. Here I find myself very much in agreement with Dale Van Kley and his argument that whilst the key concepts of the Enlightenment were so broad that they could be adapted to a variety of different political viewpoints, it was the application of ideas in specific political, religious and ideological polemical contexts that set up the "fundamental political and ideological directions of eighteenth-century France." D. Van Kley, "Church, State, and the Ideological Origins of the French Revolution: The Debate over The General Assembly of the Gallican Clergy in 1765," republished in T. C. W. Blanning, ed., *The Rise and Fall of the French Revolution* (Chicago, 1996), p. 63.

50. On the links between virtue and terror in Jacobin political language, see M. Linton, "Robespierre's Political Principles," in C. Haydon and W. Doyle, eds, *Robespierre* (Cambridge, 1999), pp. 37–53.

6. THE RELIGIOUS ORIGINS OF THE FRENCH REVOLUTION, 1560–1791
Dale Van Kley

1. On the origin of Henry's supposed saying, see M. Wolfe, *The Conversion of Henri IV: Politics, Power, and Religious Belief in Early-Modern France* (Cambridge, MA, 1993), p. 1. On the sincerity of Henry's conversion, see T. Wanneghffelen, *Ni Rome ni Genève: Les Fidèles entre deux chaires en France au XVIe siècle* (Paris, 1997), pp. 406–27; and R. Love, *Blood and Religion: The Conscience of Henry IV, 1553–1593* (Montreal and Kingston, 2001).

2. The best account of the Saint-Cloud affair is still Dom H. Leclercq, *L'Église constitutionnelle (juillet 1790–avril 1791)* (Paris, 1934), 564–98. The most recent treatment of Louis XVI's decision to flee France is T. Tackett's *When the King Took Flight* (Cambridge, MA., 2003), although Tackett does very little with the religious aspect of that flight.

3. On the novelty of the French Revolution's concept of "revolution," see K. M. Baker, "Inventing the French Revolution," in *Inventing the French Revolution* (Cambridge, 1990), pp. 203–23. See also Mona Ozouf on the related concept of "regeneration" in F. Furet and M. Ozouf, eds, *A Critical Dictionary of the French Revolution* (Cambridge, MA, 1989), p. 781–91.

4. Although this brief definition of religion owes something to Clifford Geertz's essay on "Religion as a Cultural System," in *The Interpretation of Cultures* (New York, 1973), pp. 87–125, Geertz's definition does not adequately differentiate religion from "ideology" as characterized in the same anthology of essays, pp. 193–233. This essay's emphasis on the element of transcendence as the diagnostic trait owes something to Mircea Eliade's *The Sacred and the Profane: The Nature of Religion*, trans. by W. R. Frank (San Diego, New York and London, 1987), pp. 8–18.

5. On French royal religion, see principally M. Bloch, *The Royal Touch: Sacred and Scrofula in England and France*, trans. by J. E. Anderson (London, 1971); R. Jackson, *Vive le Roi: A History of the French Coronation Oath from Charles V to Charles X* (Chapel Hill, NC, 1984).

6. On the incompatibility between Calvinism and French sacral monarchy see D. K. Van Kley. *The Religious Origins of the French Revolution: From Calvin to the Civil Constitution of the Clergy, 156–1791* (New Haven, CY, 1996), pp. 22–6 and C. Elwood, *The Body Broken: The Calvinist Doctrine of the Eucharist and the Symbolization of Power in Sixteenth-Century France* (New York, 1999).

7. The association of the king's "absolute" authority with the "will" to make law without the consent of subjects owes most of course to Jean Bodin's formative treatise, *On Sovereignty*, ed. and trans. by Julian Franklin (Cambridge, 1992).

8. R. Giesey, "The King Imagined," in Keith M. Baker, ed., *The Political Culture of the Old Regime*, vol. 1 of *The French Revolution and the Creation of Modern Political Culture* (Oxford, 1987), pp. 41–59.

9. The argument advanced here owes much to the work of Denis Crouzet, especially although not exclusively his massive and magisterial *Les Guerriers de Dieu: La Violence au temps des troubles de religion* (2 vols, Seyssel, 1990). See also R. Harding, "Revolution and Reform in the Holy League: Angers, Rennes, Nantes," JMH, 53 (September 1981), pp. 413–14.

10. On the distinction between the king's two bodies, see E. Kantorowicz, *The King's Two Bodies: A Study in Medieval Political Theology* (Princeton, NJ, 1957); and on the meaning of the royal funerary ceremony, see R. E. Giesey, *The Royal Funerary Ceremonies in Renaissance France* (Geneva, 1960).

11. For example, R. Mettam, *Power and Faction in Louis XIV's France* (Oxford, 1988); S. Kettering, *Patrons, Brokers, and Clients in Seventeenth-Century France* (Oxford, 1983); N. Henshall, *The Myth of Absolutism* (London, 1992); and H. Duchardt, "Absolutismus – Abschied von einem Epochenbegriff?," *Historische Zeitschrift*, 158 (1994), 113–22. For an excellent summary of this historiography along with a salutary corrective to it, see F. Cosandey and R. Descimon, *L'Absolutisme en France: Histoire et historiographie* (Paris, 2002), pp. 191–297.

12. A.-G. Martimort, *Le Gallicanisme de Bossuet* (Paris, 1953)

13. P. Blet, *Les Assemblées du clergé et Louis XIV de 1670 à 1693*, (Paris, 1972) p. 396.

14. See D. Parker, *The Making of French Absolutism* (London, 1990), pp. 118–45; and Cosandy and Descimon, *L'Absolutisme*, pp. 109–88.

15. See S. Hanley, *The Lit de Justice of the Kings of France: Constitutional Ideology in Legend, Ritual, and Discourse* (Princeton, NJ, 1983), 254–344; and R. Giesey, "The King Imagined."

16. I take issue here with Reinhard Koselleck's classic *Critique and Crisis: The Pathogenesis of Modern Society* (Oxford, 1988), which maintains that one of the defining characteristics of early-modern absolutism was its willingness to allow the inner conscience to remain off limits.

17. Definitions and characterizations of Jansenism are also all but innumerable, although several recent short syntheses in English are handy and helpful: W. Doyle, *Jansenism. Catholic Resistance to Authority from the Reformation to the French Revolution* (London, 2000); and L. Kolakowski, *God Owes Us Nothing* (Chicago, reprinted 1998). While Kolakowski emphasizes the similarity of Jansenism to

Calvinism – and this is a possible reading of the evidence – I have here under-scored their differences.

18. D. Garrioch, *The Formation of the Parisian Bourgeoisie, 1690–1830* (Cambridge, MA, 1997). See also M.-J. Michel, *Jansénisme à Paris, 1640–1730* (Paris, 2000).

19. On the miracles and convulsions of Saint-Médard, B. Robert Kreiser, *Miracles, Convulsions, and Ecclesiastical Politics in Early Eighteenth-Century Paris* (Princeton, NJ, 1987); and Catherine-Laurence Maire, *Les convulsions de Saint-Médard: Miracles, convulsions et prophéties à Paris au XVIIIe siècle* (Paris, 1985); and on popular politicization, A. Farge, *Subversive Words* (Cambridge, 1994).

20. R. Golden, *The Godly Rebellion: Parisian Curés and the Religious Fronde, 1652–1662* (Chapel Hill, NC, 1981), pp. 130, 143–51.

21. P. Dieudonné, *La Paix clémentine: Défaite et victoire du premier jansénisme français sous le pontificat de Clément IX (1667–1669)* (Louvain, 2003).

22. Henri-François d'Aguesseau, *Fragment inédit des mémoires du chancelier Daguesseau*, ed. by A. Gazier (Paris, 1920), p. 11.

23. C.-L. Maire, *De la cause de Dieu à la cause de la nation: Le Jansénisme au XVIIIe siècle* (Paris, 1998).

24. On the existence of such a "party" in the early eighteenth century, see D. A. Bell, *Lawyers and Citizens: The Making of a Political Elite in Old Regime France* (NewYork, 1994), pp. 1–125; and P. R. Campbell, *Power and Politics in Old-Regime France, 1720–1745* (London, 1996), pt. 2.

25. On the conduct of policy under Cardinal Fleury, see Campbell, *Power and Politics*.

26. See the evidence of this transformation in D. Van Kley, "The Ideological Origins of the French Revolution: The Debate over the General Assembly of the Gallican Clergy in 1765," JMH, 51 (December 1979), pp. 629–66.

27. Van Kley, *Religious Origins*, pp. 100–14, 155–6, 164–6.

28. On the religiously polarizing effect of the expulsion of the Jesuits else-where in Catholic Europe, see D. K. Van Kley, "Catholic Conciliar Reform in an Age of Anti-Catholic Revolution: France, Italy and the Netherlands, 1758–1801," in J. Bradley and D. K. Van Kley, eds, *Religion and Politics in Enlightenment Europe* (Notre Dame and London, 2001), pp. 69–88.

29. *Lettres à un ami sur la destruction des jésuites. Seconde lettre ou commentaire du bref de Clément XIV* (n.p., 1774), pp. 153–4.

30. Louis-Adrien Le Paige and Christophe Coudrette, *Histoire générale de la Compagnie de Jésus en France, et analyse de ses constitutions et privilèges* (4 vols, Paris, 1761), 3, p. 225.

31. *Réplique aux apologies des jésuites* (n.p, 1761–2), pt. 3, p. 52.

32. Jean Le Rond d'Alembert, *Sur la destruction des jésuites en France, par un auteur désinteressé* (n.p., 1765).

33. S. Maza, *Private Lives and Public Affairs: The Causes Célèbres of Prerevolutionary France* (Berkeley, CA, 1993).

34. For a fresh look at the more positive side of the relation between Jansenism and the Enlightenment, see M. Cottret, *Jansénismes et lumières: Pour un autre XVIIIe siècle* (Paris, 1998).

35. On the role of Jansenism in the making of the "patriot" movement, see S. M. Singham, "'A Conspiracy of Twenty Million Frenchmen': Public

Opinion, Patriotism, and the Assault on Absolutism during the Maupeou Years" (PhD, Princeton University, 1991); and D. K. Van Kley, "The Religious Origins of the Patriot and Ministerial Parties in Pre-Revolutionary France," in *Belief in History: Innovative Approaches to European and American Religion*, ed. T. Kselman (Notre Dame and London, 1991) pp. 173–236.

36. On public opinion as a factor in eighteenth-century French politics, see in general Keith M. Baker, *Inventing the French Revolution*.

37. *Nouvelles ecclésiastiques, ou mémoire pour servir à l'histoire de la bulle Unigenitus* (Utrecht: aux dépens de la Compagnie, 1728–1803), 1 January 1728, p. 2.

38. R. Darnton, *The Forbidden Best-Sellers of Pre-Revolutionary France* (New York, 1995), pp. 137–66, 197–246, 337–89; and "Reading, Writing and Publishing," in *The Literary Underground of the Old Regime* (Cambridge, MA., 1982), pp. 199–208; and J. Merrick, *The Desacralization of the French Monarchy in Eighteenth Century* (Baton Rouge, LA, 1990).

39. This reference is of course to Jacques-Bénigne Bossuet's *Politique tirée des propres paroles de l'Écriture sainte*, ed. by Jacques Le Brun (Geneva, 1967).

40. For example, T. Tackett, "Conspiracy Obsession in a Time of Revolution: French Elites and the Origins of the Terror, 1789–1792," AHR, 105 (June 2001), 691–714; and J. I. Engels, "Beyond Sacral Monarchy: A New Look at the Image of Early Modern French Monarchy," FH, 15 (2001), 139–58.

41. D. K. Van Kley, *The Damiens Affair and the Unraveling of the Old Regime* (Princeton, NJ, 1984), pp. 3–96.

42. B. Plongeron et al., *Les Défis de la modernité, 1750–1840*, vol. 10, in J.-M. Mayer, Ch. and L. Pietri, A. Vauchez, and M. Venard, eds, *Histoire du christianisme des origines à nos jours* (Paris, 1997), p. 336. Although clearly more sympathetic to the papal perspective than is Plongeron, this is also among the principal theses of G. Pelletier's recent magisterial thesis, "La Théologie et la politique du Saint-Siège devant la Révolution française, 1789–1799," 3 vols (thèse de doctorat conjoint en histoire des religions et anthropologie religieuse et en théologie, Université de Paris IV–Institut Catholique de Paris), esp. 1, pp. 169–96.

7. THE CONTESTED IMAGE: STAGE, CANVAS, AND THE ORIGINS OF THE FRENCH REVOLUTION *Mark Ledbury*

1. See "Further Reading" for this chapter.

2. K. M. Baker, ed, *The Political Culture of the Old Regime*, vol. 1 of *The French Revolution and the Creation of Modern Political Culture* (Oxford and New York, 1987–94).

3. See P. Burke, *The Fabrication of Louis XIV* (New Haven, CT and London, 1992); J.-M. Apostolidès, *Le Roi-Machine: Spectacle et politique au temps de Louis XIV* (Paris, 1981).

4. See especially B. Fort, ed, *Fictions of the French Revolution* (Evanston, IL, 1991); L. Hunt, *Politics, Culture, Class and the French Revolution* (Berkeley, CA, 1984); and also the essays in "The French Revolution in Culture: New Problems and Perspectives," special volume of ECS 22/3 (1989).

5. On genre painting as a phenomenon, see particularly the catalog of the exhibition *The Age of Watteau, Chardin and Fragonard. Masterpieces of French Genre*

Painting (eds, C. Bailey and P. Connisbee, exh. cat., Washington, National Gallery of Art, 2003), but this catalogue takes a determinedly non-political view of the paintings it describes. See also R. Rand, ed., *Intimate Encounters: Love and Domesticity in French Genre Painting* (exh. cat. Dartmouth, Hood Museum, 1997), which takes a more politically engaged view.

6. See E. Barker, "Painting and Reform in Eighteenth-century France: Greuze's *Accordée de Village*," *Oxford Art Journal*, 20/2 (1997), pp. 42–51; R. Rand, "Civil and Natural Contract in Greuze's *Accordée de Village*," *Gazette des* Beaux-Arts, 127 (May/June 1996), pp. 221–33.

7. For a still fundamental study of this genre in France see F. Gaiffe, *Le Drame en France au XVIIIe siècle* (Paris, 1907) Two fascinating modern studies of the drame are: Scott S. Bryson, *The Chastised Stage: Bourgeois Drama and the Exercise of Power* (Saratoga, CA, 1991); P. Frantz, *Esthétique du tableau dans le théâtre du XVIIIe siecle* (Paris, 1998)

8. See A. Ménil, *Diderot et le drame: théâtre et politique* (Paris, 1995)

9. It is worth noting that Diderot's own plays on this new model did not meet with grand acclaim: his first effort, *Le Fils naturel* (The Natural Son, 1757), was a stage flop, while *Le Père de Famille* (The Paterfamilias, 1758) was more successful. A thorough documentary study of the fate of these plays can be found in Anne-Marie Chouillet, "Dossier du *Fils Naturel* et du *Père de Famille*," SVEC, 208 (1982), pp. 75–126.

10. See my *Greuze, Sedaine and the Boundaries of Genre* (Oxford, 2000). The most thorough and useful edition of the play which sets it in its cultural and historical context, but without emphasizing the play's political dimensions, is J. Dunkley, ed, *Le Philosophe sans le savoir* (Egham, 1993).

11. [Louis-Sébastien Mercier] *Du Théâtre, ou nouvel essai sur l'art dramatique* (Amsterdam, 1773)

12. For new images of motherhood in eighteenth-century France, see C. Duncan, "Happy Mothers and Other New Ideas in Eighteenth-Century French Art." *Art Bulletin*, LV (December 1973), pp. 570–83; reprinted in C. Duncan, *The Aesthetics of Power* (Cambridge, 1993), p. 3–22.

13. Greuze's *La Mère bien aimée*, often seen as a lyrical homage to happy bourgeois motherhood, was in fact a family portrait of the Marquis de Laborde. See E. Munhall, ed., *Greuze the Draftsman* (exh. cat., New York and Los Angeles, 2001–2), pp. 200–3. See also C. B. Bailey, *Patriotic Taste: Collecting Modern Art in Pre-Revolutionary Paris* (New Haven, CT and London, 2002).

14. Apart from the oft-cited works of Robert Darnton, see for example, N. Rattner Gellbart, *Feminine and Opposition Journalism in Old Regime France: Le Journal des dames* (Berkeley, 1987); Jack Censer and J. Popkin, eds, *Press and Politics in Pre-Revolutionary France* (Berkeley, CA, 1987); B. Fort and J. Popkin, eds, *The Mémoires Secrets and the Culture of Publicity in Eighteenth-Century France* (Oxford, 1998); See also H. Mason, ed, *The Darnton Debate: Books and Revolution in the Eighteenth Century* (Oxford, 1998).

15. J. Habermas, *The Structural Transformation of the Public Sphere. An Enquiry into a Category of Bourgeois Society*, trans. by T. Burger (Cambridge, 1989).

16. For an eloquent argument in favour of the importance of the image, see J. Landes, *Visualizing the Nation* (Ithaca, NY, 2001), esp. pp. 1–23. For an equally eloquent and persuasive argument for a theatrical rather than a literary conception

of the prerevolutionary public sphere, see J. Ravel, *The Contested Parterre: Public Theatre and French Political Culture 1680–1791* (Ithaca, NY, 1999).

17. Figures compiled by A. D. Smith for the article "The Historical Revival in late 18th Century France and England," *Art History*, 2/3 (June 1979), pp. 156–78 and republished by Udolpho van de Sandt in his essay "Institutions et concours," in R. Michel and P. Bordes, eds, *Aux armes et aux arts* (Paris, 1989), pp. 137–68, give a figure of (+/–5 percent) 21, 950 livrets sold for the Salon of 1787. Extrapolating on the basis that two visitors attended for every livret sold (a conservative estimate) this would mean that over forty thousand people attended the Salon over the course of its duration. By any measure this is a significant number, and represents a rejoinder to the argument that paintings were seen by only an elite few.

18. These pamphlets have been much studied in recent years. See especially R. Wrigley, *The Origin of French Art Criticism from the Ancien Régime to the Restoration* (New York and Oxford, 1993); they provided the major source for perhaps the single most important work published on prerevolutionary art in the last twenty years, T. Crow's *Painters and Public Life in Eighteenth-Century Paris* (New Haven, CT and London, 1985).

19. Ravel, *Contested Parterre*.

20. For a sense of how contemporaries reacted to Figaro and its many spin-offs, see the very interesting, anonymous *Journal d'un provincial à Paris, 25 Juin–1e aout, 1784* (Ms. BNF, available through Gallica at gallica.bnf.fr), esp. ff. 17–18. *Le Mariage de Figaro* is available in the excellent French edition of Beaumarchais's works, *Oeuvres*, eds, P. Larthomas and J. Larthomas (Paris, 1988) and, in English, *Beaumarchais: The Figaro Trilogy*, trans. Coward (New York, 2003). For the circumstances of the production, see the venerable but still useful F. Gaiffe, *Les Grands évènements littéraires: Le Mariage de Figaro* (Paris, 1928).

21. Crow, *Painters and Public Life*, pp. 216–26.

22. See T. Crow, *Emulation: Making Artists for Revolutionary France* (New Haven, CT and London, 1995); A. Potts, "Beautiful Bodies and Dying Heroes," *History Workshop Journal*, 30 (1990) pp. 1–21; A. S. Godeau, *Male Trouble. A Crisis in Representation* (London, 1999)

23. See, for example, R. Wokler, "La Querelle des bouffons and the Italian Liberation of France: A Study of Revolutionary Foreplay," *Eighteenth-century Life* 11 (1987), pp. 94–116 and T. C. W. Blanning, *The Culture of Power and the Power of Culture* (Oxford, 2002), pp. 357–74.

24. S. Schama, "The Domestication of Majesty. Royal Family Portraiture 1500–1850," *Journal of Interdisciplinary History*, 17/1 (1986) pp. 155–83.

25. In Van Kley's formulation, this process can be dated to the Damiens assassination attempt of 1757. See D. Van Kley, *The Damiens Affair and the Unraveling of the Ancien Régime* (Princeton, 1984); R. Chartier, *Les Origines culturelles de la Révolution française* (Paris, 1990), pp. 145–8. For a discussion of Collé and Sedaine's works, see M. Noiray, "Quatre rois à la chasse: Dodsley, Collé, Sedaine, Goldoni," in David Charlton and Mark Ledbury, eds, *Michel-Jean Sedaine 1719–1797: Theatre, Opera and Art* (London, 2000), pp. 97–118.

26. Schama, "Domestication of Majesty."

27. On the contrasting rhetoric of the Royal Body, see T. Kaiser, *"Louis le bien aimé* and the Rhetoric of the Royal Body," in S. E. Melzer and K. Norberg, eds, *From the Royal to the Republican Body* (Berkeley, CA, 1998), pp. 131–61.

28. See the comments on the painting and the circumstances of its display in B. Fort, ed., *Les Salons des mémoires secrets 1767–1787* (Paris, 1999), pp. 317–20.

29. See, for example, R. Darnton in *The Forbidden Bestsellers of Pre-Revolutionary France* (London, 1996), pp. 85–114.

30. See (among many others) L. Price, "Vies privées et scandaleuses: Marie-Antoinette and the Public Eye," *Eighteenth Century. Theory and Interpretation*, 33/2 (Summer 1992), pp. 176–92; V. R. Gruder, "The Question of Marie Antoinette: The Queen and Public Opinion before the Revolution," FH, 16/3 (2002), pp. 269–98.

31. Darnton, *Forbidden Bestsellers*, p. 21

32. J. Goodman, "Enlightenment and Lubricity," in A. D'Souza, ed., *Self and History: A Tribute to Linda Nochlin* (London, 2001), pp. 42–53.

33. See, for example, the *Essai historique sur la vie de Marie Antoinette d'Autriche . . . pour servir à l'histoire de cette princesse* (Paris, 1789). On Marie-Antoinette and pornography, see Lynn Hunt's work (Further Reading) and especially D. Goodman, ed., *Marie-Antoinette: Writings on the Body of a Queen* (New York, 2003)

34. There is no time here to enter the debate about how to define and denote "Popular Culture," but see P. Burke's *Popular Culture in Early Modern Europe* (new edn, Cambridge, 1994) and R. Isherwood's *Farce and Fantasy: Popular Entertainment in Eighteenth-Century Paris* (Oxford, 1989)

35. Mikhail Bakhtin's influential elaboration of carnival as a concept has proved useful to cultural historians, but controversial. See his *Rabelais and his World*, trans. by H. Iswolsky (Cambridge, MA, 1967) and his *Problems of Dostoevsky's Poetics*, ed. and trans. by C. Emerson (Minneapolis, MN, 1984). For a still very useful summary of the carnival debate, see Peter Burke, *Popular Culture*.

36. B. Fort, "Voice of the Public: The Carnivalization of Salon Art in PreRevolutionary Pamphlets," ECS, 22/3 (Spring 1989), pp. 368–94, esp. pp. 383–4.

37. On these revolutionary festivals, see M. Ozouf, *La Fête révolutionnaire* (Paris, 1976) On David's part in them the fundamental work remains D. L. Dowd, *Pageant Master of the Republic. Jacques-Louis David and the French Revolution* (Lincoln, NE, 1948).

38. William Tell had become a fetish figure for the Revolution, and had been the subject of a series of dramas and visual representations from Antoine-Marin Le Mierre's drama, *Guillaume Tell* (performed 1766, published Paris, 1767, and then republished and performed, significantly, in 1793), to François André Vincent's *Guillaume Tell Upsetting Gessler's Boat* (Toulouse, Musée des Augustins), to Sedaine's "Sans-Culotte" *Opéra-Comique, Guillaume Tell* (performed 1791, 1793, published 1794).

39. On this drawing, and another for the same design, see Antoine Schnapper and Arlette Sérullaz, eds, *Jacques Louis David 1748–1825* (exh. cat., Paris and Versailles, 1989), nos 123–4, pp. 292–5, and P. Bordes, in *Aux armes et aux arts*, who makes an argument for interpreting the two versions of the design as transmitting significantly different political messages.

40. Hunt, *Politics, Culture, Class and the French Revolution*.

41. On these general trends in visual, literary and musical culture, see especially B. Jobert, ed, *l'Invention du sentiment* (exh. cat., Paris: Cité de la Musique,

2002); see also *French Painting 1774–1830: The Age of Revolution* (exh. cat., Detroit, MI, Paris, New York, 1974).

42. This image and other almanac images are discussed in an excellent essay by Abby Zanger, "Lim(b)inal images: 'Betwixt and Between' Louis XIV's Martial and Marital Bodies," in Melzer and Norberg, eds, *From the Royal to the Republican Body*, pp. 32–63. The volume is an example of the way in which cultural historians have come to stress the importance of the semiotics of the corporeal to our understandings of political change.

43. On this drawing and project, see especially, P. Bordes, *Le Serment du jeu de paume de Jacques-Louis David* (Paris, 1982).

8. THE PAMPHLET DEBATE OVER THE ORGANIZATION OF THE ESTATES GENERAL *Kenneth Margerison*

Acknowledgment

The author thanks Joshua Bashara, Christopher Blanton, Erika Galan, and Patricia Margerison for their useful commentary on an earlier version of this essay.

1. G. Lefebvre, *The Coming of the French Revolution*, trans. by R. R. Palmer (Princeton, NJ, 1947), especially pp. 76–92. For an example of Lefebvre's influence on more contemporary historians see W. Doyle, *The Oxford History of the French Revolution* (Oxford, 1989), pp. 101–8.

2. See especially K. M. Baker, ed., *The French Revolution and the Creation of Modern Political Culture: The Political Culture of the Old Regime* (Oxford, 1987), vol. 1; K. M. Baker, *Inventing the French Revolution* (Cambridge, 1990).

3. For a survey of events in the autumn of 1788 see J. Egret, *The French Prerevolution, 1787–1788*, trans. by Wesley D. Camp (Chicago, 1977), pp. 179–214.

4. On the growing importance of public opinion see K. M. Baker, "Public Opinion as Political Invention," in Baker, *Inventing the French Revolution*, pp. 167–99.

5. This debate is conveniently summarized in D. Van Kley, "New Wine in Old Wineskins: Continuity and Rupture in the Pamphlet Debate of the French Prerevolution, 1787–1789," FHS, 17 (Fall 1991), pp. 447–65. On the role of Jansenism in the political controversies of the era, see D. Van Kley, *The Religious Origins of the French Revolution: From Calvin to the Civil Constitution of the Clergy, 1560–1791* (New Haven, CT, 1996).

6. K. M. Baker, "On the Problem of the Ideological Origins of the French Revolution," in Baker, *Inventing the French Revolution*, especially pp. 17–18.

7. A.-F. Delandine, *Des Etats-généraux ou histoire des assemblées nationales en France* (Paris, 1788), pp. xiv–xxi.

8. On the relationship of Jansenism and Rousseau see Van Kley, *Religious Origins*, pp. 294–7.

9. S. Linguet, *Avis aux Parisiens* (n.p, n.d.), pp. 2, 10–11.

10. D. Wick, *A Conspiracy of Well-Intentioned Men: The Society of Thirty and the French Revolution* (New York, 1987); D. Wick, "The Court Nobility and the French Revolution: The Example of the Society of Thirty," ECS, 13 (Spring 1980), pp. 263–84.

11. Egret, for instance, identified many pamphlets which had little in common with national constitutionalism as the work of the society. *Prerevolution*, pp. 190–7.

12. K Margerison, *Pamphlets and Public Opinion: The Campaign for a Union of Orders in the Early French Revolution* (West Lafayette, IN, 1998), pp. 67–70.

13. See, for example, W. H. Sewell, Jr, *A Rhetoric of Revolution: The Abbé Sieyes and "What Is the Third Estate?"* (Durham, NC, 1994), p. 65.

14. Margerison, *Pamphlets and Public Opinion*, pp. 101–3.

15. On the duc d'Orléans see G. A. Kelly, "The Machine of the Duc d'Orléans and the New Politics," JMH 51 (December 1979), pp. 667–84.

16. For the attitudes of the deputies at Versailles see T. Tackett, *Becoming a Revolutionary: The Deputies of the French National Assembly and the Emergence of a Revolutionary Culture (1789–1790)* (Princeton, NJ, 1996).

17. For the most recent expression of this sentiment see ibid., pp. 146–8.

18. For the importance of August 4 see M. Fitzsimmons, *The Remaking of France: The National Assembly and the Constitution of 1791* (Cambridge, 1994), especially 33–68 and Fitzsimmons, *The Night the Old Regime Ended: August 4, 1789, and the French Revolution* (University Park, PA, 2003).

9. PEASANTS AND THEIR GRIEVANCES *John Markoff*

1. A. Soboul, *The French Revolution, 1787–1799* (New York, 1977), p. 8.

2. G. Lefebvre, *The Coming of the French Revolution* (Princeton, NJ, 1947), p. 142.

3. G. V. Taylor, "Revolutionary and Nonrevolutionary Content in the *Cahiers* of 1789," FHS, 7 (1972), p. 495.

4. D. M. G. Sutherland, *France, 1789–1815: Revolution and Counterrevolution* (New York, 1986), p. 439.

5. P. Jones, *The Peasantry in the French Revolution* (Cambridge, 1988); A. Ado, *Paysans en révolution: terre, pouvoir et jacquerie 1789–1794* (Paris, 1996); J. Markoff, *The Abolition of Feudalism. Peasants, Lords and Legislators in the French Revolution* (University Park, PA, 1996).

6. J. Markoff, "Revolutions," in N. J. Smelser and P. B. Baltes, *International Encyclopedia of the Social and Behavioral Sciences* (Oxford, 2002), vol. 1, pp. 637–42.

7. G. Shapiro and J. Markoff, "Officially Solicited Petitions: The *Cahiers de Doléances* as a Historical Source," *International Review of Social History* 46 (2001, Supplement), pp. 79–106.

8. G. Shapiro and J. Markoff, *Revolutionary Demands. A Content Analysis of the Cahiers de Doléances of 1789* (Stanford, CA, 1998), pp. 234–5.

9. Statistical tabulation of grievances of the sort presented here is now fairly easy to obtain using the *French Revolution Analysis System* developed by G. Shapiro

and available from him. Information may be found on the website (www. frasystem.com).

10. M. Vovelle, *The Fall of the French Monarchy, 1787–1792* (Cambridge, 1984), p. 3.

11. Vovelle, ibid., pp. 5–7.

12. F. Caussy, *Voltaire, seigneur de village* (Paris, 1912), p. 3.

13. F Pasquier and Fr. Galabert, eds, *Cahiers paroissiaux des sénéchaussées de Toulouse et de Comminges en 1789* (Toulouse, 1928), p. 7.

14. Pierre de Saint Jacob, *Les Paysans de la Bourgogne du Nord au dernier siècle de l'Ancien Régime* (Paris, 1960), p. 120.

15. Jones, *Peasantry in the French Revolution*, pp. 124–66; K. Norberg, "Dividing Up the Commons: Institutional Change in Rural France, 1789–1799," *Politics and Society*, 16 (1988), pp. 265–86.

16. O. Hufton, *The Poor of Eighteenth-Century France: 1750–1789* (Oxford, 1974); R. M. Schwartz, *Policing the Poor in Eighteenth-Century France* (Chapel Hill, NC, 1988).

17. J. Dupâquier, *Histoire de la population française*, vol.2: *De la Renaissance à 1789* (Paris, 1988), pp. 64–5.

18. P. T. Hoffman and J.-L. Rosenthal, "New Work in French Economic History," *French Historical Studies*, 23 (2000), pp. 439–53; D. R. Weir, "Les Crises économiques de la Révolution française," *Annales: ESC*, 46 (1991), pp. 917–47; G. Grantham, "The French Cliometric Revolution: A Survey of Cliometric Contributions to French Economic History," *European Review of Economic History* 1 (1997), pp. 353–405.

19. G. Bouchard, *Le village immobile; Sennely-en-Sologne au XVIIIe siècle* (Paris, 1972); L. Vardi, *The Land and the Loom. Peasants and Profits in Northern France, 1680–1800* (Durham, NC, 1993), p. 232.

20. P. T. Hoffman, *Growth in a Traditional Society. The French Countryside, 1450–1815* (Princeton, NJ, 1996), p. 135.

21. M. Bouloiseau, ed., *Cahiers de doléances du tiers état du bailliage de Rouen pour les états généraux de 1789* (Rouen, 1960), p. 308.

22. P. Mathias and P. O'Brien, "Taxation in Britain and France, 1715–1810. A Comparison of the Social and Economic Incidence of Taxes Collected for the Central Governments," *Journal of European Economic History*, 5 (1976), pp. 601–50; M. Kwass, *Privilege and the Politics of Taxation in Eighteenth-Century France. Liberté, Egalité, Fiscalité* (Cambridge, 2000).

23. Vovelle, *Fall of the French Monarchy*, pp. 12–13; Jones, *Peasantry in the French Revolution*, pp. 42–59; W. Doyle, *The Origins of the French Revolution*, 3rd edn (Oxford, 1999), pp. 181–3.

24. C. Wolikow, "Communautés territoires et villageois en France aux XVIIe et XVIIIe siècles," *Bulletin de la Société d'Histoire Moderne et Contemporaine* (1999), nos 1–2, p. 47.

25. J. Necker, *Compte rendu au roi* (Paris, 1781), appended map ("carte des gabelles").

26. J. Necker, *De l'administration des finances* (Paris, 1784), 1:195; 2:30–1, 57–8.

27. Markoff, *Abolition of Feudalism*, pp. 350–1.

28. C. A. Bouton, *The Flour War: Gender, Class and Community in Late Ancien Régime Society* (University Park, PA, 1993); "Les Mouvements de subsistance et le

problème de l'économie morale et la Révolution française," AHRF, no. 319 (2000), pp. 71–100.

29. S. L. Kaplan, *Provisioning Paris* (Ithaca, NY, 1984); J. A. Miller, *Mastering the Market: The State and the Grain Trade in Northern France, 1700–1860* (Cambridge, 1999).

30. W. Reddy, *The Rise of Market Culture: The Textile Trade and French Society, 1750–1900* (Cambridge, 1984); G. Gullickson, *The Spinners and Weavers of Auffay: Rural Industry and the Sexual Division of Labor in a French Village, 1750–1850* (Cambridge, 1986); C. Bouton, "Regions and Regionalism: The Case of France," paper presented to the 1994 meetings of the American Historical Association, San Francisco.

31. Markoff, *Abolition of Feudalism*, Fig. 6.11.

32. Robert-Thomas Lindet, *Correspondance de Thomas Lindet pendant la Constituante et la Législative (1789–1792)* (Paris, 1899), pp. 158–9.

33. This claim is based on preliminary results of a comparative study of the politics of provisioning in England, Germany, and France being carried out by J. Bohstedt, C. Bouton, M. Gailus, and M. Geyer, some of whose results are reported in Bouton, "Regions and Regionalism."

34. J.-P. Jessenne, "Le Changement rural, l'état et l'adaptation des communautés villageoises en France et en Europe du nord-ouest à la fin du XVIIIe siècle," AHRF, no. 315 (1999), p. 135.

35. R. Kagan, "Law Students and Careers in Eighteenth-Century France," P&P, 68 (1975), pp. 38–72.

36. G. Astoul, "Solidarités paysannes au pays des croquants au XVIIIe siècle," AHRF, no. 311 (1998).

37. H. Root, *Peasants and King in Burgundy. Agrarian Foundations of French Absolutism* (Berkeley, CA and Los Angeles, 1987).

38. Root, *Peasants and King*, pp. 155–204.

39. Jessenne, "Changement rural," pp. 134–5.

40. P. M. McPhee, " 'The Misguided Greed of Peasants'? Popular Attitudes to the Environment in the Revolution of 1789," FHS, 24 (2001), p. 250.

41. J.-L. Rosenthal, *The Fruits of Revolution: Property Rights, Litigation, and French Agriculture, 1700–1860* (Cambridge, 1992).

42. McPhee, " 'Misguided Greed'?," pp. 247–69; A. Corvol, *L'Homme et l'arbre sous l'Ancien Régime* (Paris, 1984).

43. I. A. Cameron, *Crime and Repression in the Auvergne and the Guyenne, 1720–1790* (Cambridge, 1981), pp. 79–88, 224–6.

44. Markoff, *Abolition of Feudalism*, p. 312.

45. J. Nicolas, "Les Émotions dans l'ordinateur: Premiers résultats d'une enquête collective," paper presented at University of Paris VII, October 1986; "Un Chantier toujours neuf," in Jean Nicolas, ed., *Mouvements populaires et conscience sociale, XVIe–XIXe siècles* (Paris, 1985), pp. 13–20.

46. Astoul, "Solidarités paysannes," p. 28.

47. Jones, *Peasantry and the French Revolution*, pp. 34–42.

48. Bouton, "Mouvements de subsistance," p. 83.

49. R. M. Schwartz, "Beyond the Parish Pump: The Politicization of the Peasantry in Burgundy, 1750–1850," pp. 120–35 in M. P. Hanagan, Leslie Page Moch, and Wayne te Brake, eds, *Challenging Authority: The Historical Study of*

Contentious Politics (Minneapolis, MN, 1998), A. Follain, "Les communautés rurales en Normandie sous l'Ancien Régime. Identité communautaire," RHMC, 45 (1998), pp. 691–721.

50. Astoul, "Solidarités paysannes," pp. 26–7.

51. J.-M. Moriceau, "Les 'Baccanals' ou grèves de moissoneurs en pays de France (seconde moitié du XVIIIe siècle)," in Nicolas, ed., *Mouvements populaires*, pp 421–34.

52. Marc Bloch, *The Historian's Craft* (New York, 1953), p. 172.

53. Markoff, *Abolition of Feudalism*, pp. 114–16; A. Crubaugh, *Balancing the Scales of Justice. Local Courts & Rural Society in Southwest France, 1750–1800* (University Park, PA, 2001).

54. R. Forster, *The Nobility of Toulouse in the Eighteenth Century: A Social and Economic Study* (Baltimore, MD, 1960), p. 29.

55. J. Bastier, *La Féodalité au siècle des lumières dans la région de Toulouse (1730–1790)* (Paris, 1975), pp. 123–5, 168–9.

56. P. Lesprand and L. Bour, eds, *Cahiers de doléances des prévôtés bailliagères de Sarrebourg et Phalsbourg et du bailliage de Lixheim pour les états généraux de 1789* (Metz, 1938), p. 187.

57. Jules-Joseph Vernier, *Cahiers de doléances du bailliage de Troyes (principal et secondaires) et du bailliage de Bar-sur-Seine pour les états généraux de 1789* (Troyes, 1909), pp. 466–7.

58. Markoff, *Abolition of Feudalism*, p. 112.

59. G. Laurent, ed., *Cahiers de doléances pour les états-généraux de 1789*, vol. 1, *Bailliage de Châlons-sur Marne* (Epernay, 1906), pp. 70–1.

60. Markoff, *Abolition of Feudalism*, p. 112.

61. A. Blossier, ed., *Cahiers de doléances du bailliage de Honfleur pour les Etats généraux de 1789* (Caen, 1913), p. 47.

62. P. Goubert, "Sociétés rurales françaises du 18e siècle: Vingt paysanneries contrastées. Quelques problèmes," in Pierre Goubert, ed., *Clio parmi les hommes: Recueil d'articles* (Paris, 1976), pp. 63–74.

63. M. Vovelle, "The Countryside and the French Peasantry in Revolutionary Iconography," in A. Forrest and P. M. Jones, eds, *Reshaping France: Town Country and Region during the French Revolution* (Manchester, 1991), pp. 26–36.

64. R. Dupuy, *De la Révolution à la Chouannerie: Paysans en Bretagne, 1788–1794* (Paris, 1988), pp. 24–32.

65. Quoted in M. Cubells, *Les Horizons de la liberté: La Naissance de la Révolution en Provence, 1787–1789* (Aix-en-Provence, 1987), p. 68.

66. Markoff, *Abolition of Feudalism*, pp. 357–9.

67. G. Lefebvre, *The Great Fear of 1789: Rural Panic in Revolutionary France* (London, 1973); C. Ramsay, *The Ideology of the Great Fear: The Soissonnais in 1789* (Baltimore, MD, 1992).

68. J. Egret, *La Révolution des notables: Mounier et les monarchiens* (Paris, 1950), p. 105.

69. T. Tackett, *Becoming a Revolutionary: The Deputies of the French National Assembly and the Emergence of a Revolutionary Culture (1789–1790)* (Princeton, NJ, 1996), pp. 171–2.

70. J. Mavidal and E. Laurent, *Archives parlementaires de 1787 à 1860*, 1st ser. (Paris, 1867–75), 8, p. 397.

10. FROM THE ESTATES GENERAL TO THE NATIONAL ASSEMBLY,
MAY 5–AUGUST 4, 1789 *Michael Fitzsimmons*

1. M. B. Garrett, *The Estates General of 1789: The Problems of Composition and Organization* (New York, 1935), pp. 25–40.
2. B. Stone, *The Parlement of Paris, 1774–1789* (Chapel Hill, NC, 1981), p. 167.
3. [Joseph-Antoine-Joachim Cérutti], *A la mémoire de feu de Monseigneur de Dauphin* (n.p., n.d.), p. xi.
4. N. Ruault, *Gazette d'un Parisien sous la Révolution: Lettres à son frère 1783–1796*, ed. by Anne Vassal (Paris, 1976), p. 126.
5. A. de Baecque, "Pamphlets: Libel and Political Mythology," in Robert Darnton and Daniel Roche, eds, *Revolution in Print: The Press in France 1775–1800* (Berkeley, CA, 1989), pp. 165–6.
6. AN AB XIX 3259, *cahier* of *bailliage* of Château-Thierry, pp. 12–13.
7. E. Dumont, *Souvenirs sur Mirabeau et sur les deux premieres assemblées legislatives*, ed. by J. Bénétruy (Paris, 1951), p. 47, trans. as *Recollections of Mirabeau and of the Two First Legislative Assemblies of the French Revolution* (London, 1832); chs 2–5, esp. pp. 35–6.
8. The comment is from Marc, marquis de Bombelles, *Journal*, ed. by Jean Grassion and Frans Durif, 5 vols (Geneva, 1977–), II: 308.
9. François Ménard de la Groye, *Correspondance (1789–1791)*, ed. by Florence Mirouse (Mayenne, 1989), p. 25.
10. *Journal d' Adrien Duquesnoy député du Tiers-état de Bar-le-Duc sur l'Assemblée constituante 3 mai 1789–3 avril 1790*, 2 vols, ed. by R. de Crèvecoeur (Paris, 1894), I: 19–20; BN MSS Nouv. Acq. Fr. 12938, fol. 9 v°.
11. G. Chaussinand-Nogaret, *The French Nobility in the Eighteenth Century: From Feudalism to Enlightenment* (Cambridge, 1985), pp. 134–7. Chaussinand-Nogaret emphasizes the ambiguity of positions in the remaining *cahiers*, but the unequivocal positions more closely reflect the situation at the Estates General. Indeed, vote by order was the dominant single stance among the nobility.
12. Arthur Young, *Travels in France during the Years 1787, 1788 & 1789*, ed. by Constantia Maxwell (Cambridge, 1929), pp. 133, 135.
13. AN W 306, dossier 377, fol. 20; Ménard de la Groye, *Correspondance*, p. 35.
14. On the vote figures, BN MSS Nouv. Acq. Fr. 12938, ff. 11, 23, on the conference votes; on the June 10 vote, Jacques-Antoine Creuzé-Latouche, *Journal des Etats-Généraux et du début de l'Assemblée nationale 18 mai–29 juillet 1789*, ed. by Jean Marchand (Paris, 1946), p. 94.
15. One term put forward and rejected, for example, was that of "Assembly representing the great majority of the French, in the absence of the representation of the least, or 96/100 of the nation." See Ruault, *Gazette*, p. 409.
16. On the sense of alarm in the nobility, see Bombelles, *Journal*, II: 336.
17. J. Hardman, *Louis XVI* (New Haven, CT, 1993), p. 150.
18. John Hardman, *French Politics 1774–1789: From the Accession of Louis XVI to the Fall of the Bastille* (London, 1995), pp. 162–7.
19. On the power that the program held at the time, see Ruault, *Gazette*, p. 140.

20. On the motivation of the clergy, see M. G. Hutt, The Role of the *Curés* in the Estates General of 1789," *Journal of Ecclesiastical History*, 6 (1955): pp. 205–14. On the separate seating arrangements for the clergy in the National Assembly, Urbain-Réné Pilastre de la Brardière and J. B. Leclerc, *Correspondance de MM. les députés des communes de la province d'Anjou avec leurs commettants rélativement aux Etats-Généraux . . . en 1789*, 10 vols (Angers, 1789–1791), I: 142–3, 205–6, 235–6.

21. Pilastre de la Brardière and Leclerc, *Correspondance*, I: 238.

22. *A MM. les citoyens de la ville de Paris* (n.p., n.d.); see also the speech of the duc d'Aiguillon in *Lettre de MM. les députés de Lyon, à leurs commettants* (n.p., n.d.) Newberry Library, FRC 4841.

23. Bibliothèque historique de la ville de Paris MS N.A. 22, ff. 1–5.

24. *Page à la cour de Louis XVI: Souvenirs du comte d'Hézecques*, ed. by Emmanuel Bourassin (Paris, 1987), pp. 137–8.

25. On the confusion surrounding the vote, as a result of which each side believed that it had prevailed, see M. P. Fitzsimmons, *The Remaking of France: The National Assembly and the Constitution of 1791* (Cambridge, 1994), p. 49.

26. Archives nationales AD[xviiic] 135, Première lettre de M. l'abbé de Bonneval, député du clergé de Paris, à ses commettants, pp. 81–2.

27. On the popular rising in Paris, see J. Godechot, *The Taking of the Bastille July 14, 1789* (New York, 1970).

28. AM Bordeaux D 227, copy of letter of Nairac, July 15, 1789; *The Papers of Thomas Jefferson*, ed. by J. Boyd (Princeton, NJ, 1950–), 15: 278, 279.

29. Bibliothèque Municipale Dijon Ms. 2522, no. 3, letter of July 30, 1789.

30. Bibliothèque historique de la ville de Paris Ms. CP 6540, letter of July 31, 1789.

31. For a more extensive consideration of the night of August 4 and its results, see M. P. Fitzsimmons, *The Night the Old Regime Ended: August 4, 1789, and the French Revolution* (University Park, PA, 2003) and P. Kessell, *La Nuit du 4 août* (Paris, 1978)

32. BM Albi Ms. 177, letter of August 8, 1789.

33. *Procès-verbal de l'Assemblée nationale*, No. 40bis (August 4, 1789), pp. 21–2.

34. Jean-Paul Rabaut de Saint-Étienne, *Précis de l'histoire de la Révolution française* (Paris, 1827), p. 201; Henri Perrin de Boussac, *Un témoin de la Révolution et l'Empire: Charles Jean-Marie Alquier (1752–1826)* (La Rochelle, 1983), p. 41.

35. Fitzsimmons, *The Remaking of France*.

36. On the coming together of the Assembly, see T. Tackett, *Becoming a Revolutionary: The Deputies of the French National Assembly and the Emergence of a Revolutionary Culture (1789–1790)* (Princeton, NJ, 1996).

37. The August decrees can be found in John Hall Stewart, *A Documentary Survey of the French Revolution* (New York, 1951), pp. 106–10.

38. Archives départementales de l'Oise J 136, doc. 77.

Further reading

INTRODUCTION THE ORIGINS OF THE FRENCH REVOLUTION IN FOCUS

The range of topics covered in the introduction is too wide for an essay on further reading. The endnotes provide the surest guide to important works of interpretation and recent research. However, everyone should become familiar with George Lefebvre's classic, *The Coming of the French Revolution*, trans. by R. R. Palmer (Princeton, NJ, 1947). Just how misleading Soboul's Marxist "catechism," as Furet called it, was, is clear from the more recent revisionist classic, W. Doyle, *The Origins of the French Revolution* (1980, 3rd edn, Oxford, 1999). The best account, rather than interpretation, of 1787–8 is still in J. Egret, *The French PreRevolution, 1787–8* (1962 in French, trans. by Wesley D. Camp, Chicago, 1977). The more recently emphasized cultural dimension is explained by R. Chartier, *The Cultural Origins of the French Revolution* (Durham, NC, 1991). An exceptional volume on a defining aspect of the Revolution is D. Van Kley, ed., *The French Idea of Freedom. The Old Regime and the Declaration of Rights of 1789* (Stanford, CA, 1994). C. Jones, *The Great Nation: France from Louis XV to Napoleon* (London, 2003), draws recent research together into a lengthy but accessible narrative. More introductory is J. R. Censer and L. Hunt, *Liberty, Equality, Fraternity: Exploring the French Revolution* (University Park, PA, 2001), which has a useful and entertaining CD-ROM included, with songs, images and documents. On the internet further reading suggestions may be found in Colin Jones's excellent guide to further reading for his book (http://www.warwick.ac.uk/staff/Colin.Jones). A course description with topics, questions and a bibliography of secondary literature as well as a nearly complete list of sources published in English, as taught by Peter Campbell, is also available (via a link at http://www.sussex.ac.uk/history/profile421.html).

1. THE FINANCIAL ORIGINS OF THE FRENCH REVOLUTION

There is no general history of French finances in the eighteenth century but a series of monographs on different aspects. For a general overview on the early modern state and finance, one can read a valuable summary by G. Ardant, "Financial Policy and Economic Infrastructure of Modern States and Nations," in C. Tilly, ed, *The Formation of National States in Western Europe* (Princeton, NJ, 1975), pp. 243–327 and the chapters on France in R. Bonney, ed, *Economic Systems and State Finance* (1999), W. M. Ormrod, M. Bonney, and R. Bonney, eds, *Crises, Revolutions and Self-sustained Growth: Essays in European Fiscal History*

1130–1830 (Stamford, England, 1999) and Bonney, ed., *Economic Systems and State Finance*. Although it deals with Great Britain, the study of J. Brewer, *The Sinews of Power: War, Money and the English State, 1683–1783* (London, 1989) remains very useful. It shows in particular how much more would be known about French finance had the archives of the *contrôle général* not been almost completely destroyed in 1793 and 1871. The article by P. Mathias and P. O'Brien, "Taxation in Britain and France, 1715–1810. A Comparison of the Social and Economic Incidence of Taxes Collected for the Central Governments," *Journal of European Economic History*, 5, No. 3 (1976), pp. 601–50, is still valuable and can be supplemented with D. Weir, "Tontines, Public Finances and Revolution in France and England, 1688–1789," JEcH, vol. 49 (June 1989), pp. 95–124 and J. Riley, "French Finances, 1727–1768," JMH, 1987, vol. LIX, pp. 224–43. In English, the best books on eighteenth-century French finances remain the monographs of J. F. Bosher, *French Finances, 1770–1795: From Business to Bureaucracy* (Cambridge, 1970) and J. C. Riley, *The Seven Years War and the Old Regime in France: The Economic and Financial Toll* (Princeton, NJ, 1986). On taxation, the study of G. T. Matthews on *The Royal General Farms in Eighteenth-Century France* (New York, 1958) has not been replaced. On direct taxation the recent book by M. Kwass, *Privilege and the Politics of Taxation in Eighteenth-Century France: Liberté, Égalité, Fiscalité* (Cambridge, 2000) offers an excellent survey of the problem of privilege and its cultural impact in France. In the past years, several articles have significantly renewed our understanding of French finance: F.-R. Velde and D. R. Weir, "The Financial Market and Government Debt Policy in France, 1746–1793," JEcH, 52 (March 1992), No. 1, pp. 1–39; M. Sonenscher, "The Nation's Debt and the Birth of the Modern Republic: The French Fiscal Deficit and the Politics of the Revolution of 1789," *History of Political Thought*, 18, No. 1 (Spring 1997), pp. 64–103 and No. 2 (Summer 1997), pp. 267–325; T. Le Goff, "How to Finance an Eighteenth-Century War," in Bonney and Ormrod, eds, *Crises, Revolutions and Self-Sustained Growth*, pp. 377–413. On the last controllers general's policy, see E. N. White, "Was There a Solution to the Ancient Régime's Financial Dilemma?," JEcH, 49, 1989, pp. 545–68 and R. D. Harris, *Necker, Reform Statesman of the Ancien Régime* (Berkeley, CA, 1979). There is no good biography of Calonne. The debates on physiocracy and its impact on financial policy should never be underestimated as is evident from S. L. Kaplan, *Bread, Politics and Political Economy in the Reign of Louis XV* (2 vols, The Hague, 1976).

In French, F. Crouzet's *La Grande Inflation. La Monnaie en France de Louis XVI à Napoléon* (Paris, 1993), pp. 17–89, offers a good introduction to the financial problems of the monarchy of the ancien régime. The old volume by M. Marion, *Histoire financière de la France*, vol. 1 (Paris, 1914) remains the only narrative of French finance before 1789. A recent study by M. Antoine, *Le coeur de l'État: Surintendance, contrôle général et intendances des finances 1552–1791* (Paris, 2003), offers an in-depth synthesis of the development of the fiscal state. On the budget, the article by M. Morineau, "Budget de l'état et gestion des finances royales en France au dix-huitième siècle," *Revue historique* (1980), 264, No. 536, pp. 289–336, is a classic. Figures on the budget and revenues can be found in J. J. Clamageran, *Histoire des impôts en France*, vol. 3 (Paris, 1876), and, for the second half of the century, in *Collection de comptes-rendus, pièces authentiques, états et tableaux, concernant les finances de France depuis 1758 jusqu'en 1787* (Paris, 1788). M. Touzery's

L'Invention de l'impôt sur le revenu (Paris, 1994) is the best study of the royal administration's attempts to reform the direct tax system. Joël Félix's *Finances et politique au siècle des lumières*. *Le Ministère L'Averdy, 1763–1768* (Paris, 1999) offers a detailed analysis of the issue of reforms and politics in the aftermath of the Seven Years' War. For a survey of French *contrôleurs généraux's* policy see F. Bayard, J. Félix, and P. Hamon's *Dictionnaire des surintendants et des contrôleurs généraux des finances, XVIe–XVIIe–XVIIIe siècles* (Paris, 2000). E. Faure's *La Disgrâce de Turgot* (Paris, 1961) and J. Egret's *Necker, Ministre de Louis XVI* (Paris, 1975) are both excellent biographies.

2. DECISION-MAKING

On decision-making in general, a brief description of the working of the royal council is provided by F-X. Emmanuelli, *État et pouvoirs dans la France des XVIe–XVIIIe siècles* (Paris, 1992), pp. 37–51. For Louis XV's reign try P. R. Campbell, *Power and Politics in Old Regime France, 1720–1745* (London and New York, 1996), esp. the introduction and chs 7, 8 ("The Political Culture of Court Society") and 14. For the later period see J. Hardman, *French Politics, 1774–1789* (London and New York, 1995) pp. 62–183. The best general introduction to foreign policy remains A. Sorel, *Europe and the French Revolution: The Political Traditions of the Old Regime*, trans. and ed. by A. Cobban and J. W. Hunt (London, 1969). On the specific question of entry into the War of American Independence, J. Dull, *The French Navy and American Independence: A Study of Arms and Diplomacy, 1774–1787* (Princeton, NJ, 1975) examines the relationship between rearmament and war, whilst the bearing of the American victory at Saratoga Springs on the French decision to enter the war is examined in C. H. Van Tyne, "French Aid Before the Alliance of 1778," AHR, 31 (1925), pp. 20–40. New light is shed on Louis XVI's role, and in particular the bearing of the Bavarian succession crisis on the decision, by J. Hardman and M. Price, eds, *Louis XVI and the Comte de Vergennes: Correspondence, 1774–1787* (Oxford, 1998). O. T. Murphy, *Charles Gravier, Comte de Vergennes* (Albany, NY, 1982) has material on the diplomatic revolution and the French entry into the American War.

Factions were generally built round individuals. For good treatments of Vergennes try Munro Price, *Preserving the Monarchy* (Cambridge, 1995), J.-F. Labourdette, "Vergennes et la cour," *Revue d'histoire diplomatique*, 1987, pp. 289–323 and Labourdette, *Vergennes, ministre principal de Louis XVI* (Paris, 1990). On Necker, R. Harris, *Necker, Reform Statesman of the Ancien Régime* (Berkeley, CA, 1979) but his acceptance of the accuracy of Necker's crucial *Compte rendu* remains controversial. There is no entirely satisfactory work on Calonne and none at all in English: the most thorough is R. Lacour-Gayet, *Calonne* (Paris, 1963). On Louis XVI (for he also had a faction or rather a king's party) see J. Hardman, *Louis XVI* (London and New Haven, CT, 1993). For an examination of the Polignac faction and how favour to it alienated the rest of the court see D. Wick, "The Court Nobility and the French Revolution: The Example of the Society of Thirty," ECS, 13, 1980, pp. 264–84. Factional maneuvers may be traced through the abbé de Véri, *Journal de l'abbé de Véri*, ed. by J. de Witte (2 vols, Paris,

1928–30); the marquis de Bombelles, *Journal*, ed. by J. Grassion and F. Durif (5 vols, Geneva, 1978–82) and *Memoirs of the Prince de Talleyrand*, ed. by the duc de Broglie, and trans. by Mrs Angus Hall, introduction by the Hon. Whitelaw Reid (5 vols, New York, 1891), vol. 1.

On the Assembly of Notables, the best general treatment is still the pioneering article by A. Goodwin, "Calonne, the Assembly of French Notables of 1787 and the Origins of the '*révolte nobiliaire*'," EHR, 240 (May 1946), pp. 202–34, 241 (September 1946), pp. 329–77. Goodwin takes the now unfashionable stance of defending Calonne. A more neutral tone is taken by J. Egret, *The French Pre-Revolution, 1787–1788*, trans. by W. Camp (Chicago and London, 1977), pp. 1–44. V. Gruder, "Paths to Political Consciousness: The Assembly of Notables and the Pre-Revolution in France," FHS, 13, 1984, pp. 323–55, shows how individual notables became radicalized during the course of the assembly. See also her articles "Les notables à la fin de l'ancien régime," *Dix-huitième siècle*, XIV (1982), pp. 45–57 and "A Mutation in Elite Political Culture: The French Notables and the Defence of Property and Participation," JMH, 55 (1984), pp. 598–634. For primary material on the assembly, try: *Journal de l'assemblée des notables de 1787* ed. by P. Chevallier (Paris, 1960), which publishes the diary of Loménie de Brienne; and John Hardman, *The French Revolution Sourcebook*, (London, 1998), pp. 18–49. John Hardman is currently completing a manuscript on the Assembly of Notables, for publication in 2006.

3. THE PARIS PARLEMENT IN THE 1780S

Two general histories of the parlement exist: J. H. Shennan, *The Parlement of Paris* (2nd edn, London, 1998), and E. Glasson, *Le parlement de Paris: Son rôle politique depuis le règne de Charles VII jusqu'à la Révolution* (2 vols, Paris, 1901). P. R. Doolin, *The Fronde* (Cambridge, MA, 1935) and R. Bickart, *The Parlement and the Notion of National Sovereignty* (Paris, 1932) give the misleading impression that the issues were all about constitutional ideology (as opposed to ideology justifying defence of jurisdiction). While offering a corrective view of the magistrates as well-meaning judges, Shennan also summarizes much of the important work by F. Bluche, *L'Origine des magistrats du Parlement de Paris au XVIIIe siècle (1715–1771)* (Paris, 1956) and Bluche, *Les Magistrats du Parlement de Paris au XVIIIe siècle (1715–1771)* (Paris, 1960). J. Félix, *Les Magistrats du parlement de Paris, 1771–1790* (Paris, 1990) follows in the footsteps of Bluche, an essential work of reference. Jean Egret was a great master of the history of the parlements and his numerous works are all important. His views are summarized in his brief but magisterial *Louis XV et l'opposition parlementaire* (Paris, 1970). A brief article from the *Revue historique* in 1952 is available in English as "Was the 'Aristocratic Revolt' Aristocratic?," in F. E. Kafker and J. M. Laux, eds, *The French Revolution: Conflicting Interpretations* (3rd edn, Malabar, FA, 1983), pp. 29–37; Egret, *The French Prerevolution* (Chicago, 1977) is exceptionally useful.

The parlement can also be approached through monographs and articles on particular periods, many of which offer interesting overall interpretations of motivation in relations with the Crown. On the earliest period considered here, the Fronde, see M. Cubells, "Le Parlement de Paris pendant la Fronde," *XVIIe siècle* (1957), pp. 171–98; A. L. Moote, "The Parliamentary Fronde and Seventeenth-Century Robe Solidarity," FHS, II, 1962–3, pp. 330–55 and Moote, *The Revolt of the Judges* (Princeton, NJ, 1971), to which should be added S. Kettering, "The Causes of the Judicial Frondes," *Canadian Journal of History*, XVII (1982), pp. 275–306. The innovative and thoughtful approach of A. N. Hamscher, *The Parlement of Paris after the Fronde, 1653–1673* (Pittsburg, PA, 1976) and *The Conseil Privé and the Parlements in the Age of Louis XIV: A Study in French Absolutism, Transactions of the American Philosophical Society*, 77, Part 2, 1987, by stressing negotiation and political management, has influenced interpretations of not only the parlement but also the "absolute" monarchy. Against this view is the recent challenging book by J. J. Hurt, *Louis XIV and the Parlements* (Manchester, 2002), whose case is built chiefly on the financial exactions of the monarchy from the magistrates. M. Antoine concedes some of his former absolutist argument to Hamscher in "Les Remontrances des cours supérieurs sous le règne de Louis XIV (1673–1715)," *Bibliothèque de l'École des chartes*, 151 (1993), pp. 87–115, but remains resolutely anti-parlementaire in his *Louis XV* (Paris, 1989). The early reign of Louis XV is dealt with by F. L. Ford., *Robe and Sword: The Regrouping of the French Aristocracy after Louis XIV* (Cambridge, MA, 1953) – a highly contentious view, and by the prosaic study of J. D. Hardy, Jr, *Judicial Politics in the Old Regime: The parlement of Paris during the Regency* (Baton Rouge, LA, 1967).

The study of particular crises has led to a move away from older interpretations. From an interpretative point of view, John Rogister's article "The Crisis of 1753–4 in France and the Debate on the Nature of the Monarchy and of the Fundamental Laws," *Studies Presented to the International Commission for the History of Representative and Parliamentary Institutions*, 59 (1977), pp. 105–20, is to be preferred to his idiosyncratic analysis, *Louis XV and the Parlement of Paris 1737–1755* (Cambridge, 1995), which also focuses on 1753–4. Doyle and Hamscher's stress upon the Crown's political management is added to in P. R. Campbell, in a London PhD thesis of 1985 developed as "Jansenism, Politics and the Parlement of Paris," published as part 2 of *Power and Politics in Old Regime France* (London, 1996) pp. 191–377. The argument is, however, developed into a case for interpreting the motivation of the majority of the judges as chiefly jurisdictional. This approach was followed up by J. Swann and applied to the 1750s and 1760s, in his important study, *Politics and the Parlement of Paris under Louis XV, 1754–1774* (Cambridge, 1995), which is also good on the Maupeou coup, and his "Power and Provincial Politics in Eighteenth-Century France: The Varenne Affair," FHS (1998), pp. 441–74. Still useful is J. Flammermont, *Le Chancelier Maupeou et les parlements* (Paris, 1883). M. G. S. Mansergh, "The Revolution of 1771 or the Exile of the Parlement de Paris" (DPhil, Oxford, 1973) is good on the role of factions. For the period from 1770 onwards, the interpretive article by W. Doyle, "The Parlements of France and the Breakdown of the Old Regime," FHS, 6 (1970), pp. 415–58, remains authoritative on Maupeou and the importance of a united ministry, but less so on the 1780s. For a well-chosen set of documents see J. Rothney, ed., *The Brittany Affair and the Crisis of the Old Regime* (Oxford, 1969). The reign of Louis XVI has been well served with the two fine studies by B. Stone, *The Parlement of Paris, 1774–89* (Chapel Hill, NC, 1981) and *The French Parlements and the Crisis of the Old Régime* (Chapel Hill, NC, 1986). The aspects of crown and faction which he largely overlooks are filled out by J. Hardman, *French Politics 1774–1789* (London, 1995) ch. 11, and M. Price, *Preserving the Monarchy* (Cambridge, 1995), ch. 7. H. Carré, *La Fin des parlements* (Paris, 1912) retains an interest.

The nature of constitutional ideology (dubbed "parlementary constitutionalism" by Dale Van Kley) is explored in A. Cocâtre-Zilgien, "Les Doctrines politiques des milieux parlementaires dans la seconde moitié du XVIIIe siècle, ou les avocats dans la bataille idéologique pré-révolutionnaire," *Annales de la Faculté de Droit et Sciences Économiques de Lille*, 1963, pp. 29–154; Fr. Olivier-Martin, *Les Parlements contre l'absolutisme au XVIII siècle* (Paris, 1988); K. M. Baker, "A Script for the French Revolution: The Political Consciousness of the abbé Mably," in Baker, *Inventing the French Revolution* (Cambridge, 1990), pp. 86–108; J. Merrick, *The Desacralization of the French Monarchy in the Eighteenth Century* (Baton Rouge, LA, 1990); D. Echeverria, *The Maupeou Revolution: A Study in the History of Libertarianism, 1770–1774* (Baton Rouge, LA, 1985); and D. Van Kley, *The Damiens Affair* (Princeton, NJ, 1984), and "New Wine in Old Wineskins: Continuity and Rupture in the Pamphlet Debate of the French Prerevolution," FHS, 17, 2 (1991), pp. 448–65. S. Hanley, *The Lit de Justice of the Kings of France* (Princeton, NJ, 1982) considers ideology expressed through ritual. Lawyers are dealt with by D. A. Bell's *Lawyers and Citizens. The Making of a Political Elite in Old Regime France* (New York, 1994) and their publications by S. Maza: "Le Tribunal de la nation: Les mémoires judiciaires et l'opinion publique à la fin de l'ancien régime," *Annales, ESC*, XLII (1987), pp. 73–90. We now know how crucial the *parti janséniste* was to the ideological and political revival of the parlement; see D. Van Kley, *The Jansenists and the Expulsion of the Jesuits* (New Haven, CT, 1975); Campbell, *Power and Politics* and Swann, *Politics and the Parlement of Paris*. Studies of provincial courts have contributed greatly to our understanding of the Parisian parlement and sometimes highlight the issue of corporate strife in evidence in Paris. The best of these are: J. Egret, *Le Parlement de Dauphiné et les affaires publiques dans la deuxième moitié du XVIIIe siècle* (2 vols, Grenoble, 1942); W. Doyle, *The Parlement of Bordeaux and the End of the Old Regime, 1771–1790* (London, 1974); M. Gresset, *Le Monde judiciaire à Besançon* (2 vols, Lille, 1975); O. Chaline, *Godart de Belbeuf. Le Parlement, le roi et les normands* (Luneray, 1996); J. Meyer, "La Noblesse parlementaire bretonne face à la Pré-révolution et aux débuts de la révolution: Du témoignage à la statistique," in R. Vierhaus, ed., *Vom ancien régime zur Französische Revolution* (Göttingen, 1978), pp. 278–317. M. Cuilleron, *Contribution à l'étude de la rébellion des cours souveraines sous le règne de Louis XV: Le Cas de la cour des aides et finances de Montauban* (Paris, 1983) reveals corporate tensions between courts. The early chapters of P. Dawson, *Provincial Magistrates and Revolutionary Politics in France, 1789–1795* (New Haven, CT, 1972) are also useful. A number of original sources, some in translation, are also cited in the endnotes to the present chapter.

4. FROM SOCIAL TO CULTURAL HISTORY

There is a large and fascinating body of literature on eighteenth-century cultural history. An engaging introduction is Emmett Kennedy, *A Cultural History of the*

French Revolution (New Haven, CT, 1989). Lynn Hunt's *Politics, Culture and Class in the French Revolution* (Berkeley, CA, 1984) deserves its place as a pioneering work in the cultural history of the Revolution. In the first half, Hunt highlights the symbolic and visual dimensions of the Revolution, supplementing written texts. Emphasizing the Revolution as a "new creation" certainly catches the elation of 1789 but this needs qualifying. Tocqueville would be a useful corrective here. Among Roger Chartier's influential works, his *The Cultural Origins of the French Revolution* (Durham, NC, 1991) draws together other work usefully, but gives an extremely bloodless account of culture, with very little sense of the *passion* invested in arguments and issues. His essays in *The Cultural Uses of Print in Early Modern France* (Princeton, NJ, 1987) are a varied and stimulating exposition of his thesis of culture as appropriation.

On cultural history see L. Hunt, *The New Cultural History* (Berkeley, CA, 1989) and more recently, L. Hunt and V. E. Bonnett, eds, *Beyond the Cultural Turn* (Berkeley, CA, 1999). See also J. H. Pittock and A. Wear, eds, *Interpretation and Cultural History* (London, 1990); P. Burke, *Varieties of Cultural History* (Cambridge, 1997); J. Neubauer, ed., *Cultural History after Foucault* (New York, 1998); and R. Chartier, *Cultural History between Practices and Representations* (Cambridge, 1988) and *On the Edge of the Cliff. History, Language and Practices* (Baltimore, MD, 1997).

The following titles can only suggest the range of approaches to this period which are available. For a fascinating entry into "daily life," D. Roche, *The People of Paris. An Essay in Popular Culture in the Eighteenth Century* (Berkeley, CA, 1987). On "street culture," A. Farge, *Fragile Lives. Violence, Power and Solidarity in 18th Century France* (Cambridge, 1993) and Farge, *Subversive Words. Public Opinion in 18th Century France* (Cambridge, 1994). See also D. Garrioch, *Neighbourhood and Community in Paris, 1740–1790* (Cambridge, 1986). On the workplace, the early chapters of W. H Sewell, Jr, *Work and Revolution in France: The Language of Labor from the Old Regime to 1848* (Cambridge, 1980) and M. Sonenscher, *Work and Wages. Natural Law, Politics and the 18th Century Trades* (Cambridge, 1989). Among works on leisure, see R. Isherwood, *Farce and Fantasy: Popular Entertainment in 18th Century Paris* (Oxford, 1986) and T. Brennan, *Public Drinking and Popular Culture in 18th Century Paris* (Princeton, NJ, 1988). For an important profession, D. A. Bell, *Lawyers and Citizens. The Making of a Political Elite in Old-Regime France* (New York, 1994). For the clergy, J. McManners, *French Ecclesiastical Society under the Ancien Regime* (Manchester, 1960). For a work focusing on the role of women in the upper ranks of cultural sociability, Dena Goodman, *The Republic of Letters. A Cultural History of the French Enlightenment* (Ithaca, NY, 1994). Dealing with *material* and institutional means of exchange, C. Hesse, *Publishing and Cultural Politics in Revolutionary Paris, 1775–1810* (Berkeley, CA, 1989). On the press, see Further Reading for chapter 8.

The theme of "the body" cuts across genres. Michel Foucault begins *Discipline and Punishment* (London, 1977) with an almost unbearable account of the "excess" of punishment inflicted on the body of a would-be assassin of Louis XV. This spectacular violence against the body compensated for the weakness of the state's more general coercive power. J. B. Landes, *Visualising the Nation: Gender, Representation and Revolution in Eighteenth-Century France* (Ithaca, NY, 2001) develops Lynn Hunt's approach, imaginatively tracing "the workings of visual culture in the passage from Old Regime to revolutionary society." Her interpretation needs to be integrated with A. de Baecque's more multidimensional *The Body Politic* (Stanford, CA, 1997). Foucault's work highlights a dark side of ancien-regime politics and contributed strongly to a reassessment of the Enlightenment. K. M. Baker and P. Reilly, eds, *What's Left of the Enlightenment?* (Stanford, CA, 2001) and D. Gordon, ed., *Postmodernism and the Enlightenment* (London, 2001) continue the debates with a variety of articles crossing disciplinary boundaries. Also stimulating is C. Adams, J. Censer, and L. Graham, eds, *Visions and Revisions of Eighteenth-Century France* (University Park, PA, 1997). But studies of individuals can also cover wide areas, including matters of truly global concern. Henri Grégoire ("a hero for our times?" asks the introduction to J. D. Popkin and Richard H. Popkin, eds, *The Abbé Grégoire and his World*, Dordrecht, 2000) embraced, before 1789, the causes of Jews and slaves.

Some problems seem perennial; violence, often with poverty, is one such problem. If the Revolution and its origins are to be placed in the *"longue durée"* – Fernand Braudel's term emphasizing that events need to be seen in a long time-span if their importance, or lack of importance, is to be accurately judged – one might cite *Mouvements populaires et conscience sociale* (Paris, 1985), covering social uprisings from the sixteenth to nineteenth centuries and the massively documented analysis by J. Nicolas, *La Rébellion française. Mouvements populaires et conscience sociale 1661–1789* (Paris, 2002). The work of Richard Cobb, for example, *The Police and the People* (Oxford, 1972), vividly describes the plight of the poor, perhaps more often subjected to violence than resisting violently, and implies little change in 1789. At the opposite extreme, Norbert Elias, *The Court Society* (Oxford, 1983) is a classic. As for the most articulate pre-revolutionary and revolutionary actors (and victors?), the middling classes, S. Maza's *The Myth of the French Bourgeoisie* (Cambridge, MA, 2003) is "an essay on the social imaginary, 1750–1850" which hardly touches "la réalité" of social or political history.

5. THE INTELLECTUAL ORIGINS OF THE FRENCH REVOLUTION

On the subject of the Enlightenment, the available field is extremely wide: one of the best works to show the diversity of thought amongst the *philosophes* remains P. Gay, *The Enlightenment: An Interpretation* (London, 1970). On the radical Enlightenment there is M. C. Jacob, *The Radical Enlightenment: Pantheists, Freemasons and Republicans* (London, 1981), though some historians have maintained that she overstates the case for the extent to which radical thought was widely circulated. On the interest of many nobles in the Enlightenment, see G. Chaussinand-Nogaret, *The French Nobility in the Eighteenth Century: From Feudalism to Enlightenment*, trans. by W. Doyle (Cambridge, 1985). On the extent to which members of the higher clergy, judiciary, and administrative functionaries proved to be the principal purchasers of the *Encyclopédie*, the flagship of the Enlightenment enterprise, see R. Darnton, *The Business of Enlightenment: A Publishing History of the Encyclopédie, 1775–1800* (Cambridge, MA, 1979). Indeed, the high cost of the first editions of the *Encyclopédie* put it outside the means of any but the most affluent members of society. The contribution of individual *philosophes* to the intellectual origins of the Revolution can be traced in the case of Montesquieu, through R. Barny, "Montesquieu dans la révolution française," *Annales historiques de la Révolution française*, 279 (1990), pp. 49–73; and N. Hampson, *Will and Circumstance: Montesquieu, Rousseau and the French Revolution* (London, 1983). A great deal of material has been generated on Rousseau's contribution to revolutionary ideology, much of it offering conflicting views. The case for Rousseau's influence as made by historians as well as contemporary witnesses, is summarized in B. Manin, in his section on Rousseau in F. Furet and M. Ozouf, eds, *Critical Dictionary of the French Revolution*, trans. by A. Goldhammer (Cambridge, MA, 1989). Other studies include R. Barny, *Prélude idéologique à la Révolution française: Le Rousseauisme avant 1789* (Paris, 1985); D. Echeverria, "The Pre-Revolutionary Influence of Rousseau's '*Contrat social*'," *Journal of the History of Ideas*, 33 (1972), pp. 543–60; D. Williams, "The Influence of Rousseau on Political Opinion, 1760–95," EHR, 48 (1933), pp. 414–30; and P. Higonnet, *Goodness Beyond Virtue: Jacobins During the French Revolution* (Cambridge, MA, 1998), pp. 319–20. Some of the articles in R. Wokler, ed., *Rousseau and Liberty* (Manchester, 1995), notably those by Mason, Wokler, and Hampsher-Monk, reassess the old problem of attributing to Rousseau a posthumous responsibility for the Revolution and the Terror. The subject continues to provoke both interest and controversy. For a recent account which argues that the revolutionaries contributed to the reinvention of Rousseau not only as a "revolutionary" but also as a "pro-Enlightenment" thinker, see G. Garrard, *Rousseau's Counter-Enlightenment: A Republican Critique of the Philosophes* (New York, 2003), pp. 35–40. J. Swenson, *On Jean-Jacques Rousseau, Considered as One of the First Authors of the Revolution* (Stanford, CA, 2000) has reconsidered the ways in which the ambivalent and often contradictory nature of Rousseau's own discourse made it possible for the revolutionaries to construct a version of it that suited their own political engagements.

The classic study on the intellectual origins of the Revolution remains D. Mornet, *Les Origines intellectuelles de la Révolution française, 1715–1787* (first published 1933, 3rd edn, Paris, 1938), though it has never been translated into English. The best introduction to the cultural origins of the Revolution in English is R. Chartier, *The Cultural Origins of the French Revolution*, trans. by L. G. Cochrane (Durham, NC, 1991). Another major study is D. Roche, *France in the Enlightenment*, trans. by Arthur Goldhammer (Cambridge, MA, 2000). There is also an impressive collection of articles in K. Baker, ed., *The French Revolution and the Creation of Modern Political Culture*, vol. 1, *The Political Culture of the Old Regime* (Oxford, 1987). Amongst the numerous works by R. Darnton, "The High Enlightenment and the Low-Life of Literature in Pre-Revolutionary France," which was republished, along with some of his other early articles in R. Darnton, *The Literary Underground of the Old Regime* (Cambridge, MA, 1982), remains seminal. His later writings have culminated in R. Darnton, *The Forbidden Best-Sellers of Pre-Revolutionary France* (London, 1996). Works that owe a considerable amount to areas first opened up by Darnton include S. Maza, *Private Lives and Public Affairs: The Causes Célèbres of Prerevolutionary France* (Berkeley, CA, 1993); J. R. Censer and J. D. Popkin, eds, *Press and Politics in Pre-Revolutionary France* (Berkeley, CA, 1987); J. R. Censer, *The French Press in the Age of Enlightenment* (London, 1994); C. Hesse, *Publishing and Cultural Politics in Revolutionary Paris, 1789–1810* (Berkeley, CA,

1993); and D. A. Bell, *Lawyers and Citizens: The Making of a Political Elite in Old Regime France* (Oxford, 1994).

The part played by "public opinion" in eighteenth-century thought is evaluated in a number of works, including Chartier, *The Cultural Origins of the French Revolution*, ch. 2, "The Public Sphere and Public Opinion." There is also M. Ozouf, "L'Opinion publique," in Baker, *The French Revolution*, vol. 1, *The Political Culture of the Old Regime*, pp. 419–34; and Baker, *Inventing the French Revolution* (Cambridge, 1990) ch. 8, "Public Opinion as Political Invention," pp. 167–99. An overview of recent developments in this field is given by J. Cowans, "Habermas and French History: The Public Sphere and the Problem of Political Legitimacy," FH, 13 (1999), pp. 134–60.

On desacralization and the attacks on the monarchy there has been a great deal of recent work. Desacralization, we should note, need not only be a consequence of scurrilous and pornographic "debunkings" of monarchy; it can also be a consequence of political maneuvering amongst the elite. Both D. Van Kley and J. Merrick have used this term to describe the effect of political dissent invoked by Jansenist and *parlementaire* disputes with the absolutist authority. On this process, see D. Van Kley, *The Religious Origins of the French Revolution: From Calvin to the Civil Constitution, 1560–1791* (New Haven, CT, 1996), ch. 4, "The Conceptual Dismantling of Sacral Absolutism," pp. 191–248; also J. Merrick, *The Desacralization of the French Monarchy in the Eighteenth Century* (Baton Rouge, LA, 1990). On the wave of criticisms of monarchical "despotism" that were generated in response to Louis XV's suppression of the Paris parlement in the so-called "Maupeou coup" of 1770–74, the key study is D. Echeverria, *The Maupeou Revolution: A Study in the History of Libertarianism* (Baton Rouge, LA, 1985). On the tendency of Louis XVI and Marie-Antoinette to alienate powerful factions at court, thereby inadvertently encouraging opposition to their monarchy, see D. L. Wick, *A Conspiracy of Well-Intentioned Men: The Society of Thirty and the French Revolution* (New York, 1987). On hostile representations of Marie-Antoinette and their corrosive impact on the political reputation of the monarchy, see the collected articles in D. Goodman, ed., *Marie-Antoinette: Writings on the Body of a Queen* (London, 2003). A more sceptical assessment of the extent and impact of the pamphlet attacks on the reputation of the queen is evident in V. Gruder, "The Question of Marie-Antoinette: The Queen and Public Opinion Before the Revolution," FH, 16, 3 (Sept. 2002), pp. 269–98. On the political background to hostility to Marie-Antoinette and its origins in deep-seated suspicions of the alliance with Austria, see T. E. Kaiser, "Who's Afraid of Marie-Antoinette? Diplomacy, Austro-phobia and the Queen," FH, 14 (2000), pp. 241–71.

There is much research now being done of the kinds of intellectual concepts that fed into the origins of the Revolution. On the early development of the tradition of natural law, see T. Hochstrasser, *Natural Law Theories in the Early Enlightenment* (Cambridge, 2000). On the complex and often problematic nature of revolutionary reinterpretations of natural law theory, see F. Gauthier, *Triomphe et mort du droit naturel en Révolution: 1789–1795–1802* (Paris, 1992). The classic account of the discourse of classical republicanism remains J. G. A. Pocock, *The Machiavellian Moment: Florentine Political Thought and the Atlantic Republican Tradition* (Princeton, NJ, 1975). For a major reassessment of the importance of classical republicanism in the writings of Mably, see J. K. Wright, *A Classical Republican in*

Eighteenth-Century France: The Political Thought of Mably (Stanford, CA, 1997). The development of the concept of political virtue into an ideological platform of revolutionary rhetoric is analyzed in M. Linton, *The Politics of Virtue in Enlightenment France* (Basingstoke, 2001). On the language of the rights of man there is D. Van Kley, ed., *The French Idea of Freedom: The Old Regime and the Declaration of Rights of 1789* (Stanford, CA, 1994) which offers a number of articles that examine the conjuncture of long-term origins with the politics of 1789.

6. THE RELIGIOUS ORIGINS OF THE FRENCH REVOLUTION, 1560–1791

Any essay on the religious origins of the French Revolution must be dependent on a working definition of religion. This essay invokes the authority of Mircea Eliade in his *The Sacred and the Profane: The Nature of Religion*, trans. by Willard R. Frank (New York and London, 1987), pp. 8–18, underscoring the element of transcendence to distinguish it from "ideology" which seems imperfectly differentiated from "religion" in Clifford Geertz's essays on the two phenomena in his *The Interpretation of Cultures* (New York, 1973). The notion that religion, specifically Christianity, might have been an agent in the secularization of politics since the sixteenth century owes most to M. Gauchet, *The Disenchantment of the World: A Political History of Religion*, trans. by Oscar Burge (Princeton, MJ, 1997), but also something to Peter Berger's more visibly Weberian *The Sacred Canopy: Elements of a Sociological Theory of Religion* (Garden City, NY, 1967).

As applied to the eighteenth-century Jansenist controversy in this chapter, Gauchet's trajectory leaves ample room for the lingering influence of religious sensibilities and their complicity in the formation of political ideologies and parties. In sharp contrast to this approach is Catherine Maire, *De la cause de Dieu à la cause de la nation: Le Jansénisme au XVIIIe siècle* (Paris, 1998), which is more heavily indebted to Gauchet's paradigm, and religion and specifically Jansenism immolate themselves in an act of self-destruction and quite simply give way to Enlightenment-inspired "ideology." These two views have recently taken the form of a no-holds-barred debate, with Maire attacking: *Le Débat*, no 130 (mai–août, 2004), pp. 133–53, and Van Kley responding: "Sur les sources religieuses et politiques de la Révolution française: Commentaires pour un débat," *Commentaire*, 27/10 (hiver 2004–05), pp. 893–915.

Related to the role of religion in political secularization is the notion that the ancien-régime monarchy had a distinct religious identity, and that it sustained a process of desacralization during the eighteenth century. The French monarchy's sacral identity found classic characterization in Marc Bloch, *The Royal Touch*, trans. by J. E. Anderson (London, 1971), a portraiture updated by R. Jackson in *Vive le Roi: A History of the French Coronation Oath from Charles V to Charles X* (Chapel Hill, NC, 1984); and C. Beaune, *Naissance de la nation France* (Paris, 1985). On the Renaissance theory of the mortal royal body's hypostatic union with the immortal Crown, see E. Kantorowicz, *The King's Two Bodies* (Princeton, MH, 1957) and R. Giesey, *The Royal Funerary Ceremonies in Renaissance France* (Geneva, 1960).

This historiography has come in for criticism by Alain Bourreau, *Le Simple Corps du roi: L'Impossible Sacralité des souverains français, Xve–XVIIIe siècle* (Paris, 1988), as has the thesis of the "desacralization" of this sacral monarchy in the eighteenth century, most notably by T. Tackett in "Conspiracy Obsession in a Time of Revolution: French Elites and the Origin of the Terror, 1789–1792," *AHR*, 105 (June 2001), pp. 691–714, and Jens Ivo Engels, "Beyond Sacral Monarchy: A New Look at the Image of Early Modern French Monarchy," *FH*, 15 (2001), pp. 139–58. That such a "desacralization" took place via the agency of religious conflict is nonetheless stoutly maintained by J. Merrick, *The Desacralization of the French Monarchy in the Eighteenth Century* (Baton Rouge, LA, 1990); P. Chaunu et al., *Le Basculement religieux de Paris au XVIIIe siècle* (Paris, 1998); and D. Van Kley in this essay and in *The Religious Origins of the French Revolution* (New Haven, CT, 1996). R. Darnton also maintains a variation on this thesis in *The Forbidden Best-Sellers of Pre-Revolutionary France* (New York, 1995), although stressing the role of "philosophical pornography" toward the end of the century.

As this chapter also argues that royal absolutism suffered a decline in the course of the religious controversies of the eighteenth century, it necessarily presupposes the existence of "absolutism" in the face of an historiographical body of empirical criticism of the concept, for example by R. Mettam, *Power and Faction in Louis XIV's France* (Oxford, 1988); S. Kettering, *Patrons, Brokers, and Clients in Seventeenth-Century France* (Oxford, 1983); and N. Henshall, *The Myth of Absolutism* (London, 1992). The present chapter takes its stand with D. Parker, *The Making of French Absolutism* (London, 1983) and, most recently, F. Cosandey and R. Descimon's *L'Absolutisme en France: Histoire et historiographie* (Paris, 2002), as well as with an older body of literature that, headed by W. Church in *Richelieu and Reason of State* (Princeton, NJ, 1972), emphasized the newness of the theoretical claims advanced by the apologists of "absolute" or "divine-right" monarchy in comparison of the accountability of the monarchy to both Church and "people" in traditional Gallican theory from before the wars of religion.

For the transition from traditional to "royal" Gallicanism, see older works by V. Martin and most briefly A-G. Martimort, *Le Gallicanisme* ("Que-sais-je?," Paris, 1973). While aware of its political ramifications, F. Oakley has recently reexamined the ecclesiastical and specifically conciliar side of Gallicanism in *The Conciliarist Tradition: Constitutionalism in the Catholic Church, 1300–1870* (Oxford and New York, 2003). But it was Q. Skinner who most memorably called attention to conciliarism's application to the state and use in justifications for resistance to the monarchy on both sides in the wars of religion in *The Age of the Reformation*, vol. 2 of *The Foundations of Modern Political Thought* (Cambridge, 1982). The monarchy's final retreat from the conciliar tenets of Gallicanism is best described by P. Blet, *Les Assemblées du clergé et Louis XIV de 1670 à 1693* (Rome, 1972).

The French wars of religion have benefited from new synthetic coverage by M. P. Holt, *The French Wars of Religion, 1562–1629* (Cambridge, 1995); and R. J. Knecht, *The French Civil Wars, 1562–1598* (Harlow, 2000). The thesis that the confrontation between Calvinism and League-like Catholicism witnessed the equal but oppositely desacralizing effect on the monarchy of two very different religious sensibilities is indebted to N. Z. Davis's classic article on "The Rites of Violence," in *Society and Culture in Early Modern France* (Stanford, CT, 1977) and the works of D. Crouzet, especially his *Jean Calvin: Vies parallèles* (Paris, 2000) and

Les Guerriers de Dieu (2 vols, Seyssel, 1990), as well as to B. B. Diefendorf's beauti-ful *Beneath the Cross: Catholics and Huguenots in Sixteenth-Century France* (Oxford and New York, 1991). On the political implications of Calvinist Eucharistic theology, an argument similar to the one in this essay has been advanced by C. Elwood, *The Body Broken: The Calvinist Doctrine of the Eucharist and the Symbolization of Power in Sixteenth-Century France* (New York, 1999).

The treatment of sixteenth-century Protestant political thought is dependent on (besides Skinner's *The Age of the Reformation*) R. Giesey, "The Monarchomach Triumvirs: Hotman, Béza and Mornay," *Bibliothèque d'Humanisme et Renaissance*, XXXII (1970), pp. 41–6; R. Kingdon, *Myths about the Saint Bartholomew's Day Massacre, 1572–1576* (Cambridge, MA, 1988); and M. Yardeni, "French Calvinist Political Thought, 1534–1715," in M. Prestwich, ed., *International Calvinism, 1541–1715* (Oxford, 1985), pp. 315–37. For the political thought of the Catholic League, this chapter is principally reliant on F. Baumgartner, *Radical Reactionaries: The Political Thought of the French Catholic League* (Geneva, 1976) and R. Mousnier, *The Assassination of Henry IV*, trans. by J. Spencer (London, 1973).

For the royal conversion to 'Catholicism as "sincere," see M .Wolfe, *The Conversion of Henry IV: Politics, Power, and Religious Belief in Early-Modern France* (Cambridge, MA, 1993), and T. Wanneglffelen, *Ni Rome ni Genève: Les Fidéles entre deux chaires en France au XVIe siécle* (Paris, 1977). The tricentennial of the revoca-tion of the Edict of Nantes prompted numbers of new books including E. Labrousse, *Essai sur la révocation de l'édit de Nantes* (Geneva and Paris, 1985); and J. Garrisson-Estèbe, *L'Édit de Nantes et sa révocation* (Paris, 1985). The quartocenten-nial of the Edict of Nantes saw the publication of B. Cottret's fine *1598. L'Édit de Nantes, pour en finir avec les guerres de religion* (n.p., 1997).

But the Bourbon monarchy never did quite finish with the wars of religion because, seeing in Jansenism a "rewarmed Calvinism," it solicited papal condemnation after condemnation and eventually persecuted the movement into a posture of political subversion. This, in short, is the trajectory traced by J. McManners's recent overview of the subject in *Church and Society in Eighteenth-Century France*, 2 vols (Oxford, 1998), vol. 2, pp. 343–559, 661–78; as by Van Kley, *The Religious Origins of the French Revolution*. While L. Kolakowski in *God Owes Us Nothing* (Chicago, reprinted 1998) highlights the similarity of Jansenism to Calvinism – a possible reading of the evidence – this chapter underscores the initial differences in a historiographical line of succession indebted to J. La Porte, *La Doctrine de Port-Royal*, 2 vols, esp. vol. 2, *La Morale d'après Arnauld* (Paris, 1951). A helpful recent comparison between French Protestantism and Jansenism is to be found in *Port-Royal et les protestants, Chroniques de Port-Royal* 47 (Paris, 1998), while renewed interest in the subject has resulted in two new short syntheses: J-P. Chantin, *Le Jansénisme: Entre hérésie imaginaire et résistance catholique, XVII–XIXe siècle* (Paris, 1996) and W. Doyle, *Jansenism* (London, 2000). Besides its similarity to Calvinism, some additional factors in the monarchy's hostility are adum-brated in P. Jansen, *Le Cardinal Mazarin et le jansénisme* (Paris, 1967); as well as in Richard Golden, *The Godly Rebellion: Parisian Curés and the Religious Fronde, 1652–1662* (Chapel Hill, NC, 1981) and Georges Hardy, *Le Cardinal de Fleury et le mouvement janséniste* (Paris, 1925).

In addition to Golden, D. Garrioch, and M-J. Michel have variously uncov-ered the social rooting of Jansenism in eighteenth-century Paris in the Parisian bourgeoisie and even popular classes in *The Formation of the Parisian Bourgeoisie, 1690–1830* (Cambridge, MA, 1997) and *Jansénisme à Paris, 1640–1730* (Paris, 2000), respectively; while B. R. Kreiser and C. Maire have demonstrated the movement's popular resonance via the miraculous in *Miracles, Convulsions, and Ecclesiastical Politics in Early Eighteenth-Century Paris* (Princeton, MJ, 1987) and *Les Convulsions de Saint-Médard* (Paris, 1985).

The movement's early juncture with Gallicanism is the subject of P. Dieudonné's *La Paix clémentine: Défaite et victoire du premier jansénisme français sous le pontificat de Clément XI (1667–1669)* (Louvain and Dudley, MA, 2003). And eighteenth-century Jansenism's tactical alliance with the Paris parlement and its "constitutionalism" has been the object of several studies: D. A. Bell, *Lawyers and Citizens* (new York, 1994); P. R. Campbell, *Power and Politics in Old-Regime France* (London, 1996); J. Swann, *Politics and the Parlement of Paris under Louis XV* (Cambridge, 1995); and D. Van Kley, *The Jansenists and the Expulsion of the Jesuits from France, 1757–1765* (New Haven, CT, 1975), which first identified the existence of a "Jansenist party" within the Order of Barristers and magistracy of the Paris Parlement. But see also the comparative perspective of a forthcoming article on "Jansenism and the International Expulsion of the Jesuits" by the same author for the new *Cambridge History of Eighteenth-Century Christianity, vol. 7, Enlightenment, Revolution, and Reawakening*, ed. by S. J. Brown and T. Tackett (Cambridge, 2006).

There is a paucity of scholarship about the "devout" side of the eighteenth-century religious and political conflict. See D. G. Thompson, "French Jesuit Leaders and the Destruction of the Jesuit Order, 1756–1762," FH, 2 (1988), pp. 237–63; and "General Ricci and the Suppression of the Jesuit Order in France, 1760–1764," *Journal of Ecclesiastical History* 37/3 (July 1986), pp. 426–41. Picking up where J. Pappas and his *Berthier's Journal de Trevoux and the Philosophes* (Geneva, 1957) left off, C. Northeast has brilliantly highlighted ground shared by the Jesuits and *philosophes* in *The Parisian Jesuits and the Enlightenment, 1700–62* (Geneva, 1991). A good study of the eighteenth-century (and anti-Jansenist) *parti dévot* still awaits its historian, although Mme A. Ravel is now writing a thesis on "Le Parti dévot à la cour de France au XVIIIe siècle" for the École des Hautes Études en Sciences Sociales in Paris. While waiting, there is much to be gleaned from L. Châtellier, *The Europe of the Devout* (Cambridge, 1989); B. Plongeron et al., *Les Défis de la modernité* (vol. 10, *Histoire du christianisme*, Paris, 1999), and D. McMahon, *Enemies of the Enlightenment: The French Counter-Enlightenment and the Making of Modernity* (New York, 2001).

The thesis of M. Cottret in *Jansénismes et lumières* (Paris, 1998) is that the Jansenist movement was hardly as imperious to the French Enlightenment as had long been thought. For the metamorphosis of Jansenism into a certain kind of "patriotism," see D. Van Kley, "The Religious Origins of the Patriot and Ministerial Parties in Pre-Revolutionary France," in T. Keselman, ed., *Belief in History* (Notre Dame and London, 1991), pp. 173–236, and S. M. Singham, "A Conspiracy of Twenty Million Frenchmen: Public Opinion, Patriotism, and the Assault on Absolutism during the Maupeou Years" (PhD dissertation, Princeton University, 1991).

For Jansenism's relation to the French Revolution's ecclesiastical legislation, namely the Civil Constitution of the Clergy, see E. Preclin's *Les Jansénistes du*

XVIIIe siècle et la Constitution civile du clergé, 1713–1791 (Paris, 1929). The Revolution's falling out with the papacy is the subject of G. Pelletier's recent *Rome et la Révolution française: La Théologie et la politique de Saint-Siège devant la Révolution française (1789–1799)* (Rome, 2004), as well as of A. Mathiez's still indispensable *Rome et le clergé français sous la Constituante* (Paris, 1911). The Revolution's break with Rome was one of the reasons for Louis XVI's attempted flight from France in 1791, on which see T. Tackett, *When the King Took Flight* (Cambridge, MA, 2003). For the religious dimension of this episode, however, it is still imperative to consult older studies, among them the concluding chapter on Dom H. Leclercq's *L'Église constitutionnelle (juillet 1790–avril 1791)* (Paris, 1934).

7. THE CONTESTED IMAGE: STAGE, CANVAS, AND THE ORIGINS OF THE FRENCH REVOLUTION

The work of Thomas Crow, Albert Boime, Régis Michel, Mary Sheriff, Carol Duncan, and Philippe Bordes, which has transformed the way we understand the art of the later eighteenth century in France, is all informed by empirical research, often of a "traditional" archival kind, but its interpretative insights are all influenced to a lesser or greater extent by various aspects of the revolution in the human sciences. In theater studies, the researches of Gregory Brown, Susan Maslan, and Jeffrey Ravel, who are equally at home in empirical scholarship and with questions of symbolic and semiotic power, have opened up new understandings of the theater world and new directions for both cultural history and theater research: see T. Crow, *Painters and Public Life in Eighteenth-Century Paris* (New Haven, CT and London, 1985); Crow, *Emulation: Making Artists for Revolutionary France* (New Haven, CT and London, 1995); R. Michel et M. C. Sahut, *David. L'Art et la politique* (Paris, 1995); R. Michel, *Le Beau Idéal* (Paris, 1979); T. Clark, *Farewell to an Idea. Episodes from a History of Modernism* (New Haven, CT and London, 2000); A. Boime, *Art in an Age of Revolution, 1750–1800* (Chicago, 1989); M. Sheriff, *Fragonard: Art and Eroticism* (Chicago, 1990); Sheriff, *The Exceptional Woman* (Chicago, 1996). On theatre see G. S. Brown, "A Field of Honor: The Cultural Politics of Playwriting in Eighteenth Century France" (PhD Dissertation, University of Columbia, 1997).

The most thoroughgoing Europe-wide synthesis of the importance of cultural manifestations and debate to the shifts which mark the end of the ancien régime is T. C. W. Blanning, *The Culture of Power and the Power of Culture* (Oxford, 2002), whose chapter on the "Cultural Origins of the French Revolution" ranges from music, literature, drama, and the visual arts, exploring them cogently in relation to the new public sphere, to oppositional politics, as well as the growth of a patriot nationalism to explore what he describes as "the haemorrhage of legitimacy from the representational culture of the old regime and the development of a new concept of national sovereignty legitimised by public opinion" (p. 426).

For an eloquent argument in favour of the importance of the image in the French Revolution, see J. Landes, *Visualizing the Nation* (Ithaca, NY, 2001), esp. pp. 1–23. For an equally eloquent and persuasive argument for a theatrical rather than a literary conception of the pre-Revolutionary public sphere, see J.

Ravel, *The Contested Parterre: Public Theatre and French Political Culture 1680–1791* (Ithaca, NY, 1999).

On genre painting as a phenomenon, see particularly the catalogue of the exhibition, *The Age of Watteau, Chardin and Fragonard. Masterpieces of French Genre Painting* (C. Bailey and P. Connisbee, eds, exh. cat., Washington, National Gallery of Art, 2003) but this catalog takes a determinedly nonpolitical view of the paintings it describes. See also Richard Rand, ed., *Intimate Encounters: Love and Domesticity in French Genre Painting* (exh. cat., Dartmouth, Hood Museum, 1997) which takes a more politically engaged view.

The critical pamphlets which provided the major source for perhaps the single most important work published on prerevolutionary art in the last twenty years, T. Crow's *Painters and Public Life*, have been much studied in recent years. See especially R. Wrigley, *The Origins of French Art Criticism from the Ancien Régime to the Restoration* (New York and Oxford, 1993). See also B. Fort, "Voice of the Public: The Carnivalization of Salon Art in PreRevolutionary Pamphlets," ECS, 22/3 (Spring 1989), pp. 368–94.

On the revolutionary festivals, see M. Ozouf, *La Fête révolutionnaire* (Paris, 1976). On David's part in them, the fundamental work remains D. L. Dowd, *Pageant Master of the Republic. Jacques-Louis David and the French Revolution* (Lincoln, NE, 1948).

The volume edited by S. E. Melzer and K. Norberg, *From the Royal to the Republican Body: Incorporating the Political in Seventeenth and Eighteenth-Century France* (Berkeley, CA, Los Angeles and London, 1998), is an example of the way in which cultural historians have come to stress the importance of the semiotics of the corporeal to our understandings of political change.

8. THE PAMPHLET DEBATE OVER THE ORGANIZATION OF THE ESTATES GENERAL

During the last two decades a vast literature has appeared on the political culture of ancien-regime France. The initial stimulus for these studies was F. Furet, *Penser la Révolution française* (Paris, 1978), translated as *Interpreting the French Revolution* (Cambridge, 1981), which first introduced historians to the concept of the revolution as an ideological struggle between competing political discourses. Equally important in providing a foundation for the study of political culture was J. Habermas, *Strukturwandel der Öffentlichkeit: Untersuchungen zu einer Kategorie der bürgerlichen Gesellschaft* (Neuwied, 1962), translated as *The Structural Transformation of the Public Sphere: An Inquiry into a Category of Bourgeois Society* (Cambridge, MA, 1989), which emphasized the development of a critically reasoning public in old-regime Europe. K. M. Baker, ed, *The French Revolution and the Creation of Modern Political Culture: The Political Culture of the Old Regime*, vol. 1 (Oxford, 1987) brings together a number of early efforts to interpret the nature of this culture. Clandestine publications and the literary *demi-monde* that produced them in the last half of the eighteenth century have been analyzed in a number of works by Robert Darnton, including *The Literary Underground of the Old Regime* (Cambridge, MA, 1982) and *The Forbidden-Best Sellers of Pre-Revolutionary France* (New York, 1996).

On the newspaper press of the era see J. Popkin, *News and Politics in the Age of Revolution: Jean Luzac's Gazette De Leyde* (Ithaca, NY, 1989) and J. Censer, *The French Press in the Age of Enlightenment* (London, 1994). D. K. Van Kley has revealed the importance of Jansenism in several works, most recently *The Religious Origins of the French Revolution: From Calvin to the Civil Constitution of the Clergy, 1560–1791* (New Haven, CT, 1996). D. A. Bell, *Lawyers and Citizens: The Making of a Political Elite in Old Regime France* (Oxford, 1994) explains the political role of the Parisian barrister, and S. Maza, *Private Lives and Public Affairs: The Causes Célèbres of Prerevolutionary France* (Berkeley, CA, 1993) analyzes the influence that these barristers exercised through the publication of their legal briefs. A stimulating analysis of the role of political culture and ideology regarding the origins and early development of the Revolution is found in K. M. Baker, *Inventing the French Revolution* (Cambridge, 1990). Most recently, D. A. Bell, *The Cult of the Nation in France: Inventing Nationalism, 1680–1800* (Cambridge, MA, 2001) investigates the development of the concept of the nation in the political culture of the ancien régime and the Revolution.

On the pamphlet literature that preceded the meeting of the Estates General in May 1789, see J. Popkin and D. K. Van Kley, "The Pre-Revolutionary Debate," in Colin Lucas, ed., *The French Revolutionary Research Collection* (Oxford, 1989), pp. 1–22; J. Popkin, "Pamphlet Journalism at the End of the Old Regime," ECS, 22 (Spring 1989), pp. 351–67; V. Gruder, "Les Pamphlets pre-Révolutionnaires: Réseau d'éducation politique et précurseurs des polémiques révolutionnaires," in P. Rétat, ed., *La Révolution du journal, 1788–1794* (Paris, 1989), pp. 13–24; and H. Chisick, "The Pamphlet Literature of the French Revolution: An Overview," HEI, 17 (March–May 1993), pp. 149–66. Works that have employed these pamphlets in an attempt to understand the origins of the Revolution and its early character include M. Garrett, *The Estates General of 1789: The Problems of Composition and Organization* (New York, 1935); H. B. Applewhite, *Political Alignment in the French National Assembly, 1789–1791* (Baton Rouge, LA, 1993); and K. Margerison, *Pamphlets and Public Opinion: A Campaign for a Union of Orders in the Early French Revolution* (West Lafayette, IN, 1998). More than a thousand of the pamphlets are available on the internet through the Bibliothèque nationale's digital library, Gallica.

On the career and influence of the abbé Sieyès, the classic study is P. Bastid, *Sieyès et sa pensée* (Paris, 1970). See also M. Forsyth, *Reason and Revolution: The Political Thought of the Abbé Sieyes* (Leicester, 1987) and most recently W. H. Sewell, Jr, *A Rhetoric of Bourgeois Revolution: The Abbé Sieyès and "What Is the Third Estate?"* (Durham, NC, 1994). For an English translation of *What Is the Third Estate?* and other pamphlets by Sieyès, see M. Sonenscher, ed., *Sieyès: Political Writings, including the Debate between Sieyès and Tom Paine in 1791* (Indianapolis, 2003).

9. PEASANTS AND THEIR GRIEVANCES

There is a long tradition of research on the French countryside that shows no signs of drying up. Considering the enormous variation in the conditions of rural life, and the changing interests of historians, there are always new books to be written. Marc Bloch's truly classic 1931 synthesis of that variety is still a good place to start: *French Rural History. An Essay on its Basic Characteristics* (Berkeley, CA and Los Angeles, 1966). For contrasting accounts of the state of the eighteenth-century rural economy, see G. Bouchard, *Le Village immobile; Sennely-en-Sologne au XVIIIe siècle* (Paris, 1972); L. Vardi, *The Land and the Loom. Peasants and Profits in Northern France, 1680–1800* (Durham, NC, 1993); and P. T. Hoffman, *Growth in a Traditional Society. The French Countryside, 1450–1815* (Princeton, NJ, 1996).

Moving easily from rural circumstances to rural rebellion are the chapters on the peasantry in G. Lefebvre's national picture, *The Coming of the French Revolution* (Princeton, NJ, 1947). The French have a particularly rich tradition of detailed studies of a single region. For one classic instance and one recent one, see Lefebvre's *Les Paysans du Nord pendant la Révolution française* (Paris, 1970) and S. Bianchi's *La Révolution et la Première République au village: Pouvoirs, votes et politisation dans les campagnes d'Ile-de-France 1787–1800* (Paris, 2002). There is still much to be done on the crucial relationships of peasants and lords, one recent fine study of which is A. Crubaugh, *Balancing the Scales of Justice: Local Courts and Rural Society in Southwest France, 1750–1800* (University Park, PA, 2001). The equally important question of the relationships of peasants and government is interestingly treated in H. Root, *Peasants and King in Burgundy. Agrarian Foundations of French Absolutism* (Berkeley, CA, 1987).

The study of rural defiance and insurrection before the revolutionary period is a fascinating genre all its own. Food riots have been the subject of much first-rate recent research. Among the most valuable as a foretaste of the revolution is C. Bouton's rich exploration of the extensive disturbances of 1775, *The Flour War: Gender, Class, and Community in Late Ancien Régime Society* (University Park, PA, 1993). On long-term changing patterns, see J. Nicolas, *La Rébellion française: Mouvements populaires et conscience sociale 1661–1789* (Paris, 2002) and Y.-M. Bercé, *Fête et révolte. Des mentalités populaires du XVIe au XVIII siècle* (Paris, 1976).

On the countryside in the early revolutionary period see Lefebvre, *The Great Fear of 1789: Rural Panic in Revolutionary France* (New York, 1973). A demonstration that new emphases by historians continue to reveal new facets to the rural revolution is provided by P. McPhee, *Revolution and Environment in Southern France, 1780–1830: Peasants, Lords, and Murder in the Corbières* (New York, 1999). On a region whose peasants were early to direct their mobilizations against the seigneurial regime, see M. Cubells, *Les Horizons de la liberté: La Naissance de la Révolution en Provence, 1787–1789* (Aix-en-Provence, 1987). For syntheses of the rural revolution, see J. Markoff, *The Abolition of Feudalism. Peasants, Lords and Legislators in the French Revolution* (University Park, PA, 1996), P. Jones, *The Peasantry in the French Revolution* (Cambridge, 1988), and – at long last translated from Russian – A. Ado, *Paysans en Révolution. Terre, pouvoir et jacquerie, 1789–1794* (Paris, 1996). On the response of the National Assembly in early August 1789, see P. Kessel, *La Nuit du 4 août 1789* (Paris, 1969) and M. Fitzsimmons, *The Night the Old Regime Ended* (University Park, PA, 2003).

For the villagers' own statements in the spring of 1789, nothing will ever replace the *cahiers de doléances* and going through any of the numerous published collections is always an eye-opener. As English-language guides to this material, see B. F. Hyslop, *A Guide to the General Cahiers of 1789, with the Texts of Unedited*

Cahiers (New York, 1986) and G. Shapiro and J. Markoff, *Revolutionary Demands. A Content Analysis of the Cahiers de Doléances of 1789* (Stanford, CA, 1998).

10. FROM THE ESTATES GENERAL TO THE NATIONAL ASSEMBLY, MAY 5–AUGUST 4, 1789

The Estates General and National Assembly have been the object of a number of studies. In this brief guide, preference is given to works in English, although French titles are occasionally offered when there is no English equivalent or in those instances in which it might particularly complement an English-language work.

The definitive starting point for study of the National Assembly is E. H. Lemay, *Dictionnaire des constituants 1789–1791* (2 vols, Oxford, 1991). With its biographies of deputies, several useful appendices, listing of archival sources, and bibliography, it completely supersedes A. Brette, *Les Constituants: Liste des députés et des suppléants élus à l'Assemblée constituante de 1789* (Paris, 1897). M. B. Garrett, *The Estates-General of 1789: The Problems of Organization and Composition* remains useful, but Kenneth Margerison, *Pamphlets and Public Opinion: The Campaign for a Union of Orders in the Early French Revolution* (West Lafayette, GA, 1998) is the more comprehensive and definitive treatment. On the role of the clergy at the Estates General, see M. G. Hutt, "The Role of the Curés in the Estates-General," *Journal of Ecclesiastical History*, 6 (1955) pp. 190–220; R. F. Nechelles, "The Curés in the Estates-General of 1789," *JMH*, 46 (1974) pp. 425–44, and N. Aston, *The End of an Elite: The French Bishops and the Coming of the Revolution. 1786–1790* (Oxford, 1992). C. Kuhlmann, "The Influence of the Breton Deputation and the Breton Club in the Revolution (April–October. 1789)," in *University of Nebraska Studies*, 2 (Lincoln, NE, 1902) pp. 207–98, was a pioneering but still serviceable examination of the efforts of that group to affect the deliberations of the Estates General and National Assembly.

K. M. Baker, *Inventing the French Revolution: Essays on French Political Culture in the Eighteenth Century* (Cambridge, 1990), is a collection of essays that provide insight into both the political origins of the Revolution and the early work of the National Assembly. Two longer-term overviews of events, one that sees the work of the National Assembly as an end and the other as a beginning, are P. M. Jones, *Reform and Revolution in France: The Politics of Transition. 1774–1791* (Cambridge, 1995), which highlights ancien-régime antecedents to several Revolutionary reforms, and I. Woloch, *The New Regime: Transformations of the French Civic Order. 1789–1820s* (New York, 1994). A briefer perspective is F. Braesch, *1789: L'Année cruciale* (Paris, 1941). E. Thompson, *Popular Sovereignty and the French Constituent Assembly. 1789–1791* (Manchester, 1952) and R. K. Gooch, *Parliamentary Government in France: Revolutionary Origins 1789–1791* (Ithaca, NY, 1960) examine the National Assembly as marking the transition to regular legislative, representative government in France.

The operation of the National Assembly is examined in A. Castaldo, *Les Méthodes de travail de la Constituante: Les Techniques délibératives de l'Assemblée nationale 1789–1791* (Paris, 1989) and E. H. Lemay and A. Patrick, *Revolutionaries at Work:*

The Constituent Assembly. 1789–1791 (Oxford, 1996). Norman Hampson, *Prelude to Terror: The Constituent Assembly and the Failure of Consensus 1789–1791* (Oxford, 1988) views the disagreements that emerged during the tenure of the National Assembly as laying the groundwork for the murderous proscriptions that ensued two and three years later. A more optimistic assessment, emphasizing the acceptance by the populace of the major reforms of the Assembly, particularly in the critical spheres of administration and the judiciary, is M. P. Fitzsimmons, *The Remaking of France: The National Assembly and the Constitution of 1791* (Cambridge, 1994). H. Applewhite, *Political Alignment in the French National Assembly 1789–1791* (Baton Rouge, LA, 1993) analyzes the lines of demarcation formed within the National Assembly and T. Tackett, *Becoming a Revolutionary: The Deputies of the French National Assembly and the Emergence of a Revolutionary Culture (1789–1790)* (Princeton, NJ, 1996) examines the manner in which the formation and operation of the Assembly produced a "Revolutionary" outlook during the first year of its existence. Two key events during the term of the National Assembly that heavily influenced it, one at the beginning and the other at the end, are studied in M. P. Fitzsimmons, *The Night the Old Regime Ended: August 4, 1789, and the French Revolution* (University Park, PA, 2003) and T. Tackett, *When the King Took Flight* (Cambridge, MA, 2003). Other treatments of the night of August 4, primarily compilations and document collections, are P. Kessel, *La Nuit du 4 août 1789* (Paris, 1969) and J.P. Hirsch, ed., *La Nuit du 4 août* (Paris, 1978). An earlier study, focusing on a conservative group in the Assembly, is J. Egret, *La Révolution des notables: Mounier et les monarchiens* (Paris, 1950), and it is complemented by R. H. Griffiths, *Le Centre perdu: Malouet et les monarchiens dans la Révolution française* (Grenoble, 1988).

The renunciations made during the meeting of the night of August 4 led to a comprehensive restructuring of the French polity. T. Margadant, *Urban Rivalries in the French Revolution* (Princeton, NJ, 1992) examines the competition unleashed among towns and cities as a result of the administrative and judicial reorganization of France enacted by the National Assembly. A. Crubaugh, *Balancing the Scales of Justice: Local Courts and Rural Society in Southwest France, 1750–1800* (University Park, PA, 2001) considers the transition of the justice system from seigneurial courts to the justice of the peace created by the National Assembly. The transformation of the judicial system in Paris is treated by A. Willis, *Crime and Punishment in Revolutionary Paris* (Westport, 1981).

Useful primary sources in English for students include Arthur Young, *Travels in France during the Years 1787, 1788 & 1789*, ed. by Constantia Maxwell (Cambridge, 1929), which offers contemporary observations just before and during the early months of the Revolution, and O. Browning, ed., *Despatches from Paris, 1784–1790* (2 vols, London, 1909–10), vol. I for 1784–87 and II for 1788–90, which reproduces the acute contemporary analysis of the British ambassadors' reports. Two other contemporary perceptions of the Estates General and National Assembly are the English translation of E. Dumont, *Recollections of Mirabeau, and of the Two First Legislative Assemblies of France by Etienne Dumont* (London, 1832), and also trans. by E. Seymour, *The Great Frenchman and the Little Genevese* (London, 1904) and A.F. Bertrand de Moleville, *Private memoirs of A.F. Bertrand de Moleville, Minister of State, 1790–1791, Relative to the Last Year of the Reign of Louis XVI*, ed. by G.K. Fortesque (2 vols, Boston, 1909). Two volumes of private correspondence afford different vantage points on the Estates General and National Assembly. The interesting evolution of a noble deputy is to be found in marquis de Ferrières, *Correspondance inédite 1789, 1790, 1791*, ed. by H. Carré (Paris, 1932), pp. 1–175, and the perceptions of a backbencher commons deputy in François Ménard de la Groye, *Correspondance (1789–1791)*, ed. by F. Mirouse (Le Mans, 1989).

Notes on Contributors

Peter Campbell at the University of Sussex has written widely on the ancien régime. His other books are *The Ancien Regime in France* (Blackwell, 1988); *Louis XIV* (Longman, 1993); *Power and Politics in Old Regime France* (Routledge, 1996).

Joël Félix is Professor of French at the University of Reading, has written *Les Magistrats du parlement de Paris, 1777–1790* (Sedopols, 1990); *Finances et politique au siècle des Lumières. Le ministère de L'Averdy, 1763–1768* (Imprìmerie nationale, 1999); and "Economy and Finances," in W. Doyle, ed., *Old Regime France* (Oxford University Press, 2001). His biography of Louis XVI is forthcoming.

Michael P. Fitzsimmons is Professor of History at Auburn University, Montgomery. He is the author of several articles and books: *The Parisian Order of Barristers and the French Revolution* (Harvard University Press, 1987); *The Remaking of France: The National Assembly and the Constitution of 1791* (Cambridge University Press, 1994); *The Night the Old Regime Ended. August 4, 1789 and the French Revolution* (Penn State Press, 2003).

John Hardman, is an authority on ancien-régime politics. He edited *French Revolution Documents*, vol. II (Blackwell, 1973), and *The French Revolution Sourcebook* (Arnold, 1999). His several books include *French Politics, 1774–89* (Longman, 1996); *Louis XVI* (Yale University Press, 1992); *Correspondance de Louis XVI et Vergennes* (Voltaire Foundation, 1999); and *Robespierre* (Longman, 2000).

Mark Ledbury is Associate Director of the Research and Academic Program at the Clark Art Institute, Williamstown, MA. Interested in art and theater in the eighteenth century, he has published several articles as well as his *Sedaine, Greuze and the Boundaries of Genre* (Voltaire Foundation, 2000); and, with David Charlton, *Michel-Jean Sedaine (1719–1797) Theatre, Opera and Art* (Ashgate, 2000).

Marisa Linton is a Senior Lecturer at the University of Kingston and is completing a book entitled *Virtuous Terror in the French Revolution*. She is author of "Robespierre's Political Principles," in C. Haydon and W.

Doyle, eds, *Robespierre* (Cambridge University Press, 1999); "Citizenship and Religious Toleration in France," in O. P. Grell and R. Porter, eds, *Toleration in Enlightenment Europe* (Cambridge University Press, 2000); and *The Politics of Virtue in Enlightenment France* (Palgrave, 2001)

Kenneth Margerison is Professor of History at Southwest Texas University, and author of several articles and books, including "Political Pamphlets, the Society of Thirty and the Failure to Create a Discourse of National Reform during the French Revolution 1788–1789," *History of European Ideas*, 17 (1993); *Pamphlets and Public Opinion. The Campaign for the Union of Orders in the Early French Revolution* (Purdue University Press, 1998); *P. L. Roederer, Political Thought and Practice during the French Revolution*, (Philadelphia, PA, 1993).

John Markoff, Professor of Sociology at the University of Pittsburgh, is the author of many articles and books, including "Peasant Grievances and Peasant Insurrection: France in 1789," *Journal of Modern History*, 62 (1990); "Violence, Emancipation and Democracy; the Countryside and the French Revolution," *American Historical Review*, 100 (1995); with G. Shapiro, *Revolutionary Demands: A Content Analysis of the cahiers de doléances of 1789* (Stanford University Press, CA, 1998); and *The Abolition of Feudalism. Peasants, Lords and Legislators during the French Revolution* (Penn State Press, 1996).

William Scott, University of Aberdeen Emeritus, has published *Terror and Repression in Revolutionary Marseilles* (Macmillan, 1973); "Cultural History French Style," *Rethinking History*, 1999; and has a forthcoming book on French political culture in the 1780s.

Dale Van Kley, Professor of Early Modern History, Ohio State University, has published many articles and books, including *The Jansenists and the Expulsion of the Jesuits from France, 1757–1765* (Yale University Press, 1975); *The Damiens Affair and the Unraveling of the Ancien Regime* (Princeton, 1984); *The French Idea of Freedom. The Old Regime and the Declaration of Rights of 1789* (Stanford, CA, 1994); and *The Religious Origins of the French Revolution: From Calvin to the Civil Constitution of the Clergy, 1560–1791* (Yale University Press, 1996).

Index